A·N·N·U·A·L EDITIONS

W9-AVJ-414

Social Psychology 01/02

Fifth Edition

EDITOR

Mark H. Davis
Eckerd College

Mark H. Davis received a doctorate in psychology from the University of Texas at Austin and is currently an associate professor at Eckerd College in St. Petersburg, Florida. He is a member of the American Psychological Association and serves as a consulting editor for the *Journal of Personality and Social Psychology*. His primary research interest is the study of empathy. He is the author of a number of articles on this topic, as well as the book, *Empathy: A Social Psychological Approach* (Westview Press, 1996).

McGraw-Hill/Dushkin
530 Old Whitfield Street, Guilford, Connecticut 06437

Visit us on the Internet
http://www.dushkin.com

Credits

1. The Self
Unit photo—© 2000 by Cleo Freelance Photography, Inc.

2. Social Cognition and Social Perception
Unit photo—© 2000 by Cleo Freelance Photography, Inc.

3. Attitudes
Unit photo—© Cindy Brown/Sweet By & By.

4. Social Influence
Unit photo—© 2000 by Cleo Freelance Photography, Inc.

5. Social Relationships
Unit photo—© 2000 by PhotoDisc, Inc.

6. Prejudice, Discrimination, and Stereotyping
Unit photo—© Cindy Brown/Sweet By & By.

7. Aggression
Unit photo—© by Zephyr Pictures.

8. Helping
Unit photo—© 2000 by PhotoDisc, Inc.

9. Group Processes
Unit photo—Courtesy of Digital Stock.

Copyright

Cataloging in Publication Data
Main entry under title: Annual Editions: Social Psychology. 2001/2002.
    1. Psychology—Periodicals. I. Davis, Mark, *comp.* II. Title: Social psychology.
302'.05   ISBN 0-07-243566-6   ISSN 0730-6962

Fifth Edition

Cover image © 2001 by PhotoDisc, Inc.

Printed in the United States of America   234567890BAHBAH543   Printed on Recycled Paper

In publishing ANNUAL EDITIONS we recognize the enormous role played by the magazines, newspapers, and journals of the public press in providing current, first-rate educational information in a broad spectrum of interest areas. Many of these articles are appropriate for students, researchers, and professionals seeking accurate, current material to help bridge the gap between principles and theories and the real world. These articles, however, become more useful for study when those of lasting value are carefully collected, organized, indexed, and reproduced in a low-cost format, which provides easy and permanent access when the material is needed. That is the role played by ANNUAL EDITIONS.

The field of contemporary social psychology is a little difficult to define. Historically, of course, it was easier. Initially, social psychology was the study of groups (or crowds, or mobs), and, in particular, the effect that groups had on individual behavior. As the years have gone by, however, social psychology has steadily expanded its focus to encompass phenomena that are less clearly "social" in nature. Social psychologists today now study a wide variety of topics, some of which necessarily involve groups (even if the group is only two people), but many of which deal with internal cognitive processes that can occur when a person is completely alone.

In fact, one way to define contemporary social psychology is this: It scientifically examines the thoughts, feelings, and actions of normal humans. As you may notice, this is an incredibly broad definition. While it eliminates persons with psychological disorders, it keeps for itself the study of virtually anything that the average person might think, feel, or do. The good news, for those about to read this book, is that many of the most interesting kinds of human activity will be represented here.

The form in which social psychological research is usually summarized and communicated is the research article, written by scientists for scientists. The goal in such writing is precision and, although it is sometimes hard to believe, clarity. Unfortunately, such writing is often impossible for a nonprofessional audience to understand or enjoy. The purpose of this volume is to provide interesting, highly readable examples of some of the ideas and insights that social psychology can offer about the human experience. The selections come primarily from magazines and newspapers in the popular press, a medium that sacrifices some detail and precision in exchange for a much livelier style of writing. My hope is that by reading these articles in conjunction with your textbook, you can have greater appreciation for just how fascinating and important the topics of social psychology can be.

This volume is divided into nine units, each of which deals with issues falling into one of con-

temporary social psychology's areas of concern. Although social psychology textbooks differ somewhat in how they "carve up" these topics, you will probably find that each of the units in this volume corresponds, at least roughly, to one of the chapters in your text. The articles generally fall into one of two categories. Some of them describe, in an interesting and readable way, social psychological research in a particular topic area. Other selections take a different approach, and explicitly try to apply social psychological findings to real-world problems and events. Some articles, of course, do both.

Although the units are organized to mirror the content usually found in social psychology textbook chapters, you might also find it useful to consult the *topic guide* that appears after the *table of contents*. This guide indicates how each article in the volume is related to a number of different topics that have traditionally been of concern to social psychology. Thus, no matter how your own textbook is organized, it should be possible to find articles in this volume that are relevant to any subject.

Also in this edition of *Annual Editions: Social Psychology 01/02* are *World Wide Web sites* that can be used to further explore the topics. These sites are cross-referenced by number in the *topic guide*.

Finally, I hope that you will take the time to provide some feedback to guide the annual revision of this anthology. You can do this by completing and returning the article rating form in the back of the book; by doing so you will help us understand which articles are effective and which are not. Your help in this revision process would be very much appreciated. Thank you.

Mark H. Davis
Editor

Contents

UNIT 1

The Self

Four articles in this section examine
the evolution of an individual's
personality and sense of self.

UNIT 2

Social Cognition
and Social
Perception

Six articles in this section discuss
how an individual gains a sense of
reality and social understanding.

The concepts in bold italics are developed in the article. For further expansion please refer to the Topic Guide and the Index.

UNIT 3

Attitudes

Three section articles discuss how individuals' attitudes can be influenced by persuasion and propaganda, but not always by added information.

The concepts in bold italics are developed in the article. For further expansion please refer to the Topic Guide and the Index.

UNIT 4

Social Influence

Four selections in this
section look at how social
dynamics influence an individual.

UNIT 5

Social
Relationships

Five articles in this section consider
the problems of social isolation and
how social affiliation and love establish
positive personal relationships.

UNIT 6

Prejudice, Discrimination, and Stereotyping

Five articles in this section
look at what influences an
individual's sense of prejudice,
discrimination, and stereotyping.

The concepts in bold italics are developed in the article. For further expansion please refer to the Topic Guide and the Index.

UNIT 7

Aggression

Four selections in this section
consider the impact of biology and
early social experiences on the level
of an individual's aggression.

The concepts in bold italics are developed in the article. For further expansion please refer to the Topic Guide and the Index.

ix

UNIT 8

Helping

Four articles in this section examine
how an individual develops a sense of
social support and personal commitment.

The concepts in bold italics are developed in the article. For further expansion please refer to the Topic Guide and the Index.

Overview   190

UNIT 9

Group Processes

Four selections in this section discuss how an individual does or does not gain a sense of the social community.

The concepts in bold italics are developed in the article. For further expansion please refer to the Topic Guide and the Index.

Topic Guide

This topic guide suggests how the selections in this book relate to the subjects covered in your course.

The Web icon (●) under the topic articles easily identifies the relevant Web sites, which are numbered and annotated on the next two pages. By linking the articles and the Web sites by topic, this ANNUAL EDITIONS reader becomes a powerful learning and research tool.

TOPIC AREA	TREATED IN	TOPIC AREA	TREATED IN
Aggression	28. Good Clean Fun? 29. Violence and Honor 30. Self-Esteem, Narcissism, and Aggression 31. Anatomy of a Violent Relationship ● **25, 26, 27**		38. Group Processes in the Resolution of International Conflicts ● **6, 7, 10, 27, 33**
Attitudes	13. Social Psychological Perspective 25. Aversive Racism and Selective Decisions ● **8, 9, 12**	**Cooperation**	36. Building Cooperation, Empathy, and Compassion 38. Group Processes in the Resolution of International Conflicts ● **25, 26, 27, 33**
Attribution	2. Culture 7. How Culture Molds Habits of Thought 8. Power of the Situation Over You 9. Inferential Hopscotch 10. New-Boy Network ● **7**	**Credibility of the Source**	12. How to Sell a Pseudoscience
		Culture	1. Nature of the Self 2. Culture 7. How Culture Molds Habits of Thought 20. Isn't She Lovely? 29. Violence and Honor ● **5, 6, 7, 10, 13, 33**
Automatic and Controlled Processing	6. Seed of Our Undoing 9. Inferential Hopscotch 23. Where Bias Begins 24. Breaking the Prejudice Habit 25. Aversive Racism and Selection Decisions ● **7, 21, 22, 23, 24**	**Decision Making**	37. Group Decision Fiascoes Continue ● **10, 33**
Bystander Intervention	34. Cause of Death: Uncertain(ty) ● **10, 33, 34**	**Discrimination**	25. Aversive Racism and Selection Decisions ● **21, 22, 23, 24**
Children and Adolescents	4. I Am Somebody! 26. Thin Ice "Stereotype Threat" 28. Good Clean Fun? 36. Building Cooperation, Empathy, and Compassion ● **3, 5, 6, 7**	**Education**	36. Building Cooperation, Empathy, and Compassion ● **21, 22**
Cognitive Bias	5. "Vividness Problem" 8. Power of the Situation Over You 27. Stereotype 39. Group Decision Fiascoes Continue ● **6, 10, 33, 34**	**Elaboration Likelihood Model**	11. Mindless Propaganda, Thoughtful Persuasion 13. Social Psychological Perspective ● **8, 9, 12**
		Emotions	6. Seeds of Our Undoing 18. Shyness: The New Solution 22. Will Your Marriage Last 31. Anatomy of a Violent Relationship 33. Morals, Apes, and Us ● **6, 15, 18, 21**
Cognitive Dissonance	13. Social Psychological Perspective	
Communities	19. Linking Up Online ● **10, 25, 26, 27, 33, 34**	**Evolutionary Psychology**	3. Making Sense of Self-Esteem 20. Isn't She Lovely? 33. Morals, Apes, and Us ● **5, 11, 14, 15, 18, 21, 22**
Compliance	15. Liking: The Friendly Thief 16. Persuasion: What Will It Take to Convince You? 17. Suspect Confessions ● **6, 7, 10, 27, 33**	**Foot-in-the-Door Technique**	12. How to Sell a Pseudoscience 16. Persuasion: What Will It Take to Convince You?
Conflict	22. Will Your Marriage Last 29. Violence and Honor 31. Anatomy of a Violent Relationship 36. Building Cooperation, Empathy, and Compassion	**Groupthink**	37. Group Decision Fiascoes Continue ● **10, 33**
		Health Psychology	13. Social Psychological Perspective ● **2, 15, 21**

● AE: Social Psychology

The following World Wide Web sites have been carefully researched and selected to support the articles found in this reader. The sites are cross-referenced by number and the Web icon (●) in the topic guide. In addition, it is possible to link directly to these Web sites through our DUSHKIN ONLINE support site at *http://www.dushkin.com/online/*.

The following sites were available at the time of publication. Visit our Web site—we update DUSHKIN ONLINE regularly to reflect any changes.

General Sources

1. Journals Related to Social Psychology
http://www.socialpsychology.org/journals.htm
Maintained by Wesleyan University, this site is a link to journals related to the study of psychology, social psychology, and sociology.

2. Psychology Web Archive
http://swix.ch/clan/ks/CPSP1.htm
The links listed at this public noncommercial site mostly focus on social psychology issues. This archive is an excellent jumping-off place for students of social psychology.

3. Social Psychology Network
http://www.socialpsychology.org
The Social Psychology Network is the most comprehensive source of social psychology information on the Internet, including resources, programs, and research.

4. Society of Experimental Social Psychology
http://www.sesp.org
SESP is a scientific organization dedicated to the advancement of social psychology.

The Self

5. FreudNet
http://plaza.interport.net/nypsan/
FreudNet is part of the Abraham A. Brill Library of the New York Psychoanalytic Institute. This site provides information on mental health, Sigmund Freud, and psychoanalysis.

Social Cognition and Social Perception

6. Cognitive and Psychological Sciences on the Internet
http://matia.stanford.edu/cogsci/
This site, maintained by Ruediger Oehlmann, is a detailed listing of cognitive psychology Web sites. Information on programs, organizations, journals, and groups is at this site.

7. Nonverbal Behavior and Nonverbal Communication
http://www3.usal.es/~nonverbal/
This fascinating site has a detailed listing of nonverbal behavior and nonverbal communication sites on the Web, including the work of historical and current researchers.

Attitudes

8. Propaganda and Psychological Warfare Research Resource
http://ww2.lafayette.edu/~mcglonem/prop.html
This Web site provides links to sites that use propaganda to influence and change attitudes. At this site, you can link to contemporary fascist, political, religious, and Holocaust revisionist propaganda.

9. The Psychology of Cyberspace
http://www.rider.edu/users/suler/psycyber/psycyber.html
This site studies the psychological dimensions of environments created by computers and online networks.

Social Influence

10. AFF Cult Group Information
http://www.csj.org
AFF's mission is to study psychological manipulation and cult groups, to assist those who have been adversely affected by a cult experience, and to educate.

11. Center for Leadership Studies
http://www.situational.com
The Center for Leadership Studies (CLS) is organized for the research and development of the full range of leadership in individuals, teams, organizations, and communities.

12. Social Influence Website
http://www.influenceatwork.com/intro.html
This Web site is devoted to social influence—the modern scientific study of persuasion, compliance, and propaganda.

Social Relationships

13. American Association of University Women
http://www.aauw.org
The AAUW is a national organization that promotes education and equity for all women and girls.

14. American Men's Studies Association
http://www.vix.com/pub/men/orgs/writeups/amsa.html
The American Men's Studies Association is an organization of scholars, therapists, and others interested in the exploration of masculinity in modern society. Click on Men's Issues.

15. Coalition for Marriage, Family, and Couples Education
http://www.smartmarriages.com
CMFCE is dedicated to bringing information about and directories of skill-based marriage education courses to the public. It hopes to lower the rate of family breakdown through couple-empowering preventive education.

16. GLAAD: Gay and Lesbian Alliance Against Defamation
http://www.glaad.org
GLAAD was formed in New York in 1985. Its mission is to improve the public's attitudes toward homosexuality and put an end to discrimination against lesbians and gay men.

17. The Kinsey Institute for Reasearch in Sex, Gender, and Reproduction
http://www.indiana.edu/~kinsey/
The purpose of the Kinsey Institute's Web site is to support interdisciplinary research and the study of human sexuality. The institute was founded by Dr. Alfred Kinsey, 1894–1956.

18. Marriage and Family Therapy on the Web
http://www.nova.edu/ssss/FT/web.html

This site is maintained by the School of Social and Systemic Studies at Nova University. It is a link to numerous marriage and family therapy resources on the Web.

19. The National Organization for Women (NOW) Home Page
http://www.now.org
NOW is the largest organization of feminist activists in the United States. It has 250,000 members and 600 chapters in all 50 states and the District of Columbia. NOW's goal has been "to take action" to bring about equality for all women.

20. The Society for the Scientific Study of Sexuality
http://www.ssc.wisc.edu/ssss/
The Society for the Scientific Study of Sexuality is an international organization dedicated to the advancement of knowledge about sexuality.

Prejudice, Discrimination, and Stereotyping

21. NAACP Online: National Association for the Advancement of Colored People
http://www.naacp.org
The principal objective of the NAACP is to ensure the political, educational, social, and economic equality of minority group citizens in the United States.

22. National Civil Rights Museum
http://www.civilrightsmuseum.org
The National Civil Rights Museum, located at the Lorraine Motel, where Dr. Martin Luther King Jr. was assassinated April 4, 1968, is the world's first and only comprehensive overview of the civil rights movement in exhibit form.

23. United States Holocaust Memorial Museum
http://www.ushmm.org
The United States Holocaust Memorial Museum is America's national institution for the documentation, study, and interpretation of Holocaust history, and serves as this country's memorial to the millions of people murdered during the Holocaust.

24. Yahoo—Social Psychology
http://www.yahoo.com/Social_Science/Psychology/ disciplines/social_psychology/
This link takes you to Yahoo!'s social psychology Web sites. Explore prejudice, discrimination, and stereotyping from this site.

Aggression

25. Contemporary Conflicts
http://www.cfcsc.dnd.ca/links/wars/index.html
This site, maintained by the Canadian Forces College/ Department of National Defence, has an interactive map listing all current world conflicts. Detailed information regarding each conflict can be accessed through this site.

26. MINCAVA: Minnesota Center Against Violence and Abuse
http://www.mincava.umn.edu
The Minnesota Center Against Violence and Abuse operates an electronic clearinghouse via the World Wide Web with access to thousands of Gopher servers, interactive discussion groups, newsgroups, and Web sites around the world. Its goal is to provide quick, user-friendly access to the extensive electronic resources on the topic of violence and abuse.

27. National Consortium on Violence Research
http://www.ncovr.heinz.cmu.edu/docs/data_mission.htm

The National Consortium on Violence Research is a newly established research and training institute that is dedicated to the scientific and advanced study of the factors contributing to interpersonal violence.

Helping

28. Americans With Disabilities Act Document Center
http://janweb.icdi.wvu.edu/kinder/
This Web site contains copies of the Americans With Disabilities Act of 1990 (ADA) and ADA regulations. This Web site also provides you with links to other Internet sources of information concerning disability issues.

29. Give Five
http://www.independentsector.org/give5/givefive.html
The Give Five Web site is a project of Independent Sector, a national coalition of foundations, voluntary organizations, and corporate giving programs working to encourage giving, volunteering, not-for-profit initiatives, and citizen action.

30. HungerWeb
http://www.brown.edu/Departments/World_Hunger_Program/
The aim of this site is to help prevent and eradicate hunger by facilitating the free exchange of ideas and information regarding the causes of and solutions to hunger. It contains primary information made available by the World Hunger Program as well as links to other sites.

31. Mandel Center for Nonprofit Organizations
http://www.cwru.edu/msass/mandelcenter/
The mission of the Mandel Center is to foster effective management, leadership, and governance of nonprofit organizations in human services, the arts, education, community development, religion, and other areas.

32. University of Maryland Diversity Database
http://www.inform.umd.edu/EdRes/Topic/Diversity/
The University of Maryland's Diversity Database is sponsored by the Diversity Initiative Program. It contains campus, local, national, and international academic material relating to age, class, disability, ethnicity, gender, national origin, race, religion, and sexual orientation.

Group Processes

33. Center for the Study of Group Processes
http://www.uiowa.edu/~grpproc/
The mission of the Center for the Study of Group Processes includes promoting basic research in the field of group processes and enhancing the professional development of faculty and students in the field of group processes.

34. Center for the Study of Work Teams
http://www.workteams.unt.edu
The Center for the Study of Work Teams is a nonprofit organization whose vision is to become the premier center for research on collaborative work systems to create learning partnerships that support the design, implementation, and development of collaborative work systems.

We highly recommend that you review our Web site for expanded information and our other product lines. We are continually updating and adding links to our Web site in order to offer you the most usable and useful information that will support and expand the value of your Annual Editions. You can reach us at: http://www.dushkin. com/annualeditions/.

www.dushkin.com/online/

Unit Selections

1. **The Nature of the Self,** Jonathan D. Brown
2. **Culture,** Ziva Kunda
3. **Making Sense of Self-Esteem,** Mark R. Leary
4. **I Am Somebody!** Christopher Shea

Key Points to Consider

❖ Think about those aspects of your life that you believe most clearly define who you are. How would they fit into William James's theory? Would they be aspects of the material self? The social? The spiritual?

❖ Of what does a person's self-concept consist? Which characteristics are the most important in determining how a person views the self? Why would people differ in the kind of characteristics they use to define the self? In particular, what differences in self-concept would you expect to find between men and women? People of different ethnic groups? People of different socioeconomic status?

❖ Is there such a thing as a "true self," or are we all social chameleons, changing our behaviors to fit whatever situation we are in? How could you tell what your "true" self is? What would make it the "true" one?

 **Links**   **www.dushkin.com/online/**

5. **FreudNet**
   http://plaza.interport.net/nypsan/

These sites are annotated on pages 4 and 5.

What are you *really* like? Are you extraverted or introverted? Are you optimistic or pessimistic? The kind of person who is spontaneous and impulsive, or the kind who is organized and orderly?

How do you define yourself? That is, if called upon to describe yourself to others, which characteristics would you mention first? Would it be personality characteristics, such as extraversion, shyness, impulsivity, and so on? Would it be physical characteristics such as your height, weight, speed, strength, or physical attractiveness? Would you mention social categories such as your sex, race, religion, or nationality? Finally, no matter which of these characteristics you focus on, what is your overall evaluation of yourself—that is, do you generally see yourself in a positive or negative light?

As you can see from these questions, there are many ways in which people can define themselves, and an issue of considerable interest to contemporary social psychologists is where these different views of the self come from and what implications they have for how we act. This interest in the individual self, however, is of relatively recent vintage; traditionally the field of social psychology placed more emphasis on the ways in which individuals are influenced by situations. That is, the traditional approach was to manipulate features of the situation and see what effect it had on behavior. Essentially, in this approach people were thought to be similar and interchangeable; the focus was on the role of environmental factors.

More recently, contemporary social psychology has recognized the important role played by stable characteristics of the individual. That is, not only do certain situations tend to make all people act alike, but some people act in consistent ways no matter what the situation. Thus, one feature of modern social psychology is the realization that personality variables—shyness, self-esteem, and many more—can be important influences on human behavior. This growing emphasis on the self has also coincided with modern social psychology devoting considerable attention to understanding the notion of self-concept: that is, how people go about acquiring self-knowledge, organizing and integrating such knowledge, and how self-information then influences our thoughts, feelings, and actions.

In the first selection in this unit, "The Nature of the Self," Jonathan Brown describes one of the more influential models for conceptualizing how the self is organized: the self theory of William James. According to James, there are three fundamental components to the self—the material, social, and spiritual. The second selection, "Culture," examines some interesting differences between Eastern and Western cultures in the way that people define the self; in particular, Westerners are more likely to see the self as independent of other people and Easterners are more likely to see the self as part of a larger social whole. The next two selections deal in different ways with the topic of self-esteem. In "Making Sense of Self-Esteem," Mark Leary offers an interesting new explanation for the purpose of self-esteem. In essence, Leary argues that our levels of self-esteem are signals to us that indicate our relative social standing. When others value us, our self-esteem rises; when others reject us, our self-esteem falls. Self-esteem is important, Leary asserts, because it is such a good gauge of our social standing, and social standing is extremely important to human beings, who are such a social species. Finally, in "I Am Somebody!" Christopher Shea describes some recent research which contradicts the generally accepted view that African Americans have lower self-esteem than white Americans. This work suggests that the link between race and self-esteem is not that simple, and that African Americans may derive their sense of self-worth from different sources than do whites.

1,5 +7 by Oct 3ʳᵈ

The Nature of the Self

THE NATURE OF THE ME*

Jonathan D. Brown

We will begin by considering the nature of *Me* . . . [W]e use this term to refer to people's ideas about who they are and what they are like. Before reading further, take a moment to reflect on how you think about yourself by completing the questionnaire shown in Table 1.

TABLE 1. Self-Exercise #1

Imagine you want someone to know what you are really like. You can tell this person 20 things about yourself. These can include aspects of your personality, background, physical characteristics, hobbies, things you own, people you are close to, and so forth—in short, anything that helps the person know what you are really like. What would you tell them?

1. Hardworking
2. Conscientious
3. Stubborn
4. Loyal
5. Giving
6. Compassionate
7. Sentimental
8. Reliable
9. Fair
10. Honest
11. Gardening
12. Writing poetry
13. Family is important to me
14. Controlling - not always aware of it
15. I like Decorating the house
16. I like football
17. I like having friend over
18. I like to cook for parties
19. Don't like lying
20. I like to be organized, better at work than at home

Excerpted from *The Self* by Jonathan Brown, pp. 20–32, published by McGraw-Hill: Boston. © 1998 by McGraw-Hill. Reprinted by permission.

Three Components of the Empirical Self

William James used the term "the empirical self" to refer to all of the various ways people think about themselves. His analysis is very broad.[1]

> The Empirical Self of each of us is all that he is tempted to call by the name of *me*. But it is clear that between what a man calls *me* and what he simply calls *mine* the line is difficult to draw. We feel and act about certain things that are ours very much as we feel and act about ourselves. Our fame, our children, the work of our hands, may be as dear to us as our bodies are, and arouse the same feelings and the same acts of reprisal if attacked. And our bodies themselves, are they simply ours, or are they *us*? (p. 291)

James went on to group the various components of the empirical self into three subcategories: (1) the material self, (2) the social self, and (3) the spiritual self.

Material Self

The material self refers to tangible objects, people, or places that carry the designation *my* or *mine*. Two subclasses of the material self can be distinguished. These are the bodily self and the extracorporeal (beyond the body) self. Rosenberg (1979) has referred to the extracorporeal self as the extended self, and we will adopt this terminology throughout the book.

The bodily component of the material self requires little explanation. A person speaks of *my arms* or *my legs*. These entities are clearly an intimate part of who we are. But our sense of self is not limited to our bodies. It extends to include other people (my children), pets (my dog), possessions (my car), places (my hometown), and the products of our labors (my painting).

It is not the physical entities themselves, however, that comprise the material self. Rather, it is our psychological ownership of them (Scheibe, 1985). For example, a person may have a favorite chair she likes to sit in. The chair itself is not part of the self. Instead, it is the sense of appropriation represented by the phrase "my favorite chair." This is what we mean when we talk about the extended self. It includes all of the people, places, and things that are *psychologically* part of who we are.

It is interesting to consider why James argued for such a sweeping definition of self. Prior to the time he wrote his book, psychological research on self was restricted to the physical self. Recall from Chapter 1 that the introspectionists had people report what they were thinking and feeling when exposed to various stimuli. Some of these reports concerned an awareness of one's bodily states. For example, a person might report that "my arms

feel heavy" or "my skin feels warm." These are aspects of self. But James wanted to expand the study of self to include nonphysical aspects of the person. He believed that the self was fluid and encompassed more than our physical bodies.

Given this fluidity, how can we tell whether an entity is part of the self? James believed we could make this determination by examining our emotional investment in the entity. If we respond in an emotional way when the entity is praised or attacked, the entity is likely to be part of the self.

> In its widest possible sense, . . . a man's Self is the sum total of all the he CAN call his, not only his body and his psychic powers, but his clothes and his house, his wife and children, his ancestors and friends, his reputation and works, his lands and horses, and yacht and bank-account. All these things give him the same emotions. If they wax and prosper, he feels triumphant; if they dwindle and die away, he feels cast down—not necessarily in the same degree for each thing, but in much the same way for all. (pp. 291–292)

Another way to determine whether something is part of the extended self is to see how we act toward it. If we lavish attention on the entity and labor to enhance or maintain it, we can infer that the entity is part of the self.

> [All of the components of the material self] are the objects of instinctive preferences coupled with the most important practical interests of life. We all have a blind impulse to watch over our body, to deck it with clothing of an ornamental sort, to cherish parents, wife and babes, and to find for ourselves a home of our own which we may live in and "improve."
>
> An equally instinctive impulse drives us to collect property; and the collections thus made become, with different degrees of intimacy, parts of our empirical selves. The parts of our wealth most intimately ours are those which are saturated with our labor . . . and although it is true that a part of our depression at the loss of possessions is due to our feeling that we must now go without certain goods that we expected the possessions to bring in their train, yet in every case there remains, over and above this, a sense of the shrinkage of our personality, a partial conversion of ourselves to nothingness, which is a psychological phenomenon by itself. (p. 293)

In addition to underscoring the important role motivation plays in identifying what is self from what is not, James also made an interesting point here about the nature of things that become part of the self. These possessions, James argued, are not simply valued for what they provide; they are also prized because they become part of us. "Not only the people but the places and things I know enlarge my Self in a sort of metaphoric way," James wrote (p. 308).

A good deal of research supports James's intuitions regarding the close connection between possessions and the self (see Belk, 1988). First, people spontaneously men-

---

[1] [I will quote liberally from James throughout this chapter. It should be noted, however, that James always uses the male personal pronoun "he," a practice inconsistent with contemporary standards. In this instance, I judged fidelity to be more important than political correctness and have reproduced his words without editing them.]

tion their possessions when asked to describe themselves (Gordan, 1968). People also amass possessions. Young children, for example, are avid collectors. They have bottle-cap collections, rock collections, shell collections, and so forth. These collections are not simply treasured for their material value (which is often negligible); instead, they represent important aspects of self. The tendency to treat possessions as part of the self continues throughout life, perhaps explaining why so many people have difficulty discarding old clothes or other possessions that have long outlived their usefulness.

There seem to be several reasons for this. First, possessions serve a symbolic function; they help people define themselves. The clothes we wear, the cars we drive, and the manner in which we adorn our homes and offices signal to ourselves (and others) who we think we are and how we wish to be regarded. People may be particularly apt to acquire and exhibit such signs and symbols when their identities are tenuously held or threatened (Wicklund & Gollwitzer, 1982). A recent Ph.D., for example, may prominently display his diploma in an attempt to convince himself (and others) that he is the erudite scholar he aspires to be. These functions support Sartre's (1958) claim that people accumulate possessions to enlarge their sense of self.

Possessions also extend the self in time. Most people take steps to ensure that their letters, photographs, possessions, and mementos are distributed to others at the time of their death. Although some of this distribution reflects a desire to allow others to enjoy the utilitarian value of these artifacts, Unruh (1983, cited in Belk, 1988) has argued that this dispersal also has a symbolic function. People seek immortality by passing their possessions on to the next generation.

People's emotional responses to their possessions also attest to their importance to the self. A person who loses a wallet often feels greater anguish over a lost photograph than over any money that is missing. Similarly, many car owners react with extreme anger (and often rage) when their cars are damaged, even when the damage is only slight in physical terms. Finally, many people who lose possessions in a natural disaster go through a grieving process similar to the process people go through when they lose a person they love (McLeod, 1984, cited in Belk, 1988).

Further evidence that possessions become part of the extended self comes from a series of investigations by Beggan (1992). In an initial study, participants were shown a variety of inexpensive objects (e.g., a key ring, plastic comb, playing cards). They were then given one object and told it was theirs to keep. Later, participants evaluated *their* object more favorably than the objects they didn't receive. A follow-up investigation found that this tendency was especially pronounced after participants had previously failed at an unrelated experimental test. There are several explanations for this "mere ownership effect," but one possibility is that once possessions

become part of the self, we imbue them with value and use them to promote positive feelings of self-worth.

Finally, the tendency to value self-relevant objects and entities even extends to letters of the alphabet. When asked to judge the pleasantness of various letters, people show enhanced liking for the letters that make up their own name particularly their own initials (Greenwald & Banaji, 1995; Nuttin, 1985, 1987). This "name letter effect" provides further support for James's assertion that our sense of self extends far beyond our physical bodies to include those objects and entities we call *ours*.

Social Self

James called the second category of the empirical self the social self. The social self refers to how we are regarded and recognized by others. (I will refer to these aspects of self as a person's *social identities*.) As before, James's analysis was very broad.

> . . . *a man has as many social selves as there are individuals who recognize him* and carry an image of him in their mind. . . . But as the individuals who carry the images fall naturally into classes, we may practically say that he has as many different social selves as there are distinct *groups* of persons about whose opinion he cares. (p. 294)

Deaux, Reid, Mizrahi, and Ethier (1995) distinguished five types of social identities: personal relationships (e.g., husband, wife), ethnic/religious (e.g., African-American, Muslim), political affiliation (e.g., Democrat, pacifist), stigmatized groups (e.g., alcoholic, criminal), and vocation/avocation (e.g., professor, artist). Some of these identities are ascribed identities (ones we are born with, such as son or daughter) and others are attained identities (ones we acquire in life, such as professor or student).

Each of thee identities is accompanied by a specific set of expectations and behaviors. We act differently in the role of "father" than in the role of "professor." Sometimes these differences are minor and unimportant; other times they are considerable and consequential.

> Many a youth who is demure enough before his parents and teachers, swears and swaggers like a pirate among his "tough" young friends. We do not show ourselves to our children as to our club-companions, to our customers as to the laborers we employ, to our own masters and employers as to our intimate friends. From this there results what practically is a division of the man into several selves; and this may be a discordant splitting, as where one is afraid to let one set of acquaintances know him as he is elsewhere; or it may be a perfectly harmonious division of labor, as where one tender to his children is stern to the soldiers or prisoners under his command. (p. 294)

The larger point James made here is a critical one. To a great extent, how we think of ourselves depends on the social roles we are playing (Roberts & Donahue, 1994). We are different *selves* in different social situations.

This can cause difficulties when we are confronted with situations in which two or more social selves are relevant. Anyone who has simultaneously been both a parent and a child at a family reunion can attest to the difficulties such situations create. We are also surprised to encounter people we typically see in only one role or situation outside of that usual setting. Students, for example, are often flustered when they see their teachers outside of the classroom (e.g., at a movie, restaurant, or sporting event). They aren't used to seeing their teachers dressed so casually and acting so informally.

The tendency for people to show different sides of themselves in different social settings raises an important question: Is there a stable, core sense of self that transcends these various social roles? Some theorists have answered this question with an emphatic "no." They have maintained that the self is comprised entirely of our various social roles, and that there is no real, true, or genuine self that exists apart from these social roles (Gergen, 1982; Sorokin, 1947). Many (if not most) other theorists reject this position as too extreme. While acknowledging that people behave differently in different social settings, these theorists also contend that there is a common sense of self that runs through these various social identities. William James was one adherent of this position. James believed that our social roles are one important aspect of self, but they are by no means the sole aspect of self nor the most important.

James went on to make an additional point about these social selves. He posited an instinctive drive to be noticed and recognized by others. We affiliate, James argued, not simply because we like company, but because we crave recognition and status.

> *A man's Social Self* is the recognition which he gets from his mates. We are not only gregarious animals, liking to be in sight of our fellows, but we have an innate propensity to get ourselves noticed, and noticed favorably, by our kind. No more fiendish punishment could be devised, were such a thing physically possible, than that one should be turned loose in society and remain absolutely unnoticed by all the members thereof. (p. 293)

To summarize, the social self includes the various social positions we occupy and the social roles we play. But it is not simply these identities, per se. It is more importantly the way we think we are regarded and recognized by others. It is how we think others *evaluate* us. These perceptions will figure prominently in our discussion of the reflected appraisal process in Chapter 3.

Spiritual Self

The third category in James's scheme is the spiritual self. The spiritual self is our *inner* self or our *psychological* self. It is comprised of everything we call *my* or *mine* that is not a tangible object, person, or place, or a social role.

Our perceived abilities, attitudes, emotions, interests, motives, opinions, traits, and wishes are all part of the spiritual self. (I will refer to these aspects of the spiritual self as our *personal identities*.) In short, the spiritual self refers to our perceived inner psychological qualities. It represents our subjective experience of ourselves—how it feels to be us.

> By the spiritual self . . . I mean a man's inner or subjective being, his psychic faculties or dispositions. . . . These psychic dispositions are the most enduring and intimate part of the self, that which we most verily seem to be. We take a purer self-satisfaction when we think of our ability to argue and discriminate, of our moral sensibility and conscience, of our indomitable will, than when we survey any of our other possessions. (p. 296)

James proposed two different ways of thinking about the spiritual self. One way (which he called the abstract way) is to consider each attribute in isolation, as distinct from the others. The other way (which he called the concrete way) is to consider the attributes as united in a constant stream.

> . . . this spiritual self may be considered in various ways. We may divide it into faculties, . . . isolating them one from another, and identifying ourselves with either in turn. This is an abstract way of dealing with consciousness . . . ; or we may insist on a concrete view, and then the spiritual self in us will be either the entire stream of our personal consciousness, or the present "segment" or "section" of that stream. . . . But whether we take it abstractly or concretely, our understanding the spiritual self at all is a reflective process, . . . the result of our abandoning the outward-looking point of view, and . . . [coming] *to think ourselves as thinkers.* (p. 296)

Finally, it's of interest to note the close connection between our possessions (which are aspects of the material self) and our emotions, attitudes, and beliefs (which are components of the spiritual self). As Abelson (1986) observed, this similarity is captured in our language. A person is said to *have* a belief, from the time the belief is first *acquired*, to the time it is *discarded* or *lost*. We also say things like "I *inherited* a view" or "I can't *buy* that!" Finally, we speak of people who have *abandoned* their convictions or *disowned* an earlier position. These terms imply that possessions and attitudes share an underlying conceptual property: They are both owned by the self (see Gilovich, 1991; Heider, 1956 for an elaboration of this view).

Tests and Refinements of James's Ideas

Does James's classification scheme describe the way you think about yourself? To answer this question, try to match the responses you gave to the questionnaire in my classes at the University of Washington, and I have found that students' answers do reliably fall into one of these three categories. The only trick is deciding which of the

TABLE 2. Gordon's (1968) Identity Classification Scheme

A. Ascribed Identities
   1. Age
   2. Sex
   3. Name
   4. Race/Ethnicity
   5. Religion

B. Roles and Memberships
   6. Kinship (family—son, daughter, brother, sister)
   7. Occupation
   8. Student
   9. Political affiliation
   10. Social status (part of the middle class; an aristocrat)
   11. Territoriality/Citizenship (from Minneapolis; an American)
   12. Actual group memberships (Boy Scout; Shriner)

C. Abstract
   13. Existential (me; an individual)
   14. Abstract (a person; a human)
   15. Ideological and belief references (liberal; environmentalist)

D. Interests and Activities
   16. Judgments, tastes, likes (a jazz fan)
   17. Intellectual concerns (interested in literature)
   18. Artistic activities (a dancer; a painter)
   19. Other activities (a stamp collector)

E. Material Possessions
   20. Possessions
   21. Physical body

F. Major Senses of Self
   22. Competence (intelligent; talented; creative)
   23. Self-determination (ambitious; hardworking)
   24. Unity (mixed up; together)
   25. Moral worth (trustworthy; honest)

G. Personal Characteristics
   26. Interpersonal style (friendly; fair; nice; shy)
   27. Psychic style (happy; sad; curious, calm)

H. External References
   28. Judgments imputed to others (admired; well-liked)
   29. Immediate situation (hungry; bored)
   30. Uncodable

Source: Copyright 1965 John Wiley & Sons, Inc. Reprinted by permission of John Wiley & Sons, Inc.

three categories is applicable. One way to make this determination is to consider whether the response is a noun or an adjective. Rosenberg (1979) notes that social identities are generally expressed as nouns and serve to place us in a broader social context (e.g., I am an American; I am a Democrat). In contrast, personal identities (aspects of what James called the spiritual self) are usually expressed as adjectives and serve to distinguish us from others (e.g., I am moody; I am responsible).

Gordon (1968) elaborated on James's scheme and produced a coding procedure with 8 major categories and 30 subcategories. This scheme is described in Table 2, and it is illustrated with a sample (composite) questionnaire in Table 3. You can compare the responses you gave with the ones shown there.

The Collective Self

James wrote at a time when psychology was the exclusive province of highly educated (and, by extension, well-to-do) males of European descent. His analysis is therefore somewhat parochial and narrow in scope. This limitation is apparent in the lack of attention James gave to people's ethnic, religious, and racial identities. These identities (termed the collective self by modern researchers) are of great significance to people, particularly those who occupy a minority status. For example, people place great importance on being "Irish," "Jewish," "an African-American," and so forth.

Two related issues regarding these collective identities have received attention. One line of research has focused

TABLE 3. Sample Response to "What Would You Tell Them" Questionnaire

Response	James	Gordon
1. smart	spiritual	competence
2. brown hair, brown eyes	material	physical body
3. friendly	spiritual	interpersonal style
4. the daughter of Italian immigrants	material	kinship
5. am a junior at the UW	social	student
6. like psychology	spiritual	interests and activities
7. am Catholic	social	religion
8. work at a daycare	social	occupation
9. love theater	spiritual	interests and activities
10. own a red Honda Accord	material	possessions
11. a member of Greenpeace	social	actual group
12. plan to become a school teacher	social (future)	occupation
13. am 22	material	age
14. am an only child	social	kinship
15. love laughing and smiling	spiritual	judgments, tastes, likes
16. responsible	spiritual	self-determination
17. a dancer	social	artistic activities
18. trustworthy	spiritual	moral worth
19. moody	spiritual	psychic style; personality
20. petite	material	physical body

on how people evaluate these specific identities. Historically, minority status has carried a negative connotation. Minorities have been stigmatized and subject to discrimination. This state of affairs led some minority group members to resent, disavow, or even turn against their ethnic identity (Lewin, 1948).

Recent years have seen a shift in these tendencies. Beginning with the Black Pride movement in the 1960s, minority groups have worked to improve the way their members evaluate their minority status. Rather than viewing their minority status as a stigma, group members are encouraged to celebrate their heritage and view their minority status as a source of pride. These efforts appear to be meeting with success. Most minority group members now evaluate their ethnic identity in positive terms (Crocker, Luhtanen, Blaine, & Broadnax, 1994; Phinney, 1990).

A second line of research has looked at how people maintain their ethnic identities when exposed to a dominant majority culture. Consider children of Latin-American descent who live in the United States today. Their Latin identity is apt to be paramount during their early (pre-school) years, as a result of housing and friendship patterns. Later, when they begin to attend school, they come into contact with the broader American culture. What happens to their ethnic identity then?

Table 4 describes four possible outcomes based on the strength of the children's identification with the majority and minority group (Phinney, 1990). Children who adopt the identity of the dominant culture, while still retaining a strong identification with their cultural background, are said to be acculturated, integrated, or bicultural. Those who abandon their ethnic identity for an American identity are said to be assimilated. Separation occurs among those who refuse to identify with the dominant culture, and those who lose their ties to both cultural groups are said to be marginalized.

Assimilation was the desired outcome for many turn-of-the century immigrants. These newly arrived Americans sought to completely immerse themselves in American culture and shed their ethnic identity. In so

TABLE 4. Four Identity Orientations Based on Degree of Identification with One's Ethnic Group and the Majority Group

| | | Identification with Ethnic Group | |
		Strong	Weak
Identification with Majority Group	Strong	Acculturated Integrated Bicultural	Assimilated
	Weak	Separated Dissociated	Marginalized

Source: Adapted from Phinney, 1990, *Psychological Bulletin, 108,* 499–514. Copyright 1990. Adapted by permission of The American Psychology Association.

doing, many changed their names, tried to lose their accents, and studiously adopted the customs and mores of American culture.

The situation today is quite different. Cultural diversity and pluralism are celebrated, and many minority group members strive to become acculturated, not assimilated. Phinney (1990) describes several behaviors that facilitate this goal, including participation in ethnic activities, continued use of one's native language, and the forging of friendship patterns with other minority group members. Ethier and Deaux (1994) found that behaviors of this sort helped Hispanic students retain their ethnic identity during their first year in predominantly Anglo universities.

Cultural Differences in Identity Importance

Cultural differences in the importance people attach to their various identities have also been the subject of research. James argued that personal identities (aspects of the spiritual self) are more important to people than are their social identities (aspects of the social self).

. . . men have arranged the various selves . . . in an hierarchical scale according to their worth. (p. 314) . . . with the bodily Self at the bottom, the spiritual Self at top, and the extracorporeal material selves and the various social selves between. (p. 313)

This hierarchical scheme varies across cultures (Markus & Kitayama, 1991; Triandis, 1989). Western countries (e.g., United States, Canada, and Western European countries) are very individualistic. They are competitive in orientation and emphasize ways in which people are different from one another. This emphasis leads citizens of these countries to place great importance on their personal identities. Eastern cultures (e.g., Japan, China, India), in contrast, tend to be more cooperative, collective, and interdependent. Instead of emphasizing the ways people are different from one another, these cultures emphasize ways in which people are linked together. Accordingly, people raised in these cultures emphasize their social identities.

An investigation by Cousins (1989) documents these tendencies. In this investigation, American and Japanese college students completed a questionnaire similar to the one you filled out earlier, and then placed a check mark next to the five responses they regarded as most self-descriptive. Researchers then classified each of the five responses according to whether it referred to a personal identity (a perceived trait, ability, or disposition), a social identity (a social role or relationship), or something else (e.g., physical characteristic). Figure 1 presents the results of this investigation. The figure shows that the American students listed personal identities (e.g., I am honest; I am smart) 59 percent of the time, but Japanese students did so only 19 percent of the time. In contrast, Japanese students listed social identities (e.g., I am a student; I am a daughter)

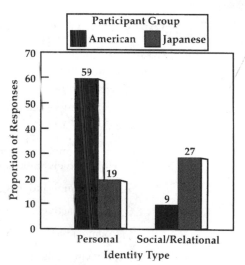

FIGURE 1. Identity statements by American and Japanese students in response to a "Who am I?" questionnaire. The data show that American students were more likely than Japanese students to describe themselves in terms of their personal attributes, whereas Japanese students were more likely than American students to describe themselves in terms of their social attributes. These findings document cross-cultural differences in the self-concept.

(Adapted from Cousins, 1989, *Journal of Personality and Social Psychology, 56,* 124–131. Copyright 1989. Adapted by permission of The American Psychological Association.)

27 percent of the time, but American students did so only 9 percent of the time. These findings document cross-cultural differences in the way people think about themselves (see also Trafimow, Triandis, & Goto, 1991).

Cousins (1989) documented another important cultural difference. People from Western cultures think of themselves as having psychological attributes that transcend particular situations. For example, when asked to describe herself, a person from a Western culture might say "I'm polite." People from Eastern cultures tend to think of themselves in relation to specific others and in specific situations; when asked to describe herself, a person from an Eastern culture might say "I'm polite at school," or "I'm polite with my father." The key difference is that the response of the person from a Western cultural background is unbounded by the situation, but the response of the person from an Eastern cultural background specifies the relational or situational context.

Individual Differences in Identity Importance

Even within cultures, people differ in the importance they attach to their various identities (Cheek, 1989; Dollinger, Preston, O'Brien, & Dilalla, 1996). Before reading further, take a moment to complete the questionnaire shown in Table 5. This questionnaire, adapted from one designed by Cheek, Tropp, Chen, and Underwood (1994), measures the weight people give to their various identities. The scale distinguishes three types of identities: personal identities (our perceived inner or psycho-

TABLE 5. Identity Questionnaire

These items describe different aspects of identity. Please read each item carefully and consider how it applies to you. Fill in the blank next to each item by choosing a number from the scale below:

1 = Not important to my sense of who I am
2 = Slightly important to my sense of who I am
3 = Somewhat important to my sense of who I am
4 = Very important to my sense of who I am
5 = Extremely important to my sense of who I am

1. __5__ My dreams and imagination.

2. __3__ My attractiveness to other people.

3. __3__ Being a part of the many generations of my family.

4. __5__ My emotions and feelings.

5. __1__ My popularity with other people.

6. __1__ My race or ethnic background.

7. __5__ My personal self-evaluations; the private opinion I have of myself.

8. __4__ My reputation; what others think of me.

9. __4__ My religion.

10. __5__ My personal values and moral standards.

11. __3__ The ways in which other people react to what I say and do.

12. __1__ My feeling of belonging to my community.

Source: Adapted from Cheek, Tropp, Chen, & Underwood, 1994. Paper presented at the 102nd Annual Convention of The American Psychological Association, Los Angeles. Reprinted by permission of Jonathan M. Cheek.

logical qualities), social identities (the way we think we are regarded and recognized by others), and collective identities (our sense of belonging to a larger social group such as our race, ethnic heritage, and religion).

To determine your score, average your responses to the four items that refer to personal identities (items 1, 4, 7, and 10), the four items that refer to social identities (items 2, 5, 8, and 11), and the four items that measure collective identities (items 3, 6, 9, and 12). Most American college students score highest on the personal identity items, but not all do. Moreover, Asian-American students place more importance on their collective identities than do European-American students, further demonstrating how cultures shape the way people think about themselves. Finally, there is evidence that, across cultures, the tendency to see oneself in relational terms (which is a component of collectivism in this scale) is more characteristic of women than of men (Kashima et al., 1995; Markus & Oyserman, 1989).

The Personal Narrative

One more issue regarding the nature of the *ME* merits consideration. To this point, we have discussed the *ME* as

if it consists of a haphazard collection of perceived possessions, social roles, and traits. This is rarely the case. Most (if not all) individuals organize the various aspects of their empirical self into a coherent pattern.

McAdams (1996) has argued that this organization is generally accomplished in the context of a personal narrative. A personal narrative is a story a person (implicitly) constructs about her life. The narrative includes the ways the person thinks of herself, as well as the person's memories, feelings, and experiences. This ongoing story contains many of the literary devices that characterize works of fiction (e.g., plots and subplots, character descriptions). Many stories also feature a critical turning point or self-defining juncture (e.g., to really know me, you need to know why I abandoned a lucrative career as a taxi driver in favor of getting a Ph.D. in psychology). In short, a personal narrative unifies and makes sense of the various aspects of a person's life, including aspects of the empirical self.

*Editor's note: This is Chapter 2 in *The Self* by Jonathan D. Brown. Other chapters that are referenced in this article may be found in that book (The McGraw-Hill Companies, 1998).

Culture

Ziva Kunda

Anyone . . . may be forgiven for assuming that social cognition research has uncovered universal principles of how people make sense of themselves and of their social worlds. But just how universal are these principles? The vast majority of social cognition research has been conducted in North America, and much of the rest has been conducted in Western Europe. Could it be that some or even most of the findings apply only to North Americans or, more broadly, to Westerners? Just how culture bound is social cognition?

Anthropologists have long noted remarkable differences in how people raised in Western cultures and those raised in Eastern cultures understand themselves and their social worlds (e.g., Shweder and LeVine 1984). To capture the flavor of these differences, consider the following anecdotes: In the United States, "the squeaky wheel gets the grease." But in Japan, "the nail that stands out gets pounded down." American parents trying to get their reluctant children to eat may urge them to think about how much more fortunate they are than all the starving children in Africa. Japanese parents faced with the same dilemma may, instead, urge their children to consider how bad the farmer who had worked so hard to produce their food would feel if they refused to eat it. An American company intent on increasing productivity asked its employees to look in the mirror before coming to work each day and tell themselves "I am beautiful" 100 times. A Japanese company with a similar intent instructed its employees to begin each day by telling a fellow employee that he or she is beautiful (these anecdotes were reported by Markus and Kitayama 1991). American children put together sports teams by appointing two captains who

Excerpted from *Social Cognition: Making Sense of People*, Chapter 11, pp. 515-533. © 1999 by The MIT Press, Cambridge, Mass. Reprinted by permission.

take turns selecting team members. Japanese children reject this method because the last picked child might feel upset. Instead, they form teams by classroom or by the Japanese equivalent of alphabetical order. American mothers want their children to grow up to be happy and successful individuals. Japanese mothers asked what they want for their children may say something like "I just want my kid to grow up so as not to be a nuisance to other people" (N.D. Kristoff, *NYT* 4.12.1998).

Such anecdotes reveal strikingly different understandings of the self and its relation to others. The American examples point to a sense of the self as distinct from others, and highlight the value of being different and special. In contrast, the Japanese examples point to a sense of the self as closely interrelated with and dependent on others, and highlight the value of harmoniously fitting in with one's group. Such differing construals of the self and society may lead to substantial differences in how people think and feel about themselves and others and in how they relate to each other.

Until relatively recently, such cultural differences were explored predominantly by anthropologists whose conclusions rested, for the most part, on observational and ethnographic data. Over the last decade or so, an increasing number of social psychologists have begun investigating the impact of culture on cognition, motivation, and emotion. Their work has resulted in the emergence of a new field, which may be termed *experimental anthropology*; it relies on the rigorous experimental methods developed by social and cognitive psychologists to explore cultural differences. The revealed cultural differences in social cognition are interesting in their own right. In many cases, they may also shed light on topics that have long been central to social psychology such as the fundamental attribution error, dissonance reduction, and the need for self-enhancement.

For example, the fundamental attribution error, that is, people's tendency to exaggerate the extent to which behavior is driven by underlying dispositions and to underestimate the extent to which it is driven by situational forces, has often been explained as resulting from basic perceptual processes. The perceiver, the argument goes, is bound to see the actor as a salient figure against a much less salient ground, the situation. Because of the relative salience of the actor, causal explanations focus on this actor's disposition. Such basic perceptual processes should be universal. Therefore, if it turns out that people in non-Western cultures are less prone than Westerners to the fundamental attribution error, this would challenge the perceptual account of this phenomenon and suggest, instead, that it is rooted in people's culture-bound beliefs and theories about what drives social behavior.

Much of the social psychological research on cultural differences has focused on East-West differences, and therefore most of this chapter will be concerned with these differences. The starting point of research on East-West differences has been the notion that the self is construed quite differently in these two cultures: North Americans and other Westerners typically view the self as independent whereas East Asians typically view the self as interdependent with others (for detailed reviews, see Markus and Kitayama 1991; Triandis 1989). After briefly outlining the basic differences between these two construals of the self, I will describe research that has investigated the implications of these differences for self-representation, attribution, and motivation.

East-West differences are presumed to be so fundamental that they affect one's very sense of selfhood and have wide-ranging implications for the way one perceives and thinks about the self and others and the way one reacts to a wide variety of social situations. Not all cultural differences are so comprehensive, though. Two cultures may differ in their understanding of a particular class of behaviors, even though they view most other aspects of social interaction similarly. Such relatively narrow cultural differences have been found to exist within the United States between Northerners and Southerners. I will describe research pointing to differences in how threats to one's honor are construed in the Northern and Southern regions of the United States, and will discuss the implications of these differences for interpersonal judgment and behavior.

East-West Differences

Independent and Interdependent Construals of the Self

The Independent Self In many Western cultures people are socialized to become unique individuals, to express their thoughts and desires, to strive to accomplish their personal goals, to self-actualize, to realize their potential. The self is viewed as an independent, autonomous, separate being defined by a unique repertoire of attributes, abilities, thoughts, and feelings (I am smart, kind, and responsible, I'm good at math, I am not very musical, I love to travel, I want to outperform my peers). One attempts to express these aspects of the self publicly and to confirm them privately through comparisons with others. It is this repertoire of internal attributes that organizes and gives meaning to one's sense of oneself. One also has knowledge about oneself in a variety of social relations (I'm competitive with my brother, witty with my best friend, shy with members of the opposite sex), but this knowledge is not viewed as central to one's core identity and is not quite as self-defining as one's more global inner attributes. Such independent construals of the self are far more common in Western than in Eastern cultures, although there are considerable variations within each culture.

The Interdependent Self I once heard a Japanese scholar remind his American audience of their sanctified rights and utmost goals, "Life, liberty, and the pursuit of happiness." Suggesting that their forefathers might have overlooked something of great importance, he asked "What about harmony?" In many non-Western societies (e.g., Japan, China, India), people are socialized to strive for harmonious relations with others, to focus on the connectedness of individuals to one another, to adjust themselves to the demands of social situations, and to try to fit in with their social group. The self is viewed as interdependent with others and is experienced as part of a social web. One's behavior, thoughts, and feelings are seen as dependent on those of others in the relationship (I respect my parents, I am sensitive to my spouse's needs, my family sees me as friendly, my coworkers think I travel too much, I want my company to outperform its rivals). One's sense of self is grounded in one's social relationships, and the most meaningful aspects of oneself are those that emerge in relation to others. As a result the self may be experienced as fluid, taking on different colorations in different social settings.

An interdependent self embraces its assigned role, focuses on social duties and obligations, and tries to figure out what others are thinking and feeling so as to best meet their expectations. One acts in accordance with one's own wishes and desires; indeed, acting on one's own wishes is viewed as infantile. Relationships, rather than being a means of realizing one's own goals, become an end in themselves, so much so that others' goals may be experienced as one's own. Note, though, that the interdependent self need not be generally more benevolent and concerned about others' welfare than is the independent self. The interdependent self is not attuned to the needs of all others, only to those of the in-group, and the in-group may be very narrowly defined.

To illustrate how the interactions among individuals with interdependent selves might differ from those among individuals with independent selves, Markus and Kitayama (1991) describe how events might unfold if a person has a friend over for lunch. An American might ask the friend "Hey, Tom, what would you like on your sandwich? I have turkey, salami, and cheese." And Tom would express his preference. The assumption underlying this interaction is that Tom has an inherent right to make a choice that reflects his preferences and desires. Although this assumption is taken for granted by individuals with independent selves, it is not shared by those with interdependent selves. If a Japanese visitor were asked "What do you want on your sandwich?" there would probably be a moment of baffled silence followed by a noncommittal "I don't know." To a Japanese, it is the host's responsibility to "read the friend's mind," figure out what the friend would like, and offer it. The friend, in turn, should accept whatever is offered with grace, and be ready to return the favor in the future. In Japan, therefore, the host might say something like "Hey, Tomio, I made you a turkey sandwich because I remember that last week you said you liked turkey more than beef." And Tomio would graciously thank the host (Markus and Kitayama 1991, p. 229).

The experience of seeing the self as crucially connected to others, knowing and trying to do what is best for them, and allowing their goals to take precedence over one's own, is not foreign to Westerners. It is not unusual, for example, for American parents to put their children's needs above their own. Still, the sense of the self as interdependent is more common and pervasive in non-Western than in Western societies. Indeed, several studies have revealed systematic differences among Americans and East Asians in the contents and richness of self-knowledge, as discussed next.

The Structure and Contents of Self-Knowledge

Relative Richness of Self-representation Think of a friend you know very well. How similar are you to this friend in shyness? How similar is your friend to you in shyness? Remarkably, Americans give somewhat different answers to these seemingly identical questions (Holyoak and Gordon 1983). When people are asked to make comparisons between a highly familiar object and a less familiar one, their responses reveal a systematic asymmetry: The unfamiliar object is judged as more similar to the familiar one than vice versa. For example, people who know more about the USA than about Mexico judge Mexico to be more similar to the USA than the USA is to Mexico. Such asymmetries are well-explained by Tversky's contrast model of similarity judgments (Tversky 1977). According to this model, when one is asked a question such as "how similar is the USA to Mexico?" perceived similarity decreases with the number of attributes that are unique to each country. However, similarity is de-

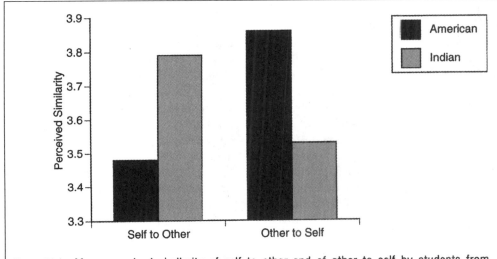

Figure 11.1 Mean perceived similarity of self to other and of other to self by students from American and Indian backgrounds. Data from Markus and Kitayama (1991, fig. 2, p. 231). Copyright © (1991) by the American Psychological Association. Reprinted with permission.

creased more by the unique attributes of the subject of the comparison (in this case, USA) than by the unique aspects of the referent (in this case, Mexico). Because we are highly familiar with the USA, we are aware that it has many unique attributes (i.e., attributes not shared with Mexico), and so we judge similarity to be relatively low. In contrast, when Mexico is the subject of the comparison (as in "How similar is Mexico to the USA), it is Mexico's unique attributes that one focuses on. Because we know little about Mexico, we can come up with only a small number of attributes unique to it, and so we judge similarity to be relatively high.

The asymmetry obtained for Americans' judgments about their similarity to a close friend therefore reveal something about the relative richness of their representations of self and other. Much like they might judge Mexico to be more similar to the USA than the USA is to Mexico, North Americans judge a friend to be more similar to the self than the self is to the friend (Holyoak and Gordon 1983). For example, I would say that you are more similar to me than I am to you (though you might think otherwise . . .). This suggests that the self is more richly represented than the other; because I know much more about my unique attributes than about yours, I judge our similarity to be lower when I am the subject of the comparison (and my unique attributes are salient) than when you are the subject of the comparison (and your unique attributes are salient).

This relatively greater richness and elaboration of self-knowledge as compared to knowledge about close others may be a by-product of a culture that promotes preoccupation with the independent self and its attributes. An interdependent culture may, instead, predispose its members toward developing an elaborate understanding of each other. Individuals whose key social tasks include fitting in with others and reading their minds to anticipate their expectations may accumulate detailed knowledge about close others. Their knowledge of others may be as rich or richer than their self-knowledge. If so, they should not show the same pattern of asymmetry in judgments about the similarity between the self and another person that North Americans tend to show.

A study reported by Markus and Kitayama (1991) supported these predictions. American students and students from India were asked to judge the similarity of the self to another person or the similarity of another person to the self. As in previous studies, the American students believed that the other was more similar to the self than the self was to the other. In contrast, as shown in figure 11.1, this pattern was reversed for the Indian students (though the reversal was not significant). This suggests that for the Indian students, the other was represented at least as richly as the self.

In sum, individuals with independent selves appear to have more rich and elaborate representations of the self than of other individuals. This relative advantage of self-representations over representations of others is eliminated and, possibly, even reversed for individuals with interdependent selves. Individuals with independent and interdependent selves differ not only in the relative richness of their self-knowledge but also in its contents, as discussed next.

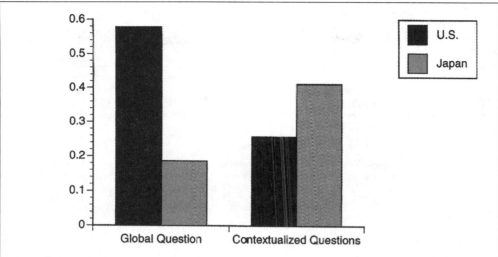

Figure 11.2 Proportion of the self-descriptions made by American students and by Japanese students that were global, unqualified attributes in response to the generalized "Who am I?" question and in response to the contextualized questions. Data from Cousins (1989, table 2, p. 127). Copyright © (1989) by the American Psychological Association. Adapted with permission.

Global versus Contextualized Self-descriptions

Imagine you were asked to generate 20 different answers to the question "Who am I?" What would you say? The kinds of responses you provide and the ease with which you can generate them may depend heavily on your cultural background. To an American, this question seems natural and obvious: it permits one to express one's stable, independent inner self. The American will likely respond with a list of global traits, abilities, and preferences. In contrast, a Japanese person confronted with the same question may find that it presupposes an unnatural separation between one's identity and one's social context. To answer the "Who am I?" question, the Japanese may feel compelled to supplement each response with an appropriate social context.

These ideas gained support from a study in which American and Japanese college students were asked to generate self-descriptions (Cousins 1989). The students first provided 20 responses to the global "Who am I?" question. Examination of the five attributes chosen by each student as most self-defining revealed that the Americans were considerably more likely than their Japanese counterparts to respond with global, unqualified traits ("I am honest," "I am easygoing"), as may be seen in figure 11.2. The Japanese students, who were relatively reluctant to describe themselves in terms of global traits, were, instead, especially likely to ground themselves in social affiliations ("a Keio student") and activities ("one who plays Mah-Jongg on Friday nights"). The Japanese students were also considerably more likely than the Americans to fall back on universal abstractions ("a living form," "a person of the twentieth century"). In short, whereas the American students responded to the "Who am I?" question mostly with global traits, the Japanese students responded mostly with social roles, activities, preferences, and abstractions.

A very different pattern emerged when the same students were given a contextualized version of the "Who am I?" questionnaire, one that asked them to describe themselves at home, at school, and with close friends. For Americans, trait terms may lose their global, cross-situational meaning when they are restricted to a particular context, because Americans conceptualize traits as transcending situations. In contrast, for Japanese individuals, the contextualized questions ground the self in its natural social situations, and provide an opportunity for reflecting on the traits one displays in each situation. Indeed, as shown in figure 11.2, Japanese students were considerably more likely than their American counterparts to answer the contextualized questions with unqualified traits (studious, quiet, boastful). Americans, in contrast, were especially likely to provide qualified responses to these contextualized questions (e.g., "I am silly with close friends"). Cousins theorized that such qualifications to an already contextualized question were intended to convey that the self in that context need not reflect one's true, context-free self.

In sum, the Americans were more likely than the Japanese to describe themselves in terms of unqualified, global traits when asked for global context-free self-descriptions, but were less likely than the Japanese to use such traits when asked to describe themselves in particular social contexts. Put differently, the American students were more likely to use traits to describe their global than their contex-

Table 11.1 Proportion of references to general dispositions and to context among American and Hindu adults asked to explain deviant and prosocial behaviors

REFERENCES TO	DEVIANT BEHAVIORS		PROSOCIAL BEHAVIORS	
	UNITED STATES	INDIA	UNITED STATES	INDIA
Dispositions	.45	.15	.35	.22
Context	.14	.32	.22	.49

Source: Data from Miller (1984, table 2, p. 967). Copyright © (1984) by the American Psychological Association, Reprinted with permission.

tualized selves, whereas the Japanese students were more likely to use traits to describe their contextualized than their global selves. These findings that the American self is conceptualized as independent of its social milieu, as comprising global, context-free attributes. In contrast, the Japanese self is conceptualized as dependent upon social situations, as comprising context-specific attributes.

Americans' view of the self as characterized by global attributes that transcend situations may be at the root of their tendency to attribute other people's behavior to stable, global attributes. East Asians, who are more likely to see the self as dependent upon one's social roles and situations, are also more likely than Americans to attribute other peoples' behaviors to their roles and situations rather than to their underlying dispositions, as discussed next.

Dispositional versus Situational Attributes

Take a moment to think of something an acquaintance of yours has done recently that you consider wrong. How do you explain your acquaintance's inappropriate behavior? The kind of explanation you come up with may depend on your cultural background. There is considerable evidence that Westerners tend to explain other people's behavior in terms of stable underlying dispositions (for a review, see Ross and Nisbett 1991). A Westerner will likely attribute an acquaintance's wrongdoing to some ingrained personality flaw: She lied because she is dishonest, he hit because he is aggressive, she insulted because she is insensitive. Such views of social behavior as driven by stable underlying dispositions may be fostered by a culture that encourages its members to view individuals as autonomous, independent agents who are separate from their social context. In contrast, a culture that encourages its members to view people as interdependent with each other and with their social environment, as many non-Western cultures do, may give rise to

very different explanations for social behavior. Non-Westerners may see other people's behavior as determined by their social roles and interpersonal situations rather than by their personalities. An East Asian may attribute an acquaintance's wrongdoing to some constraint imposed by the person's role or situation; she lied because she had to defend her client's interests, he hit because he was provoked, she insulted because she was stressed out.

Such East-West cultural differences in the way people explain everyday behaviors were demonstrated in an elegant set of studies by Joan Miller (1984). Miller recruited participants from a Western background (Americans in Chicago) and participants from an Eastern background (Hindus in Mysore, a city in South India). Each was asked to recount and explain two examples of a deviant behavior by an acquaintance and two examples of a prosocial behavior (using questions similar to the one at the start of this section). Their explanations were coded as to whether they referred to *dispositions* (e.g., proud, dishonest) or to *context,* which included interpersonal relations (e.g., "She is his aunt," "He has many enemies") as well as location in time and space (e.g., "it was early in the morning," "He lives far away from school").

There were striking differences in how Americans and Hindus explained social behavior. As may be seen in table 11.1 Americans were considerably more likely than Hindus to explain behavior as due to general dispositions whereas Hindus were considerably more likely than Americans to explain behavior as due to aspects of the context. This pattern was especially pronounced for the deviant behaviors. For these, Americans were more than three times as likely as provide dispositional than contextual explanations, whereas Hindus were more than twice as likely to provide contextual than dispositional explanations.

Interestingly, a sample of children from both cultures revealed no differences in how they explained social behavior. Cultural differences in attribution appear to emerge only in mature individuals who have been well-socialized into their culture's view of the person.

Miller reported a couple of examples that illustrate the different kinds of explanations provided by adult Americans and Hindus. One American described the following transgression:

> This involved one of the teachers I work with at school. It was a process of scheduling—something to do with scheduling. I came up with an innovative idea of organizing the scheduling, of what we should do. I talked to some of the other faculty members about it, and this first teacher picked it up and quickly went to the principal and presented it as if it were his own idea. (p. 967)

The American's explanation for this behavior was unmistakably dispositional: "He was just a very self-absorbed person. He was interested only in himself."

A rather similar transgression, also involving taking credit for someone else's ideas, was described by one Hindu participant:

> This involved a scholar in some other department, and she has got her PhD now. She wanted to publish four or five papers from her thesis. She produced some papers, but the thing is, her advisor, he put his name as first author and this young scholar as the second author. She was very hurt because that means usually the credit goes to the first author. (p. 968)

Rather than attributing this behavior to the advisor's poor character, as the American had for a similar act, this Hindu participant attributed it to social role relations: "She was his student. She would not have the power to do it (publish it) by herself."

Although these findings point to strong cultural differences in attribution, the following objection may be raised: The Americans and the Hindus may have differed not in how they explained behavior but in the kinds of behavior that they had generated; perhaps the Americans were especially likely to narrate acts that are well explained by dispositions, and the Hindus acts that are well explained by situational constraints. Maybe, if given the opportunity, even the Americans would explain the behaviors reported by the Hindus as driven mostly by situational constraints. Miller cleverly anticipated this objection and provided additional data that effectively ruled it out. In the second phase of her research, a new group of Americans listened to an experimenter read a sample of behaviors that had been generated by Hindu participants. Each of these behaviors had been explained by the Hindu participant who had originally described it as due to contextual factors rather than to dispositions (though these original explanations were not shown to the

American participants). After hearing about each behavior, the Americans were asked to explain it.

Even when trying to account for behaviors attributed by the Hindus who had generated them to contextual factors, the Americans were considerably more likely to rely on dispositional explanations than on contextual ones; on average, 36 percent of their explanations were dispositional, whereas only 17 percent were based on context. It appears that Americans are predisposed to attribute social behavior to underlying dispositions, whereas Indians are predisposed to attribute behavior to situational constraints. These differences seem to arise from deep cultural differences in the way the person is conceptualized and in how the relations between individuals and their social networks are understood.

The different theories about human nature held by Americans and East Asians color not only their understanding of relatively minor transgressions of the sort reported for acquaintances in Miller's study but also their explanations of far more deviant acts performed by strangers. Michael Morris and Kaiping Peng (1994) examined how American and Chinese individuals explain the actions of a notorious murderer. In the autumn of 1991 there were two similar, highly publicized cases of murder in the United States. In one, a Chinese graduate student at a midwestern university, who had unsuccessfully appealed his loss of an award competition and had subsequently failed to get an academic job, shot and killed his advisor, several other people, and, finally, himself. In the other case, an Irish-American postal worker in Detroit, who had lost his job, had unsuccessfully appealed the decision, and had failed to find an alternative job, shot and killed his supervisor, several other people, and, finally, himself.

Morris and Peng compared the explanations offered for these murders in an English-language newspaper (*The New York Times*) and a Chinese-language newspaper published in the United States (*World News*). All articles published in these newspapers about these two crimes were coded for the presence of dispositional and situational attributions. For the most part, the English articles were more likely than the Chinese ones to focus on both murderers' traits (e.g., "he had a short fuse"), attitudes (e.g., "personal belief that guns were an important means to redress grievances"), and psychological problems (e.g., "darkly disturbed man who drove himself to success and destruction"). In contrast, the Chinese articles were more likely than the English ones to focus on the murderer's interpersonal relationships (e.g., "did not get along with his advisor"), on circumstances (e.g., "had been recently fired"), on problems with Chinese society (e.g., "tragedy reflects lack of religion in Chinese culture"), and on aspects of American society (e.g., "murder can be traced to the availability of gun"). In short, Westerners favored dispositional accounts whereas Easterners favored situational ones.

The same pattern emerged in a subsequent study, in which Chinese and American-born graduate students at the University of Michigan read accounts of these two murders and rated the extent to which each shooting had been caused by a series of dispositional and situational factors which had been gleaned from the various newspaper articles (Morris and Peng 1994). The American students, on average, viewed dispositional explanations focusing on the murderer's pathological character as more causally important than did the Chinese students. In contrast, the Chinese students viewed situational explanations focusing on American culture and circumstances (America's individualistic values and violent movies, the recession) as more causally important than did the Americans.

These studies suggest that Westerners and Easterners subscribe to strikingly different theories about human nature, and differ markedly in their understanding of the causal underpinnings of social behavior. However, studies that involve comparisons among individuals who live in different countries, who use different languages, and who are governed by different social norms are open to a far less interesting, trivializing interpretation. Perhaps the individuals in the two cultures did not differ in their theories about human nature but, instead, differed in their understanding of the meaning and intent of the questions used by the researchers to tap their theories. Easterners, then, may hold the same theories about the causes of behavior as Westerners, but the questions they have been asked, once translated into their language and imported into their cultural context, have not adequately tapped their theories. It would be difficult to sustain this trivializing interpretation of cultural differences in attribution if it could be shown that members of the two cultures do *not* differ in their responses when asked about events for which they hold similar theories. Although Chinese and Americans differ markedly in their theories of social events, they should not differ in their theories about physical events. Therefore, if the two groups understand the attribution questions in the same way, they should provide comparable explanations for physical events even as they differ in their explanations of social events.

Following this logic, Morris and Peng (1994) created two sets of animated cartoons, one depicting social events, the other depicting physical events. The social cartoons all portrayed various interactions among a group of fish. Each showed a blue fish moving in different ways in relation to a group of other fish. In one cartoon, for example, the blue fish moved toward the group and then continued to swim along with it. In another, the group moved toward the blue fish, and the two parties than continued to swim separately. The physical cartoons all portrayed a ball-like object moving across a soccer field. In one cartoon, for example, the moving object stopped, started, and stopped again. In another, it gradually slowed down as if by friction.

The two sets of cartoons were shown to high school students in China and in the United States who were asked to rate the extent to which the movements of the blue fish (in the social scenarios) or of the round object (in the physical scenarios) were influenced by internal factors (e.g., hunger, for the fish, and internal pressure, for the ball) and the extent to which they were influenced by external factors (e.g., the other fish, for the social scenarios, and a person kicking the ball, for the physical ones). This methodology permitted cross-cultural comparisons of attributions about social and physical events. It also had the additional advantage of ensuring that, for both types of events, members of the two cultures were explaining identical scenarios.

Responses to the social events replicated the by now familiar pattern of cultural differences: On average, the Chinese respondents viewed internal factors as less influential than did the Americans and viewed the external factors as more influential than did the Americans. In contrast, the Americans and the Chinese shared the same understanding of the causes of physical events: On average, the two groups did not differ in the extent to which they viewed the internal factors or the external factors as influential.

The Chinese and American students, then, did not differ in their understanding of the questions posed to them by the investigators, nor did they differ in their views of the very nature of causality. Where they held similar theories, as they did for the physical events, they favored the same explanations. The differences in their preferred explanations of social events, therefore, can be assumed to reveal differences in their underlying theories about the nature of social events.

All these studies point to the same conclusion. Westerners tend to view social behavior as driven by internal, stable dispositions such as traits and attitudes. In contrast, Easterners tend to view social behavior as determined by the individual's interpersonal relations, roles, circumstances, and cultural milieu. This conclusion has important implications for the understanding of the fundamental attribution error, namely people's tendency to overestimate the role of dispositions in causing behavior and to underestimate the role of situations. The fundamental attribution error may be fundamental only in Western cultures, where the person is viewed as autonomous, independent, and separate from the surrounding environment. Members of Eastern cultures, where the person is viewed as intricately linked to a web of social relations and as interdependent with others, may show no similar tendency to underestimate the power of the situation.

The hypothesis that East Asians will be less prone than Americans to make the fundamental attribution error was tested in several studies (for a review, see Fiske et al. 1998). In the classic fundamental-attribution-error paradigm, participants observe a person read an essay that either supports or opposes a particular position, say a pro-Castro or an anti-Castro essay. Americans typically assume that the essay reflects the attitudes of the person who read it, even when it is clear that the person had been required to read that particular essay; for example, they believe a person who had been required to read a pro-Castro essay feels more positively about Castro than does a person who had been required to read an anti-Castro essay (for a review, see Jones 1990. In other words, they fail to appreciate the extent to which the person's actions were influenced by the situation, namely the requirements to read that particular essay. It now appears that Japanese and Korean students also make this error in the original, unmodified paradigm. However, when the paradigm is modified so that the situational constraints are highlighted, Americans continue to make the error, whereas East Asians do not (Choi and Nisbett 1998). These studies suggest that East Asians do sometimes explain behavior in terms of dispositions, much like Westerners do. However, East Asians are more likely than North Americans to pick up on cues pointing to the importance of situational constraints. When the situation is highlighted, they set aside any dispositional explanations that they may have been entertaining in favor of more appropriate situational ones.

It appears, then, that cultural differences between Western and Eastern societies result in marked differences in how people represent, understand, and think about other people and themselves. The fundamental differences in how these two cultures view human nature also appear to influence the kinds of motives that their members strive to fulfill and the social structures through which the cultures sustain these motives. . . .

Making Sense of Self-Esteem

Mark R. Leary[1]

Department of Psychology, Wake Forest University, Winston-Salem, North Carolina

Abstract

Sociometer theory proposes that the self-esteem system evolved as a monitor of social acceptance, and that the so-called self-esteem motive functions not to maintain self-esteem per se but rather to avoid social devaluation and rejection. Cues indicating that the individual is not adequately valued and accepted by other people lower self-esteem and motivate behaviors that enhance relational evaluation. Empirical evidence regarding the self-esteem motive, the antecedents of self-esteem, the relation between low self-esteem and psychological problems, and the consequences of enhancing self-esteem is consistent with the theory.

Keywords

self-esteem; self; self-regard; rejection

Self-esteem has been regarded as an important construct since the earliest days of psychology. In the first psychology textbook, William James (1890) suggested that the tendency to strive to feel good about oneself is a fundamental aspect of human nature, thereby fueling a fascination—some observers would say obsession—with self-esteem that has spanned more than a century. During that time, developmental psychologists have studied the antecedents of self-esteem and its role in human development, social psychologists have devoted attention to behaviors that appear intended to maintain self-esteem, personality psychologists have examined individual differences in the trait of self-esteem, and theorists of a variety of orientations have discussed the importance of self-regard to psychological adjustment. In the past couple of decades, practicing psychologists and social engineers have suggested that high self-esteem is a remedy for many psychological and social problems.

Yet, despite more than 100 years of attention and thousands of published studies, fundamental issues regarding self-esteem remain poorly understood. Why is self-esteem important? Do people really have a need for self-esteem? Why is self-esteem so strongly determined by how people believe they are evaluated by others? Is low self-esteem associated with psychological difficulties and, if so, why? Do efforts to enhance self-esteem reduce personal and social problems as proponents of the self-esteem movement claim?

PERSPECTIVES ON THE FUNCTION OF SELF-ESTEEM

Many writers have assumed that people seek to maintain their self-esteem because they possess an inherent "need" to feel good about themselves. However, given the apparent importance of self-esteem to psychological functioning, we must ask why self-esteem is so important and what function it might serve. Humanistic psychologists have traced high self-esteem to a congruency between a person's real and ideal selves and suggested that self-esteem signals people as to when they are behaving in self-determined, autonomous ways. Other writers have proposed that people seek high self-esteem because it facilitates goal achievement. For example, Bednar, Wells, and Peterson (1989) proposed that self-esteem is subjective feedback about the adequacy of the self. This feedback—self-esteem—is positive when the individual copes well with circumstances but negative when he or she avoids threats. In turn, self-esteem affects subsequent goal achievement; high self-esteem increases coping, and low self-esteem leads to further avoidance.

The ethological perspective (Barkow, 1980) suggests that self-esteem is an adaptation that evolved in the service of maintaining dominance in social relationships. According to this theory, human beings evolved mechanisms for monitoring dominance because dominance facilitated the acquisition of mates and other reproduction-enhancing resources. Because attention and favorable reactions from others were associated with being dominant, feelings of self-esteem became tied to social approval and deference. From this perspective, the motive to evaluate oneself positively reduces, in evolutionary terms, to the motive to enhance one's relative dominance.

One of the more controversial explanations of self-esteem is provided by terror management theory, which suggests that the function of self-esteem is to buffer people against the existential terror they experience at the prospect of their own death and annihilation (Solomon, Greenberg, & Pyszczynski, 1991). Several experiments have supported aspects of the theory, but not the strong argument that the function of the self-esteem system is to provide an emotional buffer specifically against death-related anxiety.

All of these perspectives offer insights into the nature of self-esteem, but each has conceptual and empirical difficulties (for critiques, see Leary, 1999; Leary & Baumeister, in press). In the past few years, a novel perspective—sociometer theory—has cast self-esteem in a somewhat different light as it attempts to address lingering questions about the nature of self-esteem.

SOCIOMETER THEORY

According to sociometer theory, self-esteem is essentially a psychological meter, or gauge, that monitors the quality of people's relationships with others (Leary, 1999; Leary & Baumeister, in

From *Current Directions in Psychological Science,* February 1999, pp. 32-35. © 1999 by the American Psychological Society. Reprinted by permission of Blackwell Publishers.

press; Leary & Downs, 1995). The theory is based on the assumption that human beings possess a pervasive drive to maintain significant interpersonal relationships, a drive that evolved because early human beings who belonged to social groups were more likely to survive and reproduce than those who did not (Baumeister & Leary, 1995). Given the disastrous implications of being ostracized in the ancestral environment in which human evolution occurred, early human beings may have developed a mechanism for monitoring the degree to which other people valued and accepted them. This psychological mechanism— the *sociometer*—continuously monitors the social environment for cues regarding the degree to which the individual is being accepted versus rejected by other people.

The sociometer appears to be particularly sensitive to changes in relational evaluation—the degree to which others regard their relationship with the individual as valuable, important, or close. When evidence of low relational evaluation (particularly, a decrement in relational evaluation) is detected, the sociometer attracts the person's conscious attention to the potential threat to social acceptance and motivates him or her to deal with it. The affectively laden self-appraisals that constitute the "output" of the sociometer are what we typically call self-esteem.

Self-esteem researchers distinguish between *state self-esteem*—momentary fluctuations in a person's feelings about him- or herself—and *trait self-esteem*— the person's general appraisal of his or her value; both are aspects of the sociometer. Feelings of state self-esteem fluctuate as a function of the degree to which the person perceives others currently value their relationships with him or her. Cues that connote high relational evaluation raise state self-esteem, whereas cues that connote low relational evaluation lower state self-esteem. Trait self-esteem, in contrast, reflects the person's general sense that he or she is the sort of person who is valued and accepted by other people. Trait self-esteem may be regarded as the resting state of the sociometer in the absence of incoming information relevant to relational evaluation.

SELF-ESTEEM AND ITS RELATIONSHIP TO BEHAVIOR

Sociometer theory provides a parsimonious explanation for much of what we know about self-esteem. Here I examine how sociometer theory answers four fundamental questions about self-esteem raised earlier.

The Self-Esteem Motive

As noted, many psychologists have assumed that people possess a motive or need to maintain self-esteem. According to sociometer theory, the so-called self-esteem motive does not function to maintain self-esteem but rather to minimize the likelihood of rejection (or, more precisely, relational devaluation). When people behave in ways that protect or enhance their self-esteem, they are typically acting in ways that they believe will increase their relational value in others' eyes and, thus, improve their chances of social acceptance.

The sociometer perspective explains why events that are known (or potentially known) by other people have much greater effects on self-esteem than events that are known only by the individual him- or herself. If self-esteem involved only private self-judgments, as many psychologists have assumed, public events should have no greater impact on self-esteem than private ones.

Antecedents of Self-Esteem

Previous writers have puzzled over the fact that self-esteem is so strongly tied to people's beliefs about how they are evaluated by others. If self-esteem is a *self*-evaluation, why do people judge themselves by *other* people's standards? Sociometer theory easily explains why the primary determinants of self-esteem involve the perceived reactions of other people, as well as self-judgments on dimensions that the person thinks are important to significant others. As a monitor of relational evaluation, the self-esteem system is inherently sensitive to real and potential reactions of other people.

Evidence shows that state self-esteem is strongly affected by events that have implications for the degree to which one is valued and accepted by other people (Leary, Haupt, Strausser, & Chokel, 1998; Leary, Tambor, Terdal, & Downs, 1995). The events that affect self-esteem are precisely the kinds of things that, if known by other people, would affect their evaluation and acceptance of the person (Leary, Tambor, et al., 1995). Most often, self-esteem is lowered by failure, criticism, rejection, and other events that have negative implications for relational evaluation; self-esteem rises when a person succeeds, is praised, or experiences another's love—events that are associated with relational appreciation. Even the mere possibility of rejection can lower self-esteem, a finding that makes sense if the function of the self-esteem system is to warn the person of possible relational devaluation in time to take corrective action.

The attributes on which people's self-esteem is based are precisely the characteristics that determine the degree to which people are valued and accepted by others (Baumeister & Leary, 1995). Specifically, high trait self-esteem is associated with believing that one possesses socially desirable attributes such as competence, personal likability, and physical attractiveness. Furthermore, self-esteem is related most strongly to one's standing on attributes that one believes are valued by significant others, a finding that is also consistent with sociometer theory.

In linking self-esteem to social acceptance, sociometer theory runs counter to the humanistic assumption that self-esteem based on approval from others is false or unhealthy. On the contrary, if the function of self-esteem is to avoid social devaluation and rejection, then the system must be responsive to others' reactions. This system may lead people to do things that are not always beneficial, but it does so to protect their interpersonal relationships rather than their inner integrity.

Low Self-Esteem and Psychological Problems

Research has shown that low self-esteem is related to a variety of psychological difficulties and personal problems, including depression, loneliness, substance abuse, teenage pregnancy, academic failure, and criminal behavior. The evidence in support of the link between low self-esteem and psychological problems has often been overstated; the relationships are weaker and more scattered than typically assumed (Mecca, Smelser, & Vasconcellos, 1989). Moreover, high self-esteem also has notable drawbacks. Even so, low self-esteem tends to be more strongly associated with psychological difficulties than high self-esteem.

From the standpoint of sociometer theory, these problems are caused not by low self-esteem but rather by a history of low relational evaluation, if not outright rejection. As a subjective gauge of relational evaluation, self-esteem may parallel these problems, but it is a coeffect rather than a cause. (In fact, contrary to the popular view that low self-esteem causes these problems, no direct evidence exists to document that self-esteem has any causal role in thought, emotion, or behavior.) Much research shows that interpersonal rejection results in emotional problems, difficulties relating with others, and maladaptive efforts to be accepted (e.g., excessive dependency, membership in deviant groups), precisely the concomitants of low self-esteem (Leary, Schreindorfer, & Haupt, 1995). In addition, many personal problems lower self-esteem because they lead other people to devalue or reject the individual.

Consequences of Enhancing Self-Esteem

The claim that self-esteem does not cause psychological outcomes may appear to fly in the face of evidence showing that interventions that enhance self-esteem do, in fact, lead to positive psychological changes. The explanation for the beneficial effects of programs that enhance self-esteem is that these interventions change people's perceptions of the degree to which they are socially valued individuals. Self-esteem programs always include features that would be expected to increase real or perceived social acceptance; for example, these programs include components aimed at enhancing social skills and interpersonal problem solving, improving physical appearance, and increasing self-control (Leary, 1999).

CONCLUSIONS

Sociometer theory suggests that the emphasis psychologists and the lay public have placed on self-esteem has been somewhat misplaced. Self-esteem is certainly involved in many psychological phenomena, but its role is different than has been supposed. Subjective feelings of self-esteem provide ongoing feedback regarding one's relational value vis-à-vis other people. By focusing on the monitor rather than on what the monitor measures, we have been distracted from the underlying interpersonal processes and the importance of social acceptance to human well-being.

Recommended Reading

Baumeister, R. F. (Ed.). (1993). *Self-esteem: The puzzle of low self-regard.* New York: Plenum Press.
Colvin, C. R., & Block, J. (1994). Do positive illusions foster mental health? An examination of the Taylor and Brown formulation. *Psychological Bulletin, 116,* 3–20.
Leary, M. R. (1999). (See References)
Leary, M. R., & Downs, D. L. (1995). (See References)
Mecca, A. M., Smelser, N. J., & Vasconcellos, J. (Eds.). (1989). (See References)

Note

1. Address correspondence to Mark Leary, Department of Psychology, Wake Forest University, Winston-Salem, NC 27109; e-mail: leary@wfu.edu.

References

Barkow, J. (1980). Prestige and self-esteem: A biosocial interpretation. In D. R. Omark, F. F. Strayer, & D. G. Freedman (Eds.), *Dominance relations: An ethological view of human conflict and social interaction* (pp. 319–332). New York: Garland STPM Press.
Baumeister, R. F., & Leary, M. R. (1995). The need to belong: Desire for interpersonal attachments as a fundamental human motivation. *Psychological Bulletin, 117,* 497–529.
Bednar, R. L., Wells, M. G., & Peterson, S. R. (1989). *Self-esteem: Paradoxes and innovations in clinical theory and practice.* Washington, DC: American Psychological Association.
James, W. (1890). *The principles of psychology* (Vol. 1). New York: Henry Holt.
Leary, M. R. (1999). The social and psychological importance of self-esteem. In R. M. Kowalski & M. R. Leary (Eds.), *The social psychology of emotional and behavioral problems: Interfaces of social and clinical psychology* (pp. 197–221). Washington, DC: American Psychological Association.
Leary, M. R., & Baumeister, R. F. (in press). The nature and function of self-esteem: Sociometer theory. *Advances in Experimental Social Psychology.*
Leary, M. R., & Downs, D. L. (1995). Interpersonal functions of the self-esteem motive: The self-esteem system as a sociometer. In M. H. Kernis (Ed.), *Efficacy, agency, and self-esteem* (pp. 123–144). New York: Plenum Press.
Leary, M. R., Haupt, A. L., Strausser, K. S., & Chokel, J. L. (1998). Calibrating the sociometer: The relationship between interpersonal appraisals and state self-esteem. *Journal of Personality and Social Psychology, 74,* 1290–1299.
Leary, M. R., Schreindorfer, L. S., & Haupt, A. L. (1995). The role of self-esteem in emotional and behavioral problems: Why is low self-esteem dysfunctional? *Journal of Social and Clinical Psychology, 14,* 297–314.
Leary, M. R., Tambor, E. S., Terdal, S. J., & Downs, D. L. (1995). Self-esteem as an interpersonal monitor. The sociometer hypothesis. *Journal of Personality and Social Psychology, 68,* 518–530.
Mecca, A. M., Smelser, N. J., & Vasconcellos, J. (Eds.). (1989). *The social importance of self-esteem.* Berkeley: University of California Press.
Solomon, S., Greenberg, J., & Pyszczynski, T. (1991). A terror management theory of social behavior: The psychological functions of self-esteem and cultural worldviews. *Advances in Experimental Social Psychology, 24,* 93–159.

I am somebody!

Do blacks really need to work on their self-esteem? An African-American psychologist says no.

By Christopher Shea

June 2, 2000 | Race and "self-esteem" are inextricably bound in the popular imagination. Thanks to racism and discrimination, the theory goes, a core of self-doubt lurks in the heart of every black child and young adult. If we could only raise black self-esteem, academic and economic achievement would follow.

The evidence for this line of thinking is everywhere. At Detroit's public, all-black Paul Robeson Academy, students start the day by standing up and proclaiming: "I feel like somebody. I act like somebody. Nobody can make me feel like a nobody!" Last fall, the organizers of Denver's Black Arts Festival described their mission as, in part, "building self-esteem" in young people. And newspaper profiles of black leaders invariably point out that these people possess self-esteem—taking for granted that it is an odd quality for an African-American to have.

Early academic research seemed to support the notion of low black self-esteem. Almost everyone remembers the work of psychologists Kenneth and Mamie Clark, who from 1938 to 1977 conducted experiments showing that black children preferred white dolls over black ones. The Supreme Court footnoted the work in the landmark *Brown vs. Board of Education* decision, in which the court pronounced that the assignment of black children to segregated schools "generates a feeling of inferiority . . . that may affect their hearts and minds in a way unlikely ever to be overcome."

Since then, however, psychological studies of black self-esteem have offered increasingly mixed results. And the latest study may prove to be the nail in the theory's coffin. In a recent issue of *Psychological Bulletin*, an African-American psychologist is offering what some in the field take to be the final word on the issue. Blacks don't have less self-esteem than whites, her findings show. In fact, they often have more.

Bernadette Gray-Little, a professor of psychology at the University of North Carolina at Chapel Hill, writing with graduate student Adam Hafdahl, performed a complex review of every piece of research available on black self-esteem, 261 studies in all. Other scholars have attempted similar projects, but this study stands out for its scope and statistical rigor.

"There have been inconsistencies in the results of the studies on this topic over time," says the UNC professor, who insists she entered the project with no political agenda. "I wanted to see if I could find any basis for a firm conclusion. And if inconsistencies occurred, I wanted to know when and why."

The broad trends she discerned are fairly straightforward. Before age 10, whites slightly surpass blacks in self-esteem. Everyone takes a big self-esteem hit in junior high. After that, blacks narrowly but consistently surpass whites, through age 21, the upper limit of the study.

For Sandra Graham, a professor of education at UCLA, the study is "the definitive statement on the issue." She notes that Gray-Little's findings are surprising in that they don't "fit with the prevailing perceptions of how a stigmatized person should feel about themselves."

"The prevailing view," she says, "is that society puts you in a certain place and that influences how you feel. But the research has not supported that idea."

Making use of a technique called meta-analysis, the study culled data from many studies and treated them as if they were part of one giant study—a method that increases the odds that the findings are not the result of chance. Gray-Little dices up the research in provocative ways. The self-esteem gap seems to vary along socioeconomic lines, for instance. Low-income blacks show higher self-esteem than low-income whites. The gap, however, disappears at higher income levels.

As blacks got more rights, what happened to their self-esteem?

One of the more intriguing findings-within-the-findings is that black self-esteem has not risen over time, as many psychologists had predicted. It evidently has never been low. Whatever racism's effects—and they are surely huge—this study says low valuation of oneself is simply not among them. Self-esteem is a sticky, tangled subject—a totem of the therapy industry and a call to arms in the culture wars. Cultural conservatives grind their teeth at the mere mention of the topic. And even among academics who study it, there is debate about how it should be defined and measured.

California gave self-esteem a bad name in the mid-1980s, when its governor and Legislature signed off on a "Task Force to Promote Self-Esteem and Personal and Social Responsibility." The task force quickly became a laughingstock, triggering a backlash. A vocal group of psychologists and pundits attacked self-esteem as a fuzzy concept that could not be considered in the abstract (apart from achievement). They also argued that there was no clear link between it and achievement, since many high achievers think they stink.

In a famous paper from 1996, Roy F. Baumeister, a psychologist at Case Western University, proposed that attempts to raise self-esteem might actually worsen social problems. Criminals, Klan members and Nazis, he archly noted, all most likely suffer not from too little self-esteem but from too much.

A more moderate collection of essays on self-esteem published in 1989 by University of California professors underscored just how hard it was to turn the tentative academic findings on the subject into policy. Self-esteem proved hard to divorce from behavioral problems. Did low self-esteem cause the problems or does dysfunction hurt self-esteem? Even more vexing, self-esteem didn't always correlate with social problems in the expected way. While abused or neglected kids did show low self-esteem, for example, alcoholics and child abusers didn't seem to have self-image issues (though you might wish they did).

Despite the controversies, self-esteem remains a live topic in psychology. In 1996, the National Advisory Mental Health Council, a collection of 52 top behavioral scientists, pinpointed it as one of the most promising subjects for further research. "The policy of spending vast amounts of money to raise self-esteem was way ahead of what we know about self-esteem," argues Jennifer Crocker, a professor of psychology at the University of Michigan. "But the attack on the self-esteem movement was way ahead of what we know, also."

Crocker maintains that self-esteem is not so squishy a concept after all. It's fairly stable from childhood into adulthood in most people, she says, and it correlates strongly with depressive symptoms on one hand and with psychological well-being—i.e., happiness—on the other.

To Crocker, what is most provocative about the Gray-Little study is that it poses a challenge to the standard psychological explanations of self-esteem. In the first decades of the last century, social scientists like George Herbert Mead, tinkering with ideas put forward by William James, developed the idea that self-esteem was akin to a mirror. It wasn't so much an internal gyroscope as it was a reflection of other people's views, Mead and others said. People tended to take a bead on other people's impressions of them, and internalize those opinions.

Social scientists went on to apply that theory to African-Americans in a predictable way: Low social status equaled low self-esteem. For a long time, social scientists thought they had the research to back up that assumption—namely, the Clarks' doll studies. But those studies have come under fire at least since the mid-1970s. In 1976, a Princeton psychologist, W. Curtis Banks, reviewed the Clarks' results and concluded they could have been the result of chance. Additionally, the kids in the studies often didn't understand what they were being asked to do, and often resisted making any choice at all. Efforts to study black self-esteem using surveys and questionnaires have often failed to support the Clarks' work as well.

Some critics wonder whether a quality as subtle and elusive as self-esteem can be captured by surveys in lab settings. Alvin F. Poussaint, the eminent African-American psychiatrist at Harvard Medical School, notes that black kids may have been told by their parents that they are as good as anyone else. In turn, this sentiment may show up on forms asking them if they are satisfied with themselves. But the kids may only be talking the talk.

"As a psychiatrist, I like to look at people's behavior to get a sense of their self-esteem," Poussaint says. "Let's say someone is always being self-destructive, has always given up. I work with that more than I do whether they feel good about themselves."

However, it's clearly the case that important findings in many areas, including depression, depend on self-reports. And many researchers believe that the use of surveys to study self-esteem have produced robust, replicable results.

In the new paper, Gray-Little suggests that the mirror theory of self-esteem isn't wrong. It just needs tweaking. African-Americans do, indeed, get their ideas about self-worth largely from others—but not from "society," nor from whites. It is friends, family and neighbors who project the impressions that matter. In other words, people think globally, but get their self-esteem locally.

It's a liberating concept: White Americans don't have much say in how blacks feel about themselves. But given the turmoil in some sectors of the black community—involving generational substance abuse, black-on-black crime, an epidemic of incarceration and a history of fatherless families—it seems rather counterintuitive to propose that African-American children receive more reinforcement from their families and neighborhoods than whites do.

Gray-Little's second hypothesis—that high black self-esteem may have to do with group pride—is more convincing. Marge Schott aside, most whites don't think of themselves as part of a coherent ethnic group, nor do they get satisfaction from their ethnic identification. Yet African-Americans do, on both counts.

"Blacks, a highly identifiable social group, emphasize their desirable distinctiveness," Gray-Little writes. That, she suggests, may be enough to push blacks a nose ahead of whites.

Crocker offers another explanation. She believes that self-esteem for blacks is governed by an internal gyroscope after all. And that gyroscope is religion. In surveys, many more African-Americans than whites report deriving a sense of self-worth from their religious beliefs. For believers, she suggests, it may not really matter what other people think of you so long as God is on your side. (Religion has been suggested as part of the explanation for the mysterious black-white suicide gap, too. Nearly 20 white men per 100,000 kill themselves, compared with 12.4 per 100,000 black men.)

Today, Gray-Little's findings about race seem useful and eye-opening, but someday they may seem strangely in step with the biases of our day simply because they focus on the issue of race at all. As with almost every quality, studies show the differences in self-esteem among individuals absolutely swamps differences between groups. So perhaps future research will explore the issue freed from categories like class, race and gender.

But at the very least, her study should ring the death knell for a certain journalistic cliché. The next time Colin Powell gets written up, let's hope the profile doesn't include a line noting, in a tone approaching wonder, that the man possesses self-esteem. Why wouldn't he?

About the writer
Christopher Shea is a writer living in Washington.

Unit 2

Key Points to Consider

❖ Why does vividness so strongly affect our judgments? Can you think of any ways to counteract its effects?

❖ What does it mean to say that some parts of the social inference process are "automatic" and some are "controlled"? Why is that distinction important for our understanding of the perception process?

❖ How would you summarize the phenomenon known as the "fundamental attribution error" (FAE)? Why is it considered an error? What does the East-West cultural difference tell us about the likelihood of displaying the FAE?

 **Links**   **www.dushkin.com/online/**

6. **Cognitive and Psychological Sciences on the Internet**
   http://matia.stanford.edu/cogsci/

7. **Nonverbal Behavior and Nonverbal Communication**
   http://www3.usal.es/~nonverbal/

These sites are annotated on pages 4 and 5.

Pretend that I have just asked you your position on gun control, the name of your favorite television program, and how many children you plan on having. Now assume that I also ask you to estimate what proportion of the U.S. population holds the same attitude about guns, likes the same program, or plans on having that same number of children. If you are like most people, there is a good chance that your estimates of what the general population thinks on an issue will be influenced by your own opinion. In short, most of us believe that our own attitudes and preferences are relatively common in the population, and that alternate attitudes and preferences are less common. This tendency to see our own preferences as being widely shared by others is referred to as the "false consensus effect."

This phenomenon is just one example of the kinds of topics that fall under the heading of social cognition, a broad area that may loosely be defined as how people think about the social world. That is, the emphasis in this area is on the thought processes people engage in when they think about others. The emphasis in social cognition research, then, is usually on how people think, rather than on the content of those thoughts. For example, one issue of importance to those who study social cognition is what happens to the information we acquire about other people. How is such information about people stored and organized in memory? How is it accessed and retrieved later on? After retrieval, how is it used to help us understand and interpret the world?

Pretend that you are the personnel director of a large company and have the job of interviewing hundreds of prospective employees for that company every year. The total amount of time and money that will be invested in these new employees will be enormous; thus, the consequences of hiring the wrong people will be serious. In each interview, you must try to answer a number of important questions: How honest is this candidate? How dependable? How will he or she fit in with the other employees?

This hypothetical situation is an example of social perception, or the process by which one individual makes inferences about another individual. As you might imagine, this is a very important ability for humans to have, because there are many times when it is important to reach an accurate understanding about what kind of person someone else is. When the behavior of others, such as employees and spouses, has important implications for us, then the ability to successfully predict how such people will act in the future can be critical. It should not be surprising, then, to discover that social psychology has been interested in this topic for decades.

One approach to this topic has been to study "impression formation"—the process by which we form an initial impression of someone with whom we are not familiar. Research indicates that we form such impressions quite quickly, often on the basis of

very little information. One kind of information that is often available in such situations—and that is therefore frequently used—is group membership, that is, the person's sex, race, age, social class, etc. Beyond such obvious kinds of information, we also use the person's words and actions to reach an initial impression.

The three articles included in the first part of this unit illustrate the variety of issues that have been addressed within the area of social cognition. The first selection describes the role that "vividness" plays in shaping our judgments. Because vivid or dramatic information is more easily retrieved from memory, we tend to overvalue it in our decision making, often making these judgments less accurate. The next selection addresses an important issue in contemporary social psychology, the distinction between automatic and controlled mental processes. In "The Seed of Our Undoing," Daniel Wegner describes some research he has done on the phenomenon of "ironic" mental processes—when our attempts to control our thoughts in a particular way lead to the *opposite* result. Wegner argues that this occurs because "ironic" processes automatically operate whenever we also engage in deliberate efforts at thought control. Finally, in "How Culture Molds Habits of Thought," Erica Goode presents recent evidence bearing on the issue of how culture can affect social cognition. As it turns out, Eastern and Western cultures differ markedly in their cognitive processes, especially in the way that they offer explanations for the behavior of other people.

The second subsection in this unit deals with social perception. In the first article, "The Power of the Situation Over You," Michael Lovaglia describes a well-known phenomenon in social psychology: the fundamental attribution error. This refers to the tendency (at least in Western cultures) to overemphasize the importance of a person's dispositional characteristics and to underestimate the impact that situational factors have on his or her behavior. In the second article, "Inferential Hopscotch: How People Draw Social Inferences From Behavior," the authors review recent research that indicates that drawing inferences actually consists of multiple steps. The initial step is typically rather quick and automatic; in it, the behavior is immediately interpreted as evidence of an underlying trait. In the more conscious and effortful second step, however, we deliberately try to take into account other factors that might have influenced the behavior. The third article, "The New-Boy Network," takes as its starting point a very specific kind of social inference problem: the job interview. Malcolm Gladwell describes social psychological research that documents just how quickly we are able to make snap judgments about other people, and also describes an infrequently used interview technique that may help provide better judgments than the technique typically used today.

THE "VIVIDNESS" PROBLEM

Keith E. Stanovich
University of Toronto

It is fine to point out how the existence of placebo effects renders testimonials useless as evidence, but we must recognize another obstacle that prevents people from understanding that testimonials cannot be accepted as proof of a claim. Social and cognitive psychologists have studied what is termed the *vividness effect* in human memory and decision making (see Baron, 1998; Nisbett & Ross, 1980). When faced with a problem-solving or decision-making situation, people retrieve from memory the information that seems relevant to the situation at hand. Thus, they are more likely to use the facts that are more accessible to solve a problem or make a decision. One factor that strongly affects accessibility is the vividness of information.

The problem is that there is nothing more vivid or compelling than sincere personal testimony that something has occurred or that something is true. The vividness of personal testimony often overshadows other information of much higher reliability. How often have we carefully collected information on different product brands before making a purchase, only to be dissuaded from our choice at the last minute by a chance recommendation of another product by a friend or an advertisement? Car purchases are a typical example (Nisbett & Ross, 1980). We may have read surveys of thousands of customers in *Consumer Reports* and decided on car X. After consulting the major automotive magazines and confirming that the experts also recommend car X, we feel secure in our decision—until, that is, we meet a friend at a party who knows a friend who knows a friend who bought an X and got a real lemon, spent hundreds on repairs, and would never buy another. Obviously, this single instance should not substantially affect our opinion, which is based on a survey of thousands of owners and the judgment of several experts. Yet how many of us could resist the temptation to overweight this evidence?

The auto purchase situation illustrates that the problems created by vivid testimonial evidence are not unique to psychology. For example, Stephen Budiansky (1984), Washington correspondent of the British science journal *Nature,* has summarized the situation in medicine with a statement that reinforces many of the points about science that we have discussed in previous chapters:

> Science eschews the personal. Although it is commonplace to ascribe this tendency to some fundamental coldness on the part of scientists, in fact it is really one of the great intellectual triumphs of the 20th century that scientists have learned to discount the experiences of individuals when searching for cause and effect in the natural world. The health sciences have had a particularly rough time of it; people tend to get sick for a variety of reasons and people more often than not get better no matter what "care" is prescribed. The apparently undying popularity of quack remedies, invariably supported by testimonials from satisfied customers, is vivid proof of how hard we find it to look beyond personal experience. (p. 7)

Instances of how vividness affects people's opinions are not hard to find. Reporter Haynes Johnson (1991) wrote of how President Reagan came to recognize the severity of the AIDS problem:

> [Reagan] had not realized the seriousness of AIDS until July 1985, when he saw a news report disclosing that the actor Rock Hudson had died of the disease. This was more than five years after AIDS had been identified, thousands of Americans had been infected, and AIDS had been the subject of intense national publicity.

Excerpted from *How to Think Straight About Psychology,* 6/e, chapter 4, pp. 61-70. © 2001 by Allyn & Bacon. Reprinted by permission.

When Reagan saw the news report about Hudson's death, he asked [Brigadier] General Hutton [a former doctor] to tell him about the disease. (p. 454)

In short, the constant news reports and statistics on the increasing numbers of AIDS deaths had not attracted the president's attention, but the report of a single person who was known to him did. Similarly, writer Michael Lewis (1997) describes how conservative commentator George Will—a notorious opponent of government regulation—published a column calling for mandatory air bags after seeing a death in a car crash outside of his home.

Imagine that you saw the following headline one Friday morning in your newspaper: "Jumbo Jet Crash: 413 killed." Goodness, you might think, what a horrible accident. What a terrible thing to happen. Imagine though, that the following Thursday you got up and your newspaper said, "Another Jumbo Jet Disaster: 442 Die." My God, you might think. Not another disaster! How horrible. What in the world is wrong with our air traffic system. And then imagine—please imagine as best you can—getting up the following Friday and seeing in the paper: "Third Tragic Airline Crash: 431 Dead." Not only you but the nation would be beside itself. A federal investigation would be demanded. Flights would be grounded. Commissions would be appointed. Massive lawsuits would be filed. *Newsweek* and *Time* would run cover stories. It would be the lead item on television news programs for several days. Television documentaries would explore the issue. The uproar would be tremendous.

But this is not an imaginary problem. It is real. A jumbo jet *does* crash every week. Well, not one jet, but a lot of little jets. Well, not little jets really, but little transportation devices. These devices are called passenger automobiles. And approximately 457 people die in them *each week* in the United States (23,800 people each year—37,500 if we count trucks and motorcycles; National Safety Council, 1990), enough to fill a jumbo jet.

A jumbo jet's worth of people die in passenger cars on our nation's highways every week, *yet we pay no attention*. The "Jumbo Jet's Worth of People Who Die" are not presented to us in a vivid way by the media. Hence, the 457 people who die *each week* in passenger cars (plus the additional 263 who die *each week* in trucks and on motorcycles) have no vividness for us. We don't talk about them at the dinner table as we do when a jet goes down and kills a lot of people. We do not debate the safety and necessity of car travel as we would the safety of the air traffic system if a jumbo jet crashed every week killing 400 people each time. The 457 are not on the news because they

are distributed all over the country and thus are a statistical abstraction to most of us. The media do not vividly present to us these 457 deaths because they do not happen in the same place. Instead, the media present to us (occasionally) a number (e.g., 457 per week). This *should* be enough to get us thinking, but it is not. Driving automobiles is an extremely dangerous activity, however it is measured (Lichtenstein, Slovic, Fischhoff, Layman, & Combs, 1978; National Safety Council, 1990), yet there has never been a national debate about its risk relative to the benefits involved. Is this an acceptable toll for a suburban lifestyle that demands a lot of driving? We never ask the question because no problem is recognized. No problem is recognized because the cost is not presented to us in a vivid way, as is the cost of airline crashes.

Think of the absurdity of the following example. A friend drives you 20 miles to the airport where you are getting on a plane for a trip of about 750 miles. Your friend is likely to say, "Have a safe trip," as you part. This parting comment turns out to be sadly ironic, because your friend is *three times more likely to die in a car accident on the 20-mile trip back home than you are on your flight of 750 miles* (National Safety Council, 1990). It is the vividness problem that accounts for the apparent irrationality of person A's wishing person B safety, when it is person A who is in more danger.

Misleading personal judgments based on the vividness of media-presented images are widespread. One study (MacDonald, 1990; see also Cole, 1998) surveyed parents to see which risks to their children worried them the most. Parents turned out to be most worried about their children's being abducted, an event with a probability of 1 in 700,000. In contrast, the probability of their child's being killed in a car crash, which the parents worried about much less, is well over *100 times more likely* than their being abducted (Paulos, 1988). Of course, the fears of abduction are mostly a media-created worry. The results actually suggest that, largely because of perceptions skewed by vividness effects, "American parents seem to worry about events that are least likely to happen" (MacDonald, 1990). One of the researchers lamented that this focus on worries that are "currently fashionable" misdirects the attention of parents and leads them to "ignore areas where they could have more impact, like school performance, television viewing habits, drug use and car safety" (MacDonald, 1990).

Writer Katherine Dunn (1993) recounted the fear she felt as a parent in the mid-1980s when stories of abducted children were sweeping the country. Rumors were spread that as many as 70,000 children had been snatched in malls and used by pornographers and/or tortured by strangers. Dunn reported tracking down the actual evidence by calling

the FBI. It turned out that the number 70,000 referred not to abductions but to the number of runaways and children involved in custody disputes. Regarding children being abducted by strangers—which was the heart of the rumor sweeping the country—the FBI had recorded seven such cases nationwide. It was obviously not the number of these cases that had prompted such parental fears, but the vividness of the descriptions of the harm to the children. The vastly greater danger to any child in the passenger seat of an automobile (even when buckled up) was simply not as vivid.

The previous anecdote calls to mind science writer K. C. Cole's (1998) description of the ridiculous image of a woman driving down the street with a young child romping in the front seat, arriving at a shopping mall, and then getting out and grabbing the child's hand very tightly as she worries about child kidnappers. Cole discusses some of the reasons why people misassess risk. One factor involved is that people exaggerate risks that are perceived to be beyond their control. This is one reason why airline accidents—with people strapped in seats and dependent on the skills of others, on the performance of technology, and on the weather—seem so unacceptable to people. Cole (1998) reports on a poll taken after a TWA crash in which a large majority of people were willing to pay $50 more for a round-trip airline ticket if it increased safety. Yet the same people resist safety features in automobiles that would provide a much greater increment in safety at a much lower cost.

Writer Peter Boyer (1999) describes how similar misperceptions of risk are fostered by the gun lobby in the United States which tries to keep the public focused on vivid cases of "intruders" coming through the doors of households. The not-so-subtle subtext here is that one lowers one's risk by having a gun to protect yourself. Boyer (1999) points to the irony that the gun industry tries to focus attention on "guns in the hands of bad people" when the actual statistics show that the real problem is "guns in the hands of *good* people." Criminals do not account for most gun deaths in this country. There are actually more suicides with guns than there are homicides with guns. Most gun deaths are unintentional shootings and suicides—which is why research indicates that bringing a gun into a home actually *increases* family risk.

The Overwhelming Impact of the Single Case

Psychologists have extensively studied the tendency for people's judgments to be dominated by a single, salient example when more accurate information is available. Hamill, Wilson, and Nisbett (1980) showed subjects a taped interview with a prison guard. Some subjects viewed interviews with a guard whose responses and manner suggested that he was a truly humane individual. Others viewed an interview with an extremely inhumane and disagreeable guard. The interviews modified opinions about guards in a positive or negative direction, depending on which interview had been viewed. More interesting was the fact that half the subjects received information indicating that the interview they had witnessed was a part of a large study of prison guards and that the guard they had seen was highly typical of all guards in the prison system. The other subjects were told that the guard they had viewed was highly atypical of all guards and that his behavior and opinions were very extreme, either positively or negatively, depending on the interview. The information about whether the interview they had witnessed was typical or not had no effect on the subjects' opinions about prison guards. Knowledge of the statistical reliability of the interview was overwhelmed by the reactions to the interview itself.

Wilson and Brekke (1994) demonstrated how insidious the vividness problem is and also how it influences actual consumer behavior. They investigated how people were influenced by two different types of information about two different brands (brand A and brand B) of condom. One type of information was a survey and analysis in *Consumer Reports* magazine, and the other was the opinions of two university students about their preferences for condom brands. First, Wilson and Brekke surveyed a group of subjects on which type of information they would want to be influenced by. Over 85 percent of the subjects said that they would *want* to be more influenced by the *Consumer Reports* article than by the opinions of the two students. A similar group of subjects were then recruited for a study in which they were told that they would be given, free of charge, some condoms of their own choosing. The subjects were told that they could consult either or both of two types of information: a survey and analysis in *Consumer Reports* magazine and the opinions of two university students about their preferences. Even though less than 15 percent of a similar group of subjects *wanted* to be influenced by the opinions of the two students, 77 percent of the subjects requested both types of information. Apparently the subjects could not resist seeing the testimonials even though they did not believe that they should be affected by them. And they were indeed affected by them. When the subjects chose to see both types of information and the recommendations of the two sources of information differed, 31 percent of the subjects chose the brand of condom recommended in the students testimonials over the brand recommended by *Consumer Reports*.

Another example of how people respond differently to vivid anecdotal information comes from the media coverage of the Vietnam War in the mid to late 1960s. As the war dragged on and the death toll of Americans killed continued without an end in sight, the media took to reporting the weekly number of American service personnel who had been killed that week. Week after week, the figure varied between 200 and 300, and the public, seemingly, became quite accustomed to this report. However, one week a major magazine published a spread, running on for several pages, of the individual pictures of those persons who had died in the previous week. The public was now looking, concretely, at the approximately 250 individual lives that had been lost in a typical week. The result was a major outcry against the toll that the war was taking. The 250 pictures had an effect that the weekly numbers had not had. But we, as a society, must overcome this tendency not to believe numbers—to have to *see* everything. Most of the complex influences on our society are abstractions that are accurately captured only by numbers. Until the public learns to treat abstractions as seriously as images, public opinion will be as fickle as the latest image to flicker across the screen.

But it is not only the public that is plagued by the vividness problem. Experienced clinical practitioners in both psychology and medicine struggle all the time with the tendency to have their judgment clouded by the overwhelming impact of the single case. Writer Francine Russo (1999) describes the dilemma of Wille Anderson, an oncologist at the University of Virginia. Anderson is an advocate of controlled experimentation and routinely enrolls his patients in controlled clinical trials, but he still struggles with his own reactions to single, salient cases that have an emotional impact on his decisions. Despite his scientific orientation, he admits that "when it's real people looking you in the eye, you get wrapped up in their hopes and your hopes for their hopes, and it's *hard*" (p. 36). But Anderson knows that sometime the best thing for his patients is to ignore the "real person looking you in the eye" and go with what the best evidence says. And the best evidence comes from a controlled clinical trial, not from the emotional reaction to that person looking you in the eye.

What to Do About the Vividness Problem

The vividness problem is a difficulty we all face when evaluating evidence. And in an environment saturated with media images, it is becoming increasingly difficult for society not to be dominated by the images and instead to solve its problems based on valid evidence. Writer Barry Glassner (1999) describes an all too familiar example. On an Oprah Winfrey program in 1995, information was being presented on a surgical intervention (which will here remain unnamed so as not to contribute further to a vividness effect) that had caused some controversy because some people had claimed to have been injured by it. Evidence was being presented that studies from the Mayo Clinic, Harvard, and the University of Michigan had shown no overall danger from the procedure—at which point a woman claiming to have been injured jumped up from the audience and shouted "We are the evidence. The study is us sitting here!" (Glassner, 1999, p. 164). Which do you think the television audience of millions remembered better—the study from the Mayo Clinic or the woman screaming that she had been injured?

Even though we all are prone to overestimating the value of testimonial and other single-case evidence, we can become more self-aware and more conscious of when our opinions are being overwhelmed by personal testimony or particularly vivid single cases. A column by writer Remar Sutton (1987) illustrates quite well how becoming more aware of these influences can help. He wrote about the beginning of his attempt at a major weight loss by describing how "a diving buddy" had recommended a popular book, *Fit for Life*. Sutton described seeing the authors on a talk show and mentioned that they "appeared awfully sincere, sounded authoritative, and attacked some traditional nutritional thinking." He recalled that "every time a critic attacked them, they rebutted effectively *with their own experiences* [italics added]. All of that, *and* the talk show host said he lost weight and felt better with their plan, too." In short, Sutton admitted in his column that he had become interested in the ideas in this book through his hearing of personal experiences and testimonials.

But fortunately Sutton had acquired the critical thinking skills that this book is trying to teach. He researched the information given in the book, looking for confirming evidence—not on talk shows and in popular magazines but in the peer-reviewed scientific literature. He concluded that "too many ideas presented in the book were simply not backed up by long-term controlled scientific research that was statistically valid. Indeed, most of these ideas were counter to statistically valid research." Furthermore, in the course of his research, Sutton found out that the two authors had received their nutrition certificates from a "school" in Austin, Texas, that was nothing more than a post office box!

Sutton had the insight to realize that he had been close to being "sucked in" by the quackery in the book and to ask himself, "So why did I nearly fall for the *Fit for Life* approach?" His answer provides a good review of several of the pitfalls described previously. He admitted that he "trusted [his] diving friend's recommendation based on his personal experience." He had also liked the way the authors "presented *themselves* as much as their information" and that he "believed that television . . . and large numbers of book sales made the message of *Fit for Life* legitimate."

Sutton's conclusion sums up the vividness issue nicely:

> Like it or not, personal testimonials and the sincerity of a person's presentation do not necessarily make any product or opinion accurate. Carefully designed, properly controlled, replicable studies which prove statistically valid over the long term are the only assurance any of us have that a diet or medical treatment . . . can benefit us.

Sutton ended by stating that he was still not hostile to new or innovative approaches to dieting, and he urged proponents of new approaches to write him. But he reminded them, "I'll be happy to present the opposite point of view on diet and fitness as long as the proponents of these views can point me to the reliable scientific studies that provide statistical validity for that position. Please do write, but don't forget those bibliographies."

In summary, the problems created by reliance on testimonial evidence are everpresent. The vividness of such evidence often eclipses more reliable information and obscures understanding. Psychology instructors worry that merely pointing out the logical fallacies of reliance on testimonial evidence is not enough to provide a deep understanding of the pitfalls of this type of data. What else can be done? Is there any other way to get this concept across to people? Fortunately there is an alternative—an alternative somewhat different from the academic approach. The essence of this approach is to fight vividness with vividness. To hoist testimonials by their own petard! To let testimonials devour themselves with their own absurdity. A practitioner of this approach is the one, the only, the indubitable Amazing Randi!

The Amazing Randi: Fighting Fire with Fire

James Randi is a magician and jack-of-all trades who was given a MacArthur Foundation "genius" grant. For many years, he has been trying to teach the public some basic skills of critical thinking. The Amazing Randi (his stage name) has done this by exposing the fraud and charlatanism surrounding claims of "psychic" abilities. Although he has uncovered many magicians and con-

jurors masquerading as psychics, he is best known for exposing the trickery of Uri Geller, the psychic superstar of the 1970s. Bursting on the scene with his grand claims of psychic powers, Geller captivated the media to an extraordinary degree. He was featured in newspapers, on television shows, and in major news magazines on several continents. Randi detected and exposed the common and sometimes embarrassingly simple magic tricks that Geller used to perform his psychic "feats," which included bending keys and spoons, and starting watches—mundane fare for a good magician. Since the Geller exposé, Randi has continued to use his considerable talents in the service of the public's right to know the truth in spite of itself by exposing the fallacies behind ESP, biorhythms, psychic surgery, extraterrestrials, levitation, and other pseudosciences, all marvelously detailed with great humor in his book *Flim-Flam* (1980; see also his book *The Faith Healers,* 1987, in which he exposed several bogus religious "healers" as frauds).

One of Randi's minor diversions consists of demonstrating how easy it is to garner testimonial evidence for any preposterous event or vacuous claim. His technique is to let people be swallowed up in a trap set by their own testimonials. Randi makes much use of that fascinating American cultural institution, the talk show, often appearing as a guest in the guise of someone other than himself. On a New York show a few years ago, he informed the audience that, while driving through New Jersey earlier in the day, he had seen a formation of orange V-shaped objects flying overhead in a northerly direction. Within seconds, as Randi put it, "the station switchboard lit up like an electronic Christmas tree." Witness after witness called in to confirm this remarkable sighting. Unfortunately for them, the "sighting" was only a product of Randi's imagination. Callers provided many details that Randi had "omitted," including the fact that there had been more than one pass of the "saucers." This little scam illustrates how completely unreliable are individual reports that "something happened."

In Winnipeg, Canada, Randi appeared on a radio show as an "astrographologist." A week earlier, listeners had been told to send in their handwriting samples and birth dates. Three were chosen and were contacted so that Randi could assess the "readings" of their personalities. He was hugely successful, receiving ratings from the listeners of 9, 10, and 10 on a 1-to-10 scale of accuracy. Randi did eventually reveal the secret of his method to the radio listeners. He had read, word for word, the "readings" that astrologer Sydney Omarr had given to three members

of the audience of a recent *Merv Griffin Show.*

On a different radio show, Randi demonstrated the basis of the popularity of another pseudoscience: biorhythms (Hines, 1998). One listener agreed to keep a day-by-day diary and compare it with a two-month biorhythm chart that had been prepared especially for her. Two months later, the woman called back to inform the audience that biorhythms should be taken very seriously because her chart was more than 90 percent accurate. Randi had to inform her of the silly mistake made by his secretary, who had sent someone else's chart to her, rather than her own. However, the woman did agree to evaluate the correct chart, which would be mailed to her right away, and to call back. A couple of days later, the woman called back, relieved. Her own chart was just as accurate—in fact, even *more* accurate. On the next show, however, it was discovered that, whoops, another error had been made. The woman had been sent Randi's secretary's chart, rather than her own!

Randi's biorhythm and astrographologist scams are actually examples of a phenomenon that has been termed the *P. T. Barnum* effect (Barnum, the famous carnival and circus operator, coined the statement "There's a sucker born every minute"). This effect has been extensively studied by psychologists (e.g., Dickson & Kelly, 1985), who have found that the vast majority of individuals will endorse generalized personality summaries as accurate and specific descriptions of themselves. The Barnum effect makes it easier to generate testimonials and, of course, shows why they are worthless. There are certain sets of statements and phrases that most people see as applicable to themselves (many of these phrases have been studied by psychologists; see, e.g., Dickson & Kelly, 1985; Hyman, 1981; Marks & Kammann, 1980). Anyone can feed them to a "client" as individualized psychological "analysis." The client is usually very impressed by the individualized accuracy of the "personality reading," not knowing that the same reading is being given to everyone. Of course, the Barnum effect is the basis of belief in the accuracy of palm readers and astrologers.

What Randi is trying to do in these little scams is to teach people a lesson about the worthlessness of testimonial evidence. He consistently demonstrates how easy it is to generate testimonials in favor of just about *any* bogus claim (Randi, 1983). For this reason, presenting a testimonial in support of a particular claim is meaningless. Only evidence from controlled observations is sufficient to actually *test* a claim. . . .

The Seed of Our Undoing

by Daniel M. Wegner, University of Virginia

Daniel M. Wegner is Professor of Psychology at the University of Virginia. His doctorate in psychology is from Michigan State University (1974), and his work is on the role of thought in self-control and social life. Author of *White Bears and Other Unwanted Thoughts* (1989), he also wrote *Implicit Psychology* (1977) and *A Theory of Action Identification* (Erlbaum, 1985), both with Robin R. Vallacher, and edited *The Self in Social Psychology* (1980) with Vallacher and the *Handbook of Mental Control* (1993) with James W. Pennebaker. His research has been funded by NSF and is currently funded by NIMH. He has been a Fellow of the Center for Advanced Study in the Behavioral Sciences (1996–1997), and has served as associate editor of *Psychological Review*. References to his research are available on his home page: http://wsrv.clas.Virginia.EDU/~dmw2m/

According to Aristotle, the classic Greek tragedies tell stories of good people whose nature contains the seed of their own undoing. The research that my colleagues, students, and I have been conducting on *mental control* reveals the outline of just such a seed in the psychological processes that operate when people try to control their own minds. This seed is not quite tragic, as it does not always lead to wholesale undoing. However, it is certainly ironic—and we have been using the term "ironic process" to describe it.

The Irony of Not Thinking

The possibility that there might be an ironic process in mental control is easy to grasp in the case of thought suppression. A person who is asked to stop thinking about a white bear, for example, will typically think about it repeatedly as a result. In the first studies of this phenomenon (conducted with David Schneider, Sam Carter, and Teri White), we used stream-of-consciousness reports during suppression to measure this recurrence, but this suppression-induced preoccupation has now been found with less conspicuous methods. People who are trying not to think of an emotional thought such as sex, for example, show an increase in electrodermal response—as much as they do when they are specifically trying to focus on that thought.

Under some conditions, suppression yields even more intense levels of preoccupation with a thought than does concentration. People trying not to think about a target thought show such *hyperaccessibility*—the tendency for the thought to come to mind more readily even than a thought that is the focus of intentional concentration—when they are put under an additional mental load or stress. In several studies using the Stroop color-word paradigm (conducted with Ralph Erber and Sophia Zanakos), for example, we have found that trying not to think about a target word under conditions of mental load makes people unusually slow at identifying the color in which the word is presented. The word jumps into mind before the color and interferes with naming it. By this measure, unwanted thoughts are found to be more accessible than other comparison thoughts. And the ironic effect announces itself with a reversal of this finding under load for concentration: On average, any thought at all is more accessible than the concentration target.

Both of these observations can be explained by an ironic automatic process in the mind. The attempt to suppress a thought seems to conjure up an ironic psychological process that then works against the very intention that set it in motion. The suppressed thought is brought to mind in sporadic intrusions because of this sensitivity. The attempt to concentrate on a thought, in turn, seems to introduce an ironic psychological process that works against the intention to concentrate, and that therefore enhances the accessibility of everything other than the concentration target.

Why might such ironic processes occur? One way of accounting for these findings is to suggest that ironic processes are part of the machinery of mental control. It may be that in any attempt to control our minds, two processes are instituted—an *operating process* that works quite consciously and effortfully to carry out our desire, and an *ironic process* that works unconsciously and less effortfully to check on whether the operating process is failing and needs renewal. In the case of thought suppression, for instance, the operating process involves the conscious and labored search for distracters—as we try to fasten our minds on anything other than the unwanted thought—whereas the ironic process is an automatic search for the unwanted thought itself. The ironic process is a monitor of sorts, a checker that determines whether the operating process is needed, but that also has a tendency to influence the accessibility of conscious mental contents. It ironically enhances the sensitivity of the mind to the very thought that is being suppressed.

Varieties of Irony

An ironic process theory can explain far more than the paradox of thought suppression—indeed, something like this might vex most everything we try to do with our minds. If the ironic process is inherent in the control system whereby we secure whatever mental control we do enjoy, then it ought to be evident across many domains in which we do have some success in controlling our minds. However, because the operating process requires conscious effort and mental resources, it can be undermined by distraction and evidence of ironic processes will then arise. When people undertake to control their minds while they are burdened by mental loads—such as distracters, stress, or time pressure—the result should often be the opposite of what they intend.

Studies in my laboratory have uncovered evidence of ironic effects in several domains. Ironic mood effects occur, for example, when people attempt to control their moods while they are under mental load. Individuals following instructions to try to make themselves happy become sad, whereas those trying to make themselves sad actually experience buoyed mood. Ironic effects also surface in the self-control of anxiety. People trying to relax under load show psychophysiological indications of anxiousness, whereas those not trying to relax show fewer such indications. And ironic effects also occur in the control of sleep. People who are encouraged to "fall asleep as quickly as you can" as they listen to raucous, distracting music stay awake longer than those who are not given such encouragement. Ironic effects also accrue in the control of movement, arising when people try to keep a handheld pendulum from moving in a certain direction, or when they try to keep from overshooting a golf putt. In both cases, an imposition of mental load makes individuals more likely to commit exactly the unwanted action.

Research in other laboratories has revealed further ironic effects. Studies by Neil Macrae, Galen Bodenhausen, Alan Milne, and their colleagues, for instance, have established several remarkable ironic effects in the mental control of stereotyping and prejudice. People who are trying not to stereotype a skinhead as they form an impression of him, for example, show greater stereotyping under mental load. Individuals in this circumstance have been found to avoid even sitting near the skinhead as well. And people under mental load who are specifically trying to forget the stereotypical characteristics of a person (in a directed forgetting study) have been found more likely to recall those characteristics than are people without such load.

Ironic effects observed in yet other laboratories lend further credence to the basic idea. In work by Jeff Greenberg, Tom Pyszczynski, Sheldon Solomon, Jamie Arndt and their colleagues, for example, distraction tasks imposed after people have been asked to reflect for a while on their own death have revealed high levels of accessibility of death-related thoughts. This series of experiments suggests that people who are prompted to think about death turn shortly thereafter to the strategy of suppressing such thoughts even without instruction to do so—and thus suffer ironic returns of the thought. Related findings reported by Leonard Newman, Kimberly Duff, and Roy Baumeister indicate that people under mental load who are forming impressions of a person will project a personality trait onto the target when they are suppressing thoughts of the trait—whether in response to suppression instructions, or

spontaneously because they dislike the trait in themselves

Cultivating the Seed

These studies illustrate how it is that we can, on occasion, cultivate the seed of our own undoing. To begin with, we apparently need good intentions. Like Aristotle's tragic hero, the individual attempting mental control often does so for good cause—in hopes of achieving high performance, moral ends, or at least mental peace. People often begin on the path toward ironic effects when they try to exercise good intentions—to behave effectively, to avoid prejudice, to be happy, to relax, to avoid negative thoughts or thoughts of personal shortcomings, or even just to sleep. The simple adoption of a goal is no sin, but this turns out to be the first step toward ironic effects.

The next step in cultivating the seed, as illustrated in this research, is the pursuit of such noble goals in the face of a shortage of mental resources. When there is insufficient time and thought available to achieve the chosen intention, people do not merely fail to produce the mental control they desire. Rather, the ironic process goes beyond "no change" to produce an actual reversal. The opposite happens. These studies indicate, in sum, that ironic effects are precipitated when we try to do more than we can with our minds.

Why would we do such a thing? At the extreme, we do this when we are desperate: We will try to achieve a particular sort of mental control even though we are mentally exhausted. These traits are, of course, highly reminiscent of the circumstances of many people suffering from various forms of psychological disorder. It makes sense that people who are anxious, depressed, traumatized, obsessed, or those with disorders of sleep, eating, movement, or the like, might frequently try to overcome their symptoms—and might also be inclined to

attempt such control even under adverse conditions of stress or distraction. Evidence from correlational studies conducted in my laboratory and elsewhere suggests a possible role for ironic processes in several such forms of psychopathology.

We know from such relations that attempts to avoid unwanted symptoms are often highly associated with those symptoms. The most obvious explanation of these associations is that people who experience unwanted mental states attempt to control them. But the more subtle possibility, as yet untested in large-scale studies, is that the attempt to control unwanted mental states plays a role in perpetuating them. The experiments showing that mental control attempts can yield laboratory analogs of unwanted mental states provide one basis for this conclusion.

Another line of evidence suggesting a role for ironic processes in the etiology of some disorders comes from studies of what happens when mental control is rescinded. The best examples of such work are the series of experiments by James Pennebaker and colleagues. When people in these studies are encouraged to express their deepest thoughts and feelings in writing, they experience subsequent improvements in psychological and physical health. Expressing oneself in this way involves relinquishing the pursuit of mental control, and so eliminates a key requirement for the production of ironic effects. After all, as suggested in other studies conducted in my lab with Julie Lane and Laura Smart, the motive to keep one's thoughts and personal characteristics secret is strongly linked with mental control. Disclosing these things to others, or even in writing to oneself, is the first step toward abandoning what may be an overweening and futile quest to control one's own thoughts and emotions.

When we relax the desire for the control of our minds, the seeds of our undoing may remain uncultivated, perhaps then to dry up and blow away.

How Culture Molds Habits of Thought

By ERICA GOODE

For more than a century, Western philosophers and psychologists have based their discussions of mental life on a cardinal assumption: that the same basic processes underlie all human thought, whether in the mountains of Tibet or the grasslands of the Serengeti.

Cultural differences might dictate what people thought about. Teenage boys in Botswana, for example, might discuss cows with the same passion that New York teenagers reserved for sports cars.

But the habits of thought—the strategies people adopted in processing information and making sense of the world around them—were, Western scholars assumed, the same for everyone, exemplified by, among other things, a devotion to logical reasoning, a penchant for categorization and an urge to understand situations and events in linear terms of cause and effect.

Recent work by a social psychologist at the University of Michigan, however, is turning this long-held view of mental functioning upside down.

In a series of studies comparing European Americans to East Asians, Dr. Richard Nisbett and his colleagues have found that people who grow up in different cultures do not just think about different things: they think differently.

"We used to think that everybody uses categories in the same way, that logic plays the same kind of role for everyone in the understanding of everyday life, that memory, perception, rule application and so on are the same," Dr. Nisbett said. "But we're now arguing that cognitive processes themselves are just far more malleable than mainstream psychology assumed."

A summary of the research will be published next winter in the journal Psychological Review, and Dr. Nisbett discussed the findings Sunday at the annual meetings of the American Psychological Association in Washington.

In many respects, the cultural disparities the researchers describe mirror those described by anthropologists, and may seem less than surprising to Americans who have lived in Asia. And Dr. Nisbett and his colleagues are not the first psychological researchers to propose that thought may be embedded in cultural assumptions: Soviet psychologists of the 1930's posed logic problems to Uzbek peasants, arguing that intellectual tools were influenced by pragmatic circumstances.

But the new work is stirring interest in academic circles because it tries to define and elaborate on cultural differences through a series of tightly controlled laboratory experiments. And the theory underlying the research challenges much of what has been considered gospel in cognitive psychology for the last 40 years.

"If it's true, it turns on its head a great deal of the science that many of us have been doing, and so it's sort of scary and thrilling at the same time," said Dr. Susan Andersen, a professor of psychology at New York University and an associate editor at Psychological Review.

In the broadest sense, the studies—carried out in the United States, Japan, China and Korea—document a familiar division. Easterners, the researchers find, appear to think more "holistically," paying greater attention to context and relationship, relying more on experience-based knowledge than abstract logic and showing more tolerance for contradiction. Westerners are more "analytic" in their thinking, tending to detach objects from their context, to avoid contradictions and to rely more heavily on formal logic.

In one study, for example, by Dr. Nisbett and Takahiko Masuda, a graduate student at Michigan, students from Japan and the United States were shown an animated underwater scene, in which one larger "focal" fish swam among smaller fishes and other aquatic life.

Asked to describe what they saw, the Japanese subjects were much more likely to begin by setting the scene, saying for example, "There was a lake or pond" or "The bottom was rocky," or "The water was green." Americans, in contrast, tended to begin their descriptions with the largest fish, making statements like

"There was what looked like a trout swimming to the right."

Over all, Japanese subjects in the study made 70 percent more statements about aspects of the background environment than Americans, and twice as many statements about the relationships between animate and inanimate objects. A Japanese subject might note, for example, that "The big fish swam past the gray seaweed."

"Americans were much more likely to zero in on the biggest fish, the brightest object, the fish moving the fastest," Dr. Nisbett said. "That's where the money is as far as they're concerned."

But the greater attention paid by East Asians to context and relationship was more than just superficial, the researchers found. Shown the same larger fish swimming against a different, novel background, Japanese participants had more difficulty recognizing it than Americans, indicating that their perception was intimately bound with their perception of the background scene.

When it came to interpreting events in the social world, the Asians seemed similarly sensitive to context, and quicker than the Americans to detect when people's behavior was determined by situational pressures.

Psychologists have long documented what they call the fundamental attribution error, the tendency for people to explain human behavior in terms of the traits of individual actors, even when powerful situational forces are at work. Told that a man has been instructed to give a speech endorsing a particular presidential candidate, for example, most people will still believe that the speaker believes what he is saying.

Yet Asians, according to Dr. Nisbett and his colleagues, may in some situations be less susceptible to such errors, indicating that they do not describe a universal way of thinking, but merely the way that Americans think.

In one study, by Dr. Nisbett and Dr. Incheol Choi, of Seoul National

What Americans notice: the biggest, fastest and shiniest.

University in Korea, the Korean and American subjects were asked to read an essay either in favor of or opposed to the French conducting atomic tests in the Pacific. The subjects were told that the essay writer had been given "no choice" about what to write. But subjects from both cultures still showed a tendency to "err," judging that the essay writers believed in the position endorsed in the essays.

When the Korean subjects were first required to undergo a similar experience themselves, writing an essay according to instructions, they quickly adjusted their estimates of how strongly the original essay writers believed what they wrote. But Americans clung to the notion that the essay writers were expressing sincere beliefs.

One of the most striking dissimilarities found by the researchers emerged in the way East Asians and Americans in the studies responded to contradiction. Presented with weaker arguments running contrary to their own, Americans were likely to solidify their opinions, Dr. Nisbett said, "clobbering the weaker arguments," and resolving the threatened contradiction in their own minds. Asians, however, were more likely to modify their own position, acknowledging that even the weaker arguments had some merit.

In one study, for example, Asian and American subjects were presented with strong arguments in favor of financing a research project on adoption. A second group was presented both with strong arguments in support of the project and weaker arguments opposing it.

Both Asian and American subjects in the first group expressed strong

support for the research. But while Asian subjects in the second group responded to the weaker opposing arguments by decreasing their support, American subjects increased their endorsement of the project in response to the opposing arguments.

In a series of studies, Dr. Nisbett and Dr. Kaiping Peng of the University of California at Berkeley found that Chinese subjects were less eager to resolve contradictions in a variety of situations than American subjects. Asked to analyze a conflict between mothers and daughters, American subjects quickly came down in favor of one side or the other. Chinese subjects were more likely to see merit on both sides, commenting, for example, that, "Both the mothers and the daughters have failed to understand each other."

Given a choice between two different types of philosophical argument, one based on analytical logic, devoted to resolving contradiction, the other on a dialectical approach, accepting of contradiction, Chinese subjects preferred the dialectical approach, while Americans favored the logical arguments. And Chinese subjects expressed more liking than Americans for proverbs containing a contradiction, like the Chinese saying "Too modest is half boastful." American subjects, Dr. Nisbett said, found such contradictions "rather irritating."

Dr. Nisbett and Dr. Ara Norenzayan of the University of Illinois have also found indications that when logic and experiential knowledge are in conflict, Americans are more likely than Asians to adhere to the rules of formal logic, in keeping with a tradition that in Western societies began with the Ancient Greeks.

For example, presented with a logical sequence like, "All animals with fur hibernate. Rabbits have fur. Therefore rabbits hibernate," the Americans, the researchers found, were more likely to accept the validity of the argument, separating its formal structure, that of a syllogism, from its content, which might or might not be plausible. Asians, in contrast, more frequently judged such syllogisms as invalid based on their implausibility—not all animals with fur do in fact hibernate.

While the cultural disparities traced in the researchers' work are substantial, their origins are much less clear. Historical evidence suggests that a divide between Eastern and Occidental thinking has existed at least since ancient times, a tradition of adversarial debate, formal logical argument and analytic deduction flowering in Greece, while in China an appreciation for context and complexity, dialectical argument and a tolerance for the "yin and yang" of life flourished.

How much of this East-West difference is a result of differing social and religious practices, different languages or even different geography is anyone's guess. But both styles, Dr. Nisbett said, have advantages, and both have limitations. And neither approach is written into the

genes: many Asian-Americans, born in the United States, are indistinguishable in their modes of thought from European-Americans.

Dr. Alan Fiske, an associate professor of anthropology at the University of California at Los Angeles, said that experimental research like Dr. Nisbett's "complements a lot of ethnographic work that has been done."

"Anthropologists have been describing these cultures and this can tell you a lot about everyday life and the ways people talk and interact," Dr. Fiske said. "But it's always difficult to know how to make sense of these qualitative judgments, and they aren't controlled in the same way that an experiment is controlled."

Yet not everyone agrees that all the dissimilarities described by Dr. Nesbitt and his colleagues reflect fundamental differences in psychological process.

Dr. Patricia Cheng, for example, a professor of psychology at the University of California at Los Angeles, said that many of the researchers' findings meshed with her own experience. "Having grown up in a traditional Chinese family and also being in Western culture myself," she said, "I do see some entrenched habits of interpretation of the world that are different across the cultures, and they do lead to pervasive differences."

But Dr. Cheng says she thinks that some differences—the Asian tolerance for contradiction, for example—are purely social. "There is not a difference in logical tolerance," she said.

Still, to the extent that the studies reflect real differences in thinking and perception, psychologists may have to radically revise their ideas about what is universal and what is not, and to develop new models of mental process that take cultural influences into account.

The Power of the Situation over You

Michael J. Lovaglia *University of Iowa*

INVESTIGATING THE FUNDAMENTAL ATTRIBUTION ERROR

The first studies to investigate the fundamental attribution error looked at the conclusions people draw when they watch another person's behavior. We use what people say and do as clues to discover what kind of person they are. However, we may attribute behavior to a person's character when that person had little or no control over what she did. Factors in a person's situation may have dictated her behavior. She may have had little choice but to act as she did, so her behavior would not really tell us much about the kind of person she is. Nonetheless, we will probably continue to assume that her beliefs and attitudes correspond to her behavior. Because we typically assume a correspondence between a person's behavior and attitude whether one exists or not, another term used almost interchangeably with the fundamental attribution error is *correspondence bias* (Jones 1986). Correspondence bias represents a different theoretical approach to the same research area. It helps to be familiar with both terms.

Jones and Harris (1967) set up a situation where people would judge a person's attitude based on an essay the person had written. People were asked to judge one of two essays about Fidel Castro's communist regime in Cuba. They were told that the essay they read had been written for a political science class. One essay supported Castro; the other essay attacked him. People read the essay then rated the author's true attitude toward Castro. Researchers predicted, as would most of us, that people would assume that authors of a pro-Castro essay had a pro-Castro attitude, whereas authors of an anti-Castro essay had an anti-Castro attitude. That is exactly what happened, to no one's great surprise.

When they repeated the study, Jones and Harris (1967) showed people the assignment that a teacher had given along with the essay that had been written to complete the assignment. People reading the pro-Castro essay saw that the assignment had been to "write a short cogent defense of Castro's Cuba." Similarly, people reading the anti-Castro essay saw that the assignment had been to "write a short cogent criticism of Castro's Cuba." People thus were aware that the author of the essay had little choice in the subject matter of the essay. The teacher's assignment dictated whether the essay would be pro-Castro or anti-Castro. Would people continue to assume that authors of pro-Castro essays had attitudes more favorable to Castro than did authors of anti-Castro essays? They did. Despite knowing that the essay author had little choice in the content of the essay, people continued to assume that authors of the pro-Castro essay were more pro-Castro than were authors of the anti-Castro essay. That is, despite direct evidence that a situational factor (the assignment) dictated the content of the essay, people assumed that the essay content *corresponded* to the true attitude of the writer. We now know that by ignoring the evidence of a situational cause for the essay's content, the students displayed *correspondence bias*. They committed the *fundamental attribution error.*

The scientific community did not immediately accept the existence of a widespread bias toward dispositional attributions, let alone a fundamental attribution error. Following Jones and Harris (1967), many studies were conducted that showed how correspondence bias persists in a variety of situations that restrict a person's behavior. In one study, students judged the attitude of a person reading an essay aloud. Students assumed the essay reader's attitude corresponded to the essay content even when they had been told that the speech had been written by someone else (Miller 1976).

In my social psychology classes, I demonstrate the pervasive effect of correspondence bias. Two students volunteer to present a short speech. I take them into the hallway and give each a handwritten speech on the abortion issue. One essay is prochoice, the other is prolife. The presenters then take five minutes to practice their speech. Meanwhile, in the classroom, I pass out index cards on which the students will rate their impressions of the true attitudes of the presenters toward abortion. Then the first presenter gives the prolife speech. Students rate the true attitude of the presenter on an index car and turn it in. The second presenter gives the prochoice speech. Again, students rate the true attitude of the presenter and hand in their ratings. In this situation, it is quite plausible that students rate the prochoice presenter as having a prochoice attitude and the prolife presenter as having a prolife attitude. Students, after all, may well assume that the presenters wrote the speech they were presenting, or that presenters had chosen to speak on the side of the issue that corresponded with their true attitude toward abortion.

The next part of the demonstration is more interesting. I ask for two more volunteers to give a speech. In front of the class, I ask the presenter of the prochoice speech to give the handwritten copy of the speech to the first new volunteer. I ask the presenter of the prolife speech to give the handwritten copy of that speech to the second new volunteer. It is clear to all students that I have assigned the new volunteers to speak on either the prochoice or prolife side of the issue. They had no choice in the matter. And, because students have just finished listening to the exact speeches, it is clear that the new volunteers will be reading material written by someone else. The new volunteers have a few minutes to practice their speeches. The first volunteer presents the prochoice speech and students hand in their ratings of the speaker's true attitude toward abortion. Then the second volunteer presents. Again, students rate the speaker's true attitude. In this situation, it is difficult to see how anyone would assume that speech content would necessarily correspond to the true attitudes of the speakers. After all, students had just heard another student reading the exact speech. Will students still assume that speech content corresponds to the true attitudes of the speakers? Will students rate the prochoice speaker as truly more prochoice than the prolife speaker?

Yes, students continue to display correspondence bias even when the situation dictates what the speaker will say and the students have just heard the exact words spoken by someone else. When we tally up the results in class, the pattern is the same for the second two speakers as it was for the first two speakers. The prochoice speakers are rated as having a prochoice attitude while the prolife speakers are rated as having a prolife attitude. The effect is not as dramatic for the second pair of speakers as for the first, but it is still

apparent. Students assume that a person's spoken words correspond to the attitudes that person holds. That assumption proves very difficult to counteract.

In society, correspondence bias serves to maintain power and authority relationships among people. We give people credit for being competent when in fact their social position is responsible for their performance. One striking characteristic of modern social life is that some people have power and authority over others. Parents have power over their young children. Police detectives have power over suspected criminals. Teachers have power over students. When we deal with a person who has authority over us, it can often seem that the person is smarter and more competent than we are. Instead of attributing this power to the person's position in society, we make the fundamental attribution error. We assume the person is more competent than we are because the person has power over us. We ignore the fact that people have authority because of their social position, not necessarily because of any special expertise.

One way that society gives people power over others is by granting them authority to ask questions. When a person can ask you a question and require an answer, that person has power over you. For example, on TV police dramas, suspects often have higher social status than the detective does. The suspect might be a doctor, for example. When the detective tries to interview the doctor, the doctor usually asks a lot of questions: "What is this about, Detective?" or "Why are you interviewing me?" At some point, the detective gets serious and turns the tables, saying abruptly, "Here's how this works. I ask the questions. You answer them." Suddenly the social status of the two people has been reversed. The detective has asserted his authority, transforming the high-status doctor into a low-status suspect. Teachers demonstrate their authority by requiring students to answer questions on an exam. And children dread their parents' questions: "Why are you three hours late? Where have you been? What could you possibly have been thinking?" Anyone who has been trapped answering a five-year-old's questions for an hour knows just how much power the ability to question can give a person. Five-year-olds know it too. That is one reason they ask so many questions.

Ross, Amabile, and Steinmetz (1977) showed how questions work to cement the social position of those in authority. We think that people who ask questions are more knowledgeable than are people who have to answer them. Ross, Amabile, and Steinmetz set up a "quiz game" setting in which some students would try to answer questions as contestants. Some students would ask the questions as hosts, and other students would watch the game as the audience. It is easy to see how a questioner might have an advantage in such a situation. For example, the questioner can ask very difficult questions.

Even people with little general knowledge know odd bits of information that others are not likely to know. Coming up with difficult questions is relatively easy. For example, in the study, questioners came up with questions such as "What do the initials W. H. in W. H. Auden's name stand for?" and "What is the longest glacier in the world?"

Beginning teachers soon discover a peculiar human trait. Anything we learn, no matter how complicated or difficult, seems obvious to us, even trivial, a short time after we have learned it. Because what teachers know seems obvious to them, novice teachers often make test questions too difficult for their students to answer. The teacher knows the answers, so the questions seem easy to her. The students do not know the answers and when they flunk the test, teacher and students may conclude that the class is not bright. For example, suppose you are a quiz game contestant and are asked "In what city did Sigmund Freud live and practice psychoanalysis during much of his career?" If you know the answer, it seems obvious—Vienna. You might be thinking "Everybody knows that," but you would be wrong. If you do not know the answer, the question seems impossibly difficult and even unfair. However, the person who asked the question knows the answer. Unfair or not, the questioner will seem more knowledgeable than you.

In their quiz game study, Ross, Amabile, and Steinmetz (1977) made the advantage given to questioners obvious to everyone. Students drew cards to determine who would be assigned to the various roles—questioner, answerer, or observer. Thus students realized that questioners had been chosen at random and not because they possessed any special qualification for the questioner role. Questioners were asked to come up with "challenging but not impossible" questions for the quiz game. They were asked to avoid easy questions and to create questions on topics in which they had the most knowledge. Answerers and observers also heard these instructions given to questioners. Would students still rate questioners as more knowledgeable than answerers even though the advantage given by the answerer role was made obvious? Yes. Answerers consistently rated themselves as less knowledgeable than questioners. Neutral observers also rated questioners' general knowledge superior to that of answerers. Questioners, however, may have been more aware of the advantage their position gave them. Questioners themselves did not think they were much more knowledgeable than answerers. It may be true that those in positions of great power can sometimes more clearly see the effects of situational factors. Abraham Lincoln said, "I claim not to have controlled events, but confess plainly that events controlled me" (Lincoln 1965, p. 10). Being in a position of great power, Abraham Lincoln realized how limited his power actually was.

Results of the quiz game study imply that people in a low power position, who are required to answer the questions of a person with authority over them, will come to see the authority figure as having superior general knowledge. Our correspondence bias leads us to assume that the authority figure's apparent knowledge results from her personal abilities and general competence. We ignore evidence that the authority's position makes her appear competent. When questioners appear more knowledgeable because their position gives them the power to question, their authority seems more legitimate. We tend not to notice how big an advantage social position can be. Instead, we assume that those in positions of power must be as knowledgeable and expert as they appear. More generally, we fail to notice the situational factors at work in our lives. Instead, we attribute outcomes to the personal abilities of individuals, whether to other people or ourselves. That is the fundamental attribution error.

USING SOCIAL PSYCHOLOGY TO IMPROVE YOUR LIFE

Now that we know that we have less control over our lives than we had thought, how will social psychology help us? Research on the fundamental attribution error tells us that factors in our situation are more powerful than we think they are. If situational factors are so powerful, then changing them will change our lives. If you want your life to improve, then concentrate on changing your situation. Find ways to change your situation that will have the desired effect on you.

Recall that people are about as good as their situation allows them to be. If you want to be a good person, find a situation that supports your aspirations. For example, there is a saying among professional salespeople: "If you want to be an honest salesperson, then go to work for an honest boss." The sales game is highly competitive. Intense pressure to make a sale constantly tempts salespeople to cut corners, to lie to make a sale. Professional salespeople know that individual character is no match for the constant temptation to lie unless the organization they work for encourages honesty. They have found that an honest boss ensures that their own honesty will be supported. By changing their situation (finding an honest boss) salespeople can change a basic piece of their character (personal honesty). That insight empowers us to become better people.

Here is an example of our tendency to think we have more control over events than we actually do, and how understanding social psychology can change society. Consider this statement: "Meaningful social change must rise first in the hearts and minds

of people." Most of us find it enormously appealing. We would not be surprised if a famous person had said it, perhaps Martin Luther King Jr. at the height of the civil rights movement. It conforms to personal experience. As you grow up, your ideas about who you are and what you want to do change, so you behave differently. It sounds right. Social psychology shows us that reality is much more complicated.

Successful leaders sometimes use the principles of social psychology although they may not be aware of it. Martin Lurther Kind Jr. is a good example. During the civil rights movement in the 1950s—not so long ago—most Americans felt that African Americans should be treated differently than others. African Americans were required to use separate restrooms and drinking fountains. Facilities designated for African Americans were often unavailable. Few jobs were open to them. And while many Americans of all races believed in integration as an ideal, most of them felt that nothing could be done to change racial discrimination. Today, few people in the United States believe in or condone racial discrimination. How did such a profound change occur in the attitudes and beliefs of an entire nation?

Martin Luther King's strategy during the civil rights movement played a part in changing American's attitudes toward discrimination. At the time, popular wisdom held that you cannot legislate morality. According to popular opinion, legislation outlawing discrimination would not work unless people first came to believe that discrimination was wrong. It was commonly thought that people's hearts and minds had to change before their behavior would. Martin Luther King Jr. rejected the common wisdom in formulating a strategy for the civil rights movement (Branch 1988). While he spent much of his life trying to change people's attitudes, he did not wait for people to endorse social equality for African Americans. He saw that by changing the laws that limit people's be-

havior, not only would discrimination be reduced, but eventually hearts and minds would follow. He knew that long-held beliefs and attitudes, our feelings, are highly resistant to change. He also knew that most people will obey the law. His knowledge of people told him that over time attitudes and beliefs align with behavior. We now know there was a sound basis for his strategy in social psychological research. After civil rights legislation was passed and people grew accustomed to the new rules, attitudes toward racial discrimination changed rapidly. However, there is much work left to be done. . . .

Social psychology teachers us that what we do, our behavior, has more impact over our attitudes and beliefs than we would have imagined. Common sense, after all, has told us that our attitudes and beliefs determine how we behave. However, the power of behavior to control deeply held beliefs was one of the earlier insights of the new discipline of social psychology. William James founded the first psychological laboratory in the United States at Harvard in the 1870s. In 1890, in the first American psychology textbook, he stated the principle that we can use our behavior to control our attitudes and beliefs. He said that while we cannot easily change our deeply held moral beliefs and emotionally charged attitudes,

we need only in cold blood ACT as if the thing in question were real, and keep acting as if it were real, and it will infallibly end by growing into such a connection with our life that it will become real. (James 1890/1981, p. 949)

Behavior is easier to control than beliefs and attitudes. By consciously acting in certain ways, we will eventually come to justify and believe in the attitudes implied by our behavior. For example, when I was a freshman in college, foul language was the norm. It was cool. Speaking crudely was a badge of honor. Speaking politely was considered dis-

cathy®   **by Cathy Guisewite**

Action is sometimes more important than its immediate outcome.

honest. That way of speaking became part of my identity. Swearing was who I was. Later, swearing caused problems for me. Children who heard me would use the same words I did. And I was working as a salesperson, so swearing was inappropriate on the job. I resolved to change the way I spoke. It was not particularly difficult. I reminded myself regularly not to swear and tried to think before speaking. My attitude toward swearing did not change so quickly. For a long time I felt like a phony. Blunt, coarse speech still seemed to me to be more honest and honorable. Those feelings faded the longer I went without swearing. Years later, swearing is awkward and I can make myself do it only with difficulty. My attitude toward swearing has also changed completely. It now seems unnecessary and often destructive. My behavior changed first. My attitude toward that behavior followed.

"Bring the body, the mind will follow" is a slogan used by members of Alcoholics Anonymous. Problem drinkers often feel like phonies when they try to quit drinking. They feel they are being dishonest with other people and untrue to themselves. Deeply held attitudes may be difficult to change in normal people, but where the will has been damaged by alcohol or drug use, the conscious control of beliefs is virtually absent. Instead of trying to convince newcomers that drinking is a bad idea, AA members tell them to show up at AA meetings where no one drinks. "Bring the body" means show up, act like a sober person. Stop drinking one day at a time. Eventually, if a person does not drink for a long period, drinking comes to seem foreign, unnatural. The behavior change eventually produces an attitude change. The mind follows. Problem drinkers usually associate drinking with pleasant anticipation and exhilaration, but after quitting, they slowly come to realize and understand the problems that drinking caused them. The founders of AA had studied the psychology of William James. They knew that an effective program first must change the problem behavior. Healthier attitudes toward that behavior would follow.

The same principle that made the civil rights movement successful works to keep alcoholics sober. William James's idea that changing behavior can lead to improving personal character spurred the growth of a large self-help industry in the United States. Martin Luther King Jr. showed us that we need not be imprisoned by our history of prejudice. By changing our situation, changing the legal structure of society, racial prejudice is no longer predominant. It still exists and threatens to return full-force if we are not careful. But as long as we maintain our legal structure, our laws will allow us to be better people than our traditional fears and prejudices would suggest. The insights of social psychology can work on a more personal level as well.

PERSONAL SOCIAL PSYCHOLOGY TECHNIQUE: USING AFFIRMATION

Affirmations are positive statements about the person you want to be. By affirming the kind of person we want to become, we set ourselves up to change in that direction. The technique is not new. It has been used in crude form by teachers in the United States for about as long as there have been blackboards. Picture a whitewashed rural schoolhouse. A barefoot boy in pants too short for his legs stands at the blackboard writing laboriously "I will not stick Molly's braids in the inkwell," 100 times. We now think that positive statements make more effective affirmations than negative ones; so the boy wearing flashy athletic shoes and baggy jeans might write "I will respect Molly as a person." The idea is the same. All of that writing on the blackboard is supposed to change the boy's attitude toward tormenting the girl sitting in front of him, making him a better person.

The affirmation technique gained legitimacy with William James's insight that attitudes come to correspond to behavior. Affirmations are behavior. If you repeatedly behave as if you are a certain kind of person, you grow into that kind of person. Affirmations, then, are more effective the more active you make them. Affirmations should at least be spoken clearly aloud. Better yet, write them out laboriously in the best handwriting you can muster. Write so that someone else could easily read what you have written. It is not necessary to write an affirmation 100 times. A few times a day seems sufficient to produce noticeable results.

I first used the affirmation technique as a young man selling furniture. I had fallen into the habit of using little lies to make a sale. A customer might ask, "When can I get this sofa?" I would reply, "We have a shipment coming in next week. Let me reserve one for you. We only need a 20 percent deposit with your order." I would start to fill out the paperwork. The customer would start to write a check. It was another easy sale. I knew all along that the customer's sofa would not arrive the following week. It might take about a month, but the customer did not want to wait. If I told her it would be a month, then she might keep looking until she found a store that had what she wanted in stock.

I would rationalize that technically what I said was true. We would get a shipment the following week. The customer's sofa, however, would not be on it. It was a lie. Then I would lie again when the customer called to check on the order. "Yes, we did get the shipment. Let me check the warehouse. No, your sofa did not arrive. I don't know what could have happened. I will contact the factory and get back to you." After a series of postponements and excuses, more lies, the sofa would eventually arrive. The customer would usually be happy. Rarely did a customer cancel the order even after the third or fourth delay. By then they had become committed to their purchase. The social psychology of my selling approach was sound. The ethics were not.

I never felt good about lying. I dreaded hearing the phone ring. Which customer would it be? What would I tell them this time? What had I told them last time? It was a tumultuous period in my life. I had been drinking heavily for years. I quit suddenly. I started reading books that might help me find a better way to live. One of them suggested the affirmation technique. Here is the first affirmation I tried: "I, Michael Lovaglia, am an honest and sober person." I resolved to write the affirmation at least three times a day as clearly and legibly as possible. At first it was extremely difficult. The muscles in my forearm would knot up when I tried to write those few simple words. My stomach would feel queasy. Later I found out that meant the affirmation was on target. My unconscious mind was resisting the change suggested by the affirmation. Eventually it became easier to write. My lying steadily decreased. My sales volume did go down at first but then went back up. When the phone rang at work, my anxiety level would rise, tempting me to lie. I used another affirmation to remind myself what to do: "The truth is good enough." And it was. Lying turned out to be more of a crutch than a sales tool.

Affirmations are a standard technique of the self-help industry. *The Power of Positive Thinking* by Norman Vincent Peale uses it extensively and apparently successfully. My copy of the book has a red sticker on the cover that says, OVER 5 MILLION COPIES IN PRINT. Aside from being a popular idea, it would be nice to know that affirmations also have a sound basis in social psychology. One aim of this book is to help you identify such techniques. You can concentrate on techniques that have been demonstrated to be effective and avoid the more speculative ideas in the self-improvement literature.

Attribution research explains why affirmations change our attitudes. When we observe people behaving in a certain way, we assume that their attitudes correspond to their behavior. That is correspondence bias. Our own attitudes come to correspond to our behavior in a similar way. Just as we observe others' behavior, we also observe our own behavior, at least some of the time. In some situations we may be too busy or distracted to be very good observers of what we are doing. Bem (1965, 1967) pointed out that to the extent we observe our own behavior, we will assume our attitudes correspond to that behavior. When we observe a person giving a prolife speech on abortion, we assume that person's attitude is prolife. Correspondence bias operates when we observe our own behavior as well. Bem's proposition suggests that if we make a prolife speech for whatever reason, we will observe our own behavior and assume that our attitude must be prolife. We are, or at least become, what we do. Affirmation, whether spoken or written, constitute behavior. When we observe ourselves speaking or writing about the person we want to become, we assume that we are that person. Eventually, with repeated use of the affirmation technique, the assumption about who we are becomes belief. *Affirmations allow you to grow toward the person you want to become.*

Written affirmations are effective because written evidence is hard to deny. Writing has a permanence that thought and spoken words lack. It is relatively easy to take back what you have said. "Please forgive me, I spoke without thinking" usually works if you have said something inappropriate. It is more difficult to take back what you have written. We accept that people commonly speak without thinking. We are less likely to believe they have written without thinking. Thus, as observers of our own behavior, we find written affirmations more convincing. It is as if we say to ourselves "Look how carefully I wrote this. I must have meant it." Written confessions are a good example of the power of the written word. Criminal convictions based on a written confession are almost impossible to overturn. Convictions usually stand even when it has been proved that the person convicted was coerced and confused at the time of the confession and did not know what he was signing. Juries have been known to convict on the basis of a written confession even when evidence has proven conclusively that the person who confessed could not have committed the crime. We hold people responsible for what they have written. You will hold yourself responsible for what you write about yourself. That is what makes the written affirmation a powerful tool.

Social psychological research shows why a positive affirmation is preferred over a negative one. Tell yourself to do something positive rather than to *not* do something negative. It is better to write about the person that you want to become than about the person you want to stop being. Studies have shown that using a negative word in a sentence makes the sentence harder to understand (see for example Evans 1972; Leenars, Bringmann, & Balance 1978). The danger in using negative statements as affirmation is that they require more mental processing than do positive statements. The negative statement is first seen as true, then falsified by the negative word. When my toddler is concentrating fiercely on pouring herself a glass of milk, she will usually spill it if I call out "Don't spill the milk." She understands "spill the milk" first. If she had time she would then process the "don't." But she is concentrating on her task. Before she can fully process the negative sentence, she has reacted to it as if it was positive and spills the milk. In contrast, warning her to "Be careful" will not usually produce a spill. Positive questions are easier than negative ones. Teachers know that the test question "Which of the following is *not* one of Piaget's stages of cognitive development?" will be much harder than "Which of the following is one of Piaget's stages of cognitive development?" Affirmations work the same way. A negative affirmation will probably work. It just takes more mental processing. Why put the negative statement in your mind in the first place? Concentrate on who you want to become. Sometimes, it can be difficult to frame an affirmation positively. Suppose you want to stop biting your nails. What positive affirmation would you use? It takes some thought but can usually be done. ("I, Jennie Smith, have long, elegant nails" might work.) Whenever possible use positive statements for your affirmations.

Just as a positive statement makes a deeper impression than does a negative statement, a study by Gilbert, Krull, and Malone (1990) suggests that *true* statements make a deeper impression than do *false* statements. Researchers set up a situation to investigate how we process true and false information. By default, we accept statements as true. Then, if we have evidence that the statement was false, we reclassify the statement as false. Researchers had people read a number of statements. They then received information about which were true and which were false. When given time to think about it, people could correctly identify false statements about as often as true statements. However, researchers then tried the same experiment but added a distraction. A loud noise sounded after a statement. If the statement was initially accepted as true, then the distraction should have no effect on the accurate recall of true statements. However, the distraction should serve to decrease accurate recall of false statements by preventing people from reclassifying statements from true to false. That is exactly what happened. People were able to correctly identify true statements just as often whether distracted or not. However, false statements were misclassified as true almost twice as often when people were distracted. True statements are easier to handle mentally than false ones.

One reason that bad habits are hard to break is that *not* doing something is difficult. It is hard to build an identity in a vacuum. The problem is not really quitting nail biting or smoking or drinking or using credit cards or chocolate or coffee. The problem is what to do instead. When I first quit smoking, a day would stretch out before me forever. How could a person possibly fill up all those hours without a cigarette? What was I to do? I needed an activity to fill my time while not indulging my habit. Successful addiction recovery programs—whether Alcoholics Anonymous or hospital-based treatment—recognize that a positive activity has to be substituted for the addictive behavior. For example, Alcoholics Anonymous members go to meetings instead of bars. Writing affirmations is an activity you can substitute for the habit you are trying to break. Every time you get the urge to bite your nails, you could write an affirmation instead.

Make yourself write an affirmation at least three times a day, or more often if the mood strikes you. Pick one that you think will do you some good, one that will move you closer to the kind of person you want to become. Then keep at it. It may be difficult to remember at first. If I skipped writing my affirmations one day, then I made myself write extra ones for following day. Like me, you may find it difficult to make yourself write an affirmation that challenges longheld or unconscious beliefs about yourself. I would tell myself that I did not have the time to write. Then I figured out how long it took to write an affirmation three times. Writing in longhand, as carefully and clearly as possible, it took me about two minutes. Two minutes a day to change your life.

FURTHER READING

Of General Interest

Branch, T. (1988). *Parting the waters: America in the King years, 1954–63.* New York: Simon & Schuster.

Jones, E. E. (1991). *Interpersonal perception.* New York: W. H. Freeman and Company.

Ross, L., & Nisbett, R. E. (1991). *The person and the situation: Perspectives of social psychology.* New York: McGraw-Hill.

Recent and Technical Issues

Fein, S. (1996). Effects of suspicion on attributional thinking and the correspondence bias. *Journal of Personality and Social Psychology, 70,* 1164–1184.

Gibbins, K., & Walker, I. (1996). Social roles, social norms, and self-presentation in the quiz effect of Ross, Ambaile and Steinmetz. *Journal of Social Psychology, 136,* 625–634.

Gilbert, D. T., & Malone, P. S. (1995). The correspondence bias. *Psychological Bulletin, 117,* 21–38.

Hart, A. J., & Morry, M. M. (1996). Nonverbal behavior, race, and attitude attributions. *Journal of Experimental Social Psychology, 32,* 165–179.

Miller, A. G., Ashton, W., & Mishal, M. (1990). Beliefs concerning the features of constrained behavior: A basis for the fundamental attribution error. *Journal of Personality and Social Psychology, 59,* 635–650.

Webster, D. (1993). "Motivated augmentation and reduction of the overattribution bias. *Journal of Personality and Social Psychology, 65,* 261–271.

Inferential Hopscotch: How People Draw Social Inferences From Behavior

Douglas S. Krull and Darin J. Erickson

Douglas S. Krull is an Assistant Professor of Psychology at Northern Kentucky University, Highland Heights. **Darin J. Erickson** is a graduate student at the University of Missouri, Columbia. Address correspondence to Douglas S. Krull, Department of Psychology, Northern Kentucky University, Highland Heights, KY 41099; e-mail: Krull@nku.edu.

Tim and Sue observe an anxious-looking man in a dentist's waiting room. Tim decides that the man must have an anxious personality (a trait inference). In contrast, Sue decides that the man is anxious because he is waiting to see the dentist (a situational inference). Why might Tim and Sue have drawn such different inferences? Social inference researchers have long been interested in the different inferences that people draw when they view the same behavior. Early work on social inference focused on the tendency for peoples' inferences to be biased in favor of trait inferences. For example, when members of a debate team are assigned to argue for a particular political position, observers often infer that the debaters' true attitudes match their assigned position.[1] More recently, research has focused not only on *what* people infer (i.e., the final inference), but also on *how* they infer (i.e., the process by which inferences are drawn).

THE TRAIT INFERENCE PROCESS

The vast majority of recent work on social inference has investigated the process by which people draw inferences about an actor's personality. Research suggests that the trait inference process can be thought of as composed of three states: behavior interpretation, trait inference, and situational revision.[2] First, people interpret, or derive meaning from, the actor's behavior ("John seems to be behaving in a very anxious manner"); next, they draw a trait inference that corresponds to the behavior ("John must have a very anxious personality"); finally, they may revise this inference to a greater or lesser degree by taking into account the situational forces that may have contributed to the actor's behavior ("John is waiting to see the dentist; perhaps he isn't such an anxious person after all"). These three stages seem to differ in the amount of effort required. Behavior interpretation and trait inference seem to be relatively spontaneous and effortless, whereas situational revision seems to be relatively effortful.[3] This process is depicted in Figure 1.

Stage 1: Behavior Interpretation

People tend to see what they expect to see.[4] Thus, many people in American society tend to interpret an ambiguous shove as more hostile when given by a black person than by a white person. However, people's expectations have less impact on their interpretations of behavior if the behavior is unambiguous. Trope[5] conducted an experiment in which participants interpreted facial expressions after being informed about the context in which the expressions took place. If the facial expressions were ambiguous, participants' context-based expectations influenced their interpretations of the emotions (e.g., participants interpreted a facial expression as happier if the context was "winning in a TV game show" and more fearful if the context was "a swarm of bees flying into the room"). If the facial expressions were unambiguous, participants' expectations had significantly less impact.

Stage 2: Trait Inference

People often think that you can judge a book by its cover, that people's actions reflect their personalities. Uleman, Winter, and their colleagues[6] conducted a series of investigations which suggest that when people view behavior, they may spontaneously draw inferences about the actor's personality. In these studies, participants read sentences (e.g., "The secretary solved the mystery halfway through the book") that suggest a particular trait (e.g., clever). Uleman and Winter proposed that if people spontaneously draw trait inferences upon reading the sentences (at encoding), then these traits should facilitate recall for the sentences (at retrieval). Studies of this hypothesis have found repeatedly that participants' recall is superior with trait cues than with no cues, and occasionally better with trait cues than with other types of cues (semantic), even when participants were not aware when reading the sentences that their memory for the sentences would be tested.

In a similar paradigm, Lupfer, Clark, and Hutcherson[7] conducted an experiment which suggests that trait inferences may be substantially effortless as well as spontaneous. If trait inference is substantially effortless, then people should be able to perform it even when their conscious resources are limited (i.e.,

From *Current Directions in Psychological Science*, April 1995, pp. 35–38. © 1995 by the American Psychological Society. Reprinted by permission of Blackwell Publishers.

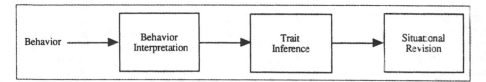

Fig. 1. The trait inference process.

when they are cognitively busy). Participants read sentences while they simultaneously rehearsed an easy set of numbers (which should not make people cognitively busy) or a difficult set of numbers (which should make people cognitively busy). Not only did trait-cued participants recall more sentences than noncued participants, but the trait-cued recall of participants in the difficult condition was not significantly different from the trait-cued recall of participants in the easy condition. This and other research suggests that when people view behavior, they may spontaneously and effortlessly interpret the behavior and infer that the actor's personality corresponds to the behavior ("John behaved in an anxious manner; John must have an anxious personality") even when they are distracted or preoccupied.

A relearning paradigm developed by Carlston and Skowronski[8] looks particularly promising for the further investigation of spontaneous trait inferences. These researchers first presented participants with person photos paired with personal statements that implied traits. For example, the following statement implies that the person in the photo is cruel: "I hate animals. Today I was walking to the pool hall and I saw this puppy. So I kicked it out of my way." Some participants were instructed to draw a trait inference (specific-impression condition), others were instructed to form an impression (general-impression condition), and others were told to simply look at the photos and statements (ostensibly to familiarize themselves with these materials for a later phase of the experiment; no-instruction condition). If these latter participants inferred traits, this would be evidence for spontaneity.

After a filler task, all participants were given photo–trait pairs and were instructed explicitly to memorize the trait associated with each photo. In some cases (relearning trials), these pairs corresponded to the photo–statement pairs presented earlier (e.g., the photo previously presented with the statement about kicking the puppy was paired with the word *cruel*). Thus, if the participants had previously inferred traits from the statements, they would be relearning the associations between the photos and the traits instead of learning these asso-

ciations for the first time. In other cases, the photo–trait pairs did not correspond to the previous photo–statement pairs (control trials). Finally, participants were shown the photos and asked to recall the traits. Recall was higher for relearning trials than for control trials, suggesting that participants had inferred traits from the initial photo–statement pairs. In addition, this finding was similar across all three conditions (specific impression, general impression, no instruction), which suggests that trait inferences had occurred in the impression conditions, and spontaneous trait inferences had occurred in the no-instruction condition. Carlston and Skowronski also ruled out several alternative explanations. Thus, these results provide strong evidence that trait inferences can be drawn spontaneously.

Stage 3: Situational Revision

People may consider the situation in which the behavior took place when they draw trait inferences, but it is not easy for them to do so. Unlike behavior interpretation and trait inference, situational revision seems to be a relatively effortful process, and so people may not complete it when they lack either the ability or the motivation to do so. A program of research conducted by Gilbert and his colleagues[3] suggests that people may be unable to complete the situational revision stage sufficiently when they are cognitively busy (when they have limited conscious resources). In one study, participants viewed several videotape clips of an anxious-appearing woman who was ostensibly discussing anxiety-provoking topics (sexual fantasies) or calm topics (world travel) with an interviewer. The film was silent, but the discussion topics appeared in subtitles. Half the participants were required to memorize these topics (cognitively busy participants), and half were not. One might expect that participants would recognize that most people would be more anxious when discussing anxiety-provoking topics than calm topics, but, remarkably, participants who attempted to memorize the discussion topics were less able than the other participants to consider the effects of the topics when drawing inferences about the target. Thus, this study

suggests that when people are preoccupied or distracted, they may draw biased trait inferences because they fail to sufficiently consider the situation in which the behavior took place.

An experiment by Webster[9] suggests that people may also revise their trait inferences insufficiently when they are unmotivated. Participants expected to answer questions about their impression of a speaker who expressed a negative view toward student exchange programs. Before viewing the speaker, participants were informed that she was required to express a negative view, but Webster predicted that unmotivated participants would be less likely than motivated participants to consider this fact, and would be more likely to infer that the speaker's view reflected her true attitude. Half of the participants expected to perform a task involving multivariate statistics after the impression formation task, whereas the other half expected to perform a task involving comedy clips after the impression formation task. Webster predicted that participants who expected to view the statistics lecture would be motivated to "stretch the fun" on the (comparatively attractive) impression formation task, whereas participants who expected to view the comedy clips would be motivated to "get the (comparatively boring) impression formation task over with." As Webster predicted, participants in the statistics conditions were better able to revise their inferences than were participants in the comedy clips condition, and were less likely to infer that the speaker's expressed view reflected her true attitude.

THE SITUATIONAL INFERENCE PROCESS

When people want to know about people, they seem to infer traits. What if people want to know about situations? Social inference researchers have learned much about the process by which people infer traits. Considerably less work has investigated how social inference proceeds when people are interested in learning about a situation, but some work suggests that situational inference may be a mirror image of the trait inference process.[10] In an experiment very similar to Gilbert's aforementioned anxious-woman experiment, participants viewed a silent videotape of an anxious-appearing interviewee. Half the participants attempted to estimate the interviewee's trait anxiety (trait goal); half attempted to estimate the degree of anxiety provoked by the interview topics (situational goal). Half of the participants in each of these conditions were made

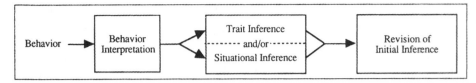

Fig. 2. The social inference process.

cognitively busy. For people with a trait goal, the results mirrored Gilbert's; that is, in an analysis that combined the dispositional and situational anxiety measures, busy participants inferred more dispositional anxiety than did nonbusy participants. However, the results were reversed for participants with a situational goal; that is, busy participants in this condition inferred more situational anxiety than did nonbusy participants. These results suggest that when people are interested in situations (rather than traits, they may spontaneously and effortlessly draw situational inferences (rather than trait inferences) from behavior. If people have the ability and motivation, they may revise these inferences by considering the actor's personality.

THE SOCIAL INFERENCE PROCESS

Considerable research suggests that when people have a trait goal, they interpret the actor's behavior, spontaneously and effortlessly draw a trait inference, and, if they have sufficient conscious resources and motivation, revise this inference by considering the situation in which the behavior took place. When people have a situational goal, they interpret the actor's behavior, may spontaneously and effortlessly draw a situational inference, and, if they have sufficient conscious resources and motivation, revise this inference by considering the actor's personality (see Fig. 2). It seems that people are able to draw either trait inferences or situational inferences from behavior when they are given either trait goals or situational goals, but what might create these goals in people's day-to-day lives? Social inference researchers have long maintained that people draw inferences to increase their ability to predict other people's behavior. Thus, a trait goal may be invoked when someone expects to interact with a person in the future ("I just met our new neighbors. They seem like friendly people"). When someone expects to enter a situation, a situational goal may be invoked ("Did you hear those people laughing? I can hardly wait to see that movie").

Even when goals are not invoked by the immediate circumstances or people's

current needs and motives, people may be predisposed to either trait inference or situational inference by their culture or personality.[11] A number of cross-cultural investigations have found that non-Westerners tend to form judgments that are more situational than those of Westerners. Shweder and Bourne[12] have suggested that non-Western people may be "culturally primed to see context and social relationships as a necessary condition for behavior," whereas Westerners may be "culturally primed to search for abstract summaries of the autonomous individual." Thus, Westerners' default process may be the trait inference process, whereas non-Westerners' default process may be the situational inference process. Even within a culture, some types of individuals may think more in terms of traits, and others may think more in terms of situational forces. For instance, Newman[13] has found that people who are high in idiocentrism (an individualist view) are more likely than people who are low in idiocentrism to infer traits spontaneously from behavior.

CONCLUSION

In the past decade or so, social inference researchers have increased their attention on the process by which people draw inferences from behavior, particularly the trait inference process. This research suggests that when people are interested in learning about another person, they may spontaneously and effortlessly interpret behavior and draw an inference about the actor's personality. They may then revise their initial inference by considering the situation in which the behavior took place if they have the ability and motivation to do so. Less research has investigated how people draw inferences when they are interested in learning about situations. However, people with a situational goal may spontaneously and effortlessly interpret behavior and draw an inference about the situation, and may revise this inference by considering the actor's personality if they have the ability and motivation to do so. Thus, it seems that the social inference process may be flexible in that people may not be compelled to always travel the same inferential road. Social inference researchers have be-

gun to investigate factors that might influence people's tendency to initially draw either trait or situational inferences (or perhaps both); some research suggests that people's current goals and motives may influence the process, and that individual differences and cultural factors may predispose people to either trait or situational inferences.

Further advances in the understanding of social inference processes and the influence of cultural factors and individual differences will have important implications at many levels of social science. Important benefits will accrue for psychologists, but also for political scientists and sociologists. For example, in politics, it may be that the tendency for conservatives to blame the poor for their plight and for liberals to blame the system reflects differences in social inference. Similarly, the default social inference process for an entire culture may influence its members' inferences and proposed solutions with regard to such ubiquitous social problems as homelessness, injustice, and violence.

Acknowledgments—We wish to thank Craig A. Anderson, Lori A. Krull, Jody C. Dill, and David Dubois for their valuable comments on earlier drafts of this manuscript.

Notes

1. This tendency to draw unwarranted trait inferences has been called correspondence bias, the fundamental attribution error, and overattribution bias. For a review, see E. E. Jones, *Interpersonal Perception* (Macmillan, New York, 1990).
2. See, e.g., D. T. Gilbert, B. W. Pelham, and D. S. Krull, On cognitive busyness: When person perceivers meet persons perceived, *Journal of Personality and Social Psychology, 54,* 733–740 (1988); Y. Trope, Identification and inferential processes in dispositional attribution, *Psychological Review, 93,* 239–257 (1986).
3. See, e.g., D. T. Gilbert, Thinking lightly about others: Automatic components of the social inference process, in *Unintended Thought: Limits of Awareness, Intention, and Control,* J. S. Uleman and J. A. Bargh, Eds. (Guilford Press, New York, 1989).
4. See, e.g., H. A. Sagar and J. W. Schofield, Racial and behavioral cues in black and white children's perceptions of ambiguously aggressive acts, *Journal of Personality and Social Psychology, 39,* 590–598 (1980). Note that contrast effects may also occur; e.g., L. L. Martin, J. J. Seta, and R. A. Crelia, Assimilation and contrast as a function of people's willingness and ability to expend effort in forming an impression, *Journal of Personality and Social Psychology, 59,* 27–37 (1990).
5. Trope, note 2.
6. For a review, see J. S. Uleman, Consciousness and control: The case of spontaneous trait inferences, *Personality and Social*

Psychology Bulletin, 13, 337–354 (1987). Note that more recent work suggests that these spontaneous inferences may often be better thought of as summaries of behavior; e.g., J. N. Bassili, Traits as action categories versus traits as person attributes in social cognition, in On-Line Cognition in Person Perception, J. N. Bassili, Ed. (Erlbaum, Hillsdale, NJ, 1989).

7. M. B. Lupfer, L. F. Clark, and H. W. Hutcherson, Impact of context on spontaneous trait and situational attributions, Journal of Personality and Social Psychology, 58, 239–249 (1990). Note that trait inferences do require some conscious resources; see J. S. Uleman, L. S. Newman, and L. Winter, Can personality traits be inferred automatically? Spontaneous inferences require cognitive capacity at encoding, Consciousness and Cognition, 1, 72–90 (1992). See Bassili, note 6.

8. D. E. Carlston and J. J. Skowronski, Savings in the re earning of trait information as evidence for spontaneous inference generation, Journal of Personality and Social Psychology, 66, 840–856 (1994).

9. D. M. Webster, Motivated augmentation and reduction of the overattribution bias, Journal of Personality and Social Psychology, 65, 261–271 (1993).

10. D. S. Krull, Does the grist change the mill?: The effect of perceiver's goal on the process of social inference, Personality and Social Psychology Bulletin, 19, 340–348 (1993). See also G. A. Quattrone, Overattribution and unit formation: When behavior engulfs the person, Journal of Personality and Social Psychology, 42, 593–607 (1982); J. D. Vorauer and M. Ross, Making mountains out of molehills: An informational goals analysis of self- and social perception, Personality and Social Psychology Bulletin, 19, 620–632 (1993).

11. See, e.g., G. J. O. Fletcher and C. Ward, Attribution theory and processes: A cross-cultural perspective, in The Cross-Cultural Challenge to Social Psychology, M. H. Bond, Ed. (Sage, Beverly Hills, CA, 1988); J. G. Miller, Culture and the development of everyday social explanation, Journal of Personality and Social Psychology, 46,

961–978 (1984). Although the terms Western and non-Western have been used for simplicity, the cultural difference is perhaps better thought of as a distinction between cultures with an independent and with an interdependent view of the self.

12. R. A. Shweder and E. Bourne, Does the concept of the person vary cross-culturally? in Cultural Conceptions of Mental Health and Therapy, A. J. Marsella and G. White, Eds. (Reidel, Boston, 1982), pp. 129–130.

13. L. S. Newman, How individualists interpret behavior: Idiocentrism and spontaneous trait inference, Social Cognition, 11, 243–269 (1993). See Bassili, note 6.

Recommended Reading

Trope, Y., and Higgins, E. T., Eds. (1993). Special issue: On Inferring Personal Dispositions from Behavior. Personality and Social Psychology Bulletin, 19.

THE NEW-BOY NETWORK

What do job interviews really tell us?

BY MALCOLM GLADWELL

Nolan Myers grew up in Houston, the elder of two boys in a middle-class family. He went to Houston's High School for the Performing and Visual Arts and then Harvard, where he intended to major in History and Science. After discovering the joys of writing code, though, he switched to computer science. "Programming is one of those things you get involved in, and you just can't stop until you finish," Myers says. "You get involved in it, and all of a sudden you look at your watch and it's four in the morning! I love the elegance of it." Myers is short and slightly stocky and has pale-blue eyes. He smiles easily, and when he speaks he moves his hands and torso for emphasis. He plays in a klezmer band called the Charvard Chai Notes. He talks to his parents a lot. He gets B's and B-pluses.

This spring, in the last stretch of his senior year, Myers spent a lot of time interviewing for jobs with technology companies. He talked to a company named Trilogy, down in Texas, but he didn't think he would fit in. "One of Trilogy's subsidiaries put ads out in the paper saying that they were looking for the top tech students, and that they'd give them two hundred thousand dollars and a BMW," Myers said, shaking his head in disbelief. In another of his interviews, a recruiter asked him to solve a programming problem, and he made a stupid mistake and the recruiter pushed the answer back across the table to him, saying that his "solution" accomplished nothing. As he remembers the moment, Myers blushes. "I was so nervous. I thought, Hmm, that sucks!" The way he says that, though, makes it hard to believe that he really was nervous, or maybe what Nolan Myers calls nervous the rest of us call a tiny flutter in the stomach. Myers doesn't seem like the sort to get flustered. He's the kind of person you would call the night before the big test in seventh grade, when nothing made sense and you had begun to panic.

I like Nolan Myers. He will, I am convinced, be very good at whatever career he chooses. I say those two things even though I have spent no more than ninety minutes in his presence. We met only once, on a sunny afternoon in April at the Au Bon Pain in Harvard Square. He was wearing sneakers and khakis and a polo shirt, in a dark-green pattern. He had a big backpack, which he plopped on the floor beneath the table. I bought him an orange juice. He fished around in his wallet and came up with a dollar to try and repay me, which I refused. We sat by the window. Previously, we had talked for perhaps three minutes on the phone, setting up the interview. Then I E-mailed him, asking him how I would recognize him at Au Bon Pain. He sent me the following message, with what I'm convinced—again, on the basis of almost no evidence—to be typical Myers panache: "22ish, five foot seven, straight brown hair, very good-looking.:)." I have never talked to his father, his mother, or his little brother, or any of his professors. I have never seen him ecstatic or angry or depressed. I know nothing of his personal habits, his tastes, or his quirks. I cannot even tell you why I feel the way I do about him. He's good-looking and smart and articulate and funny, but not so good-looking and smart and articulate and funny that there is some obvious explanation for the conclusions I've drawn about him. I just like him, and I'm impressed by him, and if I were an employer looking for bright young college graduates, I'd hire him in a heartbeat.

I heard about Nolan Myers from Hadi Partovi, an executive with Tellme, a highly touted Silicon Valley startup offering Internet access through the telephone. If you were a computer-science major at M.I.T., Harvard, Stanford, Caltech, or the

University of Waterloo this spring, looking for a job in software, Tellme was probably at the top of your list. Partovi and I talked in the conference room at Tellme's offices, just off the soaring, open floor where all the firm's programmers and marketers and executives sit, some of them with bunk beds built over their desks. (Tellme recently moved into an old printing plant—a low-slung office building with a huge warehouse attached—and, in accordance with new-economy logic, promptly turned the old offices into a warehouse and the old warehouse into offices.) Partovi is a handsome man of twenty-seven, with olive skin and short curly black hair, and throughout our entire interview he sat with his chair tilted precariously at a forty-five-degree angle. At the end of a long riff about how hard it is to find high-quality people, he blurted out one name: Nolan Myers. Then, from memory, he rattled off Myers's telephone number. He very much wanted Myers to come to Tellme.

Partovi had met Myers in January, during a recruiting trip to Harvard. "It was a heinous day," Partovi remembers. "I started at seven and went until nine. I'd walk one person out and walk the other in." The first fifteen minutes of every interview he spent talking about Tellme—its strategy, its goals, and its business. Then he gave everyone a short programming puzzle. For the rest of the hour-long meeting, Partovi asked questions. He remembers that Myers did well on the programming test, and after talking to him for thirty to forty minutes he became convinced that Myers had, as he puts it, "the right stuff." Partovi spent even less time with Myers than I did. He didn't talk to Myers's family, or see him ecstatic or angry or depressed, either. He knew that Myers had spent last summer as an intern at Microsoft and was about to graduate from an Ivy League school. But virtually everyone recruited by a place like Tellme has graduated from an élite university, and the Microsoft

summer-internship program has more than six hundred people in it. Partovi didn't even know why he liked Myers so much. He just did. "It was very much a gut call," he says.

This wasn't so very different from the experience Nolan Myers had with Steve Ballmer, the C.E.O. of Microsoft. Earlier this year, Myers attended a party for former Microsoft interns called Gradbash. Ballmer gave a speech there, and at the end of his remarks Myers raised his hand. "He was talking a lot about aligning the company in certain directions," Myers told me, "and I asked him about how that influences his ability to make bets on other directions. Are they still going to make small bets?" Afterward, a Microsoft recruiter came up to Myers and said, "Steve wants your E-mail address." Myers gave it to him, and soon he and Ballmer were E-mailing. Ballmer, it seems, badly wanted Myers to come to Microsoft. "He did research on me," Myers says. "He knew which group I was interviewing with, and knew a lot about me personally. He sent me an E-mail saying that he'd love to have me come to Microsoft, and if I had any questions I should contact him. So I sent him a response, saying thank you. After I visited Tellme, I sent him an E-mail saying I was interested in Tellme, here were the reasons, that I wasn't sure yet, and if he had anything to say I said I'd love to talk to him. I gave him my number. So he called, and after playing phone tag we talked—about career trajectory, how Microsoft would influence my career, what he thought of Tellme. I was extremely impressed with him, and he seemed very genuinely interested in me."

What convinced Ballmer he wanted Myers? A glimpse! He caught a little slice of Nolan Myers in action and—just like that—the C.E.O. of a four-hundred-billion-dollar company was calling a college senior in his dorm room. Ballmer somehow knew he liked Myers, the same way Hadi Partovi knew, and

the same way I knew after our little chat at Au Bon Pain. But what did we know? What could we know? By any reasonable measure, surely none of us knew Nolan Myers at all.

It is a truism of the new economy that the ultimate success of any enterprise lies with the quality of the people it hires. At many technology companies, employees are asked to all but live at the office, in conditions of intimacy that would have been unthinkable a generation ago. The artifacts of the prototypical Silicon Valley office—the videogames, the espresso bar, the bunk beds, the basketball hoops—are the elements of the rec room, not the workplace. And in the rec room you want to play only with your friends. But how do you find out who your friends are? Today, recruiters canvas the country for résumés. They analyze employment histories and their competitors' staff listings. They call references, and then do what I did with Nolan Myers: sit down with a perfect stranger for an hour and a half and attempt to draw conclusions about that stranger's intelligence and personality. The job interview has become one of the central conventions of the modern economy. But what, exactly, can you know about a stranger after sitting down and talking with him for an hour?

Some years ago, an experimental psychologist at Harvard University, Nalini Ambady, together with Robert Rosenthal, set out to examine the nonverbal aspects of good teaching. As the basis of her research, she used videotapes of teaching fellows which had been made during a training program at Harvard. Her plan was to have outside observers look at the tapes with the sound off and rate the effectiveness of the teachers by their expressions and physical cues. Ambady wanted to have at least a minute of film to work with. When she looked at the tapes, though, there was really only about ten seconds when the teachers were shown apart from the students.

"I didn't want students in the frame, because obviously it would bias the ratings," Ambady says. "So I went to my adviser, and I said, 'This isn't going to work.'"

But it did. The observers, presented with a ten-second silent video clip, had no difficulty rating the teachers on a fifteen-item checklist of personality traits. In fact, when Ambady cut the clips back to five seconds, the ratings were the same. They were even the same when she showed her raters just two seconds of videotape. That sounds unbelievable unless you actually watch Ambady's teacher clips, as I did, and realize that the eight seconds that distinguish the longest clips from the shortest are superfluous: anything beyond the first flash of insight is unnecessary. When we make a snap judgment, it is made in a snap. It's also, very clearly, a judgment: we get a feeling that we have no difficulty articulating.

Ambady's next step led to an even more remarkable conclusion. She compared those snap judgments of teacher effectiveness with evaluations made, after a full semester of classes, by students of the same teachers. The correlation between the two, she found, was astoundingly high. A person watching a two-second silent video clip of a teacher he has never met will reach conclusions about how good that teacher is that are very similar to those of a student who sits in the teacher's class for an entire semester.

Recently, a comparable experiment was conducted by Frank Bernieri, a psychologist at the University of Toledo. Bernieri, working with one of his graduate students, Neha Gada-Jain, selected two people to act as interviewers, and trained them for six weeks in the proper procedures and techniques of giving an effective job interview. The two then interviewed ninety-eight volunteers, of various ages and backgrounds. The interviews lasted between fifteen and twenty minutes, and afterward each interviewer filled out a six-page, five-part evaluation of the person he'd just talked to. Originally, the intention of the study was to find out whether applicants who had been coached in certain nonverbal behaviors designed to ingratiate themselves with their interviewers—like mimicking the interviewers' physical gestures or posture—would get better ratings than applicants who behaved normally. As it turns out, they didn't. But then another of Bernieri's students, an undergraduate named Tricia Prickett, decided that she wanted to use the interview videotapes and the evaluations that had been collected to test out the adage that "the handshake is everything."

"She took fifteen seconds of videotape showing the applicant as he or she knocks on the door, comes in, shakes the hand of the interviewer, sits down, and the interviewer welcomes the person," Bernieri explained. Then, like Ambady, Prickett got a series of strangers to rate the applicants based on the handshake clip, using the same criteria that the interviewers had used. Once more, against all expectations, the ratings were very similar to those of the interviewers. "On nine out of the eleven traits the applicants were being judged on, the observers significantly predicted the outcome of the interview," Bernieri says. "The strength of the correlations was extraordinary."

This research takes Ambady's conclusions one step further. In the Toledo experiment, the interviewers were trained in the art of interviewing. They weren't dashing off a teacher evaluation on their way out the door. They were filling out a formal, detailed questionnaire, of the sort designed to give the most thorough and unbiased account of an interview. And still their ratings weren't all that different from those of people off the street who saw just the greeting.

This is why Hadi Partovi, Steve Ballmer, and I all agreed on Nolan Myers. Apparently, human beings don't need to know someone in order to believe that they know someone. Nor does it make that much difference, apparently, that Partovi reached his conclusion after putting Myers through the wringer for an hour, I reached mine after ninety minutes of amiable conversation at Au Bon Pain, and Ballmer reached his after watching and listening as Myers asked a question.

Bernieri and Ambady believe that the power of first impressions suggests that human beings have a particular kind of prerational ability for making searching judgments about others. In Ambady's teacher experiments, when she asked her observers to perform a potentially distracting cognitive task—like memorizing a set of numbers—while watching the tapes, their judgments of teacher effectiveness were unchanged. But when she instructed her observers to think hard about their ratings before they made them, their accuracy suffered substantially. Thinking only gets in the way. "The brain structures that are involved here are very primitive," Ambady speculates. "All of these affective reactions are probably governed by the lower brain structures." What we are picking up in that first instant would seem to be something quite basic about a person's character, because what we conclude after two seconds is pretty much the same as what we conclude after twenty minutes or, indeed, an entire semester. "Maybe you can tell immediately whether someone is extroverted, or gauge the person's ability to communicate," Bernieri says. "Maybe these clues or cues are immediately accessible and apparent." Bernieri and Ambady are talking about the existence of a powerful form of human intuition. In a way, that's comforting, because it suggests that we can meet a perfect stranger and immediately pick up on something important about him. It means that I shouldn't be concerned that I can't explain why I like Nolan Myers, because, if such judgments are made without thinking, then surely they defy explanation.

But there's a troubling suggestion here as well. I believe that Nolan

Myers is an accomplished and likable person. But I have no idea from our brief encounter how honest he is, or whether he is self-centered, or whether he works best by himself or in a group, or any number of other fundamental traits. That people who simply see the handshake arrive at the same conclusions as people who conduct a full interview also implies, perhaps, that those initial impressions matter too much—that they color all the other impressions that we gather over time.

For example, I asked Myers if he felt nervous about the prospect of leaving school for the workplace, which seemed like a reasonable question, since I remember how anxious I was before my first job. Would the hours scare him? Oh no, he replied, he was already working between eighty and a hundred hours a week at school. "Are there things that you think you aren't good at, which make you worry?" I continued.

His reply was sharp: "Are there things that I'm not good at, or things that I can't learn? I think that's the real question. There are a lot of things I don't know anything about, but I feel comfortable that given the right environment and the right encouragement I can do well at." In my notes, next to that reply, I wrote "Great answer!" and I can remember at the time feeling the little thrill you experience as an interviewer when someone's behavior conforms with your expectations. Because I had decided, right off, that I liked him, what I heard in his answer was toughness and confidence. Had I decided early on that I didn't like Nolan Myers, I would have heard in that reply arrogance and bluster. The first impression becomes a self-fulfilling prophecy: we hear what we expect to hear. The interview is hopelessly biased in favor of the nice.

When Ballmer and Partovi and I met Nolan Myers, we made a prediction. We looked at the way he behaved in our presence—at the way he talked and acted and seemed to think—and drew conclusions about how he would behave in other situations. I had decided, remember, that Myers was the kind of person you called the night before the big test in seventh grade. Was I right to make that kind of generalization?

This is a question that social psychologists have looked at closely. In the late nineteen-twenties, in a famous study, the psychologist Theodore Newcomb analyzed extroversion among adolescent boys at a summer camp. He found that how talkative a boy was in one setting—say, lunch—was highly predictive of how talkative that boy would be in the same setting in the future. A boy who was curious at lunch on Monday was likely to be curious at lunch on Tuesday. But his behavior in one setting told you almost nothing about how he would behave in a different setting: from how someone behaved at lunch, you couldn't predict how he would behave during, say, afternoon playtime. In a more recent study, of conscientiousness among students at Carleton College, the researchers Walter Mischel, Neil Lutsky, and Philip K. Peake showed that how neat a student's assignments were or how punctual he was told you almost nothing about how often he attended class or how neat his room or his personal appearance was. How we behave at any one time, evidently, has less to do with some immutable inner compass than with the particulars of our situation.

This conclusion, obviously, is at odds with our intuition. Most of the time, we assume that people display the same character traits in different situations. We habitually underestimate the large role that context plays in people's behavior. In the Newcomb summer-camp experiment, for example, the results showing how little consistency there was from one setting to another in talkativeness, curiosity, and gregariousness were tabulated from observations made and recorded by camp counsellors on the spot. But when, at the end of the summer, those same counsellors were asked to give their final impressions of the kids, they remembered the children's behavior as being highly consistent.

"The basis of the illusion is that we are somehow confident that we are getting what is there, that we are able to read off a person's disposition," Richard Nisbett, a psychologist at the University of Michigan, says. "When you have an interview with someone and have an hour with them, you don't conceptualize that as taking a sample of a person's behavior, let alone a possibly biased sample, which is what it is. What you think is that you are seeing a hologram, a small and fuzzy image but still the whole person."

Then Nisbett mentioned his frequent collaborator, Lee Ross, who teaches psychology at Stanford. "There was one term when he was teaching statistics and one term he was teaching a course with a lot of humanistic psychology. He gets his teacher evaluations. The first referred to him as cold, rigid, remote, finicky, and uptight. And the second described this wonderful warmhearted guy who was so deeply concerned with questions of community and getting students to grow. It was Jekyll and Hyde. In both cases, the students thought they were seeing the real Lee Ross."

Psychologists call this tendency—to fixate on supposedly stable character traits and overlook the influence of context—the Fundamental Attribution Error, and if you combine this error with what we know about snap judgments the interview becomes an even more problematic encounter. Not only had I let my first impressions color the information I gathered about Myers, but I had also assumed that the way he behaved with me in an interview setting was indicative of the way he would always behave. It isn't that the interview is useless; what I learned about Myers—that he and I get along well—is something I could never have got from a résumé or by talking to his references. It's just that our conversation turns out to have been less useful, and potentially more misleading, than I had supposed. That most basic of human rituals—the conversation with a stranger—turns out to be a minefield.

Not long after I met with Nolan Myers, I talked with a human-resources consultant from Pasadena named Justin Menkes. Menkes's job is to figure out how to extract meaning from face-to-face encounters, and with that in mind he agreed to spend an hour interviewing me the way he thinks interviewing ought to be done. It felt, going in, not unlike a visit to a shrink, except that instead of having months, if not years, to work things out, Menkes was set upon stripping away my secrets in one session.

Consider, he told me, a commonly asked question like "Describe a few situations in which your work was criticized. How did you handle the criticism?" The problem, Menkes said, is that it's much too obvious what the interviewee is supposed to say. "There was a situation where I was working on a project, and I didn't do as well as I could have," he said, adopting a mock-sincere singsong. "My boss gave me some constructive criticism. And I redid the project. It hurt. Yet we worked it out." The same is true of the question "What would your friends say about you?"—to which the correct answer (preferably preceded by a pause, as if to suggest that it had never dawned on you that someone would ask such a question) is "My guess is that they would call me a people person—either that or a hard worker."

Myers and I had talked about obvious questions, too. "What is your greatest weakness?" I asked him. He answered, "I tried to work on a project my freshman year, a children's festival. I was trying to start a festival as a benefit here in Boston. And I had a number of guys working with me. I started getting concerned with the scope of the project we were working on—how much re-

sponsibility we had, getting things done. I really put the brakes on, but in retrospect I really think we could have done it and done a great job."

Then Myers grinned and said, as an aside, "Do I truly think that is a fault? Honestly, no." And, of course, he's right. All I'd really asked him was whether he could describe a personal strength as if it were a weakness, and, in answering as he did, he had merely demonstrated his knowledge of the unwritten rules of the interview.

But, Menkes said, what if those questions were rephrased so that the answers weren't obvious? For example: "At your weekly team meetings, your boss unexpectedly begins aggressively critiquing your performance on a current project. What do you do?"

I felt a twinge of anxiety. What would I do? I remembered a terrible boss I'd had years ago. "I'd probably be upset," I said. "But I doubt I'd say anything. I'd probably just walk away." Menkes gave no indication whether he was concerned or pleased by that answer. He simply pointed out that another person might well have said something like "I'd go and see my boss later in private, and confront him about why he embarrassed me in front of my team." I was saying that I would probably handle criticism—even inappropriate criticism—from a superior with stoicism; in the second case, the applicant was saying he or she would adopt a more confrontational style. Or, at least, we were telling the interviewer that the workplace demands either stoicism or confrontation—and to Menkes these are revealing and pertinent pieces of information.

Menkes moved on to another area—handling stress. A typical question in this area is something like "Tell me about a time when you had to do several things at once. How did you handle the situation? How did you decide what to do first?" Menkes says this is also too easy. "I just had to be very organized," he began again in his mock-

sincere singsong. "I had to multitask. I had to prioritize and delegate appropriately. I checked in frequently with my boss." Here's how Menkes rephrased it: "You're in a situation where you have two very important responsibilities that both have a deadline that is impossible to meet. You cannot accomplish both. How do you handle that situation?"

"Well," I said, "I would look at the two and decide what I was best at, and then go to my boss and say, 'It's better that I do one well than both poorly,' and we'd figure out who else could do the other task."

Menkes immediately seized on a telling detail in my answer. I was interested in what job I would do best. But isn't the key issue what job the company most needed to have done? With that comment, I had revealed something valuable: that in a time of work-related crisis I start from a self-centered consideration. "Perhaps you are a bit of a solo practitioner," Menkes said diplomatically. "That's an essential bit of information."

Menkes deliberately wasn't drawing any broad conclusions. If we are not people who are shy or talkative or outspoken but people who are shy in some contexts, talkative in other situations, and outspoken in still other areas, then what it means to know someone is to catalogue and appreciate all those variations. Menkes was trying to begin that process of cataloguing. This interviewing technique is known as "structured interviewing," and in studies by industrial psychologists it has been shown to be the only kind of interviewing that has any success at all in predicting performance in the workplace. In the structured interviews, the format is fairly rigid. Each applicant is treated in precisely the same manner. The questions are scripted. The interviewers are carefully trained, and each applicant is rated on a series of predetermined scales.

What is interesting about the structured interview is how narrow its objectives are. When I interviewed Nolan Myers I was groping for some kind of global sense of who he was; Menkes seemed entirely uninterested in arriving at that same general sense of me—he seemed to realize how foolish that expectation was for an hour-long interview. The structured interview works precisely because it isn't really an interview; it isn't about getting to know someone, in a traditional sense. It's as much concerned with rejecting information as it is with collecting it.

Not surprisingly, interview specialists have found it extraordinarily difficult to persuade most employers to adopt the structured interview. It just doesn't feel right. For most of us, hiring someone is essentially a romantic process, in which the job interview functions as a desexualized version of a date. We are looking for someone with whom we have a certain chemistry, even if the coupling that results ends in tears and the pursuer and the pursued turn out to have nothing in common. We want the unlimited promise of a love affair. The structured interview, by contrast, seems to offer only the dry logic and practicality of an arranged marriage.

Nolan Myers agonized over which job to take. He spent half an hour on the phone with Steve Ballmer, and Ballmer was very persuasive. "He gave me very, very good advice," Myers says of his conversations with the Microsoft C.E.O. "He felt that I should go to the place that excited me the most and that I thought would be best for my career. He offered to be my mentor." Myers says he talked to his parents every day about what to do. In February,

he flew out to California and spent a Saturday going from one Tellme executive to another, asking and answering questions. "Basically, I had three things I was looking for. One was long-term goals for the company. Where did they see themselves in five years? Second, what position would I be playing in the company?" He stopped and burst out laughing. "And I forget what the third one is." In March, Myers committed to Tellme.

Will Nolan Myers succeed at Tellme? I think so, although I honestly have no idea. It's a harder question to answer now than it would have been thirty or forty years ago. If this were 1965, Nolan Myers would have gone to work at I.B.M. and worn a blue suit and sat in a small office and kept his head down, and the particulars of his personality would not have mattered so much. It was not so important that I.B.M. understood who you were before it hired you, because you understood what I.B.M. was. If you walked through the door at Armonk or at a branch office in Illinois, you knew what you had to be and how you were supposed to act. But to walk through the soaring, open offices of Tellme, with the bunk beds over the desks, is to be struck by how much more demanding the culture of Silicon Valley is. Nolan Myers will not be provided with a social script, that blue suit and organization chart. Tellme, like any technology startup these days, wants its employees to be part of a fluid team, to be flexible and innovative, to work with shifting groups in the absence of hierarchy and bureaucracy, and in that environment, where the workplace doubles as the rec room, the particulars of your personality matter a great deal.

This is part of the new economy's appeal, because Tellme's soaring warehouse is a more productive and enjoyable place to work than the little office boxes of the old I.B.M. But the danger here is that we will be led astray in judging these newly important particulars of character. If we let personality—some indefinable, prerational intuition, magnified by the Fundamental Attribution Error—bias the hiring process today, then all we will have done is replace the old-boy network, where you hired your nephew, with the new-boy network, where you hire whoever impressed you most when you shook his hand. Social progress, unless we're careful, can merely be the means by which we replace the obviously arbitrary with the not so obviously arbitrary.

Myers has spent much of the past year helping to teach Introduction to Computer Science. He realized, he says, that one of the reasons that students were taking the course was that they wanted to get jobs in the software industry. "I decided that, having gone through all this interviewing, I had developed some expertise, and I would like to share that. There is a real skill and art in presenting yourself to potential employers. And so what we did in this class was talk about the kinds of things that employers are looking for—what are they looking for in terms of personality. One of the most important things is that you have to come across as being confident in what you are doing and in who you are. How do you do that? Speak clearly and smile." As he said that, Nolan Myers smiled. "For a lot of people, that's a very hard skill to learn. But for some reason I seem to understand it intuitively."

Unit 3

Unit Selections

11. **Mindless Propaganda, Thoughtful Persuasion,** Anthony R. Pratkanis and Elliot Aronson
12. **How to Sell a Pseudoscience,** Anthony R. Pratkanis
13. **A Social Psychological Perspective on the Role of Knowledge About AIDS in AIDS Prevention,** Marie Helweg-Larsen and Barry E. Collins

Key Points to Consider

❖ When someone is paying careful attention to a persuasive message, what implications does this have for the message's success? That is, what factors will be especially important, or unimportant, in such cases? What are the implications when the audience is not carefully attending to the message? Could persuasion still occur? What would determine whether it did or not?

❖ How would you go about "selling" a pseudoscientific belief system to someone? Which techniques do you think would be most effective? Least effective? Can you think of any examples from real life of such techniques being used? How could you use the individual's own behaviors as a means of increasing commitment?

❖ Why does providing information about AIDS, its transmission and ways to avoid it, have such a small impact on actual attitudes and behavior? Can this be explained by the traditional theories about attitudes and attitude change? Are there other factors at play as well?

 **Links**   **www.dushkin.com/online/**

8. **Propaganda and Psychological Warfare Research Resource**
   http://ww2.lafayette.edu/~mcglonem/prop.html
9. **The Psychology of Cyberspace**
   http://www.rider.edu/users/suler/psycyber/psycyber.html

These sites are annotated on pages 4 and 5.

Every year during professional football's Super Bowl, advertisers pay untold millions of dollars in order to show their commercials for beer, chips, beer, tires, beer, computers, and beer. The network showing the game also takes the opportunity to air countless advertisements promoting other programs on that network.

Every 4 years, during the presidential election, the airwaves are crowded with political advertisements in which candidates tout their own accomplishments, pose with cute children and cheering crowds, and display ominous, unflattering, black and white photographs of their opponents as grim-voiced announcers catalog the opponents' shortcomings.

The underlying reason for both of these phenomena is that the advertisers, networks, and candidates all share a common assumption: that attitudes are important. If attitudes toward a particular brand of beer can be made more favorable through cute commercials involving talking frogs, then people will buy more of that beer. If attitudes toward a television program can be made more favorable by showing funny clips from it every 12 minutes, then more people will watch the program. If attitudes toward a candidate can be made more positive—or attitudes toward the opponent more negative—then people will be more likely to vote for the candidate. To change someone's behavior, this argument goes, you must first change that person's attitude.

To one degree or another, social psychology has shared this view for decades. The study of attitudes and attitude change has been a central concern of the field for half a century—in fact, for a while that seemed to be all that social psychology studied. One major approach during this time has been to focus on where attitudes come from. The evidence from this research suggests that we acquire attitudes not only from careful consideration of the facts, but also through processes that are much less conscious and deliberate. Merely being exposed to some object frequently enough, for example, generally leads to a more favorable attitude toward it. It also appears that we sometimes arrive at our attitudes by looking at our behaviors, and then simply inferring what our attitudes must be based on our actions.

Another approach to the topic of attitudes has been to examine directly the basic assumption mentioned above, namely that attitudes are strongly associated with actual behavior. As it turns out, the link between attitudes and behavior is not as powerful or reliable as you might think, although under the right circumstances it is still possible to predict behavior from attitudes with considerable success. In fact, it is because of this link between attitudes and behavior that the last major approach to the topic—studying the factors that influence attitude *change*—has been popular for so long. Two

of the three articles in this unit, in fact, focus explicitly on the issue of persuasion; in short, how does one person convince others to change their attitudes?

In "Mindless Propaganda, Thoughtful Persuasion," Anthony Pratkanis and Elliot Aronson discuss an influential theory in contemporary social psychology, the elaboration likelihood model. According to this approach, audiences react to persuasion attempts in two basic ways—either by thinking carefully about the message and attending to its arguments, or through a much more superficial processing of the message and its content. In "How to Sell a Pseudoscience," Anthony Pratkanis outlines how someone could use social psychological principles to persuade others to accept as valid a pseudoscientific belief system. It is his belief that existing pseudosciences use precisely these techniques in their quest for new members. The final selection in this section, "A Social Psychological Perspective on the Role of Knowledge about AIDS in AIDS Prevention," examines an approach frequently used in attempts to alter nonhealthy behaviors—providing information in order to change attitudes toward the behavior. As the authors note, there is little evidence that providing such information has much influence on attitudes or behavior in the case of AIDS.

Mindless Propaganda, Thoughtful Persuasion

Anthony R. Pratkanis and
Elliot Aronson

Here are a five facts that professional persuaders have learned about modern propaganda:[1]

Ads that contain the words *new, quick, easy, improved, now, suddenly, amazing, and introducing* sell more products.

In supermarkets, merchandise placed on shelves at eye level sells best. Indeed, one study found that sales for products at waist level were only 74% as great and sales for products at floor level were only 57% as great as for those products placed at eye level.

Ads that use animals, babies, or sex appeal are more likely to sell the product than those that use cartoon characters and historical figures.

Merchandise placed at the end of a supermarket aisle or near the checkout aisle is more likely to be purchased.

Bundle pricing—for example, selling items at 2 for $1 instead of 50¢ each—often increases the customer's perception of product "value."

Why do these five techniques work? When you think about it, it makes little sense to purchase an item because it happens to be placed at the end of a supermarket aisle or on a shelf at eye level. You may not really need this conveniently located product, or the item you really want may be located on a top shelf. It makes little sense to be convinced by an ad because it uses a baby or contains certain words; such "information" is of little value in determining the quality of the product. A subtle rewording of the price does not add any value to the product. But that is the point—we consumers often don't think about the reasons we make the decisions we do. Studies show that about half of purchases in a supermarket are impulse buys and that upwards of 62% of all shoppers in discount stores buy at least one item on an unplanned basis.[2]

We often respond to propaganda with little thought and in a mindless fashion. Consider the experiments on mindlessness conducted by Ellen Langer and her colleagues.[3] Langer's collaborators walked up to persons busily using a university copy machine and said: "Excuse me: may I use the Xerox machine?" What would you do in such a situation? If you are like most people, it would depend on your mood. On some occasions you might think: *"Sure, why not? I'm a helpful person."* At other times, you might say to yourself: *"Is this person nuts or what? I got here first and have lots of work to do."* Indeed Langer's results indicate that both types of thinking were going on—a little over half of the people complied with this request.

Now, here's the interesting part. Langer found that she could get almost everyone to agree to let another person cut in front of them at the copy machine by adding one detail to the request—a *reason* for why the machine was needed. This makes sense. It takes a cold heart to deny someone, perhaps panic-stricken with an urgent need, the simple use of a copy machine. The odd thing about Langer's study is that although some of the reasons given made no sense at all, nearly everyone let the person cut in. For example, on some occasions Langer's collaborators would say, "Excuse me: May I use the Xerox machine, because I have to make copies." When you think about it, this is a pretty silly thing to say" Why would you need a copy machine if you were not planning to make copies? It is the same as no reason at all. But that is the point. Most of the people in the study did not think about it and mindlessly complied with the request.

We can also be influenced when we are being thoughtful. For example, most of us, at one time or another, have been panhandled, that is, stopped on the street by a passerby who asks for a quarter or any spare change. A common response is to ignore the request and continue to walk *mindlessly* down the street. Recently, we were panhandled in a novel manner. The panhandler asked, "Excuse me, do you have 17 cents that I could have?" What thoughts would run through your head in this situation? When it happened to us, our immediate thought was: *"Why does this person need exactly 17 cents? Is it for bus fare? Is it for a specific food purchase? Maybe the person came up short at the market."* Suddenly the panhandler was a real individual with real needs, not someone we could mindlessly pass by. We were persuaded to part with a handful of change. Intrigued, we later sent our students out on the streets to panhandle for a local charity. They found that almost twice as many people contributed when asked for 17 or 37 cents compared to those who were asked for a quarter or any spare change.[4]

People can be persuaded both when they are in a mindless state *and* when they are thoughtful, but exactly how they are influenced in either of these two states differs considerably. Richard Petty and John Cacioppo argue that there are two routes to persuasion—*peripheral* and *central*.[5] In the peripheral route, a message recipient devotes little attention and effort to processing a communication. Some examples might include watching television while doing something else or listening to a debate on an issue that you don't care much about. In the peripheral route, persuasion is determined by simple cues, such as the attractiveness of the communicator, whether or not the people around you agree with the position presented, or the pleasure and pain associated with agreeing with the position. In contrast, in the central route, a message recipient engages in a careful and thoughtful consideration of the true merits of the information presented. For example, in the central route the person may actively argue against the message, may want to know the answer to additional questions, or may seek out new information. The persuasiveness of the message is determined by how well it can stand up to this scrutiny.

Let's see how the two routes to persuasion could be used to process one of the most influential and controversial television ads of the 1988 presidential election. This ad, prepared by the Bush campaign, told the story of Willie Horton, a black man who had been sent to prison for murder. During the time when Michael Dukakis, Bush's Democratic opponent, was governor of Massachusetts, Horton was released on a prison furlough program. While on furlough, Horton fled to Maryland, where he raped a white woman after stabbing her male companion.

The ad was influential because it required little thought for a person in the peripheral route to get the point. A typical response elicited by the ad went something like this: *"Dukakis let Horton out of prison to rape and kill. Dukakis is weak on crime, especially those committed by bad, black guys."* Although the response is simple, it was nonetheless effective for George Bush. Michael Dukakis was painted as a weak leader who was soft on crime; by comparison, George Bush

looked strong and tough, capable of protecting us from the likes of Willie Horton.

However, no one was forced to think about this ad in the peripheral route. For example, in the central route to persuasion, the viewer might have asked *"Just how unusual is the Massachusetts prison furlough program? Do other states have similar programs? What is the success rate of such programs? Have instances like the Horton case happened in other states and with other governors? Can Dukakis really be held personally responsible for the decision to release Horton? How many prisoners were furloughed in Massachusetts without incident? Given that the cost of imprisoning someone for four years is approximately $88,000, or equal to the cost of four years of tuition for a student at Harvard with enough left over to buy the student a BMW upon graduation, is the furlough release program worth trying?"* In the central route, the Horton ad is potentially less effective (and might even have had the potential to damage the Bush campaign). The ad addressed few questions that a thoughtful viewer might raise.

This raises a crucial question: What determines which route to persuasion will be adopted? One factor identified by Petty and Cacioppo is the recipient's motivation to think about the message. In one experiment, Petty and Cacioppo, along with their student Rachel Goldman,[6] investigated the role of personal involvement in determining how we think about a message. Students at the University of Missouri heard a message. Students at the University of Missouri heard a message advocating that their university adopt an exam that all students would need to pass in their senior year in order to graduate. Half of the students were told that their university's chancellor was considering adopting the comprehensive exam the following year, thereby making the issue of adopting the exam personally relevant for these students. The other half were told that the changes would not take effect for ten years and thus would not affect them personally.

To see how the personal relevance of an issue influenced thinking about a communication, Petty, Cacioppo, and Goldman prepared four different versions of the comprehensive exam message. Half of the messages were attributed to a source low in expertise—a local high school class. The other half of the messages were attributed to a source high in expertise—the Carnegie Commission on Higher Education. The researchers also varied the quality of arguments in the message, with half of the messages containing weak arguments (personal opinions and anecdotes) and the other half consisting of strong arguments (statistics and other data about the value of the exam).

This simple study can tell us a lot about the way people think about a persuasive message. Suppose someone was operating in the central route to persuasion and was carefully scrutinizing the communication. When would that person be most persuaded?

Given that the person was thinking carefully, he or she would not be persuaded by weak arguments and the source of the communication would not matter much; however, a strong message that stood up to close examination would be very effective. In contrast, the content of the message would not matter much to someone who was not thinking too much about the issue; instead, someone using the peripheral route would be most persuaded by a simple device such as a source that appears to be expert.

What did Petty, Cacioppo, and Goldman find? The personal relevance of the issue determined the route to persuasion. For those students for whom the issue of comprehensive exams was personally relevant, the strength of the message's argument was the most important factor determining whether or not they were persuaded. In contrast, for those students for whom the issue of the comprehensive exam was not personally relevant, the source of the communication mattered—the source high in expertise convinced; the one from the high school class failed to do so.

Petty and Cacioppo's two routes to persuasion should alert us to two important points—one about ourselves as human beings and one about propaganda in our modern world. In many ways, we are *cognitive misers*—we are forever trying to conserve our cognitive energy.[7] Given our finite ability to process information, we often adopt the strategies of the peripheral route for simplifying complex problems; we mindlessly accept a conclusion or proposition—not for any good reason but because it is accompanied by a simplistic persuasion device.

Modern propaganda promotes the use of the peripheral route to persuasion and is designed to take advantage of the limited processing capabilities of the cognitive miser. The characteristics of modern persuasion—the message-dense environment, the thirty-second ad, the immediacy of persuasion—make it increasingly more difficult to think deeply about important issues and decisions. Given that we often operate in the peripheral route, professional propagandists have free rein to use the type of tactics described at the beginning of this chapter and throughout this book to achieve, with impunity, whatever goal they may have in mind.

We have a state of affairs that may be called the *essential dilemma of modern democracy*. On the one hand, we, as a society, value persuasion; our government is based on the belief that free speech and discussion and exchange of ideas can lead to fairer and better decision making. On the other hand, as cognitive misers we often do not participate fully in this discussion, relying instead not on careful thought and scrutiny of a message, but on simplistic persuasion devices and limited reasoning. Mindless propaganda, not thoughtful persuasion, flourishes.

The antidote to the dilemma of modern democracy is not a simple one. It requires each of us to take steps to minimize the likelihood of our processing important information in the peripheral route. This might include increasing our ability to think about an issue through education or improving our ability to detect and understand propaganda by learning more about persuasion. It may mean alerting others to the personal importance of an issue so that many more citizens are encouraged to think deeply about a proposition. It could involve restructuring the way information is presented in our society so that we have the time and the ability to think before we decide. . . . Given the stakes, it behooves each of us to think carefully about how this dilemma can best be resolved.

Notes

1. Burton, P. W. (1981). *Which ad pulled best?* Chicago: Crain; Caples, J. (1974). *Tested advertising methods.* Englewood Cliffs, NJ: Prentice-Hall; Loudon, D. L., & Della Bitta, A. J. (1984). *Consumer behavior.* New York: McGraw-Hill; Ogilvy, D. (1983). *Ogilvy on advertising.* New York: Crown.

2. Ibid.

3. Langer, E., Blank, A., & Chanowitz, B. (1978). The mindlessness of ostensibly thoughtful action: The role of "placebic" information in interpersonal interaction. *Journal of Personality and Social Psychology, 36,* 635–642.

4. Santos, M., Leve, C., & Pratkanis, A. R. (August 1991). *Hey buddy, can you spare 17 cents? Mindfulness and persuasion.* Paper presented at the annual meeting of the American Psychological Association, San Francisco.

5. Petty, R. E., & Cacioppo, J. T. (1986). The elaboration likelihood model of persuasion. In L. Berkowitz (Ed.), *Advances in experimental social psychology* (Vol. 19; pp. 123–205). New York: Academic Press; Petty, R. E., & Cacioppo, J. T. (1986). *Communication and persuasion: Central and peripheral routes to attitude change.* New York: Springer-Verlag. See also Chaiken, S. (1980). Heuristic versus systematic information processing and the use of source versus message cues in persuasion. *Journal of Personality and Social Psychology, 39,* 752–766; Chaiken, S., Liberman, A., & Eagly, A. (1989). Heuristic versus systematic information processing within and beyond the persuasion context. In J. S. Uleman & J. A. Bargh (Eds.), *Unintended thought* (pp. 212–252). New York: Guilford.

6. Petty, R. E., Cacioppo, J. T., & Goldman, R. (1981). Personal involvement as a determinant of argument-based persuasion. *Journal of Personality and Social Psychology, 41,* 847–855.

7. Fiske, S. T., & Taylor, S. E. (1991). *Social cognition.* New York: McGraw-Hill.

How to Sell a Pseudoscience

ANTHONY R. PRATKANIS

Want your own pseudoscience? Here are nine effective persuasion tactics for selling all sorts of filmflam.

Every time I read the reports of new pseudosciences in the SKEPTICAL INQUIRER or watch the latest "In Search Of"-style television show I have one cognitive response, "Holy cow, how can anyone believe that?" Some recent examples include: "Holy cow, why do people spend $3.95 a minute to talk on the telephone with a 'psychic' who has never foretold the future?" "Holy cow, why do people believe that an all uncooked vegan diet is natural and therefore nutritious?" "Holy cow why would two state troopers chase the planet Venus across state lines thinking it was an alien spacecraft?" "Holy cow, why do people spend millions of dollars each year on subliminal tapes that just don't work?"

There are, of course, many different answers to these "holy cow" questions. Conjurers can duplicate pseudoscientific feats and thus show us how slights of hand and misdirections can mislead (e.g., Randi 1982a, 1982b, 1989). Sociologists can point to social conditions that increase the prevalence of pseudoscientific beliefs (e.g., Lett 1992; Padgett and Jorgenson 1982; Victor 1993). Natural scientists can describe the physical properties of objects to show that what may appear to be supernatural is natural (e.g., Culver and Ianna 1988; Nickell 1983, 1993). Cognitive psychologists have identified common mental biases that often lead us to misinterpret social reality and to conclude in favor of supernatural phenomena (e.g., Blackmore 1992; Gilovich 1991; Hines 1988). These perspectives are useful in addressing the "holy cow" question; all give us a piece of the puzzle in unraveling this mystery.

I will describe how a social psychologist answers the holy cow question. Social psychology is the study of social influence—how human beings and their institutions influence and affect each other (see Aronson 1992; Aronson and Pratkanis 1993). For the past seven decades, social psychologists have been developing theories of social influence and have been testing the effectiveness of various persuasion tactics in their labs (see Cialdini 1984; Pratkanis and Aronson, 1992). It is my thesis that many persuasion tactics discovered by social psychologists are used

Anthony R. Pratkanis is associate professor of psychology, University of California, Santa Cruz, CA 95064. This article is based on a paper presented at the conference of the Committee for the Scientific Investigation of Claims of the Paranormal, June 23–26 1994, in Seattle, Washington.

every day, perhaps not totally consciously, by the promoters of pseudoscience (see Feynman 1985 or Hines 1988 for a definition of pseudoscience).

To see how these tactics can be used to sell flimflam, let's pretend for a moment that we wish to have our very own pseudoscience. Here are nine common propaganda tactics that should result in success.

1. Create a Phantom

The first thing we need to do is to create a phantom—an unavailable goal that looks real and possible; it looks as if it might be obtained with just the right effort, just the right belief, or just the right amount of money, but in reality it can't be obtained. Most pseudosciences are based on belief in a distant or phantom goal. Some examples of pseudoscience phantoms: meeting a space alien, contacting a dead relative at a séance, receiving the wisdom of the universe from a channeled dolphin, and improving one's bowling game or overcoming the trauma of rape with a subliminal tape.

Phantoms can serve as effective propaganda devices (Pratkanis and Farquhar 1992). If I don't have a desired phantom, I feel deprived and somehow less of a person. A pseudoscientist can take advantage of these feelings of inferiority by appearing to offer a means to obtain that goal. In a rush to enhance self-esteem, we suspend better judgment and readily accept the offering of the pseudoscience.

The trick, of course, is to get the new seeker to believe that the phantom is possible. Often the mere mention of the delights of a phantom will be enough to dazzle the new pseudoscience recruit (see Lund's 1925 discussion of wishful thinking). After all, who wouldn't want a better sex life, better health, and peace of mind, all from a $14.95 subliminal tape? The fear of loss of a phantom also can motivate us to accept it as real. The thought that I will never speak again to a cherished but dead loved one or that next month I may die of cancer can be so painful as to cause me to suspend my better judgment and hold out hope against hope that the medium can contact the dead or that Laetrile works. But at times the sell is harder, and that calls for our next set of persuasion tactics.

Gerald Fried

2. Set a Rationalization Trap

The rationalization trap is based on the premise: Get the person committed to the cause as soon as possible. Once a commitment is made, the nature of thought changes. The committed heart is not so much interested in a careful evaluation of the merits of a course of action but in proving that he or she is right.

To see how commitment to a pseudoscience can be established, let's look at a bizarre case—mass suicides at the direction of cult leader Jim Jones. This is the ultimate "holy cow" question: "Why kill yourself and your children on another's command?" From outside the cult, it appears strange, but from the inside it seems natural. Jones began by having his followers make easy commitments (a gift to the church, attending Wednesday night service) and then increased the level of commitment—more tithes, more time in service, loyalty oaths, public admission of sins and punishment, selling of homes, forced sex, moving to Guyana, and then the suicide. Each step was really a small one. Outsiders saw the strange end-product; insiders experienced an ever increasing spi-

> *"Source credibility can stop questioning. After all, what gives you the right to question a guru, a prophet, the image of the Mother Mary, or a sincere seeker of life's hidden potentials?"*

ral of escalating commitment. (See Pratkanis and Aronson 1992 for other tactics used by Jones.)

This is a dramatic example, but not all belief in pseudoscience is so extreme. For example, there are those who occasionally consult a psychic or listen to a subliminal tape. In such cases, commitment can be secured by what social psychologists call the foot-in-the-door technique (Freedman and Fraser 1966). It works this way: You start with a small request, such as accepting a free chiropractic spine exam (Barrett 1993a), taking a sample of vitamins, or completing a free personality inventory. Then a larger request follows—a $1,000 chiropractic re-alignment, a vitamin regime, or an expensive seminar series. The first small request sets the commitment: Why did you get that bone exam, take those vitamins, or complete that test if you weren't interested and didn't think there might be something to it? An all too common response, "Well gosh, I guess I am interested." The rationalization trap is sprung.

Now that we have secured the target's commitment to a phantom goal, we need some social support for the newfound pseudoscientific beliefs. The next tactics are designed to bolster those beliefs.

3. Manufacture Source Credibility and Sincerity

Our third tactic is to manufacture source credibility and sincerity. In other words, create a guru, leader, mystic, lord, or other generally likable and powerful authority, one who people would be just plain nuts if they didn't believe. For example, practitioners of alternative medicine often have "degrees" as chiropractors or in homeopathy. Subliminal tape sellers claim specialized knowledge and training in such arts as hypnosis. Advocates of UFO sightings often become directors of "research centers." "Psychic detectives" come with long résumés of police service. Prophets claim past successes. For example, most of us "know" that Jeane Dixon predicted the assassination of President Kennedy but probably don't know that she also predicted a Nixon win in 1960. As modern public relations has shown us, credibility is easier to manufacture than we might normally think (see Ailes 1988; Dilenschneider 1990).

Source credibility is an effective propaganda device for at least two reasons. First, we often process persuasive messages in a half-mindless state—either because we are not motivated to think, don't have the time to consider, or lack the abilities to understand the issues (Petty and Cacioppo 1986). In such cases, the presence of a credible source can lead one to quickly infer that the message has merit and should be accepted.

Second, source credibility can stop questioning (Kramer and Alstad 1993). After all, what gives you the right to question a guru, a prophet, the image of the Mother Mary, or a sincere seeker of life's hidden potentials? I'll clarify this point with an example. Suppose I told you that the following statement is a prediction of the development of the atomic bomb and the fighter aircraft (see Hines 1988):

> They will think they have seen the Sun at night
>
> When they will see the pig half-man:
>
> Noise, song, battle fighting in the sky perceived,
>
> And one will hear brute beasts talking.

You probably would respond: "Huh? I don't see how you get the atomic bomb from that. This could just as well be a prediction of an in-flight showing of the Dr. Doolittle movie or the advent of night baseball at Wrigley field." However, attribute the statement to Nostradamus and the dynamics change. Nostradamus was a man who supposedly cured plague victims, predicted who would be pope, foretold the future of kings and queens, and even found a poor dog lost by the king's page (Randi 1993). Such a great seer and prophet can't be wrong. The implied message: The problem is with you; instead of questioning, why don't you suspend your faulty, linear mind until you gain the needed insight?

4. Establish a Granfalloon

Where would a leader be without something to lead? Our next tactic supplies the answer: Establish what Kurt Vonnegut (1976) terms a "granfalloon," a proud and meaningless association of human beings. One of social psychology's most remarkable findings is the ease with which granfalloons can be created. For example, the social psychologist Henri Tajfel merely brought subjects into his lab, flipped a coin, and randomly assigned them to be labeled either Xs or Ws (Tajfel 1981; Turner 1987). At the end of the study, total strangers were acting as if those in their granfalloon were their close kin and those in the other group were their worse enemies.

Granfalloons are powerful propaganda devices because they are easy to create and, once established, the granfalloon defines social reality and maintains social identities. Information is dependent on the granfalloon. Since most granfalloons quickly develop outgroups, criticisms can be attributed to those "evil ones" outside the group, who are thus stifled. To maintain a desired social identity, such as that of a seeker or a New Age rebel, one must obey the dictates of the granfalloon and its leaders.

The classic séance can be viewed as an ad-hoc granfalloon. Note what happens as you sit in the dark and hear a thud. You are dependent on the group led by a medium for the interpretation of this sound. "What is it? A knee against the table or my long lost Uncle Ned? The group believes it is Uncle Ned. Rocking the boat would be impolite. Besides, I came here to be a seeker."

Essential to the success of the granfalloon tactic is the creation of a shared social identity. In creating this identity, here are some things you might want to include:

(a) rituals and symbols (e.g., a dowser's rod, secret symbols, and special ways of preparing food): these not only create an identity, but provide items for sale at a profit.

(b) jargon and beliefs that only the in-group understands and accepts (e.g., thetans are impeded by engrams, you are on a cusp with Jupiter rising): jargon is an effective means of social control since it can be used to frame the interpretation of events.

(c) shared goals (e.g., to end all war, to sell the faith and related products, or to realize one's human potential): such goals not only define the group, but motivate action as believers attempt to teach them.

(d) shared feelings (e.g., the excitement of a prophecy that might appear to be true or the collective rationalization of strange beliefs to others): shared feelings aid in the *we* feeling.

(e) specialized information (e.g., the U.S. government is in a conspiracy to cover up UFOs): this helps the target feel special because he or she is "in the know."

(f) enemies (e.g., alternative medicine opposing the AMA and the FDA, subliminal-tape companies spurning academic psychologists, and spiritualists condemning Randi and other investigators): enemies are very important because you as a pseudoscientist will need scapegoats to blame for your problems and failures.

5. Use Self-Generated Persuasion

Another tactic for promoting pseudoscience and one of the most powerful tactics identified by social psychologists is self-generated persuasion—the subtle design of the situation so that the targets persuade themselves. During World War II, Kurt Lewin (1947) was able to get Americans to eat more sweetbreads (veal and beef organ meats) by having them form groups to discuss how they could persuade others to eat sweetbreads.

Retailers selling so-called nutritional products have discovered this technique by turning customers into salespersons (Jarvis and Barrett 1993). To create a multilevel sales organization, the "nutrition" retailer recruits customers (who recruit still more customers) to serve as sales agents for the product. Customers are recruited as a test of their belief in the product or with the hope of making lots of money (often to buy more products). By trying to sell the product, the customer-turned-salesperson becomes more convinced of its worth. One multilevel leader tells his new sales agents to "answer all objections with testimonials. That's the secret to motivating people" (Jarvis and Barrett 1993), and it is also the secret to convincing yourself.

6. Construct Vivid Appeals

Joseph Stalin once remarked: "The death of a single Russian soldier is a tragedy. A million deaths is a statistic." (See Nisbett and Ross 1980.) In other words, a vividly presented case study or example can make a lasting impression. For example, the pseudosciences are replete with graphic stories of ships and planes caught in the Bermuda Triangle, space aliens examining the sexual parts of humans, weird goings-on in Borley Rectory or Amityville, New York, and psychic surgeons removing cancerous tumors.

A vivid presentation is likely to be very memorable and hard to refute. No matter how many logical arguments can be mustered to counter the pseudoscience claim, there remains that one graphic incident that comes quickly to mind to prompt the response: "Yeah, but what about that haunted house in New York? Hard to explain that." By the way, one of the best ways to counter a vivid appeal is with an equally vivid counter appeal. For example, to counter stories about psychic surgeons in the Philippines, Randi (1982a) tells an equally vivid story of a psychic surgeon palming chicken guts and then pretending to remove them from a sick and now less wealthy patient.

7. Use Pre-persuasion

Pre-persuasion is defining the situation or setting the stage so you win, and sometimes without raising so much as a valid argument. How does one do this? At least three steps are important.

First, establish the nature of the issue. For example, to avoid the wrath of the FDA, advocates of alternative medicine define the issue as health freedom (you should have the right to the health alternative of your choice) as opposed to consumer protection or quality care. If the issue is defined as freedom, the alternative medicine advocate will win because "Who is opposed to freedom?" Another example of this technique is to create a problem or disease, such as reactive hypoglycemia or yeast allergy, that then just happens to be "curable" with whatever quackery you have to sell (Jarvis and Barrett 1993).

Another way to define an issue is through differentiation. Subliminal-tape companies use product differentiation to respond to negative subliminal-tape studies. The claim: "Our tapes have a special technique that makes them superior to other tapes that have been used in studies that failed to show the therapeutic value of subliminal tapes." Thus, null results are used to make a given subliminal tape look superior. The psychic network has taken a similar approach—"Tired of those phoney psychics? Ours are certified," says the advertisement.

Second, set expectations. Expectations can lead us to interpret ambiguous information in a way that supports an original hypothesis (Greenwald, Pratkanis, Leippe, and Baumgardner 1986). For example, a belief in the Bermuda Triangle may lead us to interpret a plane crash off the coast of New York City as evidence for the Triangle's sinister effects (Kusche 1986; Randi 1982a). We recently conducted a study that showed how an expectation can lead people to think that subliminal tapes work when in fact they do not (Greenwald, Spangenberg, Pratkanis, and Eskenazi 1991; Pratkanis, Eskenazi, and Greenwald 1994; for a summary see Pratkanis 1992). In our study, expectations were established by mislabeling half the tapes (e.g., some subjects thought they had a subliminal tape to improve memory but really had one designed to increase self-esteem). The results showed that about half the subjects thought they improved (though they did not) based on how the tape was labeled (and not the actual content). The label led them to interpret their behavior in support of expectations, or what we termed an "illusory placebo" effect.

A third way to pre-persuade is to specify the decision criteria. For example, psychic supporters have developed guidelines on what should be viewed as acceptable evidence for paranormal abilities—such as using personal experiences as data, placing the burden of proof on the critic and not the claimant (see Beloff 1985) and above all else keeping James Randi and other psi-inhibitors out of the testing room. Accept these criteria and one must conclude that psi is a reality. The collaboration of Hyman and Honorton is one positive attempt to establish a fair playing field (Hyman and Honorton 1986).

8. Frequently Use Heuristics and Commonplaces

My next recommendation to the would-be pseudoscientist is to use heuristics and commonplaces. Heuristics are simple if-then rules or norms that are widely accepted; for example, if it costs more it must be more valuable. Commonplaces are widely accepted beliefs that can serve as the basis of an appeal; for example, government health-reform should be rejected because politicians are corrupt (assuming political corruption is a widely accepted belief). Heuristics and commonplaces gain their power because they are widely accepted and thus induce little thought about whether the rule or argument is appropriate.

To sell a pseudoscience, liberally sprinkle your appeal with heuristics and commonplaces. Here are some common examples.

(a) The *scarcity heuristic,* or if it is rare it is valuable. The Psychic Friends Network costs a pricey $3.95 a minute and therefore must be valuable. On the other hand, an average University of California professor goes for about 27 cents per minute and is thus of little value.[1]

(b) The *consensus or bandwagon* heuristic, or if everyone agrees it must be true. Subliminal tapes, psychic phone ads, and quack medicine (Jarvis and Barrett 1993) feature testimonials of people who have found what they are looking for (see Hyman 1993 for a critique of this practice).

(c) The *message length* heuristic, or if the message is long it is strong. Subliminal-tape brochures often list hundreds of subliminal studies in support of their claims. Yet most of these studies do not deal with subliminal influence and thus are irrelevant. An uninformed observer would be impressed by the weight of the evidence.

(d) The *representative* heuristic or if an object resembles another (on some salient dimension) then they act similarly. For example, in folk medicines the cure often resembles the apparent cause of the disease. Homeopathy is based on the notion that small amounts of substances that can cause a disease's symptoms will cure the disease (Barrett 1993b). The Chinese Doctrine of Signatures claims that similarity of shape and form determine therapeutic value; thus rhinoceros horns, deer antlers, and ginseng root look phallic and supposedly improve vitality (Tyler 1993).

(e) The *natural* commonplace, or what is natural is good and what is made by humans is bad. Alternative medicines are promoted with the word "natural." Psychic abilities are portrayed as natural, but lost, abilities. Organic food is natural. Of course mistletoe berries are natural too, and I don't recommend a steady diet of these morsels.

(f) The *goddess-within* commonplace, or humans have a spiritual side that is neglected by modern materialistic science. This commonplace stems from the medieval notion of the soul, which was modernized by Mesmer as animal magnetism and then converted by psychoanalysis into the powerful, hidden unconscious (see Fuller 1982, 1986). Pseudoscience plays to this commonplace by offering ways to tap the unconscious, such as subliminal tapes, to prove this hidden power exists through extrasensory perception (ESP) and psi, or to talk with the remnants of this hidden spirituality through channeling and the séance.

(g) The *science* commonplaces. Pseudosciences use the word "science" in a contradictory manner. On the one hand, the word "science" is sprinkled liberally throughout most pseudosciences: subliminal tapes make use of the "latest scientific technology"; psychics are "scientifically tested"; health fads are "on the cutting edge of science." On the other hand, science is often portrayed as limited. For example, one article in *Self* magazine (Sharp 1993) reported our subliminal-tapes studies (Greenwald et al. 1992; Pratkanis et al. 1994) showing no evidence that the tapes worked and then stated: "Tape makers dispute the objectivity of the studies. They also point out that science can't always explain the results of mainstream medicine either" (p. 194). In each case a commonplace about science is used: (1) "Science is powerful" and (2) "Science is limited and can't replace the personal." The selective use of these commonplaces allows a pseudoscience to claim the power of science but have a convenient out should science fail to promote the pseudoscience.

9. Attack Opponents Through Innuendo and Character Assassination

Finally, you would like your pseudoscience to be safe from harm and external attack. Given that the best defense is a good offense, I offer the advice of Cicero: "If you don't have a good argument, attack the plaintiff."

Let me give a personal example of this tactic in action. After our research showing that subliminal tapes have no therapeutic value was reported, my co-authors, Tony Greenwald, Eric Spangenberg, and Jay Eskenazi, and I were the target of many innuendoes. One subliminal newsletter edited by Eldon Taylor, Michael Urban, and others (see the *International Society of Peripheral Learning Specialists Newsletter,* August 1991) claimed that our research was a marketing study designed not to test the tapes but to "demonstrate the influence of marketing practices on consumer perceptions." The article points out that the entire body of data

presented by Greenwald represents a marketing dissertation by Spangenberg and questions why Greenwald is even an author. The newsletter makes other attacks as well, claiming that our research design lacked a control group, that we really found significant effects of the tapes, that we violated American Psychological Association ethics with a hint that an investigation would follow, that we prematurely reported our findings in a manner similar to those who prematurely announced cold fusion, and that we were conducting a "Willie Horton"-style smear campaign against those who seek to help Americans achieve their personal goals.

Many skeptics can point to similar types of attacks. In the fourteenth century, Bishop Pierre d'Arcis, one of the first to contest the authenticity of the Shroud of Turin, was accused by shroud promoters as being motivated by jealousy and a desire to possess the shroud (Nickell 1983: 15). Today, James Randi is described by supporters of Uri Geller as "a powerful psychic trying to convince the world that such powers don't exist so he can take the lead role in the psychic world" (Hines 1988: 91).

Why is innuendo such a powerful propaganda device? Social psychologists point to three classes of answers. First, innuendoes change the agenda of discussion. Note the "new" discussion on subliminal types isn't about whether these tapes are worth your money or not. Instead, we are discussing whether I am ethical or not, whether I am a competent researcher, and whether I even did the research.

Second, innuendoes raise a glimmer of doubt about the character of the person under attack. That doubt can be especially powerful when there is little other information on which to base a judgment. For example, the average reader of the subliminal newsletter I quoted probably knows little about me—knows little about the research and little about the peer review process that evaluated it, and doesn't know that I make my living from teaching college and not from the sale of subliminal tapes. This average reader is left with the impression of an unethical and incompetent scientist who is out of control. Who in their right mind would accept what that person has to say?

Finally, innuendoes can have a chilling effect (Kurtz 1992). The recipient begins to wonder about his or her reputation and whether the fight is worth it. The frivolous lawsuit is an effective way to magnify this chilling effect.

Can Science Be Sold with Propaganda?

I would be remiss if I didn't address one more issue: Can we sell science with the persuasion tactics of pseudoscience? Let's be honest; science sometimes uses these tactics.

For example, I carry in my wallet a membership card to the Monterey Bay Aquarium with a picture of the cutest little otter you'll ever see. I am in the otter granfalloon. On some occasions skeptics have played a little loose with their arguments and their name-calling. As just one example, see George Price's (1955) *Science* article attacking Rhine's and Soal's work on ESP—an attack that went well beyond the then available data. (See Hyman's [1985] discussion.)

I can somewhat understand the use of such tactics. If a cute otter can inspire a young child to seek to understand nature, then so be it. But we should remember that such tactics can be ineffective in promoting science if they are not followed up by involvement in the process of science—the process of questioning and discovering. And we should be mindful that the use of propaganda techniques has its costs. If we base our claims in cheap propaganda tactics, then it is an easy task for the pseudoscientist to develop even more effective propaganda tactics and carry the day.

More fundamentally, propaganda works best when we are half mindless, simplistic thinkers trying to rationalize our behavior and beliefs to ourselves and others. Science works best when we are thoughtful and critical and scrutinize claims carefully. Our job should be to promote such thought and scrutiny. We should be careful to select our persuasion strategies to be consistent with the goal.

Notes

I thank Craig Abbott, Elizabeth A. Turner, and Marlene E. Turner for helpful comments on an earlier draft of this article.

1. Based on 50 weeks a year at an average salary of $49,000 and a work week of 61 hours (as reported in recent surveys of the average UC faculty work load). Assuming a work week of 40 hours, the average faculty makes 41 cents a minute.

References

Ailes, R. 1988. *You Are the Message.* New York: Doubleday.

Aronson, E. 1992. *The Social Animal,* 6th ed. New York: W. H. Freeman.

Aronson, E., and A. R. Pratkanis. 1993. "What Is Social Psychology?" In *Social Psychology,* vol. 1, ed. by E. Aronson and A. R. Pratkanis, xiii–xx. Cheltenham, Gloucestershire: Edward Elgar Publishing.

Barrett, S. 1993a. "The Spine Salesmen." In *The Health Robbers,* ed. by S. Barrett and W. T. Jarvis, 161–190. Buffalo, N.Y.: Prometheus Books.

———. 1993b. "Homeopathy: Is It Medicine?" In *The Health Robbers,* ed. by S. Barrett and W. T. Jarvis, 191–202. Buffalo, N.Y.: Prometheus Books.

Beloff, J. 1985. "What Is Your Counter-Explanation? A Plea to Skeptics to Think Again." In *A Skeptic's Handbook of Parapsychology,* ed. by P. Kurtz, 359–377. Buffalo, N.Y.: Prometheus Books.

Blackmore, S. 1992. Psychic experiences: Psychic illusions. SKEPTICAL INQUIRER, 16: 367–376.

Cialdini, R. B. 1984. *Influence.* New York; William Morrow.

Culver, R. B., and P. A. Ianna. 1988. *Astrology: True or False?* Buffalo, N.Y.: Prometheus Books.

Dilenschneider, R. L. 1990. *Power and Influence.* New York: Prentice-Hall.

Feynman, R. P. 1985. *Surely You're Joking Mr. Feynman.* New York: Bantam Books.

Freedman, J., and S. Fraser. 1966. Compliance without pressure: The foot-in-the-door technique. *Journal of Personality and Social Psychology,* 4: 195–202.

Fuller, R. C. 1982. *Mesmerism and the American Cure of Souls.* Philadelphia: University of Pennsylvania Press.

_____. 1986. *Americans and the Unconscious.* New York: Oxford University Press.

Gilovich, T. 1991. *How We Know What Isn't So.* New York: Free Press.

Greenwald, A. G., E. R. Spangenberg, A. R. Pratkanis, and J. Eskenazi. 1991. Double-blind tests of subliminal self-help audiotapes. *Psychological Science,* 2: 119–122.

Greenwald, A. G., A. R. Pratkanis, M. R. Leippe, and M. H. Baumgardner. 1986. Under what conditions does theory obstruct research progress? *Psychological Review,* 93: 216–229.

Hines, T. 1988. *Pseudoscience and the Paranormal.* Buffalo, N.Y.: Prometheus Books.

Hyman, R. 1985. "A Critical Historical Overview of Parapsychology." In *A Skeptic's Handbook of Parapsychology,* ed. by P. Kurtz, 3–96. Buffalo, N.Y.: Prometheus Books.

_____. 1993. Occult health practices. In *The Health Robbers,* ed. by S. Barrett and W. T. Jarvis, 55–66. Buffalo, N.Y.: Prometheus Books.

Hyman, R., and C. Honorton. 1986. A joint communique: The Psi Ganzfeld controversy. *Journal of Parapsychology,* 56: 351–364.

Jarvis, W. T., and S. Barrett. 1993. "How Quackery Sells." In *The Health Robbers,* ed. by S. Barrett and W. T. Jarvis, 1–22. Buffalo, N.Y.: Prometheus Books.

Kramer, J., and D. Alstad. 1993. *The Guru Papers: Masks of Authoritarian Power,* Berkeley, Calif.: North Atlantic Books/Frog Ltd.

Kurtz, P. 1992. On being sued: The chilling of freedom of expression. SKEPTICAL INQUIRER, 16: 114–117.

Kusche, L. 1986. *The Bermuda Triangle Mystery Solved.* Buffalo, N.Y.: Prometheus Books.

Lett, J. 1992. The persistent popularity of the paranormal. SKEPTICAL INQUIRER, 16, 381–388.

Lewin, K. 1947. "Group Decision and Social Change." In *Readings in Social Psychology,* ed. by T. M. Newcomb and E. L. Hartley, 330–344. New York: Holt.

Lund, F. H. 1925. The psychology of belief. *Journal of Abnormal and Social Psychology,* 20: 63–81, 174–196.

Nickell, J. 1983. *Inquest on the Shroud of Turin.* Buffalo, N.Y.: Prometheus Books.

_____. 1993. *Looking for a Miracle.* Buffalo, N.Y.: Prometheus Books.

Nisbett, R., and L. Ross. 1980. *Human Inference: Strategies and Shortcomings of Social Judgment.* Englewood Cliffs, N.J.: Prentice-Hall.

Padgett, V. R., and D. O. Jorgenson. 1982. Superstition and economic threat: Germany 1918–1940. *Personality and Social Psychology Bulletin,* 8: 736–741.

Petty, R. E., and J. T. Cacioppo. 1986. *Communication and Persuasion: Central and Peripheral Routes to Attitude Change.* New York: Springer-Verlag.

Pratkanis, A. R. 1992. The cargo-cult science of subliminal persuasion. SKEPTICAL INQUIRER, 16: 260–272.

Pratkanis, A. R., and E. Aronson. 1992. *Age of Propaganda; Everyday Use and Abuse of Persuasion.* New York: W. H. Freeman.

Pratkanis, A. R., J. Eskenazi, and A. G. Greenwald. 1994. What you expect is what you believe (but not necessarily what you get): A test of the effectiveness of subliminal self-help audiotapes. *Basic and Applied Social Psychology,* 15: 251–276.

Pratkanis, A. R., and P. H. Farquhar. 1992. A brief history of research on phantom alternatives: Evidence for seven empirical generalizations about phantoms. *Basic and Applied Social Psychology,* 13: 103–122.

Price, G. R. 1955. Science and the supernatural. *Science,* 122: 359–367.

Randi, J. 1982a. *Flim-Flam!* Buffalo, N.Y.: Prometheus Books.

_____. 1982b. *The Truth About Uri Geller.* Buffalo, N.Y.: Prometheus Books.

_____. 1989. *The Faith Healers.* Buffalo, N.Y.: Prometheus Books.

_____. 1993. *The Mask of Nostradamus.* Buffalo, N.Y.: Prometheus Books.

Sharp, K. 1993. The new hidden persuaders. *Self,* March, pp. 174–175, 194.

Tajfel, H. 1981. *Human Groups and Social Categories.* Cambridge, U.K.: Cambridge University Press.

Turner, J. C. 1987. *Rediscovering the Social Group.* New York: Blackwell.

Tyler, V. E. 1993. "The Overselling of Herbs." In *The Health Robbers,* ed. by S. Barrett and W. T. Jarvis, 213–224. Buffalo, N.Y.: Prometheus Books.

Victor, J. S. 1993. *Satanic Panic: The Creation of a Contemporary Legend.* Chicago, Ill.: Open Court.

Vonnegut, K. 1976. *Wampeters, Foma, and Granfalloons.* New York; Dell.

A Social Psychological Perspective on the Role of Knowledge About AIDS in AIDS Prevention

Marie Helweg-Larsen and Barry E. Collins[1]

Department of Psychology, University of California, Los Angeles, Los Angeles, California

Widespread ignorance regarding the transmission of HIV in the mid to late 1980s was, at once, a source of despair and optimism. It was discouraging that people knew so little about HIV prevention. At the same time, one could hope that an attack on the ignorance might amount to an attack on the virus itself. Today, many health educators still believe that ignorance is at the root of the spread of the disease and continue to focus on knowledge as a central causal variable in AIDS prevention. Many AIDS interventions are based on the idea that giving people the facts about transmission of HIV will lead to positive behaviors (and ultimately behavior change). In fact, some educational programs measure their success by assessing how much people learn about AIDS rather than by assessing people's changes in attitudes or behavior per se (e.g., Farley, Pomputius, Sabella, Helgerson, & Hadler, 1991; Ganz & Greenberg, 1990).

There are a number of philosophical and practical reasons for using information-based approaches to changing health-related behavior. The idea that people will change their behavior when they are informed about the logic of doing so is consistent with the Western worldview, which places individualism, enlightenment, and reason at the center of its value system. Knowledge-based behavior change is, in theory, internalized. Thus, the new behaviors will last longer, display a greater resistance to extinction, and generalize across more situations than will new behaviors arising from other forms of social influence (e.g., reward, coercion, and compliance with authority figures). Behaviors based on these other influences may be relatively situation specific and require surveillance for compliance.

Subscribing to an information-based view, many psychologists (and nonpsychologists) believe that knowledge about disease processes is a fundamental variable in any prevention theory or intervention program. Teaching the facts is seen as essential to changing attitudes or behaviors. For example, the author of one health psychology textbook argued that "health information is the first necessary component and a key ingredient in any attempt to bring about health behavior" (DiMatteo, 1991, p. 88). Similarly, the term "AIDS knowledge" is frequently used synonymously with the term "AIDS prevention" in the public-health literature in general and the AIDS prevention literature in particular.

Unfortunately, the evidence that sex education leads to changes in behaviors intended to prevent AIDS or pregnancy is disappointing. Similarly, the many research efforts aimed specifically at examining the relation between knowledge about AIDS (including how AIDS is transmitted) and preventive behaviors suggest overwhelmingly that this relation is weak or nonexistent. A review of global perspectives on AIDS (Mann, Tarantola, & Netter, 1992) concluded that "the failure of information to lead reliably, regularly, or predictably to behavior change has been documented repeatedly in varying culture and contexts and underscores the need for a comprehensive approach to prevention" (p. 330). Surprisingly, some of the researchers who themselves have found no effects of knowledge about AIDS on AIDS-related attitudes or behaviors nevertheless have made recommendations suggesting that counselors, physicians, and other health care professionals ought to provide more information about AIDS, develop educational programs, and provide sex education (Freeman et al., 1980). Our point is not that people might not benefit from or need such information (e.g., education might help reduce the stigma against persons with AIDS). Rather, we are saying that disease-related information about AIDS seems not to be an important cause of change in sexual behavior.

Surveys indicate that the absolute level of knowledge about AIDS, transmission routes, and preventive behaviors is quite high in some populations even while the frequency of behaviors that increase the risk of contamination remains high—a fact that would preclude a

Recommended Reading

Brandt, A.M. (1987). *No magic bullet: A history of venereal disease in the United States since 1880.* New York: Oxford University Press.

Cialdini, R.B. (1993). *Influence: Science and practice* (3rd ed.). Glenview, IL: Scott, Foresman/Little, Brown.

Eagley, A., & Chaiken, S. (1992). *The psychology of attitudes.* Orlando, FL: Harcourt, Brace, & Jovanovich.

From *Current Directions in Psychological Science,* April 1997, pp. 23–26. © 1997 by the American Psychological Society. Reprinted by permission of Blackwell Publishers.

strong relationship between knowledge and preventive behaviors. For example, in one study of injection drug users, participants were randomly assigned to an AIDS education group, an AIDS education group with optional HIV testing, or a wait-list control group (Calsyn, Saxon, Freeman, & Whittaker, 1992). Four months after the intervention, a structured interview could not detect any differences between the groups in either their knowledge about AIDS or their frequency of engaging in risky behaviors. Additionally, the injection drug users were very well informed about AIDS. Between 97% and 99% correctly identified routes of contracting HIV and knew that condoms could prevent its transmission. High absolute levels of knowledge about AIDS have also been found in heterosexual adolescents (e.g., DiClemente, Forrest, Mickler, & Principal Site Investigators, 1990) and gay men (e.g., Aspinwall, Kemeny, Taylor, Schneider, & Dudley, 1991). Thus, one might simply look to these high levels of knowledge to conclude that knowing the facts about AIDS is not sufficient to cause people to change their behavior. If it were, very few people in these populations would be engaging in risky behaviors.

One of the most common reactions to a failure to find a relationship between knowing the facts abut AIDS and engaging in risky behaviors is to conclude that information is a necessary, but not a sufficient, condition for behavior change (see J.D. Fisher & Fisher, 1992, for a review). However, as we discuss next, the route to changes in behaviors related to risk of contracting HIV does not (or does not always) pass through the acquisition of knowledge about AIDS.

SOCIAL PSYCHOLOGICAL THEORIES

Within social psychology, a wealth of research on persuasion and attitude change provides clues as to (a) why and under what circumstances information per se does not necessarily lead to behavior change and (b) why uniformed people nevertheless change their attitudes or behaviors. It is not our purpose to review the literature on persuasion and attitude change here, but we provide three illustrations.

First, consider the elaboration likelihood model of attitude change (Petty & Cacioppo, 1986). In this model, it is not knowledge per se but cognitive reactions to knowledge that cause changes in attitude and behavior. The model proposes that one cannot judge how effective a message is simply by examining the information learned—one must know how

the recipient of the message reacts to that knowledge. Thus, the message may be ineffective if the person sees the information as irrelevant (e.g., "I'm young and have a strong immune system, so I need not worry") or reacts negatively rather than positively (e.g., "Condoms are too much trouble, and they make me think of death and disease"). Positive reactions, which are key to an effective message, may result from superficial cues in the message (the peripheral route to persuasion) rather than from elaborate, in-depth, thoughtful analysis of the issues (the central route to persuasion). However, research shows that peripheral routes to persuasion (such as having a famous actress promote condom use) result in attitudes that are relatively temporary, are susceptible to change, and have little impact on behavior. If the central route to persuasion does result in attitude change, such change may be relatively enduring, but the person may not have the necessary skills or self-worth to carry the belief into action (Petty, Gleicher, & Jarvis, 1993).

Ajzen's (1988) theory of planned behavior provides a second example in which increased knowledge may or may not produce behavior change. The theory of planned behavior—an extension of Ajzen and Fishbein's (1980) theory of reasoned action—suggests that a behavior follows from intention, which in turn follows from a person's attitude toward the behavior, the perceived opinions of other people (norms), and perceived control over the behavior (see W.A. Fisher, Fisher, & Rye, 1995, for an application of the theory of reasoned action to AIDS-related behavior). Based on this theory, one would predict that behavior change can be produced without attitude change if new norms can be created (e.g., "I'll start bleaching my needles, not because I personally believe it's important but because everyone wants me to") or if perceived control over the behavior changes (e.g., "Now that I can easily get condoms in vending machines in the restroom, I'll begin using them"). In sum, the theory of planned behavior and the theory of reasoned action suggest that a change in norms or perceived control might reduce the frequency of risky behaviors even if people do not learn more about AIDS.

Cognitive dissonance theory (Festinger, 1957) is a third example of a social psychological theory that suggests a mechanism for attitude and behavior change in which learning a message is not relevant. According to this theory, cognitive dissonance may be evoked when a person holds inconsistent attitudes or acts inconsistently with held attitudes. To reduce the resulting dis-

comfort, the person is motivated to change an inconsistent behavior or attitude so as to eliminate the inconsistency. Using this paradigm, Stone, Aronson, Crain, and Winslow (1994) had students develop and videotape a persuasive speech about condom use and also asked the students to think about their own past inconsistent condom use. That is, cognitive dissonance was aroused by reminding students that they were being hypocritical (promoting use even though they had not used condoms consistently in the past). This cognitive dissonance in turn increased students' resolve to use condoms in the future, and more students in this condition (compared with three control conditions) bought condoms following the experiment. The important point here is that the change in intentions (and behaviors) occurred after an apparent inconsistency became clear, not because of new information.

In sum, then, many social psychological theories provide sound theoretical reasons for why information at times does not lead to learning, attitude change, or behavior change, and why attitude and behavior change may occur without new knowledge.

NEGATIVE CONSEQUENCES OF KNOWLEDGE ABOUT AIDS

Some people might argue that even if providing the facts about AIDS is not sufficient (or necessary) to change behaviors, it certainly could not hurt for people to learn more about AIDS as long as the education does not detract from other intervention methods. But in some cases, knowledge about AIDS may inhibit preventive behaviors, such as use of condoms. For example, one study (Berrenberg et al., 1993) measured the degree to which college students felt overwhelmed and irritated by information about AIDS and desired to avoid additional information (called degree of "AIDS information saturation"). The authors found that students with a high level of AIDS information saturation rated AIDS information that was provided as less valuable, less clear, and less disturbing than did students with a lower level of AIDS saturation. The students with a high level of AIDS information saturation also reported fewer intentions to change high-risk behaviors. This study hints at the possibility that there may be negative consequences of repeatedly telling people what they already know.

Health educators who believe that rational people make rational choices once they have all the information might create interventions in which they teach individuals to use disease information to persuade their partners to use condoms. However, this approach may be problematic for several related reasons. First, the failure to use condoms is more often related to concerns regarding how one appears to other people than to lack of information about the benefits of using condoms (Leary, Tchividjian, & Kraxberger, 1994). That is, people are embarrassed to buy condoms, are embarrassed about introducing the issue to their partners, and worry about the impression they give to their partners (Helweg-Larsen & Collins, 1994). Knowing the rational reasons for using a condom may not overcome these interpersonal concerns. Second, given the powerful images associated with AIDS (e.g., being gay, promiscuous, or "unclean"), AIDS might be exactly the reason one should not use to convince one's partner to use a condom. Research on attitudes and classical conditioning suggests that one should avoid linking a desired behavior (e.g., using condoms) with an image or word (AIDS) that, rightly or wrongly, carries negative connotations.

Third, there is also emerging empirical evidence that introducing disease information in a sexual situation might in fact have adverse effects on a potential partner's perceptions of a person trying to make a good impression (Collins & Karney, 1995). In one study, students who read a scenario about a college student who mentioned to his or her partner that he or she was "worried about AIDS" judged the student as nice (responsible, sincere, clean, and conscientious) but also unexciting (dull, boring, bland, uninteresting, weak, and passive). Even when these effects were controlled statistically (the effects of the nice and exciting dimensions were statistically removed), college students still perceived a person revealing concern about AIDS to his or her partner to be promiscuous, a poor long-term romantic prospect, and less sexually attractive and less heterosexual than a person who did not mention concern about AIDS.

In sum, providing the facts about disease processes might have negative consequences under certain circumstances, especially if the recipients feel they are already overloaded with such information or if they use (or are taught to use) such information to persuade their partners to use condoms or take other precautionary measures.

CONCLUSION

Not only is knowledge about AIDS an unreliable predictor of attitudes or be-haviors, but the focus on knowledge-based approaches to behavior change might distract health educators from targeting other factors leading to risky sexual behavior—factors that predict risky behaviors better than does knowledge about AIDS. This is not to say that knowledge might not be important for purposes other than changing attitudes or behaviors. It is to say that researchers should consider a broad array of theories of behavior change, including those that do not focus on information as a determinant of such change. In addition, several social psychological theories of attitude change provide excellent information about when providing factual information is most likely to lead to changes in attitudes or behaviors. In the midst of the AIDS crisis, it is essential that specialists and nonspecialists alike become aware that knowledge is not sufficient, is not always necessary, and may in certain circumstances do more harm than good.

Acknowledgments—We thank James Shepperd and David Boninger for providing helpful comments on an earlier draft of this article. This work was supported by a California State Doctoral AIDS Research Training Grant (TG-LA022) awarded through the UCLA School of Public Health to the first author.

Note

1. Address correspondence to Marie Helweg-Larsen, University of Florida, Department of Psychology, Gainesville, FL 32611-2250, or to Barry Collins, Department of Psychology, UCLA, Los Angeles, CA 90024-1563; e-mail: helweg@psych.ufl.edu or collins@psych.ucla.edu.

References

Ajzen, I. (1988). Attitudes, personality, and behavior. Chicago: Dorsey Press.

Ajzen, I., & Fishbein, M. (1980). Understanding attitudes and predicting social behavior. Englewood Cliffs, NJ: Prentice-Hall.

Aspinwall, L.G., Kemeny, M.E., Taylor, S.E., Schneider, S.G., & Dudley, J.P. (1991). Psychosocial predictors of gay men's AIDS risk-reduction behavior. Health Psychology, 10, 432–444

Berrenberg, J.L., Dougherty, K.L., Erikson, M.S., Lowe, J.L., Pacot, D.M., & Rousseau, C.N.S. (1993, April). Saturation in AIDS education: Can we still make a difference? Paper presented at the annual meeting of the Rocky Mountain and Western Psychological Associations, Phoenix, AZ.

Calsyn, D.A., Saxon, A.J., Freeman, G., & Whittaker, S. (1992). Ineffectiveness of AIDS education and HIV antibody testing in reducing high-risk behaviors among injection drug users. American Journal of Public Health, 82, 573–575.

Collins, B.E., & Karney, B.P. (1995). Behavior change and impression management: The case of safer sex. Unpublished manuscript, University of California, Los Angeles.

DiClemente, R.J., Forrest, K.A., Mickler, S., & Principal Site Investigators. (1990). College students' knowledge and attitudes about AIDS and changes in HIV-preventive behaviors. AIDS Education and Prevention, 2, 201–212.

DiMatteo, M.R. (1991). The psychology of health, illness, and medical care. Pacific Grove, CA: Brooks/Cole.

Farley, T.A., Pomputius, P.F., Sabella, W., Helgerson, S.D., & Hadler, J.L. (1991). Evaluation of the effect of school-based education on adolescents' AIDS knowledge and attitudes. Connecticut Medicine, 55, 15–18.

Festinger, L. (1957). A theory of cognitive dissonance. Evanston, IL: Row, Peterson.

Fisher, J.D., & Fisher, W.A. (1992). Changing AIDS-risk behavior. Psychological Bulletin, 111, 455–474.

Fisher, W.A., Fisher, J.D., & Rye, B.J. (1995). Understanding and promoting AIDS-preventive behavior: Insights from the theory of reasoned action. Health Psychology, 14, 255–264.

Freeman, E.W., Rickels, k., Huggins, G. R., Mudd, E.H., Garcia, C.R., & Dickens, H.O. (1980). Adolescent contraceptive use: Comparisons of male and female attitudes and information. American Journal of Public Health, 70, 790–797.

Ganz, W., & Greenberg, B.S. (1990). The role of informative television programs in the battle against AIDS. Health Communication, 2, 199–215.

Helweg-Larsen, M., & Collins, B.E. (1994). The UCLA Multidimensional Condom Attitudes Scale: Documenting the complex determinants of condom use in college students. Health Psychology, 13, 224–237.

Leary, M.R., Tchividjian, L.R., & Kraxberger, B.E. (1994). Self-presentation can be hazardous to your health: Impression management and health risk. Health Psychology, 13, 461–470.

Mann, J.M., Tarantola, D.J.M., & Netter, T.W. (Eds.). (1992). AIDS in the world. Cambridge, MA: Harvard University Press.

Petty, R.E., & Cacioppo, J.T. (1986). Communication and persuasion: Central and peripheral routes to attitude change. New York: Springer-Verlag.

Petty, R.E., Gleicher, F., & Jarvis, W.B.G. (1993). Persuasion theory and AIDS prevention. In J.B. Pryor & J.D. Reeder (Eds.), The social psychology of HIV infection (pp. 155–182). Hillsdale, NJ: Erlbaum.

Stone, J., Aronson, E., Crain, A.L., & Winslow, M.P. (1994). Inducing hypocrisy as a means of encouraging young adults to use condoms. Personality and Social Psychology Bulletin, 20, 116–128.

Unit 4

Key Points to Consider

❖ What makes social pressures so powerful? What creates them? Can you think of any examples from your own life when you felt strong pressure to obey an authority? To go along with a friend's request when you really didn't want to? Are there any groups to which you belong that exert pressure on you to think, feel, or act in a particular way? How do you handle this?

❖ Can you think of any other compliance techniques, other than the ones outlined by Michael Lovaglia in his article, that are used by salespeople? Why don't customers see through these techniques more frequently and refuse to fall for them? What steps could customers take to protect themselves from such techniques?

❖ Are the techniques described in "Suspect Confessions" fair tactics for the police to use? Why or why not? More generally, what sort of restrictions, if any, should be placed on the use of social influence techniques in our society?

 **Links** **www.dushkin.com/online/**

These sites are annotated on pages 4 and 5.

After World War II, members of the Nazi high command were put on trial for war crimes, in particular, their genocidal slaughter of millions of "undesirables": Jews, Gypsies, and homosexuals, among others. One argument that they offered in their defense was that they were "only following orders"—that is, as soldiers during wartime they had no choice but to obey the orders of their superior officers. As a result, so the argument went, they did not bear the ultimate responsibility for their actions. This argument was not especially effective, however, and many of the defendants were convicted and, in some cases, executed for their crimes. In essence, then, the war crimes judges rejected the notion that people can give up their individual moral responsibility when they are given immoral orders.

A decade later, in one of the most famous social psychological investigations ever done, Stanley Milgram reexamined this issue, and his results were highly disturbing. Milgram found that normal everyday Americans—not Nazi monsters—would follow the orders of an experimenter to administer what they thought were extremely intense electric shocks to an innocent victim as part of a research project. In some cases, a substantial percentage of the participants would administer what they thought were 450-volt shocks to a man with a heart condition who was screaming hysterically to be released from the experiment. Although many of the participants were in a state of extreme anxiety and discomfort over their terrible behavior, they nevertheless continued to obey the experimenter. As had the Nazis during World War II, these American citizens seemed to give up their moral responsibility when they agreed to follow the orders of the experimenter.

This research is just one example, although a highly dramatic one, of the phenomenon that social psychologists call social influence—the ability of a person or group to change the behavior of others. Traditionally, a distinction has been drawn among three different types of social influence: conformity, compliance, and obedience. *Conformity* refers to those times when individuals will change their attitudes or behaviors because of perceived group pressure—that is, they feel pressure to conform to the attitude or behavior of some group that is at least somewhat important to them. If, for instance, everyone in your group of friends adopts a particular style of clothing, or adopts a particular attitude toward another group, you may feel some pressure to conform to their behavior, even if no one in the group ever asks you to. *Compliance*, on the other hand, refers to those times when individuals change their behavior in response to a direct request from others. We are often faced with direct requests intended to change our behavior, whether they come from family, friends, teachers, bosses, or door-to-door salesmen. Considerable

research has been conducted to determine what kinds of strategies by "requesters" are the most effective in prompting actual compliance. Finally, *obedience* refers to those times when individuals change their behavior in response to a direct order from another person; thus, unlike compliance, in which you are asked to make a behavioral change, in obedience you are commanded to do so. The research by Milgram is a good example of an obedience situation.

The four selections in this unit illustrate, sometimes dramatically, the powerful ways in which social influence operates. In the first, "Obedience in Retrospect," Alan Elms gives an insider's perspective on what it was like to work with Milgram on his famous studies of obedience, and on the initial reaction from other psychologists when the findings were first made known. In the second article, "Liking: The Friendly Thief," Robert Cialdini describes a powerful factor which can make us very susceptible to another person's persuasion attempts: our liking for that person. If the other person is attractive, similar to us, and somewhat ingratiating, it can be difficult to say "no" even if we want to.

In the next selection, "Persuasion: What Will It Take to Convince You?" Michael Lovaglia identifies another effective technique for gaining compliance—a technique sometimes known as the "foot-in-the-door" effect. By asking for small favors first, it is possible to gain more compliance when a big request is made later on.

In the final selection, "Suspect Confessions," Richard Jerome profiles a social psychologist who specializes in investigating a particular kind of compliance situation—the police interrogation. The work of social psychologist Richard Ofshe suggests that some of the techniques used by police during questioning can be so powerful that suspects will sometimes comply (confess) even when they are innocent of the crimes! This article provides a fascinating glimpse into just how powerful some compliance-inducing tactics can be.

Obedience in Retrospect

Alan C. Elms
University of California, Davis

Milgram's original paradigm for studying obedience to authority is briefly described, and the main results are summarized. Personal observations of the conduct of the initial studies give added context for interpreting the results. Psychologists' reactions to the Milgram experiments are discussed in terms of (1) rejecting the research on ethical grounds, (2) explaining away the results as expressions of trivial phenomena, (3) subsuming obedience to destructive authority under other explanatory rubrics, and (4) endorsing or rejecting the results in terms of their perceived social relevance or irrelevance.

The problem of obedience to authority may well be the crucial issue of our time. The experiments you took part in represent the first efforts to understand this phenomenon in an objective, scientific manner. (Stanley Milgram, *Report to Memory Project Subjects*, 1962b)

Introduction

Obedience to destructive authority was indeed a crucial social issue in 1962. The Holocaust had ended less than two decades earlier. Adolf Eichmann recently had been sentenced to death for expediting it, despite his plea that he had just been "following orders." American military advisers were being ordered to Vietnam in increasing numbers to forestall Communist control of Southeast Asia. Whether destructive obedience could reasonably be described as *the* crucial issue of the time is a judgment call; surely other issues offered competition for that status. But there can be little argument that Stanley Milgram's experiments were indeed "the first efforts to understand this phenomenon in an objective, scientific manner."

Milgram was not seeking to develop a grand theory of obedience. His main concern was with the phenomenon itself. He advised his graduate students that as they began their own research, "First decide what questions you want to answer." For him those first questions were typically substantive, not theoretical. He also told his students he sought to collect data that would still be of interest 100 years later, whatever theoretical interpretations might be made of the data. For his data on obedience, we are a third of the way through that 100 years. Those data remain of high interest indeed, offering continual challenges to our theories and to our confidence as psychologists that we really understand important aspects of human social behavior.

Milgram eventually proposed his own theoretical interpretations. But what most people still remember are the data themselves, the sheer numbers of research volunteers who obeyed every order to the very end. Before Milgram, creative writers

Quotations from unpublished correspondence of Stanley Milgram are used by permission of Alexandra Milgram.

Correspondence regarding this article should be addressed to Alan C. Elms, Department of Psychology, University of California, Davis, California 95616-8686.

had incorporated striking incidents of obedience into novels, poems, and screenplays. Historians had written factual accounts of remarkably obedient individuals and groups. Psychologists had developed F- and other scales to measure inclinations toward authoritarian tyranny and subservience. Milgram instead established a realistic laboratory setting where actual obedience and its circumstances might be closely studied.

The Obedience Paradigm

For those who have forgotten the details, and for the few who have never read them, here is the basic situation that Milgram devised. First, he advertised in the New Haven (Connecticut) daily newspaper and through direct mail for volunteers for a study of memory and learning. Volunteers were promised $4.00 for an hour of their time, plus 50 cents carfare. (At the time, $4 was well above minimum wage for an hour of work; 50 cents would have paid for a round-trip bus ride to and from most areas of New Haven.) Most of those who volunteered were scheduled by telephone to come at a given time to a laboratory on the Yale University campus.

In the basic experiments, two volunteers arrived at the laboratory at about the same time. Both were invited into the lab by the experimenter. The experimenter explained that one volunteer would be assigned the role of teacher and the other would become the learner. The teacher would administer an electric shock to the learner whenever the learner made an error, and each additional shock would be 15 volts higher than the previous one. By drawing slips of paper from a hat, one volunteer became the teacher. His first task was to help strap the arms of the other volunteer to the arms of a chair, so the electrodes from the shock generator would not fall off accidentally. The teacher was given a sample 45 volt electric shock from the shock generator, a level strong enough to be distinctly unpleasant. Then the experimenter asked the teacher to begin teaching the learner a list of word pairs. The learner did fairly well at first, then began to make frequent errors. Soon the teacher found himself administering higher and higher shock levels, according to the experimenter's instructions. (Male pronouns are used here because most volunteers were male; in only one experimental condition out of 24 were female subjects used.)

After a few shocks the learner began to object to the procedure. After more shocks and more objections, he loudly refused to participate further in the learning task, and stopped responding. If the teacher stopped giving him electric shocks at this point, the experimenter ordered the teacher to continue, and to administer stronger and stronger shocks for each failure to respond—all the way to the end of the graded series of levers, whose final labels were "Intense Shock," "Extreme Intensity Shock," "Danger: Severe Shock," and "XXX," along with voltage levels up to 450 volts. In the first experimental condition, the teacher was separated from the learner by a soundproofed wall; the learner could communicate his distress only by kicking on the wall. In subsequent conditions, teachers

could hear the learner's voice through a speaker system, or sat near the learner in the same room while the learning task proceeded, or sat next to the learner and had to force his hand down onto a shock grid if he refused to accept the shocks voluntarily.

Teachers were not told several important pieces of information until their participation in the experiment was finished. Number one, the experiment was a study of obedience to authority, not a study of memory and learning. Number two, the volunteer who assumed the role of learner was actually an experimental confederate. Number three, the only shock that anyone ever got was the 45 volt sample shock given to each teacher; the shock generator was not wired to give any shocks to the learner. Number four, the learner's kicks against the wall, his screams, his refusals to continue, were all carefully scripted and rehearsed, as were the experimenter's orders to the teacher. A number of variables could be (and were) added to the research design in different conditions, but these aspects were constant.

Observations from the Inside

The basic series of obedience experiments took place in the summer of 1961. Milgram was at that time a very junior assistant professor, 27 years old, with no professional publications yet in print. I had just finished my first year of graduate school when he hired me to be his research assistant for the summer. Stanley sent me a letter on June 27, a week before I was scheduled to return to New Haven from a brief summer vacation:

> Matters have been proceeding apace on the project. The apparatus is almost done and looks thoroughly professional; just a few small but important pieces remain to be built. It may turn out that you will build them, but that depends on factors at present unknown.
>
> The advertisement was placed in the New Haven Register and yielded a disappointingly low response. There is no immediate crisis, however, since we do have about 300 qualified applicants. But before long, in your role as Solicitor General, you will have to think of ways to deliver more people to the laboratory. This is a very important practical aspect of the research. I will admit it bears some resemblance to Mr. Eichmann's position, but you at least should have no misconceptions of what we do with our daily quota. We give them a chance to resist the commands of malevolent authority and assert their alliance with morality.
>
> . . . The goal this summer is to run from 250–300 subjects in nine or ten experimental conditions. Only if this is accomplished can the summer be considered a success. Let me know if there is something I have overlooked.

The summer was a success by any reasonable standards, if not fully by Milgram's. He had not overlooked anything procedural; even at that early state in his career, he was already the most well-organized researcher I have ever encountered. But he had hardly come close to anticipating the degree to which his subjects would yield to the commands of malevolent authority, or how readily they would abrogate their alliance with morality. Milgram knew he would get *some* obedience; in a pilot study the previous winter, he had found Yale undergraduates disturbingly willing to shock their victims. But he recognized that Yale undergraduates were a special sample in many ways; that the prototype shock generator was rather crude and perhaps not altogether convincing; and that the simulated victim's displays of pain were fairly easy to ignore. For the main experiments, Milgram auditioned and rehearsed a victim whose cries of agony were truly piercing. He recruited a larger and diverse sample of nonstudent adults from the New Haven area, ranging from blue-collar workers to professionals and from 20 to 50 years in age. He constructed a professional-looking shock generator and purchased other high-quality equipment, including a 20-pen Esterline Angus Event Recorder that registered the duration and latency of each "shock" administration to the nearest hundredth of a second. He had decided that his main dependent variable would be the mean shock level at which subjects refused to go further in each experimental condition, but he wanted to be able to examine more subtle differences in their performance as well.

In early August the curtains went up on the first official obedience experiment. (More accurately, the curtains were drawn aside; Yale's new Social Interaction Laboratory, on temporary loan from the Sociology Department, was enclosed by two-way-mirrors and heavy soundproofing curtains.) Would subjects be convinced of the reality of the learning-and-memory experiment, the shock generator, the victim's suffering? They were. Would subjects obey the experimenter? They did. How far would they go? On and on up the sequence of shock levels. Would any subjects go all the way to the end of the shock board? Yes indeed.

Behind the two-way mirrors, Stanley Milgram and I (as well as occasional visitors) watched each early subject with fascination and with our own share of tension. Stanley had made broad predictions concerning the relative amounts of obedience in different conditions, but we paid little attention to the gradual confirmation of those predictions. Instead we tried to predict the behavior of each new subject, based on his initial demeanor and the little we knew about his background. We were gratified when any subject resisted authority. Sometimes it was quiet resistance, sometimes noisy, but it was exciting each time it happened. As more and more subjects obeyed every command, we felt at first dismayed, then cynically confirmed in our bleakest views of humanity. We were distressed when some volunteers wept, appalled when others laughed as they administered shock after shock. The experimenter gave each subject a standard debriefing at the end of the hour, to minimize any continuing stress and to show that the "victim" had not been injured by the "shocks." When a subject appeared especially stressed, Milgram often moved out from behind the curtains to do an especially thorough job of reassurance and stress reduction. When a subject did something truly unexpected during the experiment—an especially resolute show of resistance, for instance, or a long laughing jag—Milgram would join the experimenter in giving the subject a detailed cross-examination about why he had displayed such behavior. For us as well as the subjects, the situation

quickly became more than an artificially structured experiment. Instead it presented slice after slice of real life, with moral decisions made and unmade very evening.

The Most Prominent Results

As matters turned out, Milgram did not need equipment sensitive enough to measure shock intervals in hundredths of a second. By the end of the second run of 40 subjects, if not before, his main dependent variable had become simply the percentage of subjects who obeyed the experimenter's commands all the way to the end of the shock series, contrasted with the percentage who disobeyed by quitting at *any* point in the whole long sequence of shock levels. In the first condition, a substantial majority of subjects (26 out of 40, or 65%) obeyed completely. That was the condition with minimal feedback from the learner—a few vigorous kicks on the wall. But wouldn't obedience drop substantially if the teacher could actually hear the learner screaming and demanding to be set free? It didn't. Twenty-five out of 40 were fully obedient in this second condition. Even when Milgram tried to encourage disobedience by having the learner claim a preexisting heart condition ("It's bothering me now!"), obedience remained at a high level: 26 of 40 subjects again (Milgram, 1974, pp. 56–57). Putting the victim in the same room and near the teacher reduced obedience somewhat, but 40% still obeyed fully. Indeed, even when teachers were ordered to press the hand of the screaming victim down onto a shock plate to complete the electrical circuit, a majority did so at least twice before quitting, and 30% obeyed in this fashion to the end of the shock board (Milgram, 1974, p. 35).

Milgram ran approximately a thousand subjects through various obedience conditions in less than a year. (The National Science Foundation, which financed the research, got its money's worth from two grants totaling about $60,000.) Each subject was run through the procedure individually, then was subjected to both immediate and follow-up questionnaires of various kinds. Milgram looked at the effects not only of the victim's physical proximity to the subject but of the experimenter's proximity, the amount of group support either for obedience or for defiance, and the learning experiment's apparent institutional backing. He made a variety of interesting findings—enough to fill a book, and more. But the data that carried the greatest impact, on other psychologists and on the general public, came from those first few experimental conditions: two-thirds of a sample of average Americans were willing to shock an innocent victim until the poor man was screaming for his life, and to go on shocking him well after he had lapsed into a perhaps unconscious silence, all at the command of a single experimenter with no apparent means of enforcing his orders.

Reactions to the Research

Once these data appeared in professional psychological journals (after initial resistance from editors), they were rather quickly disseminated through newspaper and magazine stories, editorials, sermons, and other popular media. With few exceptions, the nonprofessional citations of the experiments emphasized their social relevance: Milgram had revealed in ordinary Americans the potential for behavior comparable to that of the Nazis during the European Holocaust. (According to a *TV Guide* ad for a docudrama with William Shatner as a fictionalized Milgram, the research revealed "A world of evil so terrifying no one dares penetrate its secret. Until now!" [August 21, 1976, p. A-86].)

Psychologists responded in more diverse ways. Authors eager to enliven their introductory and social psychology textbooks soon made the obedience experiments a staple ingredient. Other psychologists seemed to regard Milgram's results as a challenge of one sort or another: conceptual, ethical, theoretical, political. The obedience studies were related, historically and procedurally, to earlier studies of social influence, but they did not fit readily into current theoretical models or research trends. Because of their rapidly achieved visibility inside and outside the field, they were soon treated as fair game for elucidation or attack by psychologists with a multitude of orientations.

Ethical Concerns

One type of response to the disturbing results of the obedience studies was to shift attention from the amounts of obedience Milgram obtained to the ethics of putting subjects through such a stressful experience. The first substantial published critique of Milgram's studies focused on the presumed psychic damage wreaked on his subjects by their ordeal (Baumrind, 1964). Milgram was not altogether surprised by such criticism; similar concerns had been expressed by several Yale faculty members during or soon after the experiments and ethical questions had been raised about the research when Milgram first applied for American Psychological Association membership. But he was disappointed that his critics did not recognize the care he had put into responding to his subjects' high stress levels immediately after their participation, as well as into checking on any lingering effects over time (Milgram, 1964). Milgram was a pioneer in the debriefing procedures that are now a matter of course in psychological experiments on human subjects—debriefing in the sense not only of questioning the subject about his or her perception of the experiment, but of providing the subject with information and encouragement that will counteract any reactions to participation that might damage the subject's self-esteem. As Milgram told me later,

> My membership application to APA was held up for one year while they investigated the ethicality of the obedience experiment. In the end, they gave me a clean bill of health and admitted me to membership. Whenever any group has seriously considered the merits and problems of the experiment, they have concluded that it was an ethical experiment. Nonetheless, isolated individuals still feel strongly enough to attack it. (Personal communication, July 3, 1969)

One consequence of those individual attacks was a set of stringent federal regulations that made it virtually impossible ever again to conduct a close replication of the Milgram studies at any U.S. educational or research institution.

Many social scientists who have considered the ethics of the obedience studies in print have taken a neutral position or have come down on the side of Milgram. But outside the field, a similar perception of appropriate research and debriefing procedures is not widespread. When I participated in a conference on social science research ethics at the Kennedy Institute of Ethics 18 years after the obedience research was completed, several philosophers and professional ethicists devoted a large part of their energies to what struck me as rather crude Milgram bashing. The research scientists at the conference were not so inclined, but they had to work hard to communicate the virtues of a set of studies that had raised important issues about both the bad and the good in human nature (Beauchamp, Faden, Wallace, & Walters, 1982).

Questions of Belief

Among the early commentaries on the research, several psychologists argued that the results were not credible because the subjects did not believe they were actually harming the victim (e.g., Orne & Holland, 1968). Milgram's own data, showing that during the experiment a very high percentage of subjects believed the victim was receiving extremely painful shocks (1974, pp. 171–174), were ignored or dismissed as attempts by the subject to give Milgram the answers he wanted. Researchers' descriptions of many subjects' visible signs of high stress were also ignored, or were assumed to be evidence merely of the subjects' enthusiastic play acting. Even a filmed record of several actual subjects (Milgram, 1965a), displaying either great stress or extraordinary improvisational acting ability, did not convince psychologists who took this dismissive position. Some critics may have assumed that the four subjects shown at length in the film, plus several others who appeared more briefly, were the most convincingly emotional subjects Milgram could find among his thousand participants. In fact, Milgram chose all of them from the 14 subjects who happened to be "selected in the normal manner for recruitment" during the two days he brought movie cameras to the laboratory (Milgram, 1965c, p. 5).

Theoretical Alternatives

Many social psychologists have accepted the ethical appropriateness of Milgram's procedures and the believability of the experimental context. Even they, however, have often redirected attention away from the specific phenomenon of destructive obedience by subsuming it under a broader theoretical approach or alternative hypothetical constructs.

Milgram was slow to offer a comprehensive theoretical account of his own. His definitions of obedience to authority, from his first to his final writings on the subject, drew upon no theoretical assumptions. Rather, they were commonsense or dictionary definitions: "Every power system implies a structure of command and action in response to the command"

(Milgram, 1961, p. 2); "If *Y* follows the command of *X* we shall say that he has obeyed *X;* if he fails to carry out the command of *X,* we shall say that he has disobeyed *X*" (Milgram, 1965b, p. 58); "[I]t is only the man dwelling in isolation who is not forced to respond, through defiance or submission, to the commands of others" (Milgram, 1974, p. 1). In his grant proposals he referred to "internal restraints" or "internal resistances" that were pitted against the acceptance of authoritative commands, but he did not specify the nature of these internal processes (Milgram, 1961, p. 3; Milgram, 1962a, p. 1). He raised the possibility of predispositional factors and of "highly complex, and possibly, idiosyncratic motive structures" (1962z, p. 17), but in the research itself he directed his efforts mainly toward identifying situational factors that increased or decreased obedience. In his most extensive early discussion of his results (Milgram, 1965b, largely written in 1962), he cited such midlevel hypothetical constructs as "empathic cues," "denial and narrowing of the cognitive field," and a varying "sense of *relatedness* between his [the subject's] own actions and the consequences of those actions for the victim" (pp. 61–63; his italics).

Though it took Milgram less than a year to run all his subjects and not much longer than that to write several papers on the results, he worked on his book about obedience for over five years. He attributed the slowness of the book's writing in part to his becoming engaged in other sorts of research. But much of his struggle with the book appears to have centered on the difficulty of developing a general theory of obedience. The principal theoretical concepts he advanced in the book, including the agentic state (Milgram, 1974, pp. 133–134) and the evolution of a potential for obedience in humans (pp. 123–125), impressed many readers rather less than the results themselves—a reaction that both frustrated and pleased the data-centric Milgram. Though he had collected demographic information on all participants and had supported my collection of personality data from subsamples of obedient and disobedient subjects (Elms & Milgram, 1965), he gave short shrift to such data in his book, concluding that "It is hard to relate performance to personality because we really do not know very much about how to measure personality" (p. 205).

Others have usefully discussed the interaction of personality and situational variables in the obedience situations (e.g., Blass, 1991). A majority of the alternative explanations, however, have stressed cognitive processes, emphasizing ways in which the subject processed information about the situation that might have justified his obedience or strengthened his resistance. Milgram viewed such alternative explanations with interest, but took steps to rule out certain of them experimentally. One of the most obvious of these alternatives was the idea that subjects might be so awed by Yale University and so certain of its virtue that they would do anything they were told within those august halls, regardless of any general proclivity toward destructive obedience. Even before this environment-based explanation of his subjects' obedience was first offered in print, Milgram had largely vitiated it by moving the experiments from the awe-inspiring Interaction Laboratory to a rather less impressive basement facility and then to the in-

tentionally unimpressive office of a fly-by-night company in industrial Bridgeport, Connecticut. He got essentially the same results in all three locations. A number of alternative or additional explanations of Milgram's results remain as operable hypotheses, but none has decisively carried the day. Their very diversity ensures that the larger audience for the research will continue to be concerned primarily about the subjects' disturbing behavior rather than about the internal processes that may have produced it.

The Question of Relevance

Finally among ways in which psychologists have responded to Milgram's findings are arguments concerning the social relevance of the experiments. Many psychologists, at least in their textbooks, have embraced his findings as being highly relevant to important social phenomena, including destructive obedience not only in totalitarian states but among American soldiers, Bosnian combatants, and suicidal religious cults. But others (including some who also argued that the research was unethical or experientially unconvincing) have denied any real social relevance. Even if subjects believed they were really shocking the victim, these psychologists say, they knew the situation must not be as bad as it appeared, because somebody would have stopped them if it was. Or the subjects were in a situation where the experimenter accepted responsibility for the effects of their behavior, so their behavior is not really relevant to real-world situations where blame is less readily transferred to another individual. Or some other rationale is advanced, presumably peculiar to the Milgram obedience situation, that somehow does not translate into real-world social dynamics. Milgram rightly dismissed all such explanations that had been advanced up to the time of his final writings, and very likely would have dismissed all subsequent ones, for two simple reasons: Any effective authority figure in the real world always finds ways to justify imposing his or her will on underlings. The underlings who obey authoritative commands in the real world always find rationales for their obedience. In most prominent real-world cases of destructive obedience that have been compared (or discompared) to the Milgram studies, the authorities were able to call upon a social rationale for their commands that was at least as strong as or stronger than that available to any psychological experimenter. In addition, they were often able to promise their followers much greater rewards for obedience and punishments for disobedience.

Stanley Milgram's research on obedience tapped into psychological processes that ranked as neither new nor extreme in the history of human behavior. A "crucial issue of our time," perhaps *the* crucial issue, obedience, unfortunately remains. Though Milgram was proud that his studies were "the first efforts to understand this phenomenon in an objective, scientific manner," he did not want them to be the last. This issue of the *Journal of Social Issues* gives strong evidence that the efforts of other researchers to expand upon his groundbreaking work will continue unabated.

References

Baumrind, D. (1964). Some thoughts on ethics of research: After reading Milgram's "Behavioral Study of Obedience." *American Psychologist, 19,* 421–423.

Beauchamp, T. L., Faden, R. R., Wallace, R. J., Jr., & Walters, I., (Eds.). (1982) *Ethical issues in social science research.* Baltimore, MD: Johns Hopkins University Press.

Blass, T. (1991). Understanding behavior in the Milgram obedience experiment: The role of personality, situations, and their interactions. *Journal of Personality and Social Psychology, 60,* 398–413.

Elms, A. C., & Milgram, S. (1965). Personality characteristics associated with obedience and defiance toward authoritative command. *Journal of Experimental Research in Personality, 1,* 282–289.

Milgram, S. (1961) *Dynamics of obedience: Experiments in social psychology.* Application for National Science Foundation research grant, Yale University.

Milgram, S. (1962a). *Obedience to authority: Experiments in social psychology.* Application for National Science Foundation grant renewal, Yale University.

Milgram, S. (1962b). *Report to Memory Project subjects.* Unpublished manuscript, Yale University.

Milgram, S. (1964). Issues in the study of obedience: A reply to Baumrind. *American Psychologist, 19,* 848–852.

Milgram, S. (1965a). *Obedience* [Film]. (Available from the Pennsylvania State University Audiovisual Services.)

Milgram, S. (1965b). Some conditions of obedience and disobedience to authority. *Human Relations, 18,* 57–76.

Milgram, S. (1965c). Study notes for "Obedience." (Distributed by the New York University Film Library.)

Milgram, S. (1974). *Obedience to authority.* New York: Harper & Row.

Orne, M. T., & Holland, C. C. (1968). On the ecological validity of laboratory deceptions. *International Journal of Psychiatry, 6,* 282–293.

ALAN C. ELMS, while a graduate student at Yale University, worked with Stanley Milgram on the first obedience studies and earned his Ph.D. under the direction of Irving L. Janis. Dr. Elms did laboratory studies of role-play-induced attitude change and interview studies of right- and left-wing political activists before he focused his work on psychobiography. He has written *Social Psychology and Social Relevance* (1972), *Personality in Politics* (1976), and *Uncovering Lives: The Uneasy Alliance of Biography and Psychology* (1994). He has taught at Southern Methodist University, has been a visiting scholar at Trinity College, Dublin, and at Harvard University, and has been a faculty member at the University of California, Davis, since 1967.

Liking
The Friendly Thief

Robert B. Cialdini
Arizona State University

The main work of a trial attorney is to make a jury like his client.
—CLARENCE DARROW

Few of us would be surprised to learn that, as a rule, we most prefer to say yes to the requests of people we know and like. What might be startling to note, however, is that this simple rule is used in hundreds of ways by total strangers to get us to comply with *their* requests.

The clearest illustration I know of the professional exploitation of the liking rule is the Tupperware party, which I consider a classic compliance setting. Anybody familiar with the workings of a Tupperware party will recognize the use of the various weapons of influence we have examined so far:

• *Reciprocity.* To start, games are played and prizes won by the party goers; anyone who doesn't win a prize gets to choose one from a grab bag so that everyone has received a gift before the buying begins.

• *Commitment.* Participants are urged to describe publicly the uses and benefits they have found for the Tupperware they already own.

Excerpted from *Influence: Science and Practice,* edited by Robert B. Cialdini, chapter 5, 143-153. © 1993 by HarperCollins College Publishers. Reprinted by permission of Addison Wesley Educational Publishers, Inc.

READER'S REPORT 5.1

From a Chicago Man

Although I've never been to a Tupperware Party, I recognized the same kind of friendship pressures recently when I got a call from a long distance phone company saleswoman. She told me that one of my buddies had placed my name on something called the "MCI Friends and Family Calling Circle."

This friend of mine, Brad, is a guy I grew up with but who moved to New Jersey last year for a job. He still calls me pretty regularly to get the news on the guys we used to hang out with. The saleswoman told me that he could save 20 percent on all the calls he made to the people on his Calling-Circle list, provided they are MCI phone company subscribers. Then she asked me if I wanted to switch to MCI to get all the blah, blah, blah benefits of MCI services, and so that Brad could save 20 percent on his calls to me.

Well, I couldn't have cared less about the benefits of MCI service; I was perfectly happy with the long distance company I had. But the part about wanting to save Brad money on our calls really got to me. For me to say that I didn't want to be in his Calling Circle and didn't care about saving him money would have sounded like a real affront to our friendship when he heard about it. So, to avoid insulting him, I told her to switch me to MCI.

I used to wonder why women would go to a Tupperware Party just because a friend was holding it, and then buy stuff they didn't want once they were there. I don't wonder anymore.

Author's note: *This reader is not alone in being able to testify to the power of the pressures embodied in MCI's Calling Circle idea. When* Consumer Reports *magazine inquired into the practice, the MCI salesperson they interviewed was quite succinct: "It works 9 out of 10 times," he said.*

• *Social proof.* Once the buying begins, each purchase builds the idea that other, similar people want the products; therefore, it must be good.

All the weapons of influence are present to help things along, but the real power of the Tupperware party comes from a particular arrangement that trades on the liking rule. Despite the entertaining and persuasive selling skills of the Tupperware demonstrator, the true request to purchase the product does not come from this stranger; it comes from a friend to every person in the room. Oh, the Tupperware representative may physically ask for each party goer's order, all right; but the more psychologically compelling requester is sitting off to the side, smiling, chatting, and serving refreshments. She is the party hostess, who has called her friends together for the demonstration in her home and who, everyone knows, makes a profit from each piece sold at the party.

By providing the hostess with a percentage of the take, the Tupperware Home Parties Corporation arranges for its customers to buy from and for a friend rather than from an unknown salesperson. In this way, the attraction, the warmth, the security, and the obligation of friendship are brought to bear on the sales setting (Taylor, 1978). In fact, consumer researchers who have examined the social ties between the hostess and the party goers in home party sales settings have affirmed the power of the company's approach: The strength of that social bond is twice as likely to determine product purchase as is preference for the product itself (Frenzen & Davis, 1990). The results have been remarkable. It

was recently estimated that Tupperware sales now exceed 2.5 million dollars a day! Indeed, Tupperware's success has spread around the world to societies in Europe, Latin America, and Asia, where one's place in a network of friends and family is more socially significant than in the United States (Markus & Kitayama, 1991; Triandis, 1995). As a result, now less than a quarter of Tupperware sales take place in North America.

What is interesting is that the customers appear to be fully aware of the liking and friendship pressures embodied in the Tupperware party. Some don't seem to mind; others do, but don't seem to know how to avoid these pressures. One woman I spoke with described her reactions with more than a bit of frustration in her voice.

> It's gotten to the point now where I hate to be invited to Tupperware parties. I've got all the containers I need; and if I wanted any more, I could buy another brand cheaper in the store. But when a friend calls up, I feel like I have to go. And when I get there, I feel like I have to buy something. What can I do? It's for one of my friends.

With so irresistible an ally as friendship, it is little wonder that the Tupperware Corporation has abandoned retail sales outlets and is pushing the home party concept. Statistics reveal that a Tupperware party now starts somewhere every 2.7 seconds. Of course, all sorts of other compliance professionals recognize the pressure to say yes to someone we know and like. Take, for instance, the growing number of charity organizations that recruit volunteers to canvass for donations close to their own homes. They understand perfectly how much more difficult it is for us to turn down a charity request when it comes from a friend or neighbor.

Other compliance professionals have found that the friend doesn't even have to be present to be effective; often, just the mention of the friends' name is enough. The Shaklee Corporation, which specializes in door-to-door sales of various home-related products, advises its salespeople to use the "endless chain" method for finding new customers. Once a customer admits that he or she likes a product, that customer can be pressed for the names of friends who would also appreciate learning about it. The individuals on that list can then be approached for sales *and* a list of their friends, who can serve as sources for still other potential customers, and so on in an endless chain.

The key to the success of this method is that each new prospect is visited by a salesperson armed with the name of a friend "who suggested I call on you." Turning the salesperson away under those circumstances is difficult; it's almost like rejecting the friend. The Shaklee sales manual insists that employees use this system: "It would be impossible to overestimate its value. Phoning or calling on a prospect and being able to say that Mr. So-and-so, a friend of his, felt he would benefit by giving you a few moments of his time is virtually as good as a sale 50 percent made before you enter."

MAKING FRIENDS TO INFLUENCE PEOPLE

Compliance practitioners' widespread use of the liking bond between friends tells us much about the power of the liking rule to produce assent. In fact, we find that such professionals seek to benefit from the rule even when already formed friendships are not present for them to employ. Under these circumstances, the professionals still make use of the liking bond by employing a compliance strategy that is quite direct: They first get us to like *them*.

There is a man in Detroit, Joe Girard, who specialized in using the liking rule to sell Chevrolets. He became wealthy in the process, making over $200,000 a year. With such a salary, we might guess that he was a high-level GM executive or perhaps the owner of a Chevrolet dealership. But no. He made his money as a salesman on the showroom floor. He was phenomenal at what he did. For twelve years straight, he won the title of "Number One Car Salesman"; he averaged more than five cars and trucks sold every day he worked; and he has been called the world's "greatest car salesman" by the *Guinness Book of World Records*.

For all his success, the formula he employed was surprisingly simple. It consisted of offering people just two things: a fair price and someone they liked to buy from. "And that's it," he claimed in an interview. "Finding the salesman you like, plus the price. Put them both together, and you get a deal."

Fine. The Joe Girard formula tells us how vital the liking rule is to his business, but it doesn't tell us nearly enough. For one thing, it doesn't tell us why customers liked him more than some other salesperson who offered a fair price. There is a crucial—and fascinating—general question that Joe's formula leaves unanswered. What are the factors that cause one person to like another? If we knew *that* answer, we would be a long way toward understanding how people such as Joe can so successfully arrange to have us like them and, conversely, how we might successfully arrange to have others like us. Fortunately, social scientists have been asking this question for decades. Their accumulated evidence has allowed them to identify a number of factors that reliably cause liking. As we will see, each is cleverly used by compliance professionals to urge us along the road to "yes."

WHY DO I LIKE YOU? LET ME LIST THE REASONS

Physical Attractiveness

Although it is generally acknowledged that good-looking people have an advantage in social interaction, recent findings indicate that we may have sorely underestimated the size and reach of that advantage. There seems to be a *click, whirr* response to attractive people. Like all *click, whirr* reactions, it happens automatically, without forethought. The response itself falls into a category that social scientists call *halo effects*. A halo effect occurs when one positive characteristic of a person dominates the way that person is viewed by others. The evidence is now clear that physical attractiveness is often such a characteristic.

Research has shown that we automatically assign to good-looking individuals such favorable traits as talent, kindness, honesty, and intelligence (for a review of this evidence, see Eagly, Ashmore, Makhijani, & Longo, 1991). Furthermore, we make these judgments without being aware that physical attractiveness plays a role in the process. Some consequences of this unconscious assumption that "good-looking equals good" scare me. For example, a study of the 1974 Canadian federal elections found that attractive candidates received more than two and a half times as many votes as unattractive candidates (Efran & Patterson, 1976). Despite such evidence of favoritism toward handsome politicians, follow-up research demonstrated that voters did not realize their bias. In fact, 73 percent of Canadian voters surveyed denied in the strongest possible terms that their votes had been influenced by physical appearance; only 14 percent even allowed for the possibility of such influence (Efran & Patterson, 1976). Voters can deny the impact of attractiveness on electability all they want, but evidence has continued to confirm its troubling presence (Budesheim & DePaola, 1994).

A similar effect has been found in hiring situations. In one study, good grooming of applicants in a simulated employment interview accounted for more favorable hiring decisions than did job qualifications—this, even though the interviewers claimed that appearance played a small role in their choices (Mack & Rainey, 1990). The advantage given to attractive workers extends past hiring day to payday. Economists examining U..S. and Canadian samples have found that attractive individuals get paid on average of 12–14 percent more than their unattractive coworkers (Hammermesh & Biddle, 1994).

Equally unsettling research indicates that our judicial process is similarly susceptible to the influences of body dimensions and bone structure. It now appears that good-looking people are likely to receive highly favorable treatment in the legal system (see Castellow, Wuensch, & Moore, 1991; and Downs & Lyons, 1990, for reviews). For example, in a Pennsylvania study (Stewart, 1980), researchers rated the physical attractiveness of 74 separate male defendants at the start of their criminal trials. When, much later, the researchers checked court records for the results of these cases, they found that the handsome men had received significantly lighter sentences. In fact, attractive defendants were twice as likely to avoid jail as unattractive defendants.[1] In another study—this one on the damages

awarded in a staged negligence trial—a defendant who was better looking than his victim was assessed an average amount of $5,623; but when the victim was more attractive of the two, the average compensation was $10,051. What's more, both male and female jurors exhibited the attractiveness-based favoritism (Kulha & Kessler, 1978).

Other experiments have demonstrated that attractive people are more likely to obtain help when in need (Benson, Karabenic, & Lerner, 1976) and are more persuasive in changing the opinions of an audience (Chaiken, 1979). Here, too, both sexes respond in the same way. In the Benson et al. study on helping, for instance, the better-looking men and women received aid more often, even from members of their own sex. A major exception to this rule might be expected to occur, of course, if the attractive person is viewed as a direct competitor, especially a romantic rival. Short of this qualification, though, it is apparent that good-looking people enjoy an enormous social advantage in our culture. They are better liked, more persuasive, more frequently helped, and seen as possessing more desirable personality traits and greater intellectual capacities. It appears that the social benefits of good looks begin to accumulate quite early. Research on elementary school children shows that adults view aggressive acts as less naughty when performed by an attractive child (Dion, 1972) and that teachers presume good-looking children to be more intelligent than their less attractive classmates (Ritts, Patterson, & Tubbs, 1992).

It is hardly any wonder, then, that the halo of physical attractiveness is regularly exploited by compliance professionals. Because we like attractive people, and because we tend to comply with those we like, it makes sense that sales training programs include grooming hints, fashionable clothiers select their floor staffs from among the good-looking candidates, and con men and women are attractive.[2]

Similarity

What if physical appearance is not much at issue? After all, most people possess average looks. Are there other factors that can be used to produce lik-

---

[1] This finding—that attractive defendants, even when they are found guilty, are less likely to be sentenced to prison—helps explain one fascinating experiment in criminology (Kurtzburg, Safar, & Cavior, 1968). Some New York City jail inmates with facial disfigurements underwent plastic surgery while incarcerated; other inmates with similar disfigurements did not. Furthermore, some members of each group received services (such as counseling, training, etc.) designed to rehabilitate them to society. One year after the inmates had been released from jail, a check of the records revealed that (except for heroin addicts) criminals given the cosmetic surgery were significantly less likely to have returned to jail. The most interesting feature of this finding was that it was equally true for those inmates who had not received the traditional rehabilitative services and for those who had. Apparently, some criminologists then argued that when it comes to ugly inmates, prisons would be better off to abandon the costly rehabilitation services they typically provide and offer plastic surgery instead; the surgery seems to be at least as effective and decidedly less expensive.

The importance of the Pennsylvania data (Stewart, 1980) is that it suggests that the argument for surgery as a means of rehabilitation may be faulty. Making ugly criminals more attractive may not reduce the chances that they will commit another crime; it may only reduce their chances of being sent to jail for it.

[2] Have you ever noticed that despite their good looks, many attractive people don't seem to share the positive impressions of their personalities and abilities that observers have? Research has not only confirmed the tenuous and inconsistent relationship between attractiveness and self-esteem (see Adams, 1977), it has also offered a possible explanation. One set of authors has produced evidence suggesting that good-looking people are aware that other people's positive evaluations of them are not based on their actual traits and abilities but are often caused by an attractiveness "halo" (Major, Carrington, & Carnevale, 1984). Consequently, many attractive people who are exposed to this confusing information may be left with an uncertain self-concept.

ing? As both researchers and compliance professionals know, there are several, and one of the most influential is similarity.

We like people who are similar to us (Byrne, 1971). This fact seems to hold true whether the similarity is in the area of opinions, personality traits, background, or lifestyle. Consequently, those who want us to like them so that we will comply with them can accomplish that purpose by appearing similar to us in a wide variety of ways.

Dress is a good example. Several studies have demonstrated that we are more likely to help those who dress like us. In one study, done in the early 1970s when young people tended to dress in either "hippie" or "straight" fashion, experimenters donned hippie or straight attire and asked college students on campus for a dime to make a phone call. When the experimenter was dressed in the same way as the student, the request was granted in more than two-thirds of the instances; when the student and requester were dissimilarly dressed, the dime was provided less than half the time (Emswiller, Deaux, & Willits, 1971). Another experiment showed how automatic our positive response to similar others can be. Marchers in an antiwar demonstration were found to be more likely to sign the petition of a similarly dressed requester *and* to do so without bothering to read it first (Suedfeld, Bochner, & Matas, 1971). *Click, whirr.*

Another way requesters can manipulate similarity to increase liking and compliance is to claim that they have backgrounds and interests similar to ours. Car salespeople, for example, are trained to look for evidence of such things while examining a customer's trade-in. If there is camping gear in the trunk, the salespeople might mention, later on, how they love to get away from the city whenever they can; if there are golf balls on the back seat, they might remark that they hope the rain will hold off until they can play the eighteen holes they scheduled for later in the day; if they notice that the car was purchased out of state, they might ask where a customer is from and report—with surprise—that they (or their spouse) were born there, too.

As trivial as these similarities may seem, they appear to work (Brewer, 1979; Tajfel, 1981). One researcher who examined the sales records of insurance companies found that customers were more likely to buy insurance when a salesperson was like them in age, religion, politics, and cigarette-smoking habits (Evans, 1963). Another researcher was able to significantly increase the percentage of people who responded to a mailed survey by changing one small feature of the request: On a cover letter, he modified the name of the survey-taker to be similar to that of the survey recipient. Thus, Robert Greer received the survey from a survey center official named Bob Gregar while Cynthia Johnston received hers from a survey center official named Cindy Johanson. In two separate studies, adding this little bit of similarity to the exchange nearly doubled survey compliance (Garner, 1999). These seemingly minor commonalties can affect decisions that go well beyond whose insurance to purchase or whose survey to complete. They can affect the decision of whose life to save. When asked to rank-order a waiting list of patients suffering from kidney disorder as to their deservingness for the next available treatment, people chose those whose political party preference matched their own (Furnham, 1996).

Because even small similarities can be effective in producing a positive response to another and because a veneer of similarity can be so easily manufactured, I would advise special caution in the presence of requesters who claim to be "just like you."[3] Indeed, it would be wise these days to be careful around salespeople who just *seem* to be just like you. Many sales training programs now urge trainees to "mirror and match" the customer's body posture, mood, and verbal style, as similarities along each of these dimensions have been shown to lead to positive results (Chartrand & Bargh, 1999; Locke & Horowitz, 1990; Woodside & Davenport, 1974).

Compliments

Actor McLean Stevenson once described how his wife tricked him into marriage: "She said she liked me." Although designed for a laugh, the remark is as instructive as it is humorous. The information that someone fancies us can be a bewitchingly effective device for producing return liking and willing compliance (Berscheid & Walster, 1978; Howard, Gengler, & Jain, 1995, 1997). So, often when people flatter us or claim affinity for us, they want something from us.

Remember Joe Girard, the world's "greatest car salesman," who says the secret of his success was getting customers to like him? He did something that, on the face of it, seems foolish and costly. Each month he sent every one of his more than 13,000 former customers a holiday greeting card containing a printed message. The holiday greeting card changed from month to month (Happy New Year, Happy Valentine's Day, Happy Thanksgiving, and so on), but the message printed on the face of the

---

[3] Additional work suggests yet another reason for caution when dealing with similar requesters: we typically underestimate the degree to which similarity affects our liking for another (Gonzales, Davis, Loney, Lukens, & Junghans, 1983).

card never varied. It read, "I like you." As Joe explained it, "There's nothing else on the card, nothin' but my name. I'm just telling 'em that I like 'em."

"I like you." It came in the mail every year, 12 times a year, like clockwork. "I like you," on a printed card that went to 13,000 other people, too. Could a statement of liking so impersonal, obviously designed to sell cars, really work: Joe Girard thought so, and a man as successful as he was at what he did deserves our attention. Joe understood an important fact about human nature: we are phenomenal suckers for flattery. Although there are limits to our gullibility—especially when we can be sure that the flatterer is trying to manipulate us (Jones & Wortman, 1973)—we tend, as a rule, to believe praise and to like those who provide it, often when it is probably untrue (Byrne, Rasche, & Kelley, 1974).

An experiment done on a group of men in North Carolina shows how helpless we can be in the face of praise. The men in the study received comments about themselves from another person who needed a favor from them. Some of the men got only positive comments, some got only negative comments, and some got a mixture of good and bad. There were three interesting findings. First, the evaluator who provided only praise was liked best by the men. Second, this tendency held true even when the men fully realized that the flatterer stood to gain from their liking him. Finally, unlike the other types of comments, pure praise did not have to be accurate to work. Positive comments produced just as much liking for the flatterer when they were untrue as when they were true (Drachman, deCarufel, & Insko, 1978).

Apparently we have such an automatically positive reaction to compliments that we can fall victim to someone who uses them in an obvious attempt to win our favor. Click, whirr. When seen in this light, the expense of printing and mailing well over 150,000 "I like you" cards each year seems neither as foolish nor as costly as before. . . .

Persuasion: What Will It Take to Convince You?

Michael J Lovaglia
University of Iowa

PERSUASION BY INCHES

Have you noticed that big building projects always seem to cost much more than was originally estimated? No matter how high the original estimate, the project almost always ends up costing millions, sometimes billions of dollars more. It is not that accurate estimates are too difficult to make. If accuracy were the problem, then the original estimate would be too high only about half the time and too low the rest. The error here is too one-sided to be accidental. Taxpayers, certainly, do not like having to pay additional billions of dollars for a new highway. Yet contractors continue to give low estimates then ask for increases along the way. No matter how annoyed people get, the practice continues. Social psychology explains why.

An initially low estimate is a powerful persuasive tool, whether you are buying a car or the government is buying a highway. When people are shopping for a car, they are often strongly attracted to one more expensive than they can easily afford. The salesperson's job is to persuade them to buy a car that will strain but not break their financial resources. Suppose you are shopping for a car. You have made a firm resolution to spend no more than $12,000. At one dealership, however, you are attracted to one that costs $16,000. You realize this is out of your price range and start to move on. At that point, salespeople are taught to ask, "Would you be interested if I could get the price of this car down to $10,900?"

Excerpted from *Knowing People: The Personal Use of Social Psychology,* 2000, Chapter 5, pp. 118-125. © 2000 by McGraw-Hill. Reprinted by permission.

There are two reasons for the salesperson's question. First, notice that it is a leading question. He did not say that he could get the price reduced by $5,000. He only asked if you would be interested. However, by asking the leading question, he implied that a price of $10,900 was at least possible. Second, you would probably answer yes to the question. (A good salesperson would already have found out that it was in your price range.) Once you agree that you are interested in that car at that price, you have made a commitment. We are all taught to keep our commitments. It is difficult for people to stop and reverse themselves once they have started something. By agreeing that you would be interested, you committed yourself in a small way to buying that car. If the salesperson is good at his job, then you will buy that car and be happy with it, but the price you pay will be closer to $16,000 than it will be to $10,900. Had the salesperson accurately estimated that you might be able to buy the car for $14,900, you would not have been interested. To the salesperson's credit, you probably like your new car more than any you could have found for less than $12,000. On the other hand, your financial situation may be shaky for a while because of it.

Cialdini, Cacioppo, Bassett, and Miller (1978) investigated why giving a very low initial cost estimate is such a persuasive technique. Researchers called people on the phone to ask them to participate in a psychology study. Half of the people were told immediately that the study would take place at 7 A.M. The early hour made it unlikely that many people would agree to participate. The rest of the people were told about the study and that it would take place at a variety of times during the day. Then all of the people in the study were asked if they would like to participate first. Only after people said that they were interested in participating were they told that they would be needed at the 7 A.M. session of the study. Researchers wanted to know if getting people to agree that they were interested in the study first, before they knew how early they would have to arrive, would increase the number who eventually showed up for a 7 A.M. study.

Cialdini and colleagues (1978) showed that giving a low initial cost estimate effectively persuaded people to participate in their study. When researchers told subjects up front that the study would take place at 7 A.M., less than a third (31 percent) agreed to participate. However, when researchers got people to agree that they were interested in participating before telling them what time the study would take place, more than half (56 percent) agreed to participate. But would more people really show up for the study after having had a chance to consider their decision? Saying yes on the phone is one thing. But if people actually get out of bed in the morning to come to a study, then they

really must have been persuaded. Cialdini and colleagues found that giving a low initial cost estimate was even more effective when it came to changing people's actual behavior. When researchers forthrightly told people about the 7 A.M. study time, less than a quarter (only 24 percent) actually showed up for the study. However, when researchers got people to agree that they were interested before telling them about the early starting time, more than half (53 percent) showed up on time. Almost all of those who agreed to participate actually appeared. Once we commit in even a small way to participating in a project, we are unlikely to drop out, even if the cost of continuing increases dramatically along the way.

MENTIONING A LITTLE TO GET A LOT

Charitable organizations that solicit contributions face an interesting dilemma. If they ask for large amounts of money from people, then more people will say no. However, if solicitors ask for small amounts, more people will say yes, but rarely will large amounts be given. How can solicitors convince as many people as possible to contribute without decreasing the average amount that each person gives?

Cialdini and Schroeder (1976) found a solution to the problem faced by charitable organizations that required adding only five words to the end of a request for a contribution: "Even a penny will help." In their study, research assistants solicited funds for the American Cancer Society. All used a standard request for funds: "Would you be willing to help by giving a donation?" However, half the research assistants added the sentence "Even a penny will help." Almost twice as many people contributed when they were told that even a penny would help. More surprisingly, their contributions were no smaller than the contributions given by those who were not told that a penny would help. Researchers concluded that mentioning the penny legitimized a small donation, making it more difficult for people to say no. However, because the amount suggested—a penny—was so small, people did not use it to estimate the size of a reasonable donation.

WHO WILL HELP YOU?

Most people realize that if you want people to help you, it is good to help them. The practice of giving and receiving gifts is universal in human culture. From a very young age, we learn to give things to people in the hope that we will get something else in return. We have no guarantee that the people we give gifts to will give us gifts in return, or give us gifts of equal value. However, we are all taught that giving gifts is a good thing and that we should not keep too close an

account of who gives us what in return. The idea is that by giving gifts we start to form lasting relationships with people. For example, in my large extended family, it would not be practical for everyone to give everyone else a Christmas present. We would all be broke and spend the whole year shopping. Instead, we draw names and everyone gives one other person a gift. I give my aunt a scarf. My nephew gives me a sweater. Almost no one gets a gift from the person to whom she or he gave one. Nonetheless, gift giving works to maintain good relationships among people. Although I do not see my relatives often, I feel comfortable asking for help from my aunt or nephew when I need it. A good way to persuade people to help you is to start by giving them a gift, doing them a favor, providing some small service.

Salespeople and charitable organizations know something more surprising about giving gifts and doing favors. Another good way to persuade people to help you in the future is to get them to do you a small favor first. This is the opposite of how we are taught the social world works. We grow up thinking that we can expect about as much help from other people as we are willing to give in return. If someone does us a favor, then that person should be less likely to do us another favor right away. It is as if we have withdrawn some of our credit in the goodwill bank account. We will not be eligible for another favor until we make a deposit by helping someone else. But there are good social psychological reasons to continue helping someone we have already helped.

Recall from a previous section that once people commit to a project, they are likely to continue with it although the cost involved inches steadily upward. We feel the same way about people, but to a greater degree. It is important to us to keep and maintain our personal relationships. So once we have committed to helping a person, we are likely to agree to help the next time we are asked. We will continue to help even though the second favor requested of us is bigger than the first. Have you noticed that if you send a small donation to a charitable organization, they will send you requests for more money every couple of months? The more money that you give, the bigger and more frequent are the requests that follow. Aren't charities worried that they will wear out donors with repeated, escalating requests for money? Apparently not.

Freedman and Fraser (1966) showed that by getting a person to do you a small favor first, you increase the chance that she will do you a bigger favor later. To test this surprising idea, researchers contacted people by telephone. Researchers wanted to find out how many people would agree to a big favor that researchers would ask of them. Researchers requested that they be allowed to enter people's homes and for several hours catalog their personal belongings. Most people would be hesitant to grant such a request over the phone. Half the people contacted were first asked for a small favor. Researchers asked people merely to answer a few questions for a consumer survey. Then, three days later, researchers called back with the big request. The rest of the people in the survey were only asked if they would agree to the big favor, allowing researchers to come to their homes and make a list of their possessions. Would more people agree to let researchers come into their houses after they had first agreed to the small favor of answering a few survey questions?

Getting people to agree to doing a small favor first had a major effect (Freedman and Fraser 1966). When people were first asked to answer a few survey questions, more than half (53 percent) later agreed to let researchers come into their homes. (Imagine how successful you would be if you called strangers and asked if you could come over and go through their stuff for a couple of hours!) In contrast, when only the large request was made, just 28 percent, a little more than a quarter, agreed to let researchers come into their homes. By asking for a small favor first, researchers nearly doubled the percentage of people who would agree to grant their major request.

The lesson is clear. If you will need someone's help in the future, get that person to help you in small ways now, thus increasing the likelihood of agreement to an important request later. Note that as with the low initial bid technique of the previous section, getting people to do you a small favor requires no pressure. Persuasion starts to occur before a request is ever made. The more people help you, the more people will want to continue helping you. They become committed to your success.

The technique of gaining people's commitment by getting them to do you a favor can work for customers as well as salespeople. The one time in my life where it seemed that I got an especially good deal on a used car is an example. I had moved back to California from Idaho. I was working, selling furniture, but I no longer needed the truck that I had used to deliver waterbeds and hot tubs. I had decided to go back to school and needed a reliable car. A few blocks from the furniture store where I worked was a car lot where a national car rental company sold the rental cars to the public after they were a couple of years old. One day, as I drove by the lot, a Mustang convertible caught my eye. What better car to drive to college in California? After driving by that car several days in a row, I wanted it badly. I stopped by the lot after work to find out more about the car. With tax and license, the total price would be a little over $9,000. The salesperson told me that I would have to get my own financing. Also, the company had a strict "one-price"

policy. Car prices were not negotiable. The best price for each car was plainly marked on it. No haggling. While this seems a fair way to sell cars, it leaves the dealer firmly in control of the ultimate price that customers pay. I decided to try a little social psychology to get the price down.

I returned to the car lot prepared to buy the car. Nonetheless, I let the salesperson go through his entire sales routine. I drove the car a second time. I let him tell me at length about the company's one-price policy that was such a benefit for customers because it relieved them of the anxiety of negotiating. We practiced putting the convertible top up and down. I asked him to show me how to operate everything on the car. I asked him to help me make sure that everything worked. In social psychological terms, I was gaining his commitment to sell me that car. Every time I asked him to help me with something, to show me something, he became a little more committed to completing the sale. The only thing salespeople have to work with is their time. While he was spending time with me, he could not work with anyone else. The more time he spent with me, the more important it was to him that our meeting result in a successful sale.

Eventually he suggested that we go to his desk to "get some information" from me. He was getting impatient. At his desk, we talked about price again. He repeated the company's no-exceptions one-price policy. No negotiating. I told him that I had already arranged a loan and that the price seemed reasonable. However, $9,000 was more than I was prepared to pay. Instead, I gave him a cashier's check for $8,000 and asked him to sell me the car for that amount. He laughed a little nervously at that point. He knew I was serious—$8,000 is a lot of money and a cashier's check has more impact than a personal check. He told me that he could not do it. It was against company policy to lower the price. I paused for what seemed like a long time, then said, "OK, let's go look at the car again." More time commitment from the salesperson.

I had already noticed a small tear in the outer shell of the convertible top, perhaps half an inch long. It seemed minor but might get worse. I pointed it out to the salesperson and asked how much a new convertible top would cost. He said that he did not know. I smiled and said, "Why don't we find out?" Back at his desk, I went through the yellow pages and asked him to call convertible top repair shops. More commitment; he was doing me a favor. We eventually agreed that a new convertible top would cost about $1,200 dollars. I suggested that we subtract the price of a new top from the price of the car and complete the sale. He said that he couldn't do that. I asked him what he could do. He said he would have to find out. Would he do that for me, please? More commitment. I told him that I was taking my new girlfriend

to lunch and would be back in an hour or two.

The salesperson had spent a substantial amount of his working day with me. He had nothing to show for it yet. He was committed. When my girlfriend and I got back from lunch, the salesperson agreed to drop the "nonnegotiable" price by $500. After a little more bargaining, I wrote him a personal check for about $150 to add to the cashier's check of $8,000 that I had already given him. I had saved about $1,000. By getting him to help me repeatedly in small ways, I gained his commitment to help me in a bigger way. When I asked him to help me get the price I wanted, he found it difficult to refuse. As for the tear in the convertible top, a tube of vinyl repair goo fixed it nicely. Many good things got started that day. I drove to college with the top down and made it to graduation. Then I married my girlfriend.

TO PERSUADE THEM, LET THEM PERSUADE YOU

Cialdini, Green, and Rusch (1992) put an interesting twist on the idea that people want to help people who have helped them. Because people feel the need to reciprocate, researchers proposed that if someone has persuaded you to do something in the past, then that person will be easier for you to persuade to do something in the future. Salespeople experience the situation often. When I sold furniture to a person in business, I felt obligated to use their services as well. When a family that owned a dry cleaners brought both dining room and living room furniture from me, I started taking my clothes to their cleaners, although it required driving across town.

Cialdini and colleagues (1992) proposed that a person would be persuaded more easily by someone who had yielded to her arguments on some unrelated topic. That is, once a person has persuaded you of something, that person will feel the need to reciprocate, return the favor, by letting you persuade her on some other issue. Researchers first asked people to give their opinions about the minimum drinking age. For half the people in the study, a research assistant at first disagreed but then admitted to bring convinced by their arguments. For the rest of the people in the study, the research assistant remained unconvinced by their arguments. Then in the second part of the study, the research assistant's opinions about whether to require comprehensive exams in college were given to people. Researchers wanted to find out if people would agree more with the researcher after the researcher had agreed with them about the drinking age issue.

After the research assistant was persuaded by their arguments, people were

Dilbert discovers the value of giving in.

DILBERT reprinted by permission of United Feature Syndicate, Inc.

more likely to be persuaded by the research assistant on a different topic. Cialdini et al. (1992) were correct. Researchers asked people to estimate how much their attitude had changed after listening to the research assistant's arguments. When the research assistant had agreed with people's opinions on the earlier topic, people reported that on average their attitudes had been changed 27 percent by the research assistant. That is, the research assistant's brief statement of her or his opinions had been highly persuasive. However, when the research assistant had been unconvinced by people's opinions on an earlier topic, people reported that on average their attitudes had been changed only 6 percent by the research assistant.

To get people to agree with you, first agree with them. The implications go well beyond any individual negotiations. These research results suggest a personal style that will increase your success in social life. Most arguments people get into are silly because the outcome doesn't matter very much. But those minor disagreements set the stage for major conflict when an important issue does arise. When I was in high school I loved to argue. I practiced and studied ways to construct a sound argument. I believed that logic would prevail. It was important for me to be right and for people to acknowledge that I was right. An implication that I had not considered was that by acknowledging I was right, people would be admitting that they were wrong. People do not like to admit that they are wrong.

For several years I argued every chance I got. It puzzled me, however, that no matter how brilliant my argument, the people I argued with never seemed to be convinced. After a particularly heated argument, I would review it in my mind for days to make sure I had been right. Yet later I would find that the person I had argued with remained unconvinced. My logic was sound enough but my social psychology was weak. I had ignored the importance of reciprocity in human relationships. To convince somebody of something, it helps to let that person convince you of something else first. And because the outcome of most arguments doesn't matter very much, it pays to agree

with other people most of the time. Save your arguments for situations where the outcome is truly important to you. Agree with people unless you have a good reason not to. Let them convince you. That was exactly the opposite of the way I had approached my relationships with people. I wanted to show people that I was right. So I argued about everything. But people were not convinced. A better way to approach the people in your life is to agree with them as much as possible. Show them how right they are. Then, when an issue comes up that is very important to you, you will be more likely to convince them that on this rare but important occasion, you might be right.

STATUS AS THE MOST SUBTLE WAY TO PERSUADE

Most of this chapter has described effective, subtle, and sometimes devious techniques that salespeople and organizations use to persuade people. You have seen how you can benefit from using similar techniques when you need to persuade someone to help you. . . . Some people do not seem to need such techniques to persuade others. The doctor merely tells you that an operation is necessary and you agree to let her remove part of your body. Why doesn't your doctor need the subtle techniques of persuasion commonly used by salespeople?

The answer is *status*. Your status is your standing within a group based on your prestige, the respect that other group members give you. Doctors have high status in our society. They are respected, honored. The magic of high status is that people will try to find out what it is you want them to do, and do it for you, without your ever having to make a request. I noticed myself doing this just last week. By watching my diet and starting to exercise, I recently lost most of the excess weight I had carried around for years. I have more energy and feel healthier. Then last week it occurred to me that I should go to my doctor for the first time in years to get a physical examination. Why should I want to go to the doctor now that I feel great? I usually avoid going when I am sick. What I really wanted was my doc-

tor's approval. I wanted the doctor to tell me what a good job I had done getting rid of that extra body fat. Her approval is important to me because of her high status. My doctor never told me I should lose weight, although she did hint last time that a little exercise would help. However, I thought my doctor would approve if I lost weight. Thus the opinion I expected her to have influenced my behavior without her having to express that opinion directly. When people have high status, their opinions count.

Techniques of persuasion can be highly effective in specific situations, but to wield real influence, a person needs high status. . . .

FURTHER READING

Of General Interest

Bacharach, S. B., Lawler, E. J. (1984). *Bargaining*. San Francisco: Jossey-Bass.

Cialdini, R. B. (1993). *Influence: Science and practice*. New York: HarperCollins.

Damasio, A. R. (1994). *Descarte's error: Emotion, reason, and the human brain*. New York: Grosset/Putnam.

Pfeffer, J. (1992). *Managing with power: Politics and influence in organizations*. Boston: Harvard Business School Press.

Recent and Technical Issues

Axsom, D., Yates, S., & Chaiken, S. (1987). Audience response as a heuristic cue in persuasion. *Journal of Personality and Social Psychology, 53,* 30–40.

Fleming, J. H., Darley, J. M., Hilton, J. L., & Kojetin, B. A. (1990.) Multiple audience problem: A strategic communication perspective on social perception. *Journal of Personality and Social Psychology, 58,* 593–609.

Frey, K. P., & Eagly, A. H. (1993). Vividness can undermine the persuasiveness of messages. *Journal of Personality and Social Psychology, 65,* 32–44.

Gorassini, D. R., Olson, J. M. (1995). Does self-perception change explain the foot-in-the-door effect? *Journal of Personality and Social Psychology, 69,* 91–105.

Kruglanski, A., Webster, D. M., & Klem, A. (1993). Motivated resistance and openness to persuasion in the presence or absence of prior information. *Journal of Personality and Social Psychology, 65,* 861–876.

Petty, R. E., Schumann, D. W., Richman, S. A., & Strathman, A. J. (1993). Positive mood and persuasion: Different roles for affect under high- and low-elaboration conditions. *Journal of Personality and Social Psychology, 64,* 5–20.

Vorauer, J. D., & Miller, D. T. (1997). Failure to recognize the effect of implicit social influence on the presentation of self. *Journal of Personality and Social Psychology, 73,* 281–295.

Zarnoth, P., & Sniezek, J. A. (1997). The social influence of confidence in group decision making. *Journal of Experimental Social Psychology, 33,* 345–366.

SUSPECT
CONFESSIONS

He's made mincemeat of false memories.
But the social psychologist Richard Ofshe has a more pressing
question: Why do innocent people admit to crimes
they didn't commit?

Richard Jerome

Richard Jerome is a senior writer at People *magazine.*

THROUGH A THICKENING FOG, RICHARD J. OFSHE WINDS HIS WHITE BMW homeward into the Oakland hills, leaving behind the University of California at Berkeley, where he is a professor of social psychology. In florid tones refined by 30 years at the lectern, Ofshe is expounding on his latest area of interest, the ways in which police interrogations can elicit false confessions. Specifically, he is bemoaning the case of Jessie Lloyd Misskelley Jr., a teen-ager from a squalid Arkansas trailer park who confessed—falsely, Ofshe maintains—to taking part in the ghastly murder of three 8-year-old boys. In spite of Ofshe's voluminous expert testimony on his behalf, Misskelley, who has an I.Q. in the 70's, was sentenced to life plus 40 years in prison.

"It was like walking straight into 'Deliverance,' " Ofshe says, casually veering around another hairpin turn. "The trial was a travesty. The conduct of the judge was outrageous."

At 54, Ofshe has acquired a muted celebrity for his work on extreme influence tactics and thought control. He shared in the 1979 Pulitzer Prize in public service after assisting The Point Reyes (Calif.) Light in its exposé of Synanon, a Bay Area drug rehabilitation group that evolved into an armed cult. More recently, Ofshe has been an aggressive and influential debunker of "recovered memory," the theory whereby long-repressed traumas are retrieved by patients undergoing what Ofshe calls exceedingly manipulative psychotherapy. As such, Ofshe is a vivid figure in "Remembering Satan," Lawrence Wright's book about the case of Paul Ingram, a former Olympia, Wash., sheriff's deputy now serving 20 years in prison primarily because he became convinced that the accusa-

tions of one of his daughters, who claimed that he had indulged in a 17-year binge of satanism, incest and infanticide, were true. Ofshe, a champion of Ingram, dissects the affair in his recent book, "Making Monsters: False Memories, Psychotherapy and Sexual Hysteria," written with Ethan Watters.

But for the most part, Ofshe has set aside violent cults and overzealous shrinks and is fixated on the third of his bêtes noires: false confessions. According to Ofshe and a considerable body of literature, modern interrogation tactics are so subtly powerful that police can—entirely unwittingly—coerce innocent suspects into admitting to the most heinous crimes. Sometimes, Ofshe says, a suspect admits guilt simply to escape the stress of the interrogation. More rarely, a suspect comes to believe that he actually committed the crime in question, though he has no memory of it.

For Ofshe, exorcising both kinds of false confession from the American justice system has become an almost obsessive quest. All told, he has consulted or testified in more than 80 criminal cases involving suspects from whom, he concluded, confessions were coerced; in most of these cases, the physical evidence strongly suggested innocence. Although he makes money at it overall—$40,000 in 1993—he sometimes works pro bono. With dark, disdaining eyes set against a shock of gray curls and a swirling beard, Ofshe looks vaguely sinister—a wily Renaissance pol, perhaps, or Claudius in a road company of Hamlet. Confession, he points out, is the anchor of a trial in which there is no hard evidence. "And false confession," he says, "ranks third after perjury and eyewitness error as a cause of wrongful convictions in American homicide cases."

His numbers are based on several studies, most recently work by the sociologist Michael L. Radelet of the University of Florida, Hugo Adam Bedau, professor of philosophy at Tufts University, and Constance E. Putnam, a Boston-based writer. In their 1992 book, "In Spite of Innocence," the authors review more than 400 cases in which innocent people were convicted of capital crimes in the United States. Fourteen percent were caused by false confession. "If it happened just one-half of 1 percent of the time," Ofshe says, "it still means that hundreds, or perhaps thousands, of people each year are being unjustly imprisoned. Even if one innocent man or woman is convicted, it's too many. And it's unnecessary because this is a fixable problem"—fixable, he adds, if only police interrogations were electronically recorded, a requirement now only in Alaska and Minnesota.

"Now I don't think for one second," Ofshe stresses, "that the detectives and prosecutors in cases of false confessions want to bring about that result. But because they don't understand the mistake as it is being made, the case moves forward and takes everyone along with it."

THE BMW IS NOW TUCKED SAFELY UNDER OFSHE'S RED FERRARI, which sits on a raised hoist in the garage of his hillside home, a quasi-Mediterranean mix of stone and stucco. Inside, rock music from a new stereo system tumbles down the coiled stairs of a three-and-a-half-story central rotunda, into a cherry-paneled library where Ofshe, propped like a pasha on a brown leather couch, surveys his domain with a reverent sigh: "I never thought I'd ever get to have a house like this."

It mirrors its inhabitant: spare, opulent, imposing yet accessible. One can well appreciate that Ofshe's fondest boyhood memory is of the austere charms of the Frick Collection mansion. His father, a dress designer, moved the family from the Bronx to Queens when Ofshe was a child. Ofshe attended Queens College, then went to graduate school at Stanford. "I honestly can't tell you now what led me to psychology," he says. "I suppose I'm a watcher. "I'm comfortable observing people and lecturing at them—but I am absolutely incapable of making small talk, a gift I consider one of the great mysteries of life."

During graduate school, Ofshe was married briefly and then, as he puts it, "got un-married." (He married his present wife, Bonnie Blair, a successful designer of sweaters, in 1981.) Ofshe gravitated toward social psychology; his work on cults grew out of a study of utopian societies he undertook in the early 1970's. One such community was Synanon, begun as a drug treatment center by Charles Dederich. But by 1978, Dederich had accumulated a substantial arsenal, as well as a large cadre of loyal followers. By this time, The Point Reyes Light, a weekly based near Ofshe's summer home, had begun an investigative series on Synanon, on which Ofshe collaborated. As a result of the media exposure, Synanon lost its tax-exempt status

and disintegrated. Dederich sued Ofshe three times unsuccessfully for libel, prompting him to retaliate with a malicious prosecution suit. " 'When this is over, I'll be the one driving the red Ferrari,' " Ofshe says he told people at the time. The Ferrari, he now confides, "accounts for a small percentage of my settlement. A very small percentage."

Material success aside, Ofshe seems to revel most in the validation of his work by respected media outlets. It takes little prodding for him to express his glee at Lawrence Wright's description of him as "Zeus-like" in "Remembering Satan"—which first appeared as an article in The New Yorker, a magazine Ofshe clearly reveres. And he is quick to point out that the television movie of Wright's book, currently being filmed, features him as the central character—as played by William Devane.

What saves this self-absorption from being insufferable is Ofshe's interest in helping people he considers innocent. He first focused on police interrogation in 1987, after a phone call from Joseph G. Donahey Jr., a veteran Florida attorney. Donahey was representing Thomas F. Sawyer, a Clearwater golf course groundskeeper who in 1986, after an uncommonly grueling 16-hour interrogation, confessed to the brutal murder of a neighbor; the police convinced Sawyer that he'd lost all memory of the incident during an alcoholic blackout. (Sawyer, against whom there was no physical evidence, had quickly recanted.) "Donahey realized something was terribly wrong with Tom's confession," Ofshe says. "At first I was skeptical. But once I read the transcript of the interrogation, it became obvious what had happened to Tom."

Ofshe spent 300 hours analyzing the Sawyer interrogation—which, by a lucky quirk, was taped in its entirety—and concluded it was "a tour de fore of psychological coercion." Sawyer's police interrogators, Peter Fire and John Dean, invited Sawyer to the station house on the premise that he was being asked to "assist" with their investigation. Then, Ofshe says, they flattered him into providing his own hypothetical murder scenario. The detectives then used leading questions to shape the groundskeeper's responses, eventually tossing his answers back as evidence of his guilt. Consider the following dialogue, slightly condensed, on the position of the victim's body:

FIRE: And he would put her in the bed how? Like she's doing what?
SAWYER: Sleeping.
FIRE: O.K. What would you put her on? Her. . . .
SAWYER: On her back.
FIRE: Put her on her back? . . .
SAWYER: I'd put her on her back sleeping.
FIRE: Put her on her back, sleeping?
SAWYER: Don't you sleep on your back?
FIRE: No. . . .
SAWYER: I don't sleep on my side.
FIRE: Well, what other way could you put her?
SAWYER: Face down.

FIRE: O.K. Face down. . . .

SAWYER: I'd put her on her stomach. . . .

FIRE: You hit the nail on the head. You put her on her stomach.

Deception, typically by lying about the presence of witnesses or physical evidence or about polygraph results, is a common interrogation tactic, Ofshe says, and it was used baldly against Sawyer. ("We found a lot of hairs and fibers on her body," Fire insisted at one point. "We have your hair. . . . There's a lot of evidence. There's a lot of evidence. A lot of evidence.")

"If you're dealing with middle-class types," Ofshe says, "or at least middle-class types socialized by my mother, they're hearing: 'It's inevitable that you'll be caught and punished to the max.' I have no interest in stripping police of tactics that make perfect sense—when those tactics are supported by compelling physical evidence. But the same things that can convince a guilty person that he's been caught can convince someone who's innocent that he's caught."

Under this intense barrage, Sawyer, who for hours steadfastly maintained his innocence, exhibited his first trace of self-doubt: "I honestly believe that I didn't do it. . . . I don't remember doing it. If I did, and I don't think I did. . . . You almost got me convinced I did, but. . . ."

"He went from straight denial to 'I couldn't have done something like this,'" Ofshe says. "And finally, when he confessed, it was so beautiful, so perfect in the way he verbalized it: 'I guess all the evidence is in, I guess I must have done it.'"

Strong evidence of a false confession, Ofshe says, is when the narrative is at odds with the known facts of the case or has been clearly fed to the suspect, however inadvertently, by the police themselves. "Sawyer was wrong about almost everything," Ofshe says, "except for several details"—like the position of the victim's body—"that were clearly introduced by Fire and Dean."

Ultimately, Ofshe's testimony helped exonerate Sawyer, whose confession was suppressed in 1989 after the groundskeeper had spent 14 months in jail awaiting trial. Shortly thereafter, Ofshe—by now increasingly sought by desperate defense attorneys—helped free Mark Nunez, Leo Bruce and Dante Parker, who, fingered by a psychiatric patient and subjected to a highly coercive interrogation, had falsely confessed to killing nine people at a Buddhist temple outside Phoenix. In Flagstaff, Ofshe was instrumental in winning the 1988 acquittal of George Abney, a graduate student with a history of depression, who had admitted to the ritualistic murder of a Navajo woman. In the Phoenix case, the real murderer was eventually caught and prosecuted.

"WHAT SOME OF THE PSYCHOLOGISTS SAY IS I PUT YOU IN A ROOM, you're all emotional and at the end of five or six hours, I've fed you everything," Lieut. Ralph M. Lacer is saying in his Oakland police office, several miles from Ofshe's home. "Well, if I was on the jury, I'd be rolling my eyes saying: 'Who is the dumb [expletive] who thinks this is gonna go over?'"

Fiftyish, ruddy and blond, the bespectacled Lacer was one of the interrogating officers in the high-profile case of Bradley Page, a handsome Berkeley student who had admitted—falsely, so Page and his attorneys maintained—to murdering his girlfriend, Roberta (BiBi) Lee, in a fit of anger in 1984. After two trials, the second of which Ofshe consulted on, Page was convicted of manslaughter. (He was released, after serving part of a six-year sentence, in February.)

Only part of the Page interrogation was recorded. From 11:50 A.M. to 1:10 P.M. on Dec. 10, 1984, Lacer and his partner, Sgt. Jerry Harris, taped Page as he gave them a firm, lucid account of his movements during the time since Lee had disappeared a month before—none of which included bludgeoning her to death. Then the detectives shut off the machine until 7:07 P.M., by which time Page was highly emotional, confessing to murder, albeit in vague, halting language peppered with "might haves," "would haves" and other subjunctive phrases that left Ofshe highly suspicious. Lacer freely acknowledges that Page's admission of guilt, made in the absence of hard evidence, was the heart and soul of the case against him. "If we hadn't gotten the confession," Lacer says, "Brad would've walked."

I raise Ofshe's argument, that taping interrogations in full might resolve any ambiguities.

"First of all, a tape is inhibiting," Lacer counters. "It's hard to get at the truth. And say we go for 10 hours—we have 10 hours of tape that maybe boil down to 15 or 20 minutes of you saying, 'Yes, I killed Johnny Jones.' You bet the public defender's going to have the jury listen to all 10 hours of that tape and by that time the jury won't remember what it's all about."

According to Lacer, the craft of interrogation is learned through experience. "Every day when you stop someone on the street, you're interrogating them," he says. "'Where do you live? Where you headed to?' We definitely try to establish rapport—basically, I want to get you to talk to me. But when we bring a suspect in, we keep the room bare, a table and two or three chairs, a locked door."

I glance around, aware for the first time that the interview is unfolding in the ideal interrogation setting. I ask Lacer what would happen if a person being questioned invokes his constitutional right of silence or, if he is not under arrest, his right to simply walk out the door.

"Well, that would be the end of the situation," he says. "But many times it won't happen, and here's why: I see you've got a wedding ring on, Rich. Well, say Mrs. Rich ends up dead in the house. We call you down and you say, 'I don't think I want to talk to you guys, I'm out of here.' Well, the thing is, your in-laws find out that you took that route and they know right away who killed your wife.

"Now most of the time, the suspect will set up barriers. Like you got your legs crossed—that's kind of a psychological barrier. And I lean forward, violate your personal space, get closer and closer and pretty soon we're nose to nose." As Lacer edges toward me, his eyes, though still genial, bear into mine.

"Now remember, I'm just talking, not yelling or bullying," he says. "It's not going to help matters if I suddenly say '[Expletive], that's a [expletive] black sweater you have on—I threw away the last black sweater I had like that!' " You can maybe bully a little bit verbally by saying: 'Rich, that last story was [expletive]. Let's not even go into that again.' " Lacer's eyes turn caustic through his aviator glasses.

"Now as far as yelling," he says, chummy again, "about the only time we do it here in Oakland is if someone's talking over you or if they're going off on a tangent, and I'd say, 'Hey Rich, let's get back to the *subject!*' " His voice slices through the claustrophobia of the room—a ferocity all the more unnerving because it booms from Lacer's amiable shell.

"We've been in a room together for a while, Rich," he says, chuckling. "Do you feel like confessing to anything?"

"LACER RATIONALIZES THAT SOMEONE LIKE BRADLEY PAGE—OR YOU AND I—cannot be made to confess," Ofshe says on the day after my encounter with the Oakland lieutenant. "Because it is in many ways one of the worst professional error you can make—like a physician amputating the wrong arm."

Prevention, he adds, is surprisingly simple: "Above all, no confession ought be accepted unless it has been corroborated with clear-cut and powerful evidence. And you must never instigate a high-pressure, accusatory interrogation unless you have a good and sound reason to do it."

Another safeguard, Ofshe reiterates, is to record interrogations. Early last year, the professor helped win a significant victory in the same Clearwater courthouse where the Sawyer case was heard. Relying substantially on Ofshe's testimony, Judge Claire K. Luten formed a forceful opinion that the confession of Francis Dupont, an alcoholic drifter who had admitted to murdering a friend, was psychologically coerced. Moreover, Luten ruled that the failure to tape the interrogation of Dupont was in direct violation of due process.

"I'd be content to devote myself to that issue until I am too old to work on it," Ofshe says.

In a sense, this is Ofshe's moment, for never has the nation been more attuned to what happens in a courtroom. Yet for the plain citizen—the juror—he is also a problematic figure, a bearded academic speaking in tones of unassailable authority about social psychology, a discipline that resounds with squishy inexactitude. Ofshe's theories about false confession, however well researched, risk being perceived as just another set of legal loopholes. And his "one innocent man or woman" might well be shrugged off—probably not worth the trouble and surely not worth the risk.

For which reason Ofshe emphasizes the most basic preventive to false confession: if you find yourself being questioned about a crime you know you did not commit, resist at all costs the impulse to be helpful, no matter how charming or forbidding the interrogator might be.

"I tell my classes," Ofshe says, "that if they ever find themselves in that situation, remember the four magic words of the criminal justice system: 'I want a lawyer.' "

Unit 5

Key Points to Consider

❖ What do you think of the argument that spending time on the Internet can interfere with "normal" social life and thus have a negative effect on a person's feelings? What would be the strongest evidence for such a proposition? What complicating factors would have to be taken into consideration when testing this idea? Do you think that particular kinds of people-shy people, for instance-might be drawn to such technology?

❖ What do you think of the evolutionary psychologists' explanation for some of the findings regarding physical attractiveness? What is their strongest evidence? Their weakest evidence? Can their findings be explained in any other way?

❖ Do any of the "love stories" described by Robert Sternberg seem to characterize romantic relationship with which you are familiar? Are there any stories which are not included which seem important?

 **Links**   **www.dushkin.com/online/**

These sites are annotated on pages 4 and 5.

A young man stands on a narrow suspension bridge that stretches over a river 230 feet below. The bridge is only 5 feet wide, over 400 feet long, and it constantly swings and sways in the wind. Even for someone without a fear of heights, crossing this bridge while looking at the river far below is definitely an arousing experience. In fact, a considerable number of the people who visit this popular tourist spot every year find themselves unable to cross the bridge at all. While standing on the bridge, the young man is approached by an attractive young woman who asks him to participate in a psychology research project she is working on—all he has to do is write a brief imaginative story in response to a picture she gives him. He does so, and when he is finished, the experimenter gives him her phone number in case he wants to learn more about the experiment.

A few miles away, another young man stands on another bridge—but this one is not scary at all. It is solidly built, does not sway and wobble, and stands only 10 feet above a peaceful stream. The same attractive woman approaches this man with the same request, and, again she gives him her phone number when the experiment ends. Who do you think is more likely to call the young woman later? When this experiment was actually carried out, the results were clear—men on the arousing bridge were much more likely than men on the safe bridge to call the female experimenter later on. Not only that, but the stories the men on the arousing bridge wrote were noticeably different; they contained significantly more references to sex. In short, the men on the arousing bridge apparently reacted in a very different way to the young woman—they experienced a greater sense of physical attraction to her, and acted on that attraction later on by calling her up. Even though men on the sturdy bridge met the same young woman, they did not experience the same physical attraction.

This experiment is just one example of some of the work done by psychologists who study social relationships. This area of social psychology turns out to be a very broad one indeed, and a wide variety of topics fall under its umbrella. One research question, for example, that has attracted a lot of attention is this: What are the factors that influence the initial attraction (both romantic and nonromantic) that we feel for another person? Considerable research indicates that being similar to the other person is important, as is the sheer physical attractiveness of that other. Living or working in close proximity to other people also increases the likelihood of attraction to them.

Other researchers have tackled issues such as identifying the processes that are important for maintaining friendships over time. The level of self-disclosure in the relationship seems to be important, as does the general feeling by both participants that what they are receiving from the relationship is roughly equivalent to what their partner is receiving; that is, issues of fairness seem to play a crucial role. Still, other investigators have concerned themselves with the question of long-term romantic relationships: which factors lead to initial romantic attraction; which factors contribute to long-term satisfaction; and, how do couples deal with conflict and disagreements in long-term relationships?

The selections in this unit are divided into two subsections, the first of which addresses the "dark side" of social life: feelings of shyness and social isolation. The first selection, "Shyness: The New Solution," is a description by psychologist Bernardo Carducci of his work in the area of shyness. He discusses some of the causes of shyness, as well as some of its consequences. He also offers some techniques for coping with this common problem. The second article, "Linking Up Online," describes some of the recent research that has examined the possible connection between heavy use of the Internet and feelings of loneliness and isolation. The early research is somewhat contradictory, and this article sifts through the data.

The second subsection focuses exclusively on romantic relationships. In "Isn't She Lovely?" Brad Lemley summarizes recent research regarding the evolutionary perspective on physical attractiveness: what makes men attractive to women, and women attractive to men. The evolutionary view is that physical features serve as indicators of physical and reproductive fitness to potential mates, and that certain features are therefore universal indicators of attractiveness. In "What's Your Love Story?" noted psychologist Robert Sternberg discusses one of the ways in which he has tried to understand romantic love-through the use of narratives, or "stories," that people tell to make sense of their romantic relationships. Sternberg argues that these narratives can be very revealing, and stresses the importance of both partners having compatible "love stories." Finally, in "Will Your Marriage Last," writer Aviva Patz considers the work of Ted Huston, whose research attempts to predict—at very early stages in relationships—their likely success.

Shyness:
The New Solution

The results of a recent survey are shaking up our ideas about shyness and pointing to a surprising new approach for dealing with it.

BY BERNARDO CARDUCCI, PH.D.

At the core of our existence as human beings lies a powerful drive to be with other people. There is much evidence that in the absence of human contact people fall apart physically and mentally; they experience more sickness, stress and suicide than well-connected individuals. For all too many people, however, shyness is the primary barrier to that basic need.

For more than two decades, I have been studying shyness. In 1995, in an article in PSYCHOLOGY TODAY, I, along with shyness pioneer Philip Zimbardo, Ph.D., summed up 20 years of shyness knowledge and research, concluding that rates are rising. At the same time, I ran a small survey that included five open-ended questions asking the shy to tell us about their experiences.

The thousands of responses we received have spawned a whole new generation of research and insight. In addition to the sheer volume of surveys, my colleague and I were surprised at the depth of the comments, often extending to five or 10 handwritten pages. It was as if we had turned on a spigot, allowing people to release a torrent of emotions. They understood that we were willing to listen. For that reason, perhaps, they were not at all shy about answering. This article represents the first analysis of their responses.

The New View

"My ex-wife picked me to marry her, so getting married wasn't a problem. I didn't want to get divorced, even though she was cheating on me, because I would be back out there trying to socialize. [But] I have a computer job now, and one of my strengths is that I work well alone."

Traditionally, shyness is viewed as an intrapersonal problem, arising within certain individuals as a result of characteristics such as excessive self-consciousness, low self-esteem and anticipation of rejection. The survey responses have shown, however, that shyness is also promoted by outside forces at work in our culture, and perhaps around the globe.

In addition, our research has led us to conclude that there is nothing at all wrong with being shy. Certainly shyness can control people and make them ineffective in classroom, social and business situations. Respondents told us that they feel imprisoned by their shyness. It is this feeling that seems to be at the core of their pain. But ironically, we find that the way to break out of the prison of shyness may be to embrace it thoroughly. There are many steps the shy can take to develop satisfying relationships without violating their basic nature.

The Cynically Shy

"My shyness has caused major problems in my personal/social life. I have a strong hate for most people. I also have quite a superiority complex. I see so much stupidity and ignorance in the world that I feel superior to virtually everyone out there. I'm trying [not to], but it's hard."

Of the many voices of shy individuals we "heard" in response to our survey, one in particular emerged very clearly. Among the new patterns our analysis identified was a group I call the cynically shy. These are people who have been rejected by their peers because of their lack of social skills. They

The Eight Habits of Highly Popular People

By Hara Estroff Marano

If you were ever the last person picked for a team or asked to dance at a party, you've probably despaired that popular people are born with complete self-confidence and impeccable social skills. But over the past 20 years, a large body of research in the social sciences has established that what was once thought the province of manna or magic is now solidly our own doing—or undoing. Great relationships, whether friendships or romances, don't fall out of the heavens on a favored few. They depend on a number of very sophisticated but human-scale social skills. These skills are crucial to developing social confidence and acceptance. And it is now clear that everyone can learn them.

And they should. Recent studies illustrate that having social contact and friends, even animal ones, improves physical health. Social ties seem to impact stress hormones directly, which in turn affect almost every part of our body, including the immune system. They also improve mental health. Having large social networks can help lower stress in times of crisis, alleviate depression and provide emotional support.

Luckily, it's never too late to develop the tools of the socially confident. Research from social scientists around the world, including relationship expert John Gottman, Ph.D., and shyness authority Bernardo Carducci, Ph.D., show that the most popular people follow these steps to social success:

1. Schedule Your Social Life

It is impossible to hone your social skills without investing time in them. Practice makes perfect, even for the socially secure. Accordingly, the well-liked surround themselves with others, getting a rich supply of opportunities to observe interactions and to improve upon their own social behaviors.

You need to do the same. Stop turning down party invitations and start inviting people to visit you at home. Plan outings with close friends or acquaintances you'd like to know better.

2. Think Positive

Insecure people tend to approach others anxiously, feeling they have to prove that they're witty or interesting. But self-assured people expect that others will respond positively—despite the fact that one of the most difficult social tasks is to join an activity that is already in progress.

3. Engage in Social Reconnaissance

Like detectives, the socially competent are highly skilled at information gathering, always scanning the scene for important details to guide their actions. They direct their focus outward, observing others and listening actively.

Socially skilled people are tuned in to people's expression of specific emotions, sensitive to signals that convey such information as what people's interests are, whether they want to be left alone or whether there is room in an activity for another person.

To infer correctly what others must be feeling, the socially confident are also able to identify and label their own experience accurately. That is where many people, particularly men, fall short.

Good conversationalists make comments that are connected to what is said to them and to the social situation. The connectedness of their communication is, in fact, one of its most outstanding features. Aggressive people actually make more attempts to join others in conversation but are less successful at it than the socially adept because they call attention to themselves, rather than finding a way to fit into ongoing group activity. They might throw out a statement that disrupts the conversation, or respond contentiously to a question. They might blurt something about the way they feel, or shift the conversation to something of interest exclusively to themselves.

"You don't have to be interesting. You have to be interested," explains John Gottman, Ph.D., professor of psychology at the University of Washington. "That's how you have conversations."

4. Enter Conversations Gracefully

Timing is everything. After listening and observing on the perimeter of a group they want to join, the socially competent look for an opportunity to step in, knowing it doesn't just happen. It usually appears as a lull in the conversation.

Tuned in to the conversational or activity theme, the deft participant asks a question or elaborates on what someone else has already said. This is not the time to shift the direction of the conversation, unless it comes to a dead halt. Then it might be wise to throw out a question, perhaps something related to events of the day, and, if possible, something tangentially related to the recent discussion. The idea is to use an open-ended question that lets others participate. "Speaking of the election, what does everybody think about so-and-so's decision not to run?"

"People admire the person who is willing to take a risk and throw out a topic for conversation, but you have to make sure it has general appeal," says Bernardo Carducci, Ph.D., director of the Shyness Research Institute at Indiana University Southeast. Then you are in the desirable position of having rescued the group, which confers immediate membership and acceptance. Once the conversation gets moving, it's wise to back off talking and give others a chance. Social bores attempt to dominate a discussion. The socially confident know that the goal is to help the group have a better conversation.

5. Learn to Handle Failure

It is a fact of life that everyone will sometimes be rejected. Rebuffs happen even to popular people. What distinguishes the socially confident from mere mortals is their reaction to rejection. They don't attribute it to internal causes, such as their own unlikability or inability to make friends. They assume it can result from many factors—incompatibility, someone else's bad mood, a misunderstanding. And some conversations are just private.

Self-assured people become resilient, using the feedback they get to shape another go at acceptance. Studies show that when faced with failure, those who are well-liked turn a negative response into a counterproposal. They say things like, "Well, can we make a date for next week instead?" Or they move onto another group in the expectation that not every conversation is closed. (continued)

And should they reject others' bids to join with them, they do it in a polite and positive way. They invariably offer a reason or counter with an alternative idea: "I would love to talk with you later."

6. Take Hold of Your Emotions

Social situations are incredibly complex and dynamic. One has to pay attention to all kinds of verbal and nonverbal cues, such as facial expression and voice tone, interpret their meaning accurately, decide on the best response for the scenario, and then carry out that response—all in a matter of microseconds. No one can pay attention to or correctly interpret what is going on, let alone act skillfully, without a reasonable degree of control over their own emotional states, especially negative emotions such as anger, fear, anxiety—the emotions that usually arise in situations of conflict or uncertainty.

Recently, studies have found that people who are the most well-liked also have a firm handle on their emotions. It isn't that they internalize all their negative feelings. Instead, they shift attention away from distressing stimuli toward positive aspects of a situation. In other words, they have excellent coping skills. Otherwise, they become overly reactive to the negative emotions of others and may resort to aggression or withdraw from social contact.

7. Defuse Disagreements

Since conflict is inevitable, coping with confrontations is one of the most critical of social skills. It's not the degree of conflict that sinks relationships, but the ways people resolve it. Disagreements, if handled well, can help people know themselves better, improve language skills, gain valuable information and cement their relationships.

Instead of fighting fire with fire, socially confident people stop conflict from escalating; they apologize, propose a joint activity, make a peace offering of some kind, or negotiate. And sometimes they just change the subject. That doesn't mean that they yield to another's demands. Extreme submissiveness violates the equality basic to healthy relationships—and a sense of self-worth.

As people gain social competence, they try to accommodate the needs of both parties. Managing conflict without aggression requires listening, communicating—arguing, persuading—taking the perspective of others, controlling negative emotions, and problem-solving. Researchers have found that when people explain their point of view in an argument, they are in essence making a conciliatory move. That almost invariably opens the door for a partner to offer a suggestion that ends the standoff.

8. Laugh A Little

Humor is the single most prized social skill, the fast track to being liked—at all ages. Humor works even in threatening situations because it defuses negativity. There's no recipe for creating a sense of humor. But even in your darkest moments, try to see the lighter side of a situation.

If you need more help, call the American Psychological Association at 1-800-964-2000 for a referral to a therapist near you. For further resources check http://www.shyness.com/.

---

do not feel connected to others—and they are angry about it. They feel a sense of alienation. And like the so-called trench coat mafia in Littleton, Colorado, they adapt a stance of superiority as they drift away from others.

Their isolation discourages them from having a sense of empathy, and this leads them to dehumanize others and take revenge against them. This process is the same one used by the military to train young boys to kill. The difference is, the military is now in your house, on your TV, in your video games.

Inside the Shy Mind

"As we talked, I felt uneasy. I worried about how I looked, what I said, how I said what I said, and so forth. Her compliments made me uncomfortable."

One of the solutions to shyness is a greater understanding of its internal dynamics. It is important to note that a critical feature of shyness is a slowness to warm up. Shy people simply require extra time to adjust to novel or stressful situations, including even everyday conversations and social gatherings.

They also need more time to master the developmental hurdles of life. The good news is that shy people eventually achieve everything that everyone else does—they date, marry, have children. The bad news is, it takes them a little longer.

An unfortunate consequence of the shy being on this delayed schedule is that they lack social support through many important life experiences. When they start dating and want to talk about first-date jitters, for example, their peers will be talking about weddings. As a result, the shy may need to take an especially active role in finding others who are in their situation. One way is to build social support by starting groups of like-minded people. Another is to seek out existing groups of shy people, perhaps via the Internet. While technology often works against the shy, it can also lend them an unexpected helping hand.

Our research reveals the fact that the shy tend to make unrealistic social comparisons. In a room full of others, their attention is usually drawn to the most socially outstanding person, the life of the party—against whom they compare themselves, unfavorably, of course. This is just a preemptive strike. Typically, they compound the negative self-appraisal by attributing their own comparatively poor performance to enduring and unchangeable internal characteristics—"I was born shy" or "I don't have the gift of gab." Such attributions only heighten self-consciousness and inhibit performance.

The shy are prone to such errors of attribution because they believe that they are always being evaluated by others. Self-consciously focused on their own shortcomings, they fail to look around and notice that most people are just like them—listeners, not social standouts. Our surveys show that 48% of people are shy. So not only are the shy not alone, they probably have plenty of company at any social function.

The No. 1 problem area for the shy is starting a relationship. Fifty-eight percent told us they have problems with introductions; they go to a party but nothing happens. Forty percent said their problem was social; they had trouble developing friendships. Only seven percent of the shy have a problem with intimacy. If you get into an intimate relationship, shyness no longer seems to be a problem. Unfortunately, it's hard to get there.

The New Cultural Climate

It is no secret that certain technological advances—the Internet, e-mail, cell phones—are changing the conditions of the culture we live in, speeding it up and intensifying its complexity. This phenomenon, dubbed hyperculture, has trickled down to alter the nature of day-to-day interactions, with negative consequences for the shy. In this cultural climate, we lose patience quickly because we've grown accustomed to things happening faster and faster. We lose tolerance for those who need time to warm up. Those who are not quick and intense get passed by. The shy are bellwethers of this change: They are the first to feel its effects. And so it's not surprising that hyperculture is actually exacerbating shyness, in both incidence and degree.

Another effect of hyperculture is what I call identity intensity. Our society is not only getting faster, it is getting louder and brighter. It takes an increasingly powerful personality to be recognized. We see this in the emergence of shock jocks like Howard Stern and outrageous characters like Dennis Rodman. People have to call attention to themselves in ways that are more and more extreme just to be noticed at all. That, of course, puts the shy at a further disadvantage.

We are also undergoing "interpersonal disenfranchisement." Simply put, we are disconnecting from one another. Increasingly, we deal with the hyperculture cacophony by cocooning—commuting home with headphones on while working on our laptops. We go from our cubicle to the car to our gated community, maintaining contact with only a small circle of friends and family. As other people become just e-mail addresses or faceless voices at the other end of electronic transactions, it becomes easier and easier to mistreat and disrespect them. The cost of such disconnection is a day-to-day loss of civility and an increase in rudeness. And, again, the shy pay. They are the first to be excluded, bullied or treated in a hostile manner.

As we approach the limits of our ability to deal with the complexities of our lives, we begin to experience a state of anxiety. We either approach or avoid. And, indeed, we are seeing both phenomena—a polarization of behavior in which we see increases in both aggression, marked by a general loss of manners that has been widely observed, and in withdrawal, one form of which is shyness. Surveys we have conducted reliably show that over the last decade and a half, the incidence of shyness has risen from 40% to 48%.

So it is no accident that the pharmaceutical industry has chosen this cultural moment to introduce the antidepressant Paxil as a treatment for social phobia. Paxil is touted as a cure for being "allergic to people." One of the effects of hyperculture is to make people impatient for anything but a pill that instantly reduces their anxiety level.

The use of Paxil, however, operates against self-awareness. It makes shyness into a medical or psychiatric problem, which it has never been. It essentially labels as pathology what is a personality trait. I think it is a mistake for doctors to hand out a physiological remedy when we know that there are cognitive elements operating within individuals, communication difficulties existing between individuals, and major forces residing outside of individuals that are making it difficult for people to interact.

It is much easier for the shy to take a pill, doctors figure, than for them to take the time to adjust to their cautious tendencies, modify faulty social comparisons or learn to be more civil to others. The promise of Paxil does not include teaching the shy to develop the small talk skills they so desperately need.

Strategies of the Shy

"I have tried to overcome my shyness by being around people as much as possible and getting involved in the conversation; however, after a few seconds, I become quiet. I have a problem keeping conversation flowing."

In our survey, we asked people what they do to cope with their shyness. What we found surprised us. The shy put a lot of effort into overcoming their shyness, but the strategies they use are largely ineffective, sometimes even counterproductive. Occasionally their solutions are potentially dangerous.

Ninety-one percent of shy respondents said they had made at least some effort to overcome their shyness. By far, the top technique they employ is forced extroversion. Sixty-seven percent of them said they make themselves go to parties, bars, dances, the mall—places that will put them in proximity to others. That is good. But unfortunately, they expect the others to do all the work, to approach them and draw them out of their isolation. Simply showing up is not enough. Not only is it ineffective, it cedes control of interactions to others.

But it exemplifies the mistaken expectations the shy often have about social life. Hand in hand with the expectation that others will approach them is their sense of perfectionism. The shy believe that anything they say has to come out perfect, sterling, supremely witty, as if everyday life is some kind of sitcom. They believe that everybody is watching and judging them—a special kind of narcissism.

> **Once the shy learn to focus more on the lives of other people, shyness no longer controls them.**

Their second most popular strategy is self-induced cognitive modification: thinking happy thoughts, or the "Stuart Smalley Effect"—remember the sketch from *Saturday Night Live?* "I'm

> # Shy people tend either to reveal information about themselves too quickly, or hold back and move too slowly.

good enough, I'm smart enough, and, doggone it, people like me." Twenty-two percent of the shy try to talk themselves into not being shy. But just talking to yourself doesn't work. You have to know how to talk to other people. And you have to be around other people. The shy seldom combine extroversion with cognitive modification.

Fifteen percent of the shy turn to self-help books and seminars, which is great. But not enough people do it.

And about 12 % of the shy turn to what I call liquid extroversion. They are a distinct population of people, who, often beginning in adolescence, ingest drugs or alcohol to deal with their shyness. They self-medicate as a social lubricant, to give them courage. And while it may remove inhibitions, it doesn't provide them with what they desperately need—actual social skills, knowledge about how to be with others. Further, drinking interferes with their cognitive functioning.

Liquid extroversion poses the great danger of overconsumption of alcohol. Indeed, we have found in separate studies that a significant proportion of problem drinkers in the general population are shy.

But "shy alcoholics" tell us they do not like having to drink to perform better; they feel uneasy and lack confidence in their true selves. They begin to believe that people will like them only if they are outgoing, not the way they really are. Interestingly, the largest program for problem drinkers, Alcoholics Anonymous, works squarely against shy people. Whereas the shy are slow to warm up, AA asks people to stand up right away, to be highly visible, to immediately disclose highly personal information. It is my belief that there needs to be an AA for the shy, a program that takes into consideration the nature and dynamics of shyness. A meeting might, for example, begin by having a leader speak for the first 45 minutes while people get comfortable, followed by a break in which the leader is available to answer questions. That then paves the way for a general question-and-answer period.

Cyberbonding

"I can be anyone I want to be on the Internet and yet mostly be myself, because I know I will never meet these people I'm talking with and can close out if I get uncomfortable."

"I think the Internet hinders people in overcoming their shyness. You can talk to someone but you don't have to actually interact with them. You can sit in your room and not REALLY socialize."

Another strategy of the shy is electronic extroversion. The Net is a great social facilitator. It enables people to reach out to many others and join in at their own speed, perhaps observing in a chat room before participating. Still, Internet interaction requires less effort than face-to-face interaction, so it may increase their frustration and cause difficulties in real-life situations where social skills are not only required, but born and learned.

We know that people start out using the Internet for informational purposes, then progress to use that is social in nature, such as entering chat rooms; some then progress to personal use, talking about more intimate topics and disclosing information about themselves. The danger of electronic extroversion is that anonymity makes it easy for the shy to misrepresent themselves and to deceive others, violating the trust that is the foundation of social life.

And talk about disconnecting. The irony of a World Wide Web packed with endless amounts of information is that it can also be isolating. As individuals head to their own favorite bookmarked sites, they cut out all the disagreement of the world and reinforce their own narrow perspective, potentially leading to alienation, disenfranchisement and intolerance for people who are different.

In addition, the shy are more vulnerable to instant intimacy because of their lack of social know-how. Normally, relationships progress by way of a reasonably paced flow of self-disclosure that is reciprocal in nature. A disclosure process that moves too quickly—and computer anonymity removes the stigma of getting sexually explicit—doesn't just destroy

SHYNESS SURVEY

- 64% of shy individuals view their shyness as a result of external factors beyond their control, such as early family experiences, overprotective parents or peer victimization.

- 24% attribute shyness to internal factors within their control, such as intrapersonal difficulties, like low self-esteem and high self-consciousness, or interpersonal difficulties, like poor social skills and dating difficulties.

- 62% experience feelings of shyness daily.

- 82% report shyness as an undesirable experience.

- **Types of Individuals who make the shy feel shy:**

75% strangers
71% persons of the opposite sex, in a group
65% persons of the opposite sex, one-on-one
56% persons of the same sex, in a group
45% relatives, other than immediate family
38% persons of the same sex, one-on-one
22% their parents
20% siblings

- 46% believe their shyness can be overcome.

- 7.2% do not believe their shyness can be overcome.

- 85% are willing to work seriously at overcoming shyness.

courtship; it is a reliable sign of maladjustment. Shy people tend either to reveal information about themselves too quickly, or hold back and move too slowly.

Like most cultural influences, the Internet is neither devil nor angel. It's a social tool that works in different ways, depending on how it's used.

The Solution to Shyness

"I was very shy as a kid. Every situation scared me if it required interacting with others. After high school and into college, I became much less shy. I consciously made each interaction an exercise in overcoming shyness. Just talking to people I didn't know, getting a part-time job, volunteering. I had always been afraid to sing in front of people, but now I sing all the time. That's a big deal to me."

Every shy person believes that shyness is a problem located exclusively within the self. But our work suggests that the solution to shyness lies outside the self. To break free of the prison of shyness, you must stop dwelling on your own insecurities and become more aware of the people around you.

Through our survey, we have identified a group of people we call the successfully shy. Essentially, they recognize that they are shy. They develop an understanding of the nature and dynamics of shyness, its impact on the body, on cognitive processes and on behavior. And they take action based on that self-awareness. The successfully shy overcome their social anxiety by letting go of their self-consciousness, that inward focus of attention on the things they can't do well (like tell a joke). They accept that they aren't great at small talk or that they get so nervous in social situations that they can't draw on what is inside their mind. Or that they are paying so much attention to their feelings that they don't pay full attention to the person they're talking to. In place of self-consciousness, they substitute self-awareness. Rather than becoming anxious about their silence in a conversation, they plan ahead of time to have something to say, or rehearse asking questions. They

arrive early at parties to feel comfortable in their new setting. By contrast, less successful shy people arrive late in an effort to blend in.

The fact is, these are the same kinds of strategies that non-shy people employ. Many of them develop a repertoire of opening gambits for conversation. When among others, they engage in social reconnaissance—they wait to gather information about speakers and a discussion before jumping in.

The successfully shy also take steps at the transpersonal level, getting involved in the lives of others. They start small, making sure their day-to-day exchanges involve contact with other people. When they pick up a newspaper, for instance, they don't just put their money on the counter. They focus on the seller, thanking him or her for the service. This creates a social environment favorable to positive interactions. On a larger scale, I encourage volunteering. Once the shy are more outwardly focused on the lives of other people, shyness no longer controls them.

The successfully shy don't change who they are. They change the way they think and the actions they make. There is nothing wrong with being shy. In fact, I have come to believe that what our society needs is not less shyness but a little more.

Bernardo Carducci, Ph.D., is the director of the Shyness Research Institute at Indiana University Southeast. His last article for Psychology Today, *also on shyness, appeared in the December 1995 issue.*

READ MORE ABOUT IT

Shyness: A Bold New Approach, Bernardo J. Carducci, Ph.D. (HarperCollins, 1999)

The Shy Child, Philip G. Zimbardo, Ph.D., Shirley L. Radl (ISHK Book Service, 1999)

Linking up online

Is the Internet enhancing interpersonal connections or leading to greater social isolation?

BY REBECCA A. CLAY

Leslie, a graduate student in psychology at a Midwestern university, couldn't find anyone she was interested in dating. Then she placed a personal ad on a Web site for singles. Not long after, she received an e-mail that changed her life. Although she and her correspondent had completely different backgrounds—he didn't have a college degree, for instance—they quickly discovered they shared interests and values.

Today they're in love. "If you looked at how different our backgrounds were, nobody would ever have matched us up," says Leslie. "Even though we lived in the same town, we never would have met except through the Internet."

As Leslie's story illustrates, e-mail and other Internet technologies are changing friendship and romance, both online and in the real world. But while Leslie's story has a happy ending, others do not. Some confront disappointment when they come face to face with online correspondents; others use cyber-affairs to avoid working through problems with their real-life partners.

No one knows for sure what the long-term effects of forming and developing Internet relationships will be. Does using this technology ultimately enhance interpersonal connection or lead to greater social

isolation? And is online sexuality pathological or healthy?

With the number of Americans online growing every day, these questions have become urgent.

"As we integrate Internet use into our culture, we've got to maximize its potential benefits and mitigate any possible adverse consequences," says Russ Newman, PhD, JD, executive director for professional practice at APA. "If we just proceed blindly down the Internet road, we could find ourselves in 10 or 20 years having radically changed the way people relate to each other and realizing we're stuck with those changes. As experts in behavior and relationships, psychologists have an important role to play in making sure that doesn't happen."

Isolation or connection?

Psychologists are already hard at work studying the Internet's effects. So far, their findings have been mixed.

The first study to specifically examine the Internet's impact on emotional well-being was the widely publicized 1998 study by Robert Kraut, PhD, Sara Kiesler, PhD, and colleagues at Carnegie Mellon University's Human Computer Interaction Institute. Their "HomeNet" project focused on 169 individuals in 93 Pittsburgh families recruited from schools and community

groups as they began using the Internet. Logging programs recorded Internet use by individual family members, who assessed their own well-being and social involvement at the project's beginning, one year later and two years later.

To the researchers' surprise, they discovered that greater use of the Internet resulted in small but statistically significant increases in depression and loneliness and decreases in social engagement. Internet users, the researchers hypothesized in their *American Psychologist* report (No. 53, p. 1017–1031), were replacing the intimate, supportive relationships of real life with shallower relationships online.

The findings set off a firestorm. Critics pointed to the study's lack of random selection and a control group, which the researchers say they couldn't afford. Others noted the participants had a high degree of social connectedness to begin with and simply moved closer to the mean. Not so, say the researchers. Such an explanation, they say, doesn't address the fact that individuals with high use experienced greater declines and that those who were depressed or lonely didn't start using the Internet more.

A recent study conducted on behalf of the Stanford Institute for the Quantitative Study of Society seems to corroborate the "HomeNet" findings, although the project focused on the Internet's societal rather than psychological impact.

In the study, a company called Inter-Survey provided Internet access and equipment that allows users to go online via their televisions to a nationally representative sample of 2,689 households containing both Internet users and nonusers. An Internet-based survey revealed that 55 percent of the 4,113 adults in these households used the Internet. Of these, about a third spent more than five hours a week online.

About a quarter of these regular Internet users reported that their time online had reduced the amount of time they spent interacting with family and friends in person and on the phone. Eight percent said they spent less time attending social events.

Like the Carnegie Mellon study, these preliminary results have attracted controversy. Some critics point to research that conflicts with these negative findings. Others note that Internet users may simply find online relationships more rewarding than those available in their offline lives. Even one of the study's authors admits that Internet use had some positive benefits, with the most enthusiastic Internet users also reporting less time watching television and caught in traffic.

"There's a big gap in the research," says Linda A. Jackson, PhD, a psychology professor at Michigan State University in East Lansing.

Although the Carnegie Mellon study is the only one that has systematically tracked Internet use via computer-logging, she says, several surveys and ethnographic studies have suggested that Internet use actually enhances people's well-being and social contacts.

To help answer the question, Jackson is now trying to replicate the HomeNet study. With funding from the National Science Foundation, she is engaged in a pilot study that will use computer-logging to track the psychosocial effects of 18 months of Internet use on 45 African-American families and 45 white families.

Other researchers already have evidence that counters what they call the "apocalyptic" claims the HomeNet study and similar research have aroused.

Research scientist Katelyn Y.A. McKenna, PhD, and professor John A. Bargh, PhD, of New York University's psychology department compare the Internet's bad press to the fear of new technology that once prompted people to resist telephones in the belief that people could eavesdrop on their homes even with the phone on the hook.

McKenna and Bargh have conducted research that provides a very different picture of the Internet's impact on relationships. In a manuscript submitted for publication, they describe a recent study that found people were indeed using the Internet to form close relationships. Using data from 568 surveys from participants in randomly selected news groups, they discovered that the Internet provided a safe way for socially anxious and lonely people to form and maintain relationships. Of critical importance was their ability to express what they considered their real selves online.

These are not just virtual relationships, the researchers emphasize. Fifty-four percent of respondents later met their Internet friends face to face. Sixty-three percent had talked on the phone. And these relationships lasted. A two-year follow-up study revealed that 57 percent of the relationships formed online had not only continued but actually increased in intimacy.

Romantic relationships fared particularly well, says McKenna. Seventy percent of the romantic relationships formed online still existed at the two-year follow-up. Some participants had even married. These results are in marked contrast to the fate of couples who meet in a more traditional manner, says McKenna, pointing to a study that found that more than half of romantic relationships dissolve after two years.

"Online relationships begin on the basis of similar interests and values," says McKenna. "They allow people to bypass physical appearance and other

'gating' mechanisms that might prevent them from even giving the other person the time of day in real life."

Arguing that the Carnegie Mellon team's results held true only for the teen-agers in the group, McKenna and Bargh emphasize the importance of not making blanket statements.

"For some people, the Internet can be a great medium for making connections, widening their social circles and enriching their lives," says McKenna, citing single working mothers and the elderly as examples. "For others, it may be problematic."

For communications expert Judee K. Burgoon, PhD, conflicting findings like these underline the fact that the Internet's effect on relationships isn't inherently good or bad.

"You can't give a simple answer to that question," says Burgoon, a professor of communication and family studies at the University of Arizona in Tucson. "It all depends on how people are using the technology."

Take e-mail, she says. The lack of facial and verbal cues, for instance, can create greater intimacy or lead to misunderstandings. E-mail can facilitate relationships by allowing people to take the time to say what they mean and to communicate without the intrusion of day-to-day tensions and grievances. It can also encourage people to idealize their correspondent and lose sight of the real person behind the e-mail address. Of course, says Burgoon, the people you meet online may not even be who you think they are. In one online game, a computer program posing as "Julia" attracted the intense and persistent attentions of several male participants.

"We're only beginning to study the Internet," says Burgoon. "As the technology changes, we'll come to different conclusions than we had even two years ago."

Obsession or exploration?

That's certainly true when it comes to discussions of online sexuality, says Alvin Cooper, PhD, clinical director of the San Jose Marital and Sexuality Centre in the heart of Silicon Valley.

"We're only beginning to study the Internet. As the technology changes, we'll come to different conclusions than we had even two years ago."

Judee K. Burgoon
University of Arizona, Tucson

Cooper used to believe the hype about the dangers of online sexuality. Once he started investigating, however, he found a much more nuanced picture of how the Internet actually affects the 20 percent of users who now go online for sexual purposes. While the Internet can destroy lives, he says, it also provides a powerful tool for enhancing users' sexual relationships.

As Cooper describes in *Professional Psychology* (Vol. 30, No. 2, p. 154–164), he developed an extensive questionnaire and put an announcement on an online news site to recruit participants who had used the Internet for sexual pursuits at least once. The 9,177 people who responded revealed that the vast majority used pornography, sexual chat rooms and other online sexual activities the same way they used *Baywatch*—as casual recreation. Only the 8 percent of users who spent more than 11 hours a week on online sexuality reported that these ac-

tivities caused psychological distress and interfered with other parts of their lives.

The Internet may also pose risks to relationships that wouldn't otherwise have had problems except for what Cooper calls the "triple A" of the Internet: access, affordability and anonymity. A husband having a fight with his wife, for instance, probably won't take the trouble to punish his wife by going out to a bar to pick up a woman. Going into the other room, logging on and acting out sexual scenarios with virtual partners, however, is much easier.

But the "triple A" has plenty of positive effects, Cooper emphasizes. Users can go online to safely explore their fantasies or try new sexual experiences. Sexually disenfranchised groups, such as gays, lesbians and transgendered individuals, can create virtual communities. People with health problems, sexual dysfunction or histories of rape or abuse can find support from others. And many in what Cooper calls our "sexually illiterate" society can benefit from the sex information available online.

"After all, if you want to learn how to bake a cake, you can ask your mother or a neighbor," he says. "If you want to learn about oral sex, who are you going to ask?"

The future

The Internet has already revolutionized sexual relationships, says Cooper, citing cyber-affairs and virtual sex as

examples. In just a few years, he predicts, people will use specialized equipment to have real sex over the Internet. Instead of simply masturbating as they type, he says, people will be able to send and receive actual sexual sensations.

Jim Blascovich, PhD, professor of psychology at the University of California at Santa Barbara, is one of the people who may help make such scenarios possible. In the Research Center for Virtual Environments and Behavior he co-founded at the university, he and his colleagues have created an immersive virtual environment that allows people to "be" in the same room no matter where they're located in the real world. Now he's trying to represent people's images three dimensionally.

The technology will have tremendous implications for online relationships, says Blascovich. Instead of talking by phone, for instance, people could come together in a virtual room and be able to see each other's non-verbal reactions.

"I can only speculate at this point, but this technology will have a major impact," says Blascovich, adding that this capability is only a few years away. "Whatever you can do on the Internet, for good or for bad, will be magnified a thousandfold by immersive virtual environments."

Rebecca A. Clay is a writer in Washington, D.C.

Isn't She Lovely?

If you think that physical appeal is strictly a matter of personal taste and cultural bias, think again. Who you find attractive, say psychobiologists, is largely dictated by evolutionary needs and hardwired into your brain

BY BRAD LEMLEY

She's cute, no question. Symmetrical features, flawless skin, looks to be 22 years old—entering any meat-market bar, a woman lucky enough to have this face would turn enough heads to stir a breeze. But when Victor Johnston points and clicks, the face on his computer screen morphs into what a mesmerized physicist might call a discontinuous state of superheated, crystallized beauty. "You can see it. It's just so extraordinary," says Johnston, a professor of biopsychology at New Mexico State University who sounds a little in love with his creation.

The transformation from pretty woman to knee-weakening babe is all the more amazing because the changes wrought by Johnston's software are, objectively speaking, quite subtle. He created the original face by digitally averaging 16 randomly selected female Caucasian faces. The morphing program then exaggerated the ways in which female faces differ from male faces, creating, in human-beauty-science parlance, a "hyperfemale." The eyes grew a bit larger, the nose narrowed slightly, the lips plumped, and the jaw contracted. These are shifts of just a few millimeters, but experiments in this country and Scotland are suggesting that both males and females find "feminized" versions of averaged faces more beautiful.

Johnston hatched this little movie as part of his ongoing study into why human beings find some people attractive and others homely. He may not have any rock-solid answers yet, but he is far from alone in attempting to apply scientific inquiry to so ambiguous a subject. Around the world, researchers are marching into territory formerly staked out by poets, painters, fashion mavens, and casting directors, aiming to uncover the underpinnings of human attractiveness.

The research results so far are surprising—and humbling. Numerous studies indicate that human beauty may not be simply in the eye of the beholder or an arbitrary cultural artifact. It may be an ancient, hardwired, universal, and potent behavior-driver, on a par with hunger or pain, wrought through eons of evolution that rewarded reproductive winners and killed off losers. If beauty is not truth, it may be health and fertility: Halle Berry's flawless skin may rivet moviegoers because, at some deep level, it persuades us that she is parasite-free and consequently good mating material. Acquired, individual preferences factor in, but research increasingly indicates that their influence is much smaller than many of us would care to know. While romantic writers blather about the transcendence of beauty, Elizabethan poet Edmund Spenser more than 400 years ago pegged the emerging scientific thesis: "Beauty is the bait which with delight allures man to enlarge his kind."

Implications of human-beauty research range from the practical—providing cosmetic surgeons with pretty-people templates—to the political and philosophical. Landmark studies show that attractive males and females not only garner more attention from the opposite sex, they also get more affection from their mothers, more money at work, more votes from the electorate, more leniency from judges, and are generally regarded as more kind, competent, healthy, confident, and intelligent than their big-nosed, weak-chinned counterparts. (Beauty is considered such a valuable trait by some that one entrepreneur recently put up a Web site offering to auction off the unfertilized ova of models.)

Human attractiveness research is a relatively young and certainly contentious field—the allure of hyperfemales, for example, is still hotly debated—but those on its front lines agree on one point: We won't conquer "looks-ism" until we understand its source. As psychologist Nancy Etcoff, author of the 1999 book *Survival of the Prettiest*, puts it: "The idea that beauty is unimportant or a cultural construct is the real beauty myth. We have to understand beauty, or we will always be enslaved by it."

THE MODERN ERA OF BEAUTY STUDIES got a big push 20 years ago with an awkward question in a small, airless room at Louisiana State University in

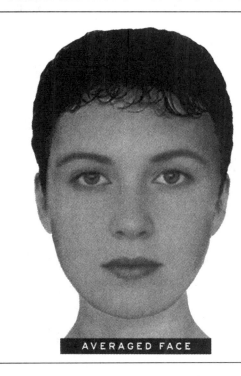

'Both sexes find the feminized picture attractive, but only males react emotionally'

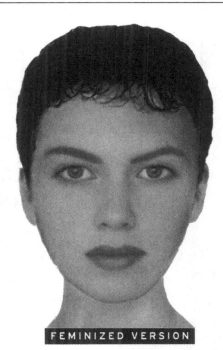

AVERAGED FACE

FEMINIZED VERSION

COURTESY VICTOR JOHNSTON

BiosycholoIgist Johnston creates the face on the left by digitally morphing 16 female Caucasian faces. Then he warped it by subtly exaggerating the ways in which female faces differ from males faces, making the brows more arched, the eyes bigger, the nose and jaw narrower, and the lips fuller. Both male and female students judged the resulting face, right, as more attractive. In Johnston's view, the experiment confirms that the hyperfemale embodies even more allure because of her promise of extraordinary fertility.

Baton Rouge. Psychology graduate student Judith Langlois was defending her doctoral dissertation—a study of how preschool children form and keep friendships—when a professor asked whether she had factored the kids' facial attractiveness into her conclusions. "I thought the question was way off the mark," she recalls. "It might matter for college students, but little kids?" After stammering out a noncommittal answer—and passing the examination—she resolved to dig deeper, aiming to determine the age at which human beings could perceive physical attractiveness.

Langlois, who had joined the faculty at the University of Texas at Austin, devised a series of experiments. In one, she had adults rate photos of human faces on a spectrum from attractive to unattractive. Then she projected pairs of high- and low-rated faces in front of 6-month-old infants. "The result was straightforward and unambiguous," she declares. "The babies looked longer at the attractive faces, regardless of the gender, race, or age of the face." Studies with babies as young as 2 months old yielded similar results. "At 2 months, these babies hadn't been reading *Vogue* magazine," Langlois observes dryly.

Her search for the source of babies' precocious beauty-detection led her all the way back to nineteenth-century research conducted by Sir Francis Galton, an English dilettante scientist and cousin of Charles Darwin. In the late 1870s, Galton created crude, blurry composite faces by melding mug-shot photographs of various social subgroups, aiming to prove that each group had an archetypal face. While that hypothesis fizzled—the average criminal looked rather like the average vegetarian—Galton was shocked to discover that these averaged faces were better looking than nearly all of the individuals they comprised. Langlois replicated Galton's study, using software to form digitally averaged faces that were later judged by 300 people to be more attractive than most of the faces used to create them.

Human beings may be born "cognitive averagers," theorizes Langlois. "Even very young infants have seen thousands of faces and may have already constructed an average from them that they use for comparison."

Racial preferences bolster the idea, say some scientists. History shows that almost universally when one race first comes into contact with another, they mutually regard each other as homely, if not freakish. Etcoff relates that a delegation of Japanese samurai visiting the United States in 1860 observed that Western women had "dogs' eyes," which they found "disheartening." Early Western visitors to Japan thought the natives' epicanthic folds made the eyes appear sleepy and small. In each case, Etcoff surmises, the unfamiliar race most likely veered from the internal, averaged ideal.

But why would cognitive averaging have evolved? Evolutionary biology holds that in any given population, extreme characteristics tend to fall away in favor of average ones. Birds with unusually long or short wings die more often in storms. Human babies who are born larger or smaller than average are less likely to survive. The ability to form an average-mate template would have conveyed a singular survival advantage.

Inclination toward the average is called koinophilia, from the Greek words *koinos,* meaning "usual," and *philos,* meaning "love." To Langlois, humans are clearly koinophiles. The remaining question is whether our good-mate template is acquired or innate. To help solve the mystery, Langlois's doctoral student Lisa Kalakanis has presented babies who are just 15 minutes old with paired images of attractive and homely faces. "We're just starting to evaluate that data," says Langlois.

But koinophilia isn't the only—or even supreme—criterion for beauty that evolution has promoted, other scientists argue. An innate yearning for symmetry is a major boon, contend biologists Anders Moller and Randy Thornhill, as asymmetry can signal malnutrition, disease, or bad genes. The two have found that asymmetrical animals, ranging from barn swallows to lions, have fewer offspring and shorter lives. Evolution would also logically instill an age preference. Human female fertility peaks in the early 20s, and so do assessments of female attractiveness. Between 1953 and 1990, the average age of *Playboy* centerfold models—who are presumably selected solely for sexual appeal—was 21.3 years. Similarly, Johnston has found that the beauty of a Japanese female face is judged to be at its peak when its perceived age is 22.4 years. Because men are fertile throughout most of their adult lives, their attractiveness ratings—while dropping as they age past their late 20s—remain relatively higher as their perceived age increases. As Johnston puts it, "Our feelings of beauty are exceptionally well tuned to the age of maximum fertility."

STILL, A SPECIES CAN STAGNATE WITHOUT some novelty When competition for mates is intense, some extreme traits might help to rivet a roving eye. "A male peacock is saying, 'Look at me, I have this big tail. I couldn't grow a tail this big if I had parasites,'" says Johnston. "Even if the trait is detrimental to survival, the benefit in additional offspring brought about by attracting females can more than compensate for the decrease in longevity" The concept seems applicable to humans, too, because it helps to resolve a nagging flaw in average-face studies. In many of them, "there were always a few individual faces in the population that were deemed even prettier than the average," says Etcoff. "If average were always best, how could that be?"

Psychologist David Perrett of the University of St. Andrews in Scotland aimed to find out by creating two averaged faces—one from a group of women rated attractive and another from men so judged. He then compared those faces with averaged faces constructed from a larger, random set of images. The composites of the beautiful people were rated more appealing than those made from the larger, random population. More surprising, when Perrett exaggerated the ways in which the prettiest fe-

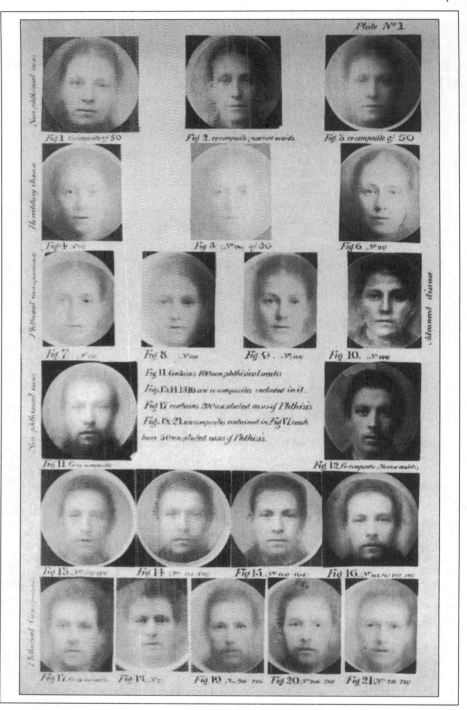

Francis Galton figured that photographically melding the faces of criminals, consumptives, and so on would yield an archetypal image for each group. But, he concluded, the resulting faces were not categorically unique. He also observed that these averaged faces were surprisingly better looking than most of humanity.

male composite differed from the average female composite, the resulting face was judged to be even more attractive.

"It turned out that the way an attractive female face differs from an average one is related to femininity," says Perrett. "For example, female eyebrows are more arched than males'. Exaggerating that difference from the average increases

femininity," and, in tandem, the attractiveness rating. In the traffic-stopping female face created for this experiment, 200 facial reference points all changed in the direction of hyperfemininity: larger eyes, a smaller nose, plumper lips, a narrower jaw, and a smaller chin.

"All faces go through a metamorphosis at puberty," observes Johnston. "In

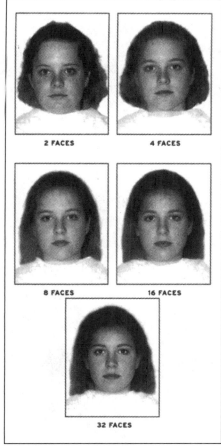

2 FACES   4 FACES

8 FACES   16 FACES

32 FACES

COURTESY JUDITH LANGLOIS

Is deviation from the average more appealing than just plain averageness? Definitely not, declares researcher Judith Langlois. Indeed, she argues, the more faces you mate together, the more beautiful the image becomes because it literally becomes *more* average. "Averaging two faces is not enough to make an attractive face," she says. "But when you get up to 32 faces, you end up with a face that is pretty darned attractive." As proof of her premise, she offers the above series of composite faces.

males, testosterone lengthens the jaw. In females, estrogen makes the hips, breasts, and lips swell." So large lips, breasts, and hips combined with a small jaw "are all telling you that I have an abundant supply of estrogen, so I am a fertile female." Like the peacock, whose huge tail is a mating advantage but a practical hindrance, "a small jaw may not, in fact, be as efficient for eating," Johnston says. But it seems attractive because it emphasizes *la différence;* whatever survival disadvantage comes along with a small jaw is more than made up for by the chance to produce more babies, so the trait succeeds.

Along with his morphing program, Johnston approached the hyperfemale hypothesis through another route. Start-

As the world becomes more egalitarian, beauty becomes more inclusive

ing with 16 computer-generated random female Caucasian faces, he had visitors to his Web site rate the attractiveness of each face on a scale of one to nine. A second generation of faces was then computed by selecting, crossing, and mutating the first generation in proportion to beauty ratings. After 10,000 people from around the world took part in this merciless business, the empirically derived fairest-of-them-all was born. Facial measurements confirm that she is decidedly hyperfemale. While we might say she is beautiful, Johnston more accurately notes that the face displays "maximum fertility cues."

Johnston's findings have set off a ruckus among beauty scientists. In a paper titled "Attractive Faces Really Are Only Average," Langlois and three other researchers blast the notion that a deviation from the average—what they term "facial extremes"—explains attractiveness better than averageness does. The findings of Perrett and his team, she says, are "artifacts of their methodology," because they used a "forced-choice" scenario that prevented subjects from judging faces as equally attractive. "We did the same kind of test, but gave people a rating scale of one to five," says Langlois. "When you do it that way, there is no significant difference—people would tell us that, basically, the two faces looked like twins." Langlois argues that if extremes create beauty, "then people with micro-jaws or hydrocephalic eyes would be seen as the most beautiful, when, in fact, eyes that are too big for a head make that head unattractive."

But for Etcoff, circumstantial evidence for the allure of some degree of hyperfemininity is substantial. "Female makeup is all about exaggerating the feminine. Eye makeup makes the brow thinner, which makes it look farther from the eye," which, she says, is a classic difference between male and female faces. From high hair (which skews facial proportions in a feminine direction, moving up the center of gravity) to collagen in lips to silicone in breasts, women instinctively exaggerate secon-

dary female sex characteristics to increase their allure. "Langlois is simply wrong," declares Johnston. In one of his studies, published last year in *Psychophysiology,* both male and female subjects rated feminized pictures as more attractive. Further, male subjects attached to electrical-brain-activity monitors showed a greater response in the P3 component, a measure of emotional intensity. "That is, although both sexes know what is attractive, only the males exhibit an emotional response to the feminized picture," Johnston says.

AND WHAT ABOUT MALE ATTRACTIVENESS? IT stands to reason that if men salivate for hyperfemales, women should pursue hypermales—that is, men whose features exaggerate the ways in which male faces differ from female ones. Even when adjusted for differing overall body size, the average male face has a more pronounced brow ridge, more sunken eyes, and bushier brows that are set closer to the eyes. The nose and mouth are wider, the lower jaw is wider and longer. Ramp up these features beyond the norm, and you've got a hunk, right?

There's no question that a dose of this classic "maleness" does contribute to what is now called handsome. Actor Brad Pitt, widely regarded as a modern paradigm of male attractiveness, is a wide-jaw guy. Biologically speaking, he subconsciously persuades a female that he could chew more nutrients out of a leafy stalk than the average potential father of her children—a handy trait, in hunter-gatherer days anyway, to pass on to progeny.

But a woman's agenda in seeking a mate is considerably more complex than simply whelping strong-jawed kids. While both men and women desire healthy, fertile mates, a man can—and, to some extent, is biologically driven to—procreate with as many women as possible. Conversely a woman, "thinks about the long haul," notes Etcoff. "Much of mate choice is about finding a helpmate to bring up the baby." In several studies, women presented with the hypermale face (the "Neanderthal type" as Etcoff puts it) judged its owner to be uncaring, aggressive, and unlikely to be a good father.

Female preferences in male faces oscillate in tandem with the menstrual cycle, suggests a study conducted by Perrett and Japanese researchers and published last June in *Nature*. When a woman is ovulating, she tends to prefer men with more masculine features; at less fertile times in her monthly cycle, she favors male faces with a softer, more feminine look. But amid the hoopla that this widely publicized finding generated, a critical fact was often overlooked. Even the "more masculine" face preferred by the ovulating women was 8 percent feminized from the male average (the less masculine face was 15 to 20 percent feminized). According to Perrett's study, even an averagely masculine face is too male for comfort.

To further complicate the male-appeal picture, research indicates that, across the board in mating species, an ugly guy can make up ground with status and/or wealth. Etcoff notes that female scorpion flies won't even look at a male unless his gift—a tasty bit of insect protein—is at least 16 square millimeters wide. The human situation isn't all that different. Anthropologist John Marshall Townsend showed photos of beautiful and homely people to men and women, and described the people in the photos as being in training for either low-, medium-, or high-paying positions—waiter, teacher, or doctor. "Not

surprisingly, women preferred the best-looking man with the most money," Etcoff writes, "but below him, average-looking or even unattractive doctors received the same ratings as very attractive teachers. This was not true when men evaluated women. Unattractive women were not preferred, no matter what their status."

IT'S ALL A BIT BLEAK. TALK TO ENOUGH PSY-chobiologists, and you get the impression that we are all rats—reflexively, unconsciously coupling according to obscure but immutable circuitry. But beauty researchers agree that, along with natural selection and sexual selection, learned behaviors are at least part of the attractiveness radar. In other words, there is room for individuality—perhaps even a smattering of mystery—in this business of attraction between humans.

"Human beauty really has three components," says Johnston. "In order of importance, there's natural selection, which leads to the average face and a limited age range. Then there's sexual selection," which leads men, at least, to be attracted to exaggerated feminine traits like the small lower jaw and the fuller lips. "Finally, there's learning. It's a fine-tuning mechanism that allows you to become even more adapted to your environment and culture. It's why one person can say 'She's beautiful' and another can say, 'She's not quite right for me.'"

The learned component of beauty detection is perhaps most evident in the give-and-take between races. While, at first meeting, different racial groups typically see each other as unattractive, when one race commands economic or political power, members of other races tend to emulate its characteristics: Witness widespread hair straightening by American blacks earlier in this century. Today, black gains in social equity are mirrored by a growing appreciation for the beauty of such characteristically black features as relatively broader noses and tightly curled hair. "Race is a cultural overlay on beauty and it's shifting," says Etcoff.

She adds that human appearance is about more than attracting sex partners. "There was a cartoon in the *New Yorker*. A mother and daughter are in a checkout line. The girl is saying to the cashier, 'Oh, no, I *do* look like my mother, with her *first* nose!' As we make ourselves more beautiful, we take away things like family resemblance, and we may realize that's a mistake. Facial uniqueness can be a wonderful emotional tag. Human beings are always looking for kinship as well as beauty."

Midway between goats and gods, human beings can find some accommodation between the notion that beauty is all and that it is nothing. "Perhaps it's best to enjoy the temporary thrill, to enjoy being a mammal for a few moments, and then do a reality check and move on," writes Etcoff. "Our brains cannot help it, but we can."

What's Your Love Story?

In your relationship, are you a cop, a comedian, a prince or a martyr? Robert J. Sternberg, Ph.D., reveals how you can use your "love story" to find your perfect match.

BY ROBERT J. STERNBERG, PH.D.

Relationships can be as unpredictable as the most suspense-filled mystery novel. Why do some couples live happily ever after, while others are as star-crossed as Romeo and Juliet? Why do we often seem destined to relive the same romantic mistakes over and over, following the same script with different people in different places, as if the fate of our relationships, from courtship to demise, were written at birth?

Perhaps because, in essence, it is. As much as psychologists have attempted to explain the mysteries of love through scientific laws and theories, it turns out that the best mirrors of the romantic experience may be *Wuthering Heights,*

Casablanca and *General Hospital.* At some level, lay people recognize what many psychologists don't: that the love between two people follows a story. If we want to understand love, we have to understand the stories that dictate our beliefs and expectations of love. These stories, which we start to write as children, predict the patterns of our romantic experiences time and time again. Luckily, we can learn to rewrite them.

I came up with the theory of love as a story because I was dissatisfied—not only with other people's work on love, but also with my own. I had initially proposed a triangular theory of love, suggesting that it comprises three elements: intimacy, passion and commitment. Different loving relationships have different combinations of these elements. Complete love requires all three elements. But the theory leaves an important question unanswered: what makes a person the kind of lover they are? And what attracts them to other lovers? I had to dig deeper to understand the love's origins. I found them in stories.

My research, which incorporates studies performed over the past decade with hundreds of couples in Connecticut, as well as ongoing studies, has shown that people describe love in many ways. This description reveals their love story. For example, someone who strongly agrees with the statement "I believe close relationships are like good partnerships" tells a business story; someone who says they end up with partners who scare them—or that they like intimidating their partner—enacts a horror story.

Couples usually start out being physically attracted and having similar interests and values. But eventually, they may notice something missing in the relationship. That something is usually story compatibility. A couple whose stories don't match is like two characters on one stage acting out different plays—they may look right at first glance, but there is an underlying lack of coordination to their interaction.

This is why couples that seem likely to thrive often do not, and couples that seem unlikely to survive sometimes do. Two people may have similar outlooks, but if one longs to be rescued like Julia Roberts in *Pretty Woman* and the other wants a partnership like the lawyers on the television show *The Practice,* the relationship may not go very far. In contrast, two people with a war story like the bickering spouses in *Who's Afraid of Virginia Woolf* may seem wildly incompatible to their friends, but their shared need for combat may be what keeps their love alive.

More than anything, the key to compatibility with a romantic partner is whether our stories match. To change the pattern of our relation-

ships, we must become conscious of our love stories, seek people with compatible tales, and replot conclusions that aren't working for us.

The Beginning of the Story

We start forming our ideas about love soon after birth, based on our inborn personality, our early experiences and our observations of our parents' relationships, as well as depictions of romance in movies, television and books. We then seek to live out these conceptions of love ourselves.

Based on interviews I conducted in the 1990s, asking college students to write about their romantic ideals and expectations, I have identified at least 25 common stories which people use to describe love. (There are probably many more.)

Some stories are far more popular than others. In 1995, one of my students, Laurie Lynch, and I identified some of the most common tales by asking people to rate, on a scale of one to seven, the extent to which a group of statements characterized their relationships. Their highest-ranked statements indicated their personal love story. Among the most popular were the travel story ("I believe that beginning a relationship is like starting a new journey that promises to be both exciting and challenging"), the gardening story ("I believe any relationship that is left unattended will not survive") and the humor story ("I think taking a relationship too seriously can spoil it"). Among the least popular were the horror story ("I find it exciting when I feel my partner is somewhat frightened of me," or "I tend to end up with people who frighten me"), the collectibles story ("I like dating different partners simultaneously; each partner should fit a particular need") and the autocratic government story ("I think it is more efficient if one person takes control of the important decisions in a relationship").

Another study of 43 couples, conducted with Mahzad Hojji, Ph.D., in 1996, showed that women prefer the travel story more than men, who pre-

fer the art ("Physical attractiveness is the most essential characteristic I look for in a partner"), collectibles and pornography ("It is very important to be able to gratify all my partner's sexual desires and whims," or "I can never be happy with a partner who is not very adventurous in his or her sex life") stories. Men also prefer the sacrifice story ("I believe sacrifice is a key part of true love"). Originally, we had expected the opposite. Then we realized that the men reported sacrificing things that women did consider significant offerings.

No one story guarantees success, our study showed. But some stories seem to predict doom more than others: the business, collectibles, government, horror, mystery, police ("I believe it is necessary to watch your partner's every move" or "My partner often calls me several times a day to ask what I am doing"), recovery ("I often find myself helping people get their life back in order" or "I need someone to help me recover from my painful past"), science fiction ("I often find myself attracted to individuals who have unusual and strange characteristics") and theater stories ("I think my relationships are like plays" or "I often find myself attracted to partners who play different roles").

How Stories Spin Our Relationships

When you talk to two people who have just split up, their breakup stories often sound like depictions of two completely different relationships. In a sense they are. Each partner has his or her own story to tell.

Most important to a healthy, happy relationship is that both partners have compatible stories—that is, compatible expectations. Indeed, a 1998 study conducted with Mahzad Hojjat, Ph.D., and Michael Barnes, Ph.D., indicated that the more similar couples' stories were, the happier they were together.

Stories tend to be compatible if they are complementary roles in a single story, such as prince and princess, or if the stories are similar enough that they can be merged into a new and unified story. For example, a fantasy story can merge with a gardening story because one can nourish, or garden, a relationship while dreaming of being rescued by a knight on a white steed. A fantasy and a business story are unlikely to blend, however, because they represent such different ideals–fate-bound princes and princesses don't work at romance!

Of course, story compatibility isn't the only ingredient in a successful relationship. Sometimes, our favorite story can be hazardous to our well-being. People often try to make dangerous or unsatisfying stories come true. Thus, someone who has, say, a horror or recovery story may try to turn a healthy relationship into a Nightmare on Elm Street. People complain that they keep ending up with the same kind of bad partner, that they are unlucky in love. In reality, luck has nothing to do with it: They are subconsciously finding people to play out their love stories, or foisting their stories on the people they meet.

Making Happy Endings

Treating problems in relationships by changing our behaviors and habits ultimately won't work because crisis comes from the story we're playing out. Unless we change our stories, we're treating symptoms rather than causes. If we're dissatisfied with our partner, we should look not at his or her faults, but at how he or she fits into our expectations.

To figure out what we want, we need to consider all of our past relationships, and we should ask ourselves what attributes characterized the people to whom we felt most attracted, and what attributes characterized the people in whom we eventually lost interest. We also need to see which romantic tale we aim to tell–and whether or not it has the potential to lead to a "happily ever after" scenario (see box, "Find Your Love Story").

Once we understand the ideas and beliefs behind the stories we accept as our own, we can do some replotting. We can ask ourselves what we like and don't like about our current story, what hasn't been working in our relationships, and how we would like to change it. How can we rewrite the scenario? This may involve changing stories, or transforming an existing story to make it more practical. For example, horror stories may be fantasized during sexual or other activity, rather than actually physically played out.

We can change our story by experimenting with new and different plots. Sometimes, psychotherapy can help us to move from perilous stories (such as a horror story) to more promising ones (such as a travel story). Once we've recognized our story–or learned to live a healthy one of our choosing–we can begin to recognize elements of that story in potential mates. Love mirrors stories because it is a story itself. The difference is that we are the authors, and can write ourselves a happy ending.

Robert J. Sternberg is IBM Professor of Psychology and Education in the department of psychology at Yale University.

READ MORE ABOUT IT

Love Is a Story, Robert J. Sternberg, Ph.D. (Oxford University Press, 1998)

A Natural History of Love, Diane Ackerman (Random House, 1994

Find Your Love Story

Adapted from *Love Is a Story* by Robert J. Sternberg, Ph.D.

Rate each statement on a scale from 1 to 9, 1 meaning that it doesn't characterize your romantic relationships at all, 9 meaning that it describes them extremely well. Then average your scores for each story. In general, averaged scores of 7 to 9 are high, indicating a strong attraction to a story, and 1 to 3 are low, indicating little or no interest in the story. Moderate scores of 4 to 6 indicate some interest, but probably not enough to generate or keep a romantic interest. Next, evaluate your own love story. (There are 12 listed here; see the book for more.)

STORY #1

5

1. I enjoy making sacrifices for the sake of my partner.
2. I believe sacrifice is a key part of true love.
3. I often compromise my own comfort to satisfy my partner's needs.
Score:__

The *sacrifice story* can lead to happy relationships when both partners are content in the roles they are playing, particularly when they both make sacrifices. It is likely to cause friction when partners feel compelled to make sacrifices. Research suggests that relationships of all kinds are happiest when they are roughly equitable. The greatest risk in a sacrifice story is that the give-and-take will become too out of balance, with one partner always being the giver or receiver.

STORY #2

1

Officer:
1. I believe that you need to keep a close eye on your partner.
2. I believe it is foolish to trust your partner completely.
3. I would never trust my partner to work closely with a person of the opposite sex. Score:__

Suspect:
1. My partner often calls me several times a day to ask exactly what I am doing.
2. My partner needs to know everything that I do.

3. My partner gets very upset if I don't let him or her know exactly where I have been. **Score:__**

Police stories do not have very favorable prognoses because they can completely detach from reality. The police story may offer some people the feeling of being cared for. People who are very insecure relish the attention that they get as a "suspect," that they are unable to receive in any other way. But they can end up paying a steep price. As the plot thickens, the suspect first begins to lose freedom, then dignity, and then any kind of self-respect. Eventually, the person's mental and even physical well-being may be threatened.

STORY #3

1. I believe that, in a good relationship, partners change and grow together.
2. I believe love is a constant process of discovery and growth.
3. I believe that beginning a relationship is like starting a new journey that promises to be both exciting and challenging. **Score:__**

Travel stories that last beyond a very short period of time generally have a favorable prognosis, because if the travelers can agree on a destination and path, they are already a long way toward success. If they can't, they often find out quite quickly that they want different things from the relationship and split up. Travel relationships tend to be dynamic and focus on the future. The greatest risk is that over time one or both partners will change the destination or path they desire. When people speak of growing apart, they often mean that the paths they wish to take are no longer the same. In such cases, the relationship is likely to become increasingly unhappy, or even dissolve completely.

STORY #4

Object:
1. The truth is that I don't mind being treated as a sex toy by my partner.
2. It is very important to me to gratify my partner's sexual desires and whims, even if people might view them as debasing.

3. I like it when my partner wants me to try new and unusual, and even painful, sexual techniques. **Score:__**

Subject:
1. The most important thing to me in my relationship is for my partner to be an excellent sex toy, doing anything I desire.
2. I can never be happy with a partner who is not very adventurous in sex.
3. The truth is that I like a partner who feels like a sex object. **Score:__**

There are no obvious advantages to the **pornography story.** The disadvantages are quite clear, however. First, the excitement people attain is through degradation of themselves and others. Second, the need to debase and be debased is likely to keep escalating. Third, once one adopts the story, it may be difficult to adopt another story. Fourth, the story can become physically as well as psychologically dangerous. And finally, no matter how one tries, it is difficult to turn the story into one that's good for psychological or physical well-being.

STORY #5

Terrorizer:
1. I often make sure that my partner knows that I am in charge, even if it makes him or her scared of me.
2. I actually find it exciting when I feel my partner is somewhat frightened of me.
3. I sometimes do things that scare my partner, because I think it is actually good for a relationship to have one partner slightly frightened of the other. **Score:__**

Victim:
1. I believe it is somewhat exciting to be slightly scared of your partner.
2. I find it arousing when my partner creates a sense of fear in me.
3. I tend to end up with people who sometimes frighten me. **Score:__**

The horror story probably is the least advantageous of the stories. To some, it may be exciting. But the forms of terror needed to sustain the excitement tend to get out of control and to put their participants, and even sometimes those around them, at both psychological and

physical risk. Those who discover that they have this story or are in a relationship that is enacting it would be well-advised to seek counseling, and perhaps even police protection.

STORY #6

Co-dependent:
1. I often end up with people who are facing a specific problem, and I find myself helping them get their life back in order.
2. I enjoy being involved in relationships in which my partner needs my help to get over some problem.
3. I often find myself with partners who need my help to recover from their past. **Score:__**

Person in recovery:
1. I need someone who will help me recover from my painful past.
2. I believe that a relationship can save me from a life that is crumbling around me.
3. I need help getting over my past. **Score:__**

The main advantage to the **recovery story** is that the co-dependent may really help the other partner to recover, so long as the other partner has genuinely made the decision to recover. Many of us know individuals who sought to reform their partners, only to experience total frustration when their partners made little or no effort to reform. At the same time, the co-dependent is someone who needs to feel he or she is helping someone, and gains this feeling of making a difference to someone through the relationship. The problem: Others can assist in recovery, but the decision to recover can only be made by the person in need of recovery. As a result, recovery stories can assist in, but not produce, actual recovery.

STORY #7

1. I believe a good relationship is attainable only if you spend time and energy to care for it, just as you tend a garden.
2. I believe relationships need to be nourished constantly to help weather the ups and downs of life.
3. I believe the secret to a successful relationship is the care that partners take of each other and of their love. **Score:__**

The biggest advantage of a **garden story** is its recognition of the importance of nurture. No other story involves this amount of care and attention. The biggest potential disadvantage is that a lack of spontaneity or boredom may develop. People in garden stories are not immune to the lure of extramarital relationships, for example, and may get involved in them to generate excitement, even if they still highly value their primary relationship. In getting involved in other relationships, however, they are putting the primary relationship at risk. Another potential disadvantage is that of smothering—that the attention becomes too much. Just as one can overwater a flower, one can overattend a relationship. Sometimes it's best to let things be and allow nature to take its course.

STORY #8

1. I believe that close relationships are partnerships.
2. I believe that in a romantic relationship, just as in a job, both partners should perform their duties and responsibilities according to their "job description."
3. Whenever I consider having a relationship with someone, I always consider the financial implications of the relationship as well. **Score:__**

A business story has several potential advantages, not the least of which is that the bills are more likely to get paid than in other types of relationships. That's because someone is always minding the store. Another potential advantage is that the roles tend to be more clearly defined than in other relationships. The partners are also in a good position to "get ahead" in terms of whatever it is that they want. One potential disadvantage occurs if only one of the two partners sees their relationship as a business story. The other partner may quickly become bored and look for interest and excitement outside the marriage. The story can also turn sour if the distribution of authority does not satisfy one or both partners. If the partners cannot work out mutually compatible roles, they may find themselves spending a lot of time fighting for position. It is important to maintain the option of flexibility.

STORY #9

1. I think fairy tales about relationships can come true.
2. I do believe that there is someone out there for me who is my perfect match.
3. I like my relationships to be ones in which I view my partner as something like a prince or princess in days of yore. **Score:__**

The **fantasy story** can be a powerful one. The individual may feel swept up in the emotion of the search for the perfect partner or of developing the perfect relationship with an existing partner. It is probably no coincidence that in literature most fantasy stories take place before or outside of marriage: Fantasies are hard to maintain when one has to pay the bills, pack the children off to school and resolve marital fights. To maintain the happy feeling of the fantasy, therefore, one has to ignore, to some extent, the mundane aspects of life. The potential disadvantages of the fantasy relationship are quite plain. The greatest is the possibility for disillusionment when one partner discovers that no one could fulfill the fantastic expectations that have been created. This can lead partners to feel dissatisfied with relationships that most others would view as quite successful. If a couple can create a fantasy story based on realistic rather than idealistic ideas, they have the potential for success; if they want to be characters in a myth, chances are that's exactly what they'll get: a myth.

STORY #10

1. I think it is more interesting to argue than to compromise.
2. I think frequent arguments help bring conflictive issues into the open and keep the relationship healthy.
3. I actually like to fight with my partner. **Score:__**

The **war story** is advantageous in a relationship only when both partners clearly share it and want the same thing. In these cases, threats of divorce and worse may be common, but neither partner would seriously dream of leaving: They're both having too much fun, in their own way. The major disadvantage, of course, is that the story often isn't shared, leading to intense and sustained conflict that can leave the partner without the war story feeling devastated much of the time. People can find themselves in a warring relationship without either of them having war as a preferred story. In such cases, the constant fighting may make both partners miserable. If the war continues in such a context, there is no joy in it for either partner.

STORY #11

Audience:
1. I like a partner who is willing to think about the funny side of our conflicts.
2. I think taking a relationship too seriously can spoil it; that's why I like partners who have a sense of humor.
3. I like a partner who makes me laugh whenever we are facing a tense situation in our relationship. **Score:__**

Comedian:
1. I admit that I sometimes try to use humor to avoid facing a problem in my relationship.
2. I like to use humor when I have a conflict with my partner because I believe there is a humorous side to any conflict.
3. When I disagree with my partner, I often try to make a joke out of it. **Score:__**

The **humor story** can have one enormous advantage: Most situations do have a lighter side, and people with this story are likely to see it. When things in a relationship become tense, sometimes nothing works better than a little humor, especially if it comes from within the relationship. Humor stories also allow relationships to be creative and dynamic. But the humor story also has some potential disadvantages. Probably the greatest one is the risk of using humor to deflect important issues: A serious conversation that needs to take place keeps getting put off with jokes. Humor can also be used to be cruel in a passive-aggressive way. When humor is used as a means of demeaning a person to protect the comedian from responsibility ("I was only joking"), a relationship is bound to be imperiled. Thus, moderate amounts are good for a relationship, but excessive amounts can be deleterious.

STORY #12

1. I think it is okay to have multiple partners who fulfill my different needs.
2. I sometimes like to think about how many people I could potentially date all at the same time.

3. I tend and like to have multiple intimate partners at once, each fulfilling somewhat different roles.
Score:__

There are a few advantages to a **collection story**. For one thing, the collector generally cares about the collectible's physical well-being, as appearance is much of what makes a collection shine. The collector also finds a way of meeting multiple needs. Usually those needs will be met in parallel—by having several intimate relationships at the same time—but a collector may also enter into serial monogamous relationships, where each successive relationship meets needs that

the last relationship did not meet. In a society that values monogamy, collection stories work best if they do not become serious or if individuals in the collection are each viewed in different lights, such as friendship or intellectual stimulation. The disadvantages of this story become most obvious when people are trying to form serious relationships. The collector may find it difficult to establish intimacy, or anything approaching a complete relationship and commitment toward a single individual. Collections can also become expensive, time-consuming, and in some cases illegal (as when an individual enters into multiple marriages simultaneously).

Will Your Marriage Last?

New studies show that the newlywed years can foretell the long-term outcome of almost every marriage. What do your newlywed years predict for you?

By Aviva Patz

What if I told you that there is a man in America who can predict, from the outset, whether or not your marriage will last? He doesn't need to hear you arguing; he doesn't need to know what you argue about. He doesn't even care whether you argue at all.

I was dubious, too, but I was curious enough to attend a lecture on the subject at the most recent American Psychological Association convention in Boston. Ted Huston, Ph.D., a professor of human ecology and psychology at the University of Texas at Austin, was showcasing the results of a long-term study of married couples that pierces the heart of social psychological science: the ability to forecast whether a husband and wife, two years after taking their vows, will stay together and whether they will be happy.

My press pass notwithstanding, I went to the seminar for reasons of my own. Fresh out of college I had gotten married—and burned. Some part of me was still reeling from three years of waking up angry every morning, not wanting to go home after work, feeling lonely even as my then husband sat beside me. I went because I have recently remarried and just celebrated my one-year anniversary. Needless to say, I'd like to make this one work. So I scribbled furiously in my notebook, drinking in the graphs and charts—for psychology, for husbands and wives everywhere, but mostly for myself.

Huston, a pioneer in the psychology of relationships, launched the Processes of Adaptation in Intimate Relationships (the "PAIR Project") in 1981, in which he followed 168 couples—drawn from marriage license records in four counties in a rural and working-class area of Pennsylvania—from their wedding day through 13 years of marriage.

Through multiple interviews, Huston looked at the way partners related to one another during courtship, as newlyweds and through the early years of marriage. Were they "gaga?" Comfortable? Unsure? He measured their positive and negative feelings for each other and

BLISS OR BUST?
TAKE THE MARRIAGE QUIZ

Created for PSYCHOLOGY TODAY by Ted Huston, Ph.D., Shanna Smith, Sylvia Niehuis, Christopher Rasmussen and Paul Miller

Circle the answer that best describes your level of agreement with each of the following statements:

Part 1 Our Relationship As Newlyweds

1. As newlyweds, we were constantly touching, kissing, pledging our love or doing sweet things for one another.
Strongly disagree (1 pt.) Disagree (2 pts.) Agree (3 pts.) Strongly agree (4 pts.)

2. As newlyweds, how often did you express criticism, anger, annoyance, impatience or dissatisfaction to one another?
Often (1 pt.) Sometimes (2 pts.) Rarely (3 pts.) Almost never (4 pts.)

3. As newlyweds, my partner and I felt we belonged together; we were extremely close and deeply in love.
Disagree (1 pt.) Mildly agree (2 pts.) Agree (3 pts.) Strongly agree (4 pts.)

4. As a newlywed, I think one or both of us were confused about our feelings toward each other, or worried that we were not right for each other.
Strongly agree (1 pt.) Agree (2 pts.) Disagree (3 pts.) Strongly disagree (4 pts.)

Part 2 Our Relationship By Our Second Anniversary

1. By our second anniversary, we were disappointed that we touched, kissed, pledged our love or did sweet things for one another less often than we had as newlyweds.
Strongly disagree (1 pt.) Disagree (2 pts.) Agree (3 pts.) Strongly agree (4 pts.)

2. By our second anniversary, we expressed criticism, anger, annoyance, impatience or dissatisfaction a lot more than we had as newlyweds.
Strongly disagree (1 pt.) Disagree (2 pts.) Agree (3 pts.) Strongly agree (4 pts.)

3. By our second anniversary, we felt much less belonging and closeness with one another than we had before.
Disagree (1 pt.) Mildly agree (2 pts.) Agree (3 pts.) Strongly agree (4 pts.)

4. By our second anniversary, I felt much more confused or worried about the relationship than I did as a newlywed.

Strongly disagree (1 pt.) Disagree (2 pts.) Agree (3 pts.) Strongly agree (4 pts.)

Scoring: Add up the points that correspond to your answers in Part 1. If you scored between 4 and 8, place yourself in Group "A." If you scored between 9 and 16, place yourself in Group "B." Now add up the points that correspond to your answers in Part 2. If you scored between 4 and 8, place yourself in Group "C.' If you scored between 9 and 16, place yourself in Group "D.'

Your Results: Find the type of marriage first by considering your score in part 1 (either A or B) in combination with your score in part 2 (either C or D): If you scored A + C, read "Mixed Blessings"; If you scored A + D, read "Disengaging Duo"; If you scored B + C, read "A Fine Romance"; If you scored B + D, read "Disaffected Lovers."

Disaffected Lovers
The contrast between the giddiness you felt as newlyweds and how you felt later may cause disenchantment. While you and your spouse are still affectionate and in love, there are clouds behind the silver lining. You may bicker and disagree, which, combined with a loss of affection and love in your relationship, could give rise to the first serious doubts about your future together.

Food for Thought: Your relationship may be at risk for eventual divorce. But the pattern of decline early on does not have to continue. Ask yourself: Did we set ourselves up for disappointment with an overly romantic view of marriage? Did we assume it would require little effort to sustain? Did we take each other for granted? Did our disappointment lead to frustration and anger? Will continued bickering erode the love we have left?

A Fine Romance
You have a highly affectionate, loving and harmonious marriage. It may have lost a touch of its initial glow as the mundane realities of marriage have demanded more of your time. But you feel a certain sense of security in the marriage. The relationship's gifts you unwrapped as newlyweds continue to delight.

Food for Thought: You have the makings of a happy, stable marriage. The cohesive partnership you have maintained bodes well for its future. You will not always be happy—all marriages go through rough periods. But

Continued on next page

your ability to sustain a healthy marriage over the critical first two years suggests that you and your partner operate together like a thermostat in a home—when it's chilly, you identify the source of the draft and eliminate it, and when it's hot, you find ways to circulate cool air.

Mixed Blessings

Your marriage is less enchanting and filled with more conflict and ambivalence than Western society's romantic ideal, but it has changed little over its first two years, losing only a modicum of "good feeling." It seems to coast along, showing few signs that it will deteriorate further or become deeply distressed.

Food for Thought: This relationship may not be the romance you envisioned, but it just might serve you well. Many people in such relationships are content, finding their marriage a reassuringly stable foundation that allows them to devote their attention to career, children or other pursuits. Other people in these relationships are slightly dissatisfied, but stay married because the

rewards outweigh the drawbacks. A few people may eventually leave such marriages in search of a "fine romance."

Disengaging Duo

You and your mate are not overly affectionate and frequently express displeasure with one another. In contrast to those in a marriage of "mixed blessings," the love you once felt diminished soon after the wedding, and you became more ambivalent about the relationship. You may already have a sense that your relationship is on shaky ground.

Food for Thought: Your relationship may be in immediate trouble. You may have married hoping that problems in the relationship would go away after the wedding, but they didn't. Ask yourself: Did I see our problems coming while we were dating? Did I think they would dissolve with marriage? What kinds of changes would I need to see in my partner in order to be happy? How likely are they to occur? How bad

---

observed how those feelings changed over time. Are newlyweds who hug and kiss more likely than other couples to have a happy marriage, he wondered, or are they particularly susceptible to divorce if their romance dissipates? Are newlyweds who bicker destined to part ways?

Since one in two marriages ends in divorce in this country, there ought to be tons of research explaining why. But the existing literature provides only pieces of the larger puzzle.

Past research has led social scientists to believe that newlyweds begin their life together in romantic bliss, and can then be brought down by their inability to navigate the issues that inevitably crop up during the marriage. When Benjamin Karny and Thomas Bradbury did a comprehensive review of the literature in 1995, they confirmed studies such as those of John Gottman and Neil Jacobson, maintaining that the best predictors of divorce are interactive difficulties, such as frequent expressions of antagonism, lack of respect for each other's ideas and similar interpersonal issues.

But most of this research was done on couples who had been married a

number of years, with many of them already well on their way to divorce. It came as no surprise, then, that researchers thought their hostility toward one another predicted the further demise of the relationship.

> ... the major distinguishing factor between those who divorced and those who remained married was the amount of change in the relationship over the first two years.

Huston's study was unique in that it looked at couples much earlier, when they were courting and during the initial years of marriage, thus providing the first complete picture of the earliest stages of distress. Its four main findings were quite surprising.

First, contrary to popular belief, Huston found that many newlyweds are far from blissfully in love. Second, couples whose marriages begin in romantic bliss are particularly divorce-prone because such intensity is too hard to maintain. Believe it or not, marriages that start out with less "Hollywood romance" usually have more promising futures. Accordingly, and this is the third major finding, spouses in lasting but lackluster marriages are not prone to divorce, as one might suspect; their marriages are less fulfilling to begin with, so there is no erosion of a Western-style romantic ideal. Lastly, and perhaps most importantly, it is the loss of love and affection, not the emergence of interpersonal issues, that sends couples journeying toward divorce.

By the end of Huston's study in 1994, the couples looked a lot like the rest of America, falling into four groups. They were either married and happy; married and unhappy; divorced early, within seven years; or divorced later, after seven years—and each category showed a distinct pattern.

Those who remained happily married were very "in love" and affec-

Believe it or not, marriages that start out with less 'Hollywood romance' usually have more promising futures.

tionate as newlyweds. They showed less ambivalence, expressed negative feelings less often and viewed their mate more positively than other couples. Most importantly, these feelings remained stable over time. By contrast, although many couples who divorced later were very affectionate as newlyweds, they gradually became less loving, more negative, and more critical of their spouse.

Indeed, Huston found that how well spouses got along as newlyweds affected their future, but the major distinguishing factor between those who divorced and those who remained married was the amount of change in the relationship over its first two years.

"The first two years are key—that's when the risk of divorce is particularly high," he says. "And the changes that take place during this time tell us a lot about where the marriage is headed."

What surprised Huston most was the nature of the changes that led to divorce: The experiences of the 56 participating couples who divorced showed that loss of initial levels of love and affection, rather than conflict, was the most salient predictor of distress and divorce. This loss sends the relationship into a downward spiral, leading to increased bickering and fighting, and to the collapse of the union.

"This ought to change the way we think about the early roots of what goes wrong in marriage," Huston said. "The dominant approach has been to work with couples to resolve conflict, but it should focus on pre-

serving the positive feelings. That's a very important take-home lesson."

"Huston's research fills an important gap in the literature by suggesting that there is more to a successful relationship than simply managing conflict," said Harry Reis, Ph.D., of the University of Rochester, a leading social psychologist.

"My own research speaks to 'loss of intimacy,' in the sense that when people first become close they feel a tremendous sense of validation from each other, like their partner is the only other person on earth who sees things as they do. That feeling sometimes fades, and when it does, it can take a heavy toll on the marriage."

Social science has a name for that fading dynamic—"disillusionment": Lovers initially put their best foot forward, ignoring each other's—and the relationship's—shortcomings. But after they tie the knot, hidden aspects of their personalities emerge, and idealized images give way to more realistic ones. This can lead to disappointment, loss of love and, ultimately, distress and divorce.

When Marriage Fails

The story of Peter and Suzie, participants in the PAIR Project, shows classic disillusionment. When they met, Suzie was 24, a new waitress at the golf course where Peter, then 26, played. He was "awed" by her beauty. After a month the two considered themselves an exclusive couple. Peter said Suzie "wasn't an airhead; she seemed kind of smart, and she's pretty." Suzie said Peter "cared a lot about me as a person, and was willing to overlook things."

By the time they strolled down the aisle on Valentine's Day in 1981, Peter and Suzie had dated only nine months, experiencing many ups and downs along the way.

Huston says couples are most vulnerable to disillusionment when their courtship is brief. In a whirlwind romance, it's easy to paint an unrealistically rosy picture of the relationship, one that cannot be sustained.

Sure enough, reality soon set in for Peter and Suzie. Within two years, Suzie was less satisfied with almost every aspect of their marriage. She expressed less affection for Peter and felt her love decline continuously. She considered him to have "contrary" traits, such as jealousy and possessiveness, and resented his propensity to find fault with her.

Peter, for his part, was disappointed that his wife did not become the flawless parent and homemaker he had envisioned.

Another danger sign for relationships is a courtship filled with drama and driven by external circumstances. For this pair, events related to Peter's jealousy propelled the relationship forward. He was the force behind their destroying letters and pictures from former lovers. It was a phone call between Suzie and an old flame that prompted him to bring up the idea of marriage in the first place. And it was a fit of jealousy—over Suzie's claiming to go shopping and then coming home suspiciously late—that convinced Peter he was ready to marry.

Theirs was a recipe for disaster: A short courtship, driven largely by Peter's jealousy, enabled the pair to ignore flaws in the relationship and in each other, setting them up for disappointment. That disappointment eroded their love and affection, which soured their perception of each other's personalities, creating feelings of ambivalence.

Ten years after saying "I do," the disaffected lovers were in the midst of divorce. When Suzie filed the papers, she cited as the primary reason a gradual loss of love.

Our culture is also to blame... for perpetuating the myth of storybook romance, which is more likely to doom a marriage than strengthen it.

The parallels between Peter and Suzie's failed marriage and my own are striking: My courtship with my first husband was short, also about nine months. Like Peter, I had shallow criteria: This guy was cool; he had long hair, wore a leather jacket, played guitar and adored the same obscure band that I did.

When it came time to build a life together, however, we were clearly mismatched. I wanted a traditional family with children; he would have been happy living on a hippie commune. In college, when we wanted to move in together, we thought our parents would be more approving if we got engaged first. So we did, even though we weren't completely sold on the idea of marriage.

The road to divorce was paved early, by the end of the first year: I had said I wanted us to spend more time together; he accused me of trying to keep him from his hobbies, and told me, in so many words, to "get a life." Well I did, and, two years later, he wasn't in it.

When Marriage Succeeds

While the disillusionment model best describes those who divorce, Huston found that another model suits those who stay married, whether or not they are happy: The "enduring dynamics model," in which partners establish patterns of behavior early and maintain them over time, highlights

stability in the relationship—the feature that distinguishes those who remain together from those who eventually split up.

The major difference between the unhappily married couples and their happy counterparts is simply that they have a lower level of satisfaction across the board. Yet, oddly enough, this relative unhappiness by itself does not doom the marriage. "We have a whole group of people who are stable in unhappy marriages and not necessarily dissatisfied," Huston said. "It's just a different model of marriage. It's not that they're happy about their marriage, it's just that the discontent doesn't spill over and spoil the rest of their lives."

And while all married couples eventually lose a bit of that honeymoon euphoria, Huston notes, those who remain married don't consider this a crushing blow, but rather a natural transition from "romantic relationship" to "working partnership." And when conflict does arise, they diffuse it with various constructive coping mechanisms.

Nancy and John, participants in Huston's study, are a shining example of happy, healthy balance. They met in February 1978 and were immediately attracted to each other. John said Nancy was "fun to be with" and he "could take her anywhere." Nancy said John always complimented her and liked to do things she enjoyed, things "other guys wouldn't do."

During their courtship, they spent a lot of time together, going to dances at their high school and hanging out with friends. They became comfortable with each other and began to openly disclose their opinions and feelings, realizing they had a lot in common and really enjoyed each other's company.

John paid many surprise visits to Nancy and bought her a number of gifts. Toward the end of the summer, John gave Nancy a charm necklace with a "genuine diamond." She recalls his saying: "This isn't your ring, honey, but you're going to get one." And she did. The two married on Jan. 17, 1981, nearly three years after they began dating.

The prognosis for this relationship is good. Nancy and John have a "fine romance"—a solid foundation of love and affection, built on honesty and intimacy. A three-year courtship enabled them to paint realistic portraits of one another, lessening the chances of a rude awakening after marriage.

In 1994, when they were last interviewed, Nancy and John were highly satisfied with their marriage. They were very compatible, disagreeing only about politics. Both felt they strongly benefited from the marriage and said they had no desire to leave.

When the seminar ends, I can't get to a pay phone fast enough. After two rings, the phone is answered. He's there, of course. Dependable. Predictable. That's one of the things that first set my husband apart. At the close of one date, he'd lock in the next. "Can I see you tomorrow for lunch?" "Will you have dinner with me next week?"

Unlike the fantasy-quality of my first marriage, I felt a deep sense of comfort and companionship with him, and did not harbor outrageous expectations. We exchanged vows three and a half years later, in August 1998.

There at the convention center, I try to tell my husband about Huston's study, about the critical first few years, about "enduring dynamics." It all comes out in a jumble.

"You're saying we have a good marriage, that we're not going to get divorced?" he asks.

"Yes," I say breathlessly, relieved of the burden of explanation.

"Well I'm glad to hear that," he says, "but I wasn't really worried."

Sometimes I wonder: Knowing what I know now, could I have saved my first marriage? Probably not. Huston's research suggests that the harbingers of disaster were present even before my wedding day.

And he blames our culture. Unlike many other world cultures, he says, Western society makes marriage the key adult relationship, which puts a lot of pressure on people to marry. "People feel they have to find a way to get there and one way is to force it, even if it only works for the time being," he says.

Our culture is also to blame, Huston says, for perpetuating the myth of storybook romance, which is more likely to doom a marriage than strengthen it. He has few kind words for Hollywood, which brings us unrealistic, unsustainable passion.

So if your new romance starts to resemble a movie script, try to re-member: The audience never sees what happens after the credits roll.

Aviva Patz is the executive editor of PSYCHOLOGY TODAY.

READ MORE ABOUT IT

When Love Dies: The Process of Marital Disaffection, Karen Kayser, Ph.D. (Guildford Press, 1993)

Fighting For Your Marriage: Positive Steps For Preventing Divorce and Preserving A Lasting Love, H. Markman, S. Stanley and S. Blumberg (Jossey-Bass, 1994)

Unit 6

Unit Selections

Key Points to Consider

❖ What kind of evidence supports the view that both prejudiced and nonprejudiced people are familiar with negative racial stereotypes? Do you agree that nonprejudiced people must deliberately and consciously attempt to substitute tolerant values for their own unconscious stereotyped beliefs? Does this research suggest any possible solutions to the problem of prejudice in society?

❖ Not all discrimination is blatant. What subtle forms of discrimination can you identify in today's society toward women, minorities, or any other group? Is any form of discrimination ever justified? Why, or why not?

❖ Besides men and women, what other social groups are depicted in the media in ways that might perpetuate stereotypes? Racial groups? Occupations? Different age groups? How powerful do you think such depictions are? What are all the ways (positive and negative) that stereotypes can affect the individual who is being stereotyped?

 **Links**   **www.dushkin.com/online/**

These sites are annotated on pages 4 and 5.

In colonial America, relatively few people were allowed to vote. Women could not. Blacks could not. Even white men, if they lacked property, could not. It took many years, the Civil War, and the passage of constitutional amendments for this particular form of discrimination to eventually pass from the scene. Even so, many would argue today that discrimination against women, minorities, and those at the lower end of the economic spectrum continues, although usually in less obvious forms. The tendency for humans to make negative judgments about others on the basis of their membership in some social group, and then to act on those judgments, is a powerful one.

As the title implies, this unit covers three distinct but related topics: prejudice, discrimination, and stereotyping. *Prejudice* refers to the negative attitude that is directed toward some people simply because they are members of some particular social group. Thus, the feelings of distaste that one might experience when encountering a member of some minority group would be an example of prejudice. In such a case, the prejudiced feelings would also probably influence the way in which our hypothetical person evaluated and judged everything that the minority group member did. In contrast, *discrimination* refers to a negative action directed toward the members of some particular social group. That is, while prejudice refers only to negative feelings, discrimination crosses the line into actual behavior. Thus, yelling a racial slur, or failing to hire someone because of her religion, would be examples of discrimination. As you might imagine, however, those who hold prejudiced attitudes are generally more likely to engage in discriminatory behavior as well. The third concept, *stereotyping,* is more cognitive in tone than the other two. Stereotyping refers to the tendency that people have to see all members of a specific social group as being alike—that is, to not recognize the differences that exist and to exaggerate the similarities. Thus, stereotypes per se are distinct from the negative feelings and negative behavior that characterize prejudice and discrimination.

The first subsection in this unit considers the topic of prejudice, and both articles are concerned with a recent and highly influential approach to studying prejudice. In "Where Bias Begins: The Truth About Stereotypes," Annie Murphy Paul reports on research suggesting that everyone—prejudiced and nonprejudiced alike—is aware of racial stereotypes

and has that knowledge automatically activated by encountering a member of that race. What distinguishes prejudiced and nonprejudiced people is what comes next: prejudiced people largely accept those stereotypes and act on them, while nonprejudiced people consciously inhibit these initial responses and substitute other, more tolerant values. In the second selection, "Breaking the Prejudice Habit," psychologist Patricia Devine takes this argument a bit further and describes some of her own research that supports the idea that nonprejudiced people often find themselves wrestling with conflicting impulses: their immediate prejudiced reaction and their conscious rejection of that response.

The second subsection tackles the issue of discrimination. In "Aversive Racism and Selection Decisions: 1989 and 1999," John Dovidio and Samuel Gaertner examine racial attitudes (prejudice) and predicted behavior (discrimination) at two time points 10 years apart. Expressions of overt prejudice among college students declined over that time period, but subtle measures of discrimination did not—indicating that the link between attitudes and behavior is not a simple one.

The third subsection consists of two articles that address stereotyping. The first, "Thin Ice: 'Stereotype Threat' and Black College Students," is by the noted social psychologist Claude Steele, and describes his research into the concept of stereotype threat: the idea that fear of confirming a negative stereotype about a group to which one belongs can lead to serious changes in the individual. In particular, people may psychologically distance themselves from identities which are threatened in this way, much to the detriment of the person. Then, in "Stereotype," Ziva Kunda discusses some of the ways in which stereotypes persist over time, despite their frequent inaccuracy.

Prejudice, Discrimination, and Stereotyping

WHERE BIAS BEGINS:
THE TRUTH ABOUT STEREOTYPES

Psychologists once believed that only bigoted people used stereotypes. Now the study of unconscious bias is revealing the unsettling truth: We all use stereotypes, all the time, without knowing it. We have met the enemy of equality, and the enemy is us.

By Annie Murphy Paul

Mahzarin Banaji doesn't fit anybody's idea of a racist. A psychology professor at Yale University, she studies stereotypes for a living. And as a woman and a member of a minority ethnic group, she has felt firsthand the sting of discrimination. Yet when she took one of her own tests of unconscious bias, "I showed very strong prejudices," she says. "It was truly a disconcerting experience." And an illuminating one. When Banaji was in graduate school in the early 1980s, theories about stereotypes were concerned only with their explicit expression: outright and unabashed racism, sexism, anti-Semitism. But in the years since, a new approach to stereotypes has shattered that simple notion. The bias Banaji and her colleagues are studying is something far more subtle, and more insidious: what's known as automatic or implicit stereotyping, which, they find, we do all the time without knowing it. Though out-and-out bigotry may be on the decline, says Banaji, "if anything, stereotyping is a bigger problem than we ever imagined."

Previously researchers who studied stereotyping had simply asked people to record their feelings about minority groups and had used their answers as an index of their attitudes. Psychologists now understand that these conscious replies are only half the story. How progressive a person seems to be on the surface bears little or no relation to how prejudiced he or she is on an unconscious level—so that a bleeding-heart liberal might harbor just as many biases as a neo-Nazi skinhead.

As surprising as these findings are, they confirmed the hunches of many students of human behavior. "Twenty years ago, we hypothesized that there were people who said they were not prejudiced but who really did have unconscious negative stereotypes and beliefs," says psychologist Jack Dovidio, Ph.D., of Colgate University. "It was like theorizing about the existence of a virus, and then one day seeing it under a microscope."

The test that exposed Banaji's hidden biases—and that this writer took as well, with equally dismaying results—is typical of the ones used by automatic stereotype researchers. It presents the subject with a series of positive or negative adjectives, each paired with a characteristically "white" or "black" name. As the name and word appear together on a computer screen, the person taking the test presses a key, indicating whether the word is good or bad. Meanwhile, the computer records the speed of each response.

A glance at subjects' response times reveals a startling phenomenon: Most people who participate in the experiment—even some African-Americans—respond more quickly when a positive word is paired with a white name or a negative word with a black name. Because our minds are more accustomed to making these associations, says Banaji, they process them more rapidly. Though the words and names aren't subliminal, they are presented so quickly that a subject's ability to make deliberate choices is diminished—allowing his or her underlying assumptions to show through. The same technique can be used to measure stereotypes about many different social groups, such as homosexuals, women, and the elderly.

THE UNCONSCIOUS COMES INTO FOCUS

From these tiny differences in reaction speed—a matter of a few hundred milliseconds—the study of automatic stereotyping was born. Its immediate ancestor was the cognitive revolution of the 1970s, an explosion of psychological research into the way people think. After decades dominated by the study of observable behavior, scientists wanted a closer look at the more mysterious operation of the human brain. And the development of computers—which enabled scientists to display information

LIKE THE CULTURE, OUR MINDS ARE SPLIT ON THE SUBJECTS OF RACE, GENDER, SEXUAL ORIENTATION.

very quickly and to measure minute discrepancies in reaction time—permitted a peek into the unconscious.

At the same time, the study of cognition was also illuminating the nature of stereotypes themselves. Research done after World War II—mostly by European émigrés struggling to understand how the Holocaust had happened—concluded that stereotypes were used only by a particular type of person: rigid, repressed, authoritarian. Borrowing from the psychoanalytic perspective then in vogue, these theorists suggested that biased behavior emerged out of internal conflicts caused by inadequate parenting.

The cognitive approach refused to let the rest of us off the hook. It made the simple but profound point that we all use categories—of people, places, things—to make sense of the world around us. "Our ability to categorize and evaluate is an important part of human intelligence," says Banaji. "Without it, we couldn't survive." But stereotypes are too much of a good thing. In the course of stereotyping, a useful category—say women—becomes freighted with additional associations, usually negative. "Stereotypes are categories that have gone too far," says John Bargh, Ph.D., of New York University. "When we use stereotypes, we take in the gender, the age, the color of the skin of the person before us, and our minds respond with messages that say hostile, stupid, slow, weak. Those qualities aren't out there in the environment. They don't reflect reality."

Bargh thinks that stereotypes may emerge from what social psychologists call in-group/out-group dynamics. Humans, like other species, need to feel that they are part of a group, and as villages, clans, and other traditional groupings have broken down, our identities have attached themselves to more ambiguous classifications, such as race and class. We want to feel good about the group we belong to—and one way of doing so is to denigrate all those who aren't in it. And while we tend to see members of our own group as individuals, we view those in out-groups as an undifferentiated—stereotyped—mass. The categories we use have changed, but it seems that stereotyping itself is bred in the bone.

Though a small minority of scientists argues that stereotypes are usually accurate and can be relied upon without reservations, most disagree—and vehemently. "Even if there is a kernel of truth in the stereotype, you're still applying a generalization about a group to an individual, which is always incorrect," says Bargh. Accuracy aside, some believe that the use of stereotypes is simply unjust. "In a democratic society people should be judged as individuals and not as members of a group," Banaji argues. "Stereotyping flies in the face of that ideal."

PREDISPOSED TO PREJUDICE

The problem, as Banaji's own research shows, is that people can't seem to help it. A recent experiment provides a good illustration. Banaji and her colleague, Anthony Greenwald, Ph.D., showed people a list of names—some famous, some not. The next day the subjects returned to the lab and were shown a second list, which mixed names from the first list with new ones. Asked to identify which were famous, they picked out the Margaret Meads and the Miles Davises—but they also chose some of the names on the first list, which retained a lingering familiarity that they mistook for fame. (Psychologists call this the "famous overnight-effect.") By a margin of two-to-one, these suddenly "famous" people were male.

Participants weren't aware that they were preferring male names to female names, Banaji stresses. They were simply drawing on an unconscious stereotype of men as more important and influential than women. Something similar happened when she showed subjects a list of people who might be criminals: without knowing they were doing so, participants picked out an overwhelming number of African-American names. Banaji calls this kind of stereotyping implicit, because people know they are making a judgment—but just aren't aware of the basis upon which they are making it.

Even further below awareness is something that psychologists call automatic processing, in which stereotypes are triggered by the slightest interaction or encounter. An experiment conducted by Bargh required a group of white participants to perform a tedious computer task. While performing the task, some of the participants were subliminally exposed to pictures of African-Americans with neutral expressions. When the subjects were then asked to do the task over again, the ones who had been exposed to the faces reacted with more hostility to the request—because, Bargh believes, they were responding in kind to the hostility which is part of the African-American stereotype. Bargh calls this the "immediate hostile reaction," which he believes can have a real effect on race relations. When African-Americans accurately perceive the hostile expressions that their white counterparts are unaware of, they may respond with hostility of their own—thereby perpetuating the stereotype.

Of course, we aren't completely under the sway of our unconscious. Scientists think that the automatic activation of a stereotype is immediately followed by a conscious check on unacceptable thoughts—at least in people who think that they are not prejudiced. This internal censor successfully restrains overtly biased responses. But there's still the danger of leakage, which often shows up in nonverbal behavior: our expressions, our stance, how far away we stand, how much eye contact we make.

The gap between what we say and what we do can lead African-Americans and whites to come away with very different impressions of the same encounter, says Jack Dovidio. "If I'm a white person talking to an African-American, I'm probably monitoring my conscious beliefs very carefully and making sure everything I say agrees with all the positive things I want to express," he says. "And I usually believe I'm pretty successful because I hear the right words coming out of my mouth." The listener who is paying attention to non-verbal behavior, however, may be getting quite the opposite message. An African-American student of Dovidio's recently told him that when she was growing up, her mother had taught her to observe how white people moved to gauge their true feelings toward

THE CATEGORIES WE USE HAVE CHANGED, BUT STEREOTYPING ITSELF SEEMS TO BE BRED IN THE BONE.

WE HAVE TO CHANGE HOW WE THINK WE CAN INFLUENCE PEOPLE'S BEHAVIORS. IT WOULD BE NAIVE TO THINK THAT EXHORTATION IS ENOUGH.

blacks. "Her mother was a very astute amateur psychologist—and about 20 years ahead of me," he remarks.

WHERE DOES BIAS BEGIN?

So where exactly do these stealth stereotypes come from? Though automatic-stereotype researchers often refer to the unconscious, they don't mean the Freudian notion of a seething mass of thoughts and desires, only some of which are deemed presentable enough to be admitted to the conscious mind. In fact, the cognitive model holds that information flows in exactly the opposite direction: connections made often enough in the conscious mind eventually become unconscious. Says Bargh: "If conscious choice and decision making are not needed, they go away. Ideas recede from consciousness into the unconscious over time."

Much of what enters our consciousness, of course, comes from the culture around us. And like the culture, it seems that our minds are split on the subjects of race, gender, class, sexual orientation. "We not only mirror the ambivalence we see in society, but also mirror it in precisely the same way," says Dovidio. Our society talks out loud about justice, equality, and egalitarianism, and most Americans accept these values as their own. At the same time, such equality exists only as an ideal, and that fact is not lost on our unconscious. Images of women as sex objects, footage of African-American criminals on the six o'clock news,—"this is knowledge we cannot escape," explains Banaji. "We didn't choose to know it, but it still affects our behavior."

We learn the subtext of our culture's messages early. By five years of age, says Margo Monteith, Ph.D., many children have definite and entrenched stereotypes about blacks, women, and other social groups. Adds Monteith, professor of psychology at the University of Kentucky: "Children don't have a choice about accepting or rejecting these conceptions, since they're acquired well before they have the cognitive abilities or experiences to form their own beliefs." And no matter how progressive the parents, they must compete with all the forces that would promote and perpetuate these stereotypes: peer pressure, mass media, the actual balance of power in society. In fact, prejudice may be as much a result as a cause of this imbalance. We

create stereotypes—African-Americans are lazy, women are emotional—to explain why things are the way they are. As Dovidio notes, "Stereotypes don't have to be true to serve a purpose."

WHY CAN'T WE ALL GET ALONG?

The idea of unconscious bias does clear up some nettlesome contradictions. "It accounts for a lot of people's ambivalence toward others who are different, a lot of their inconsistencies in behavior," says Dovidio. "It helps explain how good people can do bad things." But it also prompts some uncomfortable realizations. Because our conscious and unconscious beliefs may be very different—and because behavior often follows the lead of the latter—"good intentions aren't enough," as John Bargh puts it. In fact, he believes that they count for very little. "I don't think free will exists," he says, bluntly—because what feels like the exercise of free will may be only the application of unconscious assumptions.

Not only may we be unable to control our biased responses, we may not even be aware that we have them. "We have to rely on our memories and our awareness of what we're doing to have a connection to reality," says Bargh. "But when it comes to automatic processing, those cues can be deceptive." Likewise, we can't always be sure how biased others are. "We all have this belief that the important thing about prejudice is the external expression of it," says Banaji. "That's going to be hard to give up."

One thing is certain: We can't claim that we've eradicated prejudice just because its outright expression has waned. What's more, the strategies that were so effective in reducing that sort of bias won't work on unconscious beliefs. "What this research is saying is that we are going to have to change dramatically the way we think we can influence people's behaviors," says Banaji. "It would be naive to think that exhortation is enough." Exhortation, education, political protest—all of these hammer away at our conscious beliefs while leaving the bedrock below untouched. Banaji notes, however, that one traditional remedy for discrimination—affirmative action—may still be effective since it bypasses our unconsciously compromised judgment.

But some stereotype researchers think that the solution to automatic stereotyping lies in the process itself. Through practice, they say people can weaken the mental links that connect minorities to negative stereotypes and strengthen the ones that connect them to positive conscious beliefs. Margo Monteith explains how it might work. "Suppose you're at a party and someone tells a racist joke—and you laugh," she says. "Then you realize that you shouldn't have laughed at the joke. You feel guilty and become focused on your thought processes. Also, all sorts of cues become associated with laughing at the racist joke: the person who told the joke, the act of telling jokes, being at a party drinking." The next time you encounter these cues, "a warning signal of sorts should go off—'wait, didn't you mess up in this situation before?'—and your responses will be slowed and executed with greater restraint."

That slight pause in the processing of a stereotype gives conscious, unprejudiced beliefs a chance to take over. With time, the tendency to prevent automatic stereotyping may itself become automatic. Monteith's research suggests that, given enough motivation, people may be able to teach themselves to inhibit prejudice so well that even their tests of implicit bias come clean.

The success of this process of "de-automatization" comes with a few caveats, however. First, even its proponents concede that it works only for people disturbed by the discrepancy between their conscious and unconscious beliefs, since unapologetic racists or sexists have no motivation to change. Second, some studies have shown that attempts to suppress stereotypes may actually cause them to return later, stronger than ever. And finally, the results that Monteith and other researchers have achieved in the laboratory may not stick in the real world, where people must struggle to maintain their commitment to equality under less-than-ideal conditions.

Challenging though that task might be, it is not as daunting as the alternative researchers suggest: changing society itself. Bargh, who likens de-automatization to closing the barn door once the horses have escaped, says that "it's clear that the way to get rid of stereotypes is by the roots, by where they come from in the first place." The study of culture may someday tell us where the seeds of prejudice originated; for now the study of the unconscious shows us just how deeply they're planted.

Breaking the Prejudice Habit

Patricia G. Devine, PhD,
University of Wisconsin, Madison

Patricia G. Devine, PhD, is Professor of Psychology at the University of Wisconsin, Madison. Before becoming Professor, she was a Visiting Fellow at Yale University and an Associate Professor at Wisconsin.

Dr. Devine received the Gordon Allport Intergroup Relations Prize from the Society for the Psychological Study of Social Issues in 1990 and the APA Distinguished Scientific Award for Early Career Contribution to Psychology in 1994. She is the author or coauthor of several journal articles and is the coeditor of *Social Cognition: Impact on Social Psychology* (Academic Press, 1994). Her research interests include prejudice and intergroup relations, stereotyping, dissonance, and resistance to persuasion. Dr. Devine received her PhD in Social Psychology from Ohio State University in 1986.

Legal scholars, politicians, legislators, social scientists, and lay people alike have puzzled over the paradox of racism in a nation founded on the fundamental principle of human equality. Legislators responded with landmark legal decisions (e.g., Supreme Court ruling on school desegregation and the Civil Rights laws) that made overt discrimination based on race illegal. In the wake of the legislative changes, social scientists examined the extent to which shifts in whites' attitudes kept pace with the legal changes. The literature, however, reveals conflicting findings. Whereas overt expressions of prejudice on surveys declined (i.e., verbal reports), more subtle indicators (i.e., nonverbal measures) continue to reveal prejudice even among those who say they renounced prejudice. A central challenge presented to contemporary prejudice researchers is to explain the disparity between verbal reports and the more subtle measures.

Some reject the optimistic conclusion suggested by survey research and argue that prejudice in America is not declining; it is only changing form—becoming more subtle and disguised. By this argument, most (if not all) Americans are assumed to be racist, with only the *type* of racism differing between people. Such conclusions are based on the belief that *any* response that results in differential treatment between groups is taken as evidence of prejudice. However, this definition fails to consider *intent* or *motive* and is based on the assumption that nonthoughtful (e.g., nonverbal) responses are, by definition, more trustworthy than thoughtful responses. Indeed, nonverbal measures are assumed to be good indicators of prejudice precisely because they do not typically involve careful thought and people do not control them in the same way that they can control their verbally reported attitudes.

Rather than dismiss either response as necessarily untrustworthy, my colleagues and I have tried to understand the origin of both thoughtful and nonthoughtful responses. By directly addressing the disparity between thoughtful and nonthoughtful responses, our approach offers a more optimistic analysis regarding prospects for prejudice reduction than the extant formulations. To foreshadow, our program of research has been devoted to understanding (a) how and why those who truly renounce prejudice may continue to experience prejudice-like thoughts and feelings and (b) the nature of the rather formidable challenges and obstacles that must be overcome before one can succeed in reducing the disparity between thoughtful and nonthoughtful responses.

Automatic and Controlled Processes in Prejudice

The distinction between automatic and controlled cognitive processes has been central to our analysis in prejudice reduction. Automatic processes occur unintentionally, spontaneously, and unconsciously. We have evidence that both low- and high-prejudiced people are vulnerable to automatic stereotype activation. Once the stereotype is well learned, its influence is hard to avoid because it so easily comes to mind. Controlled processes, in contrast, are under the intentional control of the individual. An important aspect of such processes is that their initiation and use requires time and sufficient cognitive *capacity*. Non-prejudiced responses require inhibiting the spontaneously activated stereotypes and deliberately activating personal beliefs to serve as the basis for responses. Without sufficient time or cognitive capacity, responses may well be stereotype-based and, there-fore, appear prejudiced.

The important implication of the automatic/controlled process distinc-tion is that if one looks only at nonthoughtful, automatic responses, one may well conclude that all white Americans are prejudiced. We have found important differences between low- and high-prejudiced people based on the personal beliefs that each hold, despite similar knowledge of and vulnerability to the activation of cultural stereotypes. Furthermore, low-prejudiced people have estab-lished and internalized nonprejudiced personal standards for how to treat members of stereotyped groups. When given sufficient time, low-prejudiced people censor responses based on the stereotype and, instead, respond based on their beliefs. High-prejudiced peo-ple, in contrast, do not reject the stereotype and are not personally moti-vated to overcome its effect on their behavior.

A strength of this approach is that it delineates the role of both thought-ful and nonthoughtful processes in re-sponse to stereotyped group members. Eliminating prejudice requires over-coming a lifetime of socialization ex-periences, which, unfortunately, promote prejudice. We have likened reducing prejudice to the breaking of a habit in that people must first make a decision to eliminate the habit and then *learn* to inhibit the habitual (prejudiced) responses. Thus, the change from being prejudiced to non-prejudiced is not viewed as an all or none event, but as a process during which the low-prejudiced person is es-pecially vulnerable to conflict be-tween his or her enduring negative responses and endorsed nonprejudiced beliefs. For those who renounce preju-dice, overcoming the "prejudice habit" presents a formidable task that is likely to entail a great deal of inter-nal conflict over a protracted period of time.

Prejudice With and Without Compunction

In subsequent work, we examined the nature and consequences of the in-ternal conflict associated with preju-dice reduction. Specifically, we have focused on the challenges faced by those individuals who have internal-ized nonprejudiced personal standards and are trying to control their preju-diced responses, but sometimes fail. We have shown that people high and low in prejudice (as assessed by a self-report technique) have qualita-tively different affective reactions to the conflict between their verbal re-ports concerning how they *should* re-spond in situations involving contact with members of stereotyped groups and how they say they actually *would* respond. Low-prejudiced people, for example, believe that they should not feel uncomfortable sitting next to an African American on a bus. High-prejudiced people disagree, indicating that it's acceptable to feel uncomfort-able in this situation. When actual re-sponses violate personal standards, low-prejudiced people experience guilt or "prejudice with compunc-tion," but high-prejudiced individuals do not. For low-prejudiced people, the coexistence of such conflicting re-actions threatens their nonprejudiced self-concepts. Moreover, these guilt feelings play a functional role in help-ing people to "break the prejudice habit." That is, violations combined with guilt have been shown to help low-prejudiced people to use controlled processes to inhibit the prejudiced re-sponses and to replace them with re-sponses that are based on their personal beliefs.

Interpersonal Dynamics of Intergroup Contact

Until recently, our research has fo-cused rather exclusively on the nature of internal conflict associated with prejudice reduction efforts. However, many of the challenges associated with prejudice reduction are played out in the interpersonal arena, and we believe it's important to explore the relevance of our work to issues of in-tergroup tension. Thus, one of our cur-rent lines of research is devoted to exploring the nature of the challenges created by the intergroup contact when people's standards are "put on the line."

In interpersonal intergroup contact situations, we have found that al-though low-prejudiced people are highly motivated to respond without prejudice, there are few guidelines for "how to do the intergroup thing well." As a result, many experience doubt and uncertainty about how to express their nonprejudiced attitudes in intergroup situations. Thus, for low-prejudiced people, their high motiva-tion to respond without prejudice may actually interfere with their efforts to convey accurately their nonprejudiced intentions. Under these circumstances, they become socially anxious; this anxiety disrupts the typically smooth and coordinated aspects of social inter-action. Their interaction styles be-come awkward and strained, resulting in nonverbal behaviors such as de-creased eye contact and awkward speech patterns. These are exactly the types of subtle responses that have typically been interpreted as signs of prejudice or antipathy. Indeed, it is not possible to distinguish between the type of tension that arises out of antipathy toward the group or social anxiety based on these signs alone.

We argue that it may be important to acknowledge that there are qualita-tively distinct forms of intergroup ten-sion experienced by majority group members, which are systematically re-lated to their self-reported level of prejudice. For some, the tension can arise out of antipathy, as was always thought in the prejudice literature, but for others, the tension arises out of anxiety over trying to do the inter-group thing well. Functionally then, we have different starting points for trying to reduce intergroup tension. Strategies for attempting to reduce in-tergroup tension differ when the problem is conceived as one of improving skills rather than one of changing negative attitudes.

Conclusion

To sum up, although it is not easy and clearly requires effort, time, and practice, prejudice appears to be a habit that can be broken. In contrast to the prevailing, pessimistic opinion that little progress is being made toward the alleviation of prejudice, our program of research suggests that many people appear to be embroiled in the difficult or arduous process of overcoming their prejudices. During this process, low-prejudiced people are confronted with rather formidable challenges from within, as people battle their spontaneous reactions, and from the interpersonal settings in which people's standards are put on the line. We are sanguine that by developing a realistic analysis of the practical challenges faced by those who renounce prejudice, we may be able to identify strategies that may facilitate their prejudice reduction efforts.

It is important to recognize that we are not claiming to have solved the problem of intergroup prejudice, nor are we suggesting that prejudice has disappeared. The past several years have witnessed a disturbing increase in the incidence of hate crimes against minorities. And a sizable proportion of white Americans continue to embrace old-fashioned forms of bigotry. Nevertheless, we hope that by developing an understanding of the challenges associated with breaking the prejudice habit, we may gain insight into the reasons low-prejudiced people establish and internalize nonprejudiced standards. Armed with this knowledge, we may be able to encourage high-prejudiced people to renounce prejudice. And when they do, we will be in a better position to understand their challenges and, perhaps, to assist them in their efforts.

AVERSIVE RACISM AND SELECTION DECISIONS: 1989 AND 1999

John F. Dovidio[1] and Samuel L. Gaertner[2]

[1]Colgate University and [2]University of Delaware

Abstract—*The present study investigated differences over a 10-year period in whites' self-reported racial prejudice and their bias in selection decisions involving black and white candidates for employment. We examined the hypothesis, derived from the aversive-racism framework, that although overt expressions of prejudice may decline significantly across time, subtle manifestations of bias may persist. Consistent with this hypothesis, self-reported prejudice was lower in 1998–1999 than it was in 1988–1989, and at both time periods, white participants did not discriminate against black relative to white candidates when the candidates' qualifications were clearly strong or weak, but they did discriminate when the appropriate decision was more ambiguous. Theoretical and practical implications are considered.*

In part because of changing norms and the Civil Rights Act and other legislative interventions that have made discrimination not simply immoral but also illegal, overt expressions of prejudice have declined significantly over the past 35 years (Schuman, Steeh, Bobo, & Krysan, 1997). Discrimination, however, continues to exist and affect the lives of people of color and women in significant ways (Hacker, 1995). What accounts for this discrepancy? One possibility is that it represents a change in the nature of racial prejudice. Contemporary forms of prejudice may be less conscious and more subtle than the overt, traditional form (Gaertner & Dovidio, 1986; Sears, van Laar, Carillo, & Kosterman, 1997). For these more subtle forms of prejudice, discrimination is expressed in indirect and rationalizable ways, but the consequences of these actions (e.g., the restriction of economic opportunity) may be as sig-

nificant for people of color and as pernicious as the consequences of the traditional, overt form of discrimination (Dovidio & Gaertner, 1998).

In the present research, we examined the issue of changes in expressed prejudice and discrimination from the perspective of one modern form of prejudice, aversive racism. Aversive racism (see Gaertner & Dovidio, 1986) is hypothesized to characterize the racial attitudes of many whites who endorse egalitarian values, who regard themselves as nonprejudiced, but who discriminate in subtle, rationalizable ways. Specifically, the present research explored both the overt expression of racial attitudes and discrimination in simulated employment decisions for two samples across a 10-year period, from 1988–1989 to 1998–1999.

According to the aversive-racism perspective, many people who explicitly support egalitarian principles and believe themselves to be nonprejudiced also unconsciously harbor negative feelings and beliefs about blacks and other historically disadvantaged groups. Aversive racists thus experience ambivalence

Address correspondence to John F. Dovidio, Department of Psychology, Colgate University, Hamilton, NY 13346; e-mail: jdovidio@mail.colgate.edu.

From *Psychological Science*, July 2000, pp. 315-319. © 2000 by the American Psychological Society. Reprinted by permission.

between their egalitarian beliefs and their negative feelings toward blacks. In contrast to the traditional emphasis on the psychopathological aspects of prejudice, the aversive-racism framework suggests that biases related to normal cognitive, motivational, and sociocultural processes may predispose a person to develop negative racial feelings (see Gaertner & Dovidio, 1986). Nevertheless, egalitarian traditions and norms are potent forces promoting racial equality (e.g., Kluegel & Smith, 1986). As a consequence of these widespread influences promoting both negative feelings and egalitarian beliefs, aversive racism is presumed to characterize the racial attitudes of a substantial portion of well-educated and liberal whites in the United States (Gaertner & Dovidio, 1986).

The aversive-racism framework further suggests that contemporary racial bias is expressed in indirect ways that do not threaten the aversive racist's nonprejudiced self-image. Because aversive racists consciously recognize and endorse egalitarian values, they will not discriminate in situations in which they recognize that discrimination would be obvious to others and themselves—for example, when the appropriate response is clearly dictated. However, because aversive racists do possess negative feelings, often unconsciously, discrimination occurs when bias is not obvious or can be rationalized on the basis of some factor other than race. We have found support for this framework across a range of experimental paradigms (see Dovidio & Gaertner, 1998; Gaertner & Dovidio, 1986).

Because the negative consequences of aversive racism are expressed in ways that are not easily recognizable (by oneself, as well as by others) as racial bias, traditional techniques for eliminating bias by emphasizing the immorality of prejudice and illegality of discrimination are not effective for combating contemporary racism: "Aversive racists recognize prejudice is bad, but they do not recognize that they are prejudiced. . . . Like a virus that has mutated, racism has also evolved into different forms that are more difficult not only to recognize but also to combat" (Dovidio & Gaertner, 1998, p. 25). Thus, direct and overt expressions of prejudice, such as self-reported attitudes, are more amenable to change and pressures of increasingly egalitarian norms (Kluegel & Smith, 1986) than are indirect manifestations of racism because they are more easily recognized as racial biases.

The present research was designed to extend the research on aversive racism by exploring changes, over a 10-year period, in expressed racial attitudes and patterns of discrimination in hiring recommendations for a black or white candidate for a position as a peer counselor. Two measures were taken from two comparable student samples 10 years apart. One measure was self-reported racial prejudice. The other measure involved decisions in a simulated employment context. Participants were asked to use interview excerpts to evaluate candidates for a new program for peer counseling at their university. Three profiles were developed: One reflected clearly strong qualifications (pretested as being accepted 85–90% of the time across two samples), one represented clearly weak qualifications (pretested as being accepted 10–20% of the time), and the third involved marginally acceptable but ambiguous qualifications (pretested as being accepted about 50–65% of the time). Participants evaluated a single candidate who was identifiable as black or white from information in the excerpt.

With respect to expressed racial attitudes, we predicted, on the basis of continued emphasis on egalitarian values in the United States (Schuman et al., 1997), that the general trend toward the expression of less prejudiced attitudes (Dovidio & Gaertner, 1998; Schuman et al., 1997) would be reflected across our two samples. Whereas expressed prejudice was expected to decline, we hypothesized that subtle, covert forms of discrimination would persist. Specifically, we predicted, on the basis of previous work on aversive racism as well as work showing that racial stereotypes are most influential in ambiguous situations (see Fiske, 1998), that discrimination against black applicants would occur when the match between the candidate's qualifications and the position criteria was unclear—in the ambiguous-qualifications condition—but not when candidates were clearly well qualified or unqualified for the position.

METHOD

Participants

Participants were 194 undergraduates at a Northeastern liberal arts college during the 1988–1989 academic year ($n = 112$; 48 white male and 64 white female undergraduates) or the 1998–1999 academic year ($n = 82$; 34 white male and 48 white female undergraduates). Participants were enrolled in the university's introductory psychology class, and admissions data indicated that the student populations were scholastically (e.g., standardized-test scores, high school grades) and demographically (e.g., geographical, sex, and racial distributions; socioeconomic status) comparable across the two time periods. Involvement in the study partially satisfied one option for a course requirement. Self-reported prejudice scores were available for 77% ($n = 86$) of participants in 1988–1989 and 87% ($n = 71$) of participants in 1998–1999.

Procedure

During mass pretesting sessions, participants were administered, along with several other surveys, questionnaires assessing their racial attitudes. For the present study, we examined responses to three racial-attitude items (Weigel & Howes, 1985) that were the same at both testing periods: "Blacks shouldn't push themselves where they are not wanted," "I would probably feel somewhat self-conscious dancing with a black person in a public place," and "I would mind it if a black family with about the same income and education as my own would move next door to my home." Responses were on a scale from 1 (disagree strongly) to 5 (agree strongly) (Cronbach's alpha = .71 overall).

Later, during an experimental session, participants (from 1 to 8 per session) were informed that they would be asked questions about "the desirability and feasibility of a peer counseling program and the qualities of personnel." They were randomly assigned to one of six conditions in a 3 (qualifications: clearly strong, ambiguous, clearly weak) × 2 (race of candidate) design. Thirty to 34 participants were assigned to each condition. After reading a 120-word description of an ostensibly new program, each participant was asked to evaluate a candidate from a previous round of applicants on the basis of interview excerpts. These excerpts were systematically varied to manipulate the strength of the candidate's qualifications. For the candidate with strong qualifications, leadership experiences included being co-captain of the swim team in high school and being a member of the disciplinary board in college; his self-description was "sensitive, intelligent, and relaxed." In response to the question "If a female student came to you because she was pregnant, what would you do?" this candidate was quoted as saying, "Explain options to her and ask her if she would like the telephone number of the health center." For the candidate with ambiguous qualifications, the candidate's leadership experiences included only being co-captain of the swim team in high school; his self-description was "sensitive, intelligent, and emotional." In response to the question about the female student who might be pregnant, this candidate said, "Ask her if she would like the telephone number of the health center." For the candidate with weak qualifications, the leadership experiences included being co-captain of the chess team in high school; his self-description was "independent, forthright, and intense." This candidate's response to the question about the student's pregnancy was, "Tell her that is too personal and that she must talk with her parents."

The race of the applicant was varied by the list of his activities. Black candidates listed membership in the Black Student Union, whereas white students listed fraternity membership (which was almost exclusively white on campus).

The final versions of the three "interview excerpts" were pretested with 20 undergraduate students from each time period. They were given all three excerpts, in random order and without racially identifying information. Undergraduates at both time periods clearly distinguished among strong, ambiguous, and weak qualifications. The strongly qualified candidate was recommended for the peer counselor program by 85% and 90% of the pretest participants at the two time periods, respectively; the candidate with ambiguous qualifications was recommended by 50% and 65% of these participants; and the candidate with weak qualifications was recommended by 20% and 10% of these students.

In the main study, students evaluated the candidates by rating them on a series of scales. The first item assessed perceptions of whether the candidate was qualified for the position, on a scale from 1 (not at all) to 10 (extremely); this item served as a check on the manipulation of the interview excerpts. The last two items represented the primary dependent measures. They asked whether participants would recommend the candidate for the position (yes or no) and how strongly they would recommend the candidate (on a scale from 1, not at all, to 10, very strongly). On the last page of the booklet, participants read, "When reading a resumé or transcript, people often form a visual image of a person. Based on the information provided, what image of the applicant have you formed?" A question about the candidate's race was included among other items about his imagined physical characteristics.

RESULTS

The manipulations of race and qualifications were effective. Participants identified the candidate as being white 100% of the time in the white-candidate condition and as being black 97% of the time in the black-candidate condition. Preliminary analyses of the yes/no recommendations and their strength revealed no systematic effects for the sex of the participant. Consequently, this factor was not included in subsequent analyses. A 3 (qualifications: clearly strong, ambiguous, clearly weak) × 2 (race of candidate) × 2 (time: 1988–1989, 1998–1999) analysis of variance demonstrated the expected main effect of manipulated qualifications on perceived qualifications, $F(1, 182) = 62.92$, $p < .001$ ($Ms = 7.21$ vs. 6.38 vs. 3.98; see Table 1). This main effect was uncomplicated by any interactions. Each of the three qualifications conditions differed significantly from the other two according to Scheffé post hoc tests.

The $3 \times 2 \times 2$ analysis of variance performed on the strength of recommendations revealed the anticipated main effect for qualifications, $F(1, 182) = 81.15$, $p < .001$ (see Table 1). Participants recommended candidates in the strong-qualifications condition most highly ($M = 6.85$), candidates in the ambiguous-qualifications condition next most highly ($M = 5.36$), and those in the weak-qualifications condition least highly ($M = 3.15$). Scheffé tests demonstrated that these means differed significantly from each other. There was no main effect for the candidate's race ($F < 1$), but the predicted Qualifications × Race of Candidate interaction was obtained, $F(2, 182) = 6.08$, $p < .003$. Planned comparisons revealed no significant difference in the strength of recommendations for black and white candidates who had strong qualifications ($Ms = 7.18$ vs. 6.52, $p > .10$) or who had weak qualifications ($Ms = 3.50$ vs. 2.81, $p > .10$). However, as predicted, ambiguously qualified black candidates were recommended significantly less strongly than were comparable white candidates ($Ms = 4.82$ vs. 5.91), $t(64) = 2.79$, $p < .001$. In addition, Scheffé tests comparing the strengths of participants' recommendations revealed that when the applicant was white, participants responded to ambiguous qualifications more as if these qualifications were strong (difference between means = 0.61, n.s.; Table 1) than as if they were weak (difference = 3.10, $p < .05$). When the applicant was black, however, participants reacted to ambiguous qualifications more like weak qualifications (difference between means = 1.32, n.s.) than like strong qualifications (difference = 2.36, $p < .05$).

Moreover, the Qualifications × Race of Candidate interaction was comparable across participants in the 1988–1989 and the 1998–1999 samples: The Qualifications × Race of Candidate × Time interaction did not approach significance, $F(2, 182) = 0.61$, $p > .54$. The Qualifications × Race of Candidate

Table 1. *Perceived qualifications and candidate recommendations as a function of the candidate's qualifications and race*

Condition	Perceived qualifications[a] 1988–1989	1998–1999	Both	Strength of recommendation[a] 1988–1989	1998–1999	Both	Percentage recommended 1988–1989	1998–1999	Both
Clearly strong qualifications									
White candidate	7.32	6.93	7.15	6.74	6.21	6.52	89	79	85
	(1.46)	(2.06)	(1.72)	(1.41)	(2.09)	(1.72)			
Black candidate	7.79	6.60	7.27	7.32	7.00	7.18	95	87	91
	(1.23)	(1.77)	(1.58)	(1.67)	(1.60)	(1.62)			
Ambiguous qualifications									
White candidate	6.45	5.85	6.21	6.05	5.69	5.91	75	77	76
	(1.11)	(1.68)	(1.36)	(1.73)	(1.60)	(1.67)			
Black candidate	6.72	6.33	6.55	5.06	4.53	4.82	50	40	45
	(1.32)	(1.59)	(1.44)	(1.39)	(1.64)	(1.51)			
Clearly weak qualifications									
White candidate	3.90	3.67	3.81	3.05	2.42	2.81	5	8	6
	(2.00)	(2.27)	(2.07)	(1.65)	(1.68)	(1.66)			
Black candidate	4.24	4.08	4.17	3.29	3.77	3.50	12	15	13
	(1.75)	(2.06)	(1.86)	(1.69)	(1.69)	(1.68)			

[a]Table entries are means, with standard deviations in parentheses. Reponses were on a scale from 1 (*not at all qualified* or *not at all recommended*) to 10 (*extremely qualified* or *very strongly recommended*).

interaction was marginally significant for participants in 1988–1989, $F(2, 106) = 2.54$, $p < .083$; it was significant for participants in the 1998–1999 sample alone, $F(2, 76) = 3.94$, $p < .024$ (see Table 1).

Log-linear analyses, paralleling those for the strength of recommendations, were conducted on the dichotomous (yes/no) recommendation measure. These analyses yielded the same pattern of results. Overall, candidates in the strong qualifications condition were recommended most frequently (88%), those in the ambiguous-qualifications condition were recommended next most frequently (61%), and those in the weak-qualifications condition were recommended least frequently (10%), $\chi^2(2, N = 194) = 80.37$, $p < .001$. The Qualifications × Race of Candidate interaction was also obtained, $\chi^2(2, N = 194) = 6.75$, $p < .035$. Black and white candidates were recommended equivalently often in the strong-qualifications (91% vs. 85%) and weak-qualifications (13% vs. 6%) conditions ($ps > .50$), but blacks were recommended less often than whites in the ambiguous-qualifications condition (45% vs. 76%), $\chi^2(1, N = 66) = 6.35$, $p < .012$. Again, the interaction was not moderated by the time period in which the data were collected; the three-way interaction did not approach significance ($p > .50$). Taken together, the results for the strength of recommendations and the yes/no measure offer support for the hypotheses.

For the participants for whom prejudice scores were available, the 3 (qualifications) × 2 (race of candidate) × 2 (time: 1988–1989, 1998–1999) analysis of variance demonstrated only a main effect for time, $F(1, 145) = 8.31$, $p < .005$. As expected, participants in the 1988–1989 had higher prejudice scores than those in 1998–1999 ($Ms = 1.84$ vs. 1.54). In addition, for both ratings of qualifications and recommendations, 3 × 2 × 2 × 2 (prejudice) analyses of variance, classifying participants in the two samples as high or low in prejudice on the basis of median splits, were performed. There were no significant effects for prejudice qualifying the results reported earlier. However, overall, participants higher in prejudice (as a continuous variable) recommended black candidates less strongly than participants lower in prejudice, $r(79) = -.24$, $p < .05$. The correlation between prejudice and strength of recommendation was nonsignificant for white applicants, $r(74) = .05$, $p > .50$.

DISCUSSION

Overall, the pattern of results supports the hypothesis derived from the aversive-racism framework. As predicted from that framework, and consistent with other theories of modern racism (e.g., McConahay, 1986), and the influence of stereotyping (Fiske, 1998), bias against blacks in simulated hiring decisions was manifested primarily when a candidate's qualifications for the position were ambiguous. When a black candidate's credentials clearly qualified him for the position, or when his credentials clearly were not appropriate, there was no discrimination against him. Moreover, as expected, self-reported expressions of prejudice declined significantly across the 10-year period. Taken together, these contrasting trends for self-reported prejudice and discrimination in simulated employment decisions support our hypothesis that the development of contemporary forms of prejudice, such as aversive racism, may account—at least in part—for the persistence of racial disparities in society despite significant decreases in expressed racial prejudice and stereotypes. However, this finding does not imply that old-fashioned racism is no longer a problem. In fact, the overall negative correlation between expressed prejudice and recommendations for black candidates suggests that traditional racism is a force that still exists and that can operate independently of contemporary forms of racism.

One potential alternative explanation for the results of the employment decision is that the credentials in the clear-qualifications condition were so extreme that ceiling and floor effects suppressed the variance in responses and reduced the likelihood of obtaining differences as a function of the candidate's race. Although plausible, this explanation is not supported empirically. The strength-of-recommendation measure could range from 1 to 10, and the means in the strong-qualifications condition (6.52 for white candidates and 7.18 for black candidates) and the weak-qualifications condition (2.81 for white candidates and 3.50 for black candidates) did not closely approach these scale endpoints. This restricted-range interpretation would also suggest that the within-condition standard deviations would be substantially lower in the clear-qualifications conditions than in the ambiguous-qualifications condition. As illustrated in Table 1, this was not the case. The standard deviations were similar for both white candidates (1.72 and 1.66 vs. 1.67) and black candidates (1.62 and 1.68 vs. 1.51); there was no statistical evidence of heterogeneity of within-group variances. Thus, this extremity explanation cannot readily account for the obtained pattern of results.

In addition, although we had predicted, on the basis of the ambiguity versus clarity of appropriate decisions, that discrimination against blacks would be unlikely to occur when qualifications were either clearly weak or clearly strong, other perspectives could suggest that bias would occur in these conditions. In the weak-qualifications condition, the black candidate's clear lack of credentials could have provided an ostensibly nonracial justification for particularly negative evaluations. Although a floor effect offers one potential explanation for the lack of difference in this condition, as we noted earlier, the within-cell standard deviations do not readily support this interpretation. Another possibility is that because the black candidate did not display obviously negative qualities, but rather insufficiently positive ones, excessive devaluation of this candidate was difficult to rationalize. Contemporary racism is hypothesized to involve sympathy for blacks (Katz, Wackenhut, & Hass, 1986), as well as cautiousness by whites about being too negative in evaluations of blacks (and thus appearing biased); either or both of these factors could have limited the negativity of response to blacks when qualifications were weak and could account for the slightly more positive response to black than to white candidates in this condition (see Table 1). In addition, sympathy and concerns about being too harsh in evaluations are particularly likely to occur when the relevance to the evaluator and the challenge to the status quo are minimal (see Dovidio & Gaertner, 1996; McConahay, 1986). Participants were not led to believe that their responses would directly influence the outcome of the particular candidate's application in the current study. Under conditions of greater relevance to the evaluator, greater bias toward either highly qualified or underqualified blacks may occur as a function of direct or symbolic threats (Dovidio & Gaertner, 1996).

The overall pattern of results obtained in the present study also helps to illuminate some of the processes underlying the effects of aversive racism. In particular, participants' ratings of the candidates' qualifications were not directly influenced by race: Participants rate the objective qualifications of blacks and whites equivalently. The effect of race seemed to occur not in how the qualifications were perceived, but in how they were considered and weighed in the recommendation decisions. We (Gaertner et al., 1997) have proposed, for example, that the effects of aversive racism may be rooted substantially in intergroup biases based on social categorization processes. These biases reflect in-group favoritism as well as out-group derogation. Along these lines, Hewstone (1990) found that people tend to judge a potentially negative behavior as more negative and intentional, and are more likely to attribute the behavior to the person's personality, when the behavior is performed by an out-group member than when it is performed by an in-group member. Thus, when given latitude for interpretation, as in the ambiguous-qualifications condition, whites may give white candidates the "benefit of the doubt," a benefit that is not extended to out-group members (i.e., to black candidates). As a consequence, as demonstrated in the present study, moderate qualifications are responded to as if they were strong qualifications when the candidate is white, but as if they were weak qualifications when the candidate is black.

The subtle, rationalizable type of bias demonstrated in the present study, which is manifested in terms of in-group favoritism, can pose unique challenges to the legal system. As Krieger (1998) observed, "Title VII is poorly equipped to control prejudice resulting from in-group favoritism" (p. 1325). Identifying the existence and persistence of subtle bias associated with aversive racism can thus help to demonstrate that discrimination is not "a thing of the past" and can encourage renewed efforts to develop techniques to combat contemporary racial bias.

ACKNOWLEDGMENTS

We express our appreciation to Marnie Tobriner and Abby Russin for their assistance in the collection of the data and to Gifford Weary and three anonymous reviewers for their helpful and insightful comments on an earlier version of the manuscript. The research and preparation of this manuscript were supported by National Institute of Mental Health Grant MH48721.

REFERENCES

Dovidio, J.F., & Gaertner, S.L. (1996). Affirmative action, unintentional racial biases, and intergroup relations. *Journal of Social Issues, 52*(4), 51–75.

Dovidio, J.F., & Gaertner, S.L. (1998). On the nature of contemporary prejudice: The causes, consequences, and challenges of aversive racism. In J. Eberhardt & S.T. Fiske (Eds.), *Confronting racism: The problem and the response* (pp. 3–32). Newbury Park, CA: Sage.

Fiske, S. (1998). Stereotyping, prejudice, and discrimination. In D. Gilbert, S. Fiske, & G. Lindzey (Eds.), *The handbook of social psychology* (4th ed., Vol. 2, pp. 357–411). New York: McGraw-Hill.

Gaertner, S.L. & Dovidio, J.F. (1986). The aversive form of racism. In J.F. Dovidio & S.L. Gaertner (Eds.), *Prejudice, discrimination, and racism* (pp. 61–89). Orlando, FL: Academic Press.

Gaertner, S.L., Dovidio, J.F., Banker, B., Rust, M., Nier, J., Mottola, G., & Ward, C. (1997). Does racism necessarily mean anti-blackness? Aversive racism and pro-whiteness. In M. Fine, L. Powell, L. Weis, & M. Wong (Eds.), *Off white* (pp. 167–178). London: Routledge.

Hacker, A. (1995). *Two nations: Black and White, separate, hostile, unequal.* New York: Ballantine Books.

Hewstone, M. (1990). The "ultimate attribution error"? A review of the literature on intergroup attributions. *European Journal of Social Psychology, 20,* 311–335.

Katz, I., Wackenhut, J., & Hass, R.G. (1986). Racial ambivalence, value duality, and behavior. In J.F. Dovidio & S.L. Gaertner (Eds.), *Prejudice, discrimination, and racism* (pp. 35–59). Orlando, FL: Academic Press.

Kluegel, J.R., Smith, E.R. (1986). *Beliefs about inequality: America's views of what is and what ought to be.* New York: Aldine de Gruyter.

Krieger, L.H. (1998). Civil rights perestroika: Intergroup relations after affirmative action. *California Law Review, 86,* 1251–1333.

McConahay, J.B. (1986). Modern racism, ambivalence, and the modern racism scale. In J.F. Dovidio & S.L. Gaertner (Eds.), *Prejudice, discrimination, and racism* (pp. 91–125). Orlando, FL: Academic Press.

Schuman, H., Steeh, C., Bobo, L., & Krysan, M. (1997). *Racial attitudes in America: Trends and interpretations.* Cambridge, MA: Harvard University Press.

Sears, D.O., van Laar, C., Carillo, M., & Kosterman, R. (1997). Is it really racism? The origin of white Americans' opposition to race-targeted policies. *Public Opinion Quarterly, 61,* 15–53.

Weigel, R.H., & Howes, P.W. (1985). Conceptions of racial prejudice: Symbolic racism reconsidered. *Journal of Social Issues, 41*(3), 117–138.

(RECEIVED 8/4/99; REVISION ACCEPTED 1/20/00)

THIN ICE:

"STEREOTYPE THREAT" AND BLACK COLLEGE STUDENTS

by CLAUDE M. STEELE

When capable black college students fail to perform as well as their white counterparts, the explanation often has less to do with preparation or ability than with the threat of stereotypes about their capacity to succeed. Educators at Stanford who tested this hypothesis report their findings and propose solutions

Claude M. Steele is the Lucie Stern Professor in the Social Sciences at Stanford University. His articles have appeared in *The New York Times* and *The American Prospect*.

THE buildings had hardly changed in the thirty years since I'd been there. "There" was a small liberal-arts school quite near the college that I attended. In my student days I had visited it many times to see friends. This time I was there to give a speech about how racial and gender stereotypes, floating and abstract though they might seem, can affect concrete things like grades, test scores, and academic identity. My talk was received warmly, and the next morning I met with a small group of African-American students. I have done this on many campuses. But this time, perhaps cued by the familiarity of the place, I had an experience of déjà vu. The students expressed a litany of complaints that could have come straight from the mouths of the black friends I had visited there thirty years earlier: the curriculum was too white, they heard too little black music, they were ignored in class, and too often they felt slighted by faculty members and other students. Despite the school's recruitment efforts, they were a small minority. The core of their social life was their own group. To relieve the dysphoria, they went home a lot on weekends.

I found myself giving them the same advice my father gave me when I was in college: lighten up on the politics, get the best education you can, and move on. But then I surprised myself by saying, "To do this you have to learn from people who part of yourself tells you are difficult to trust."

Over the past four decades African-American college students have been more in the spotlight than any other American students. This is because they aren't just college students; they are a cutting edge in America's effort to integrate itself in the thirty-five years since the passage of the Civil Rights Act. These students have borne much of the burden for our national experiment in racial integration. And to a significant degree the success of the experiment will be determined by their success.

Nonetheless, throughout the 1990s the national college-dropout rate for African-Americans has been 20 to 25 percent higher than that for whites. Among those who

 From *The Atlantic Monthly,* August 1999, pp. 44-47, 50-54. © 1999 by Claude Steele. Reprinted by permission.

finish college, the grade-point average of black students is two thirds of a grade below that of whites.

A recent study by William Bowen and Derek Bok, reported in their book *The Shape of the River*, brings some happy news: despite this underachievement in college, black students who attend the most selective schools in the country go on to do just as well in postgraduate programs and professional attainment as other students from those schools. This is a telling fact in support of affirmative action, since only these schools use affirmative action in admissions. Still, the underperformance of black undergraduates is an unsettling problem, one that may alter or hamper career development, especially among blacks not attending the most selective schools.

Attempts to explain the problem can sound like a debate about whether America is a good society, at least by the standard of racial fairness, and maybe even about whether racial integration is possible. It is an uncomfortably finger-pointing debate. Does the problem stem from something about black students themselves, such as poor motivation, a distracting peer culture, lack of family values, or—the unsettling suggestion of *The Bell Curve*—genes? Or does it stem from the conditions of blacks' lives: social and economic deprivation, a society that views blacks through the lens of diminishing stereotypes and low expectations, too much coddling, or too much neglect?

In recent years this debate has acquired a finer focus: the fate of middle-class black students. Americans have come to view the disadvantages associated with being black as disadvantages primarily of social and economic resources and opportunity. This assumption is often taken to imply that if you are black and come from a socioeconomically middle-class home, you no longer suf-

---

The finger-pointing debate over the underperformance of black undergraduates has missed one big culprit—"stereotype threat." This is the threat of being viewed through the lens of a negative stereotype, or the fear of doing something that would inadvertantly confirm that stereotype.

---

fer a significant disadvantage of race. "Why should the son of a black physician be given an advantage in college admission over the son of a white delivery-truck driver?" This is a standard question in the controversy over affirmative action. And the assumption behind it is that surely in today's society the disadvantages of race are overcome when lower socioeconomic status is overcome.

But virtually all aspects of underperformance—lower standardized-test scores, lower college grades, lower graduation rates—persist among students from the African-American middle class. This situation forces on us

an uncomfortable recognition: that beyond class, something racial is depressing the academic performance of these students.

Some time ago I and two colleagues, Joshua Aronson and Steven Spencer, tried to see the world from the standpoint of these students, concerning ourselves less with features of theirs that might explain their troubles than with features of the world they see. A story I was told recently depicts some of these. The storyteller was worried about his friend, a normally energetic black student who had broken up with his longtime girlfriend and had since learned that she, a Hispanic, was now dating a white student. This hit him hard. Not long after hearing about his girlfriend, he sat through an hour's discussion of *The Bell Curve* in his psychology class, during which the possible genetic inferiority of his race was openly considered. Then he overheard students at lunch arguing that affirmative action allowed in too many underqualified blacks. By his own account, this young man had experienced very little of what he thought of as racial discrimination on campus. Still, these were features of his world. Could they have a bearing on his academic life?

My colleagues and I have called such features "stereotype threat"—the threat of being viewed through the lens of a negative stereotype, or the fear of doing something that would inadvertently confirm that stereotype. Everyone experiences stereotype threat. We are all members of some group about which negative stereotypes exist, from white males and Methodists to women and the elderly. And in a situation where one of those stereotypes applies—a man talking to women about pay equity, for example, or an aging faculty member trying to remember a number sequence in the middle of a lecture—we know that we may be judged by it.

Like the young man in the story, we can feel mistrustful and apprehensive in such situations. For him, as for African-American students generally, negative stereotypes apply in many situations, even personal ones. Why was that old roommate unfriendly to him? Did that young white woman who has been so nice to him in class not return his phone call because she's afraid he'll ask her for a date? Is it because of his race or something else about him? He cannot know the answers, but neither can his rational self fully dismiss the questions. Together they raise a deeper question: Will his race be a boundary to his experience, to his emotions, to his relationships?

With time he may weary of the extra vigilance these situations require and of what the psychologists Jennifer Crocker and Brenda Major have called the "attributional ambiguity" of being on the receiving end of negative stereotypes. To reduce this stress he may learn to care less about the situations and activities that bring it about—to realign his self-regard so that it no longer depends on how he does in the situation. We have called this psychic adjustment "disidentification." Pain is lessened by ceasing to identify with the part of life in which the pain occurs. This withdrawal of psychic investment may be supported by other members of the stereotype-threatened group—even to the point of its becoming a group norm. But not caring can mean not being motivated. And this can have real costs. When stereotype threat affects school life, disidentification is a high price to pay for psychic comfort. Still, it is a price that groups contending with powerful negative stereotypes about their abilities—women in advanced math, African-Americans in all academic areas—may too often pay.

MEASURING STEREOTYPE THREAT

CAN stereotype threat be shown to affect academic performance? And if so, who would be most affected—stronger or weaker students? Which has a greater influence on academic success among black college students—the degree of threat or the level of preparation with which they enter college? Can the college experience be redesigned to lessen the threat? And if so, would that redesign help these students to succeed academically?

As we confronted these questions in the course of our research, we came in for some surprises. We began with what we took to be the hardest question: Could something as abstract as stereotype threat really affect something as irrepressible as intelligence? Ours is an individualistic culture; forward movement is seen to come from within. Against this cultural faith one needs evidence to argue that something as "sociological" as stereotype threat can repress something as "individualistic" as intelligence.

To acquire such evidence, Joshua Aronson and I (following a procedure developed with Steven Spencer) designed an experiment to test whether the stereotype threat that black students might experience when taking a difficult standardized test could depress their performance on the test to a statistically reliable degree. In this experiment we asked black and white Stanford students into our laboratory and gave them, one at a time, a thirty-minute verbal test made up of items from the advanced Graduate Record Examination in literature. Most of these students were sophomores, which meant that the test was particularly hard for them—precisely the feature, we reasoned, that would make this simple testing situation different for our black participants than for our white participants.

In matters of race we often assume that when a situation is objectively the same for different groups, it is *experienced* in the same way by each group. This assumption might seem especially reasonable in the case of "standardized" cognitive tests. But for black students, difficulty with the test makes the negative stereotype relevant as an interpretation of their performance, and of them. They know that they are especially likely to be seen as having limited ability. Groups not stereotyped in

this way don't experience this extra intimidation. And it is a serious intimidation, implying as it does that they may not belong in walks of life where the tested abilities are important—walks of life in which they are heavily invested. Like many pressures, it may not be experienced in a fully conscious way, but it may impair their best thinking.

This is exactly what Aronson and I found. When the difficult verbal test was presented as a test of ability, black students performed dramatically less well than white students, even though we had statistically matched the two groups in ability level. Something other than ability was involved; we believed it was stereotype threat.

But maybe the black students performed less well than the white students because they were less motivated, or because their skills were somehow less applicable to the advanced material of this test. We needed some way to determine if it was indeed stereotype threat that depressed the black students' scores. We reasoned that if stereotype threat had impaired their performance on the test, then reducing this threat would allow their performance to improve. We presented the same test as a laboratory task that was used to study how certain problems are generally solved. We stressed that the task did not measure a person's level of intellectual ability. A simple instruction, yes, but it profoundly changed the meaning of the situation. In one stroke "spotlight anxiety," as the psychologist William Cross once called it, was turned off—and the black students' performance on the test rose to match that of equally qualified whites.

Aronson and I decided that what we needed next was direct evidence of the subjective state we call stereotype threat. To seek this, we looked into whether simply sitting down to take a difficult test of ability was enough to make black students mindful of their race and stereotypes about it. This may seem unlikely. White students I have taught over the years have sometimes said that they have hardly any sense of even having a race. But blacks have many experiences with the majority "other group" that make their race salient to them.

We again brought black and white students in to take a difficult verbal test. But just before the test began, we gave them a long list of words, each of which had two letters missing. They were told to complete the words on this list as fast as they could. We knew from a preliminary survey that twelve of the eighty words we had selected could be completed in such a way as to relate to the stereotype about blacks' intellectual ability. The fragment "—ce," for example, could become "race." If simply taking a difficult test of ability was enough to make black students mindful of stereotypes about their race, these students should complete more fragments with stereotype-related words. That is just what happened. When black students were told that the test would measure ability, they completed the fragments with significantly more stereotype-related words than when they were told that it was not a measure of ability.

Whites made few stereotype-related completions in either case.

What kind of worry is signaled by this race consciousness? To find out, we used another probe. We asked participants on the brink of the difficult test to tell us their preferences in sports and music. Some of these, such as basketball, jazz, and hip-hop, are associated with African-American imagery, whereas others, such as tennis, swimming, and classical music, are not. Something striking emerged: when black students expected to take a test of ability, they spurned things African-American, reporting less interest in, for instance, basketball, jazz, and hip-hop than whites did. When the test was presented as unrelated to ability, black students strongly preferred things African-American. They eschewed these things only when preferring them would encourage a stereotypic view of themselves. It was the spotlight that they were trying to avoid.

STEREOTYPE THREAT VERSUS SELF-FULFILLING PROPHECY

ANOTHER question arises: Do the effects of stereotype threat come entirely from the fear of being stereotyped, or do they come from something internal to black students—self-doubt, for example?

Beginning with George Herbert Mead's idea of the "looking-glass self," social psychology has assumed that one's self-image derives in large part from how one is viewed by others—family, school, and the broader society. When those views are negative, people may internalize them, resulting in lower self-esteem—or self-hatred, as it has been called. This theory was first applied to the experience of Jews, by Sigmund Freud and Bruno Bettelheim, but it was also soon applied to the experience of African-Americans, by Gordon Allport, Frantz Fanon, Kenneth Clark, and others. According to the theory, black students internalize negative stereotypes as performance anxiety and low expectations for achievement, which they then fulfill. The "self-fulfilling prophecy" has become a commonplace about these students. Stereotype threat, however, is something different, something external: the situational threat of being negatively stereotyped. Which of these two processes, then, caused the results of our experiments?

Joshua Aronson, Michael Lustina, Kelli Keough, Joseph Brown, Catherine Good, and I devised a way to find out. Suppose we told white male students who were strong in math that a difficult math test they were about to take was one on which Asians generally did better than whites. White males should not have a sense of group inferiority about math, since no societal stereotype alleges such an inferiority. Yet this comment would put them under a form of stereotype threat: any faltering on the test could cause them to be seen negatively from the standpoint of the positive stereotype about Asians and math ability. If stereotype threat alone—in the absence of any internalized self-doubt—was capable of disrupting test performance, then white males taking the test after this comment should perform less well than white males taking the test without hearing the comment. That is just what happened. Stereotype threat impaired intellectual functioning in a group unlikely to have any sense of group inferiority.

In science, as in the rest of life, few things are definitive. But these results are pretty good evidence that stereotype threat's impairment of standardized-test performance does not depend on cueing a pre-existing anxiety. Steven Spencer, Diane Quinn, and I have shown how stereotype threat depresses the performance of accomplished female math students on a difficult math test, and how that performance improves dramatically when the threat is lifted. Jean-Claude Croizet, working in France with a stereotype that links poor verbal skills with lower-class status, found analogous results: lower-class college students performed less well than upper-class college students under the threat of a stereotype-based judgment, but performed as well when the threat was removed.

Is everyone equally threatened and disrupted by a stereotype? One might expect, for example, that it would affect the weakest students most. But in all our research the most achievement-oriented students, who were also the most skilled, motivated, and confident, were the most impaired by stereotype threat. This fact had been under our noses all along—in our data and even in our theory. A person has to care about a domain in order to be disturbed by the prospect of being stereotyped in it. That is the whole idea of disidentification—protecting against stereotype threat by ceasing to care about the domain in which the stereotype applies. Our earlier experiments had selected black students who identified with verbal skills and women who identified with math. But when we tested participants who identified less with these domains, what had been under our noses hit us in the face. None of them showed any effect of stereotype threat whatsoever.

These weakly identified students did not perform well on the test: once they discovered its difficulty, they stopped trying very hard and got a low score. But their performance did not differ depending on whether they felt they were at risk of being judged stereotypically.

WHY STRONG STUDENTS ARE STEREOTYPE-THREATENED

THIS finding, I believe, tells us two important things. The first is that the poorer college performance of black students may have another source in addition to the one—lack of good preparation and, perhaps, of identification with school achievement—that is commonly understood. This additional source—the threat of being negatively stereotyped in the environment—has not been well understood. The distinction has important policy implications: different kinds of students may require different pedagogies of improvement.

The second thing is poignant: what exposes students to the pressure of stereotype threat is not weaker academic identity and skills but stronger academic identity and skills. They may have long seen themselves as good students—better than most. But led into the domain by their strengths, they pay an extra tax on their investment—vigilant worry that their future will be compromised by society's perception and treatment of their group.

This tax has a long tradition in the black community. The Jackie Robinson story is a central narrative of black life, literature, and journalism. *Ebony* magazine has run a page for fifty years featuring people who have broken down one or another racial barrier. Surely the academic vanguard among black college students today knows this tradition—and knows, therefore, that the thing to do, as my father told me, is to buckle down, pay whatever tax is required, and disprove the damn stereotype.

That, however, seems to be precisely what these students are trying to do. In some of our experiments we administered the test of ability by computer, so that we could see how long participants spent looking at different parts of the test questions. Black students taking the test under stereotype threat seemed to be trying too hard rather than not hard enough. They reread the questions, reread the multiple choices, rechecked their answers, more than when they were not under stereotype threat. The threat made them inefficient on a test that, like most standardized tests, is set up so that thinking long often means thinking wrong, especially on difficult items like the ones we used.

Philip Uri Treisman, an innovator in math workshops for minority students who is based at the University of Texas, saw something similar in his black calculus students at the University of California at Berkeley: they worked long hours alone but they worked inefficiently—for example, checking and rechecking their calculations against the correct answers at the back of the book, rather than focusing on the concepts involved. Of course, trying extra hard helps with some school tasks. But under stereotype threat this effort may be misdirected. Achievement at the frontier of one's skills may be furthered more by a relaxed, open concentration than by a strong desire to disprove a stereotype by not making mistakes.

Sadly, the effort that accompanies stereotype threat exacts an additional price. Led by James Blascovich, of the University of California at Santa Barbara, we found that the blood pressure of black students performing a difficult cognitive task under stereotype threat was elevated compared with that of black students not under stereotype threat or white students in either situation.

In the old song about the "steel-drivin' man," John Henry races the new steam-driven drill to see who can dig a hole faster. When the race is over, John Henry has prevailed by digging the deeper hole—only to drop dead. The social psychologist Sherman James uses the term "John Henryism" to describe a psychological syndrome that he found to be associated with hypertension in several samples of North Carolina blacks: holding too rigidly to the faith that discrimination and disadvantage can be overcome with hard work and persistence. Certainly this is the right attitude. But taken to extremes, it can backfire. A deterioration of performance under stereotype threat by the skilled, confident black students in our experiments may be rooted in John Henryism.

This last point can be disheartening. Our research, however, offers an interesting suggestion about what can be done to overcome stereotype threat and its detrimental effects. The success of black students may depend less on expectations and motivation—things that are thought to drive academic performance—than on trust that stereotypes about their group will not have a limiting effect in their school world.

HOW TO REDUCE STEREOTYPE THREAT

PUTTING this idea to the test, Joseph Brown and I asked, How can the usual detrimental effect of stereotype threat on the standardized-test performance of these students be reduced? By strengthening students' expectations and confidence, or by strengthening their trust that they are not at risk of being judged on the basis of stereotypes? In the ensuing experiment we strengthened or weakened participants' confidence in their verbal skills, by arranging for them to have either an impressive success or an impressive failure on a test of verbal skills, just before they took the same difficult verbal test we had used in our earlier research. When the second test was presented as a test of ability, the boosting or weakening of confidence in their verbal skills had no effect on performance: black participants performed less well than equally skilled white participants. What does this say about the commonsense idea that black students' academic problems are rooted in lack of self-confidence?

What did raise the level of black students' performance to that of equally qualified whites was reducing stereotype threat—in this case by explicitly presenting the test as racially fair. When this was done, blacks performed at the same high level as whites even if their self-confidence had been weakened by a prior failure.

These results suggest something that I think has not been made clear elsewhere: when strong black students sit down to take a difficult standardized test, the extra

Our research bears a practical message: although stereotypes held by the larger society may be hard to change, it is possible to create educational niches in which negative stereotypes are not felt to apply— and which permit a sense of trust that would otherwise be difficult to sustain.

apprehension they feel in comparison with whites is less about their own ability than it is about having to perform on a test and in a situation that may be primed to treat them stereotypically. We discovered the extent of this apprehension when we tried to develop procedures that would make our black participants see the test as "race-fair." It wasn't easy. African-Americans have endured so much bad press about test scores for so long that, in our experience, they are instinctively wary about the tests' fairness. We were able to convince them that our test was race-fair only when we implied that the research generating the test had been done by blacks. When they felt trust, they performed well regardless of whether we had weakened their self-confidence beforehand. And when they didn't feel trust, no amount of bolstering of self-confidence helped.

Policies for helping black students rest in significant part on assumptions about their psychology. As noted, they are typically assumed to lack confidence, which spawns a policy of confidence-building. This may be useful for students at the academic rearguard of the group. But the psychology of the academic vanguard appears different—underperformance appears to be rooted less in self-doubt than in social mistrust.

Education policy relevant to non-Asian minorities might fruitfully shift its focus toward fostering racial trust in the schooling situation—at least among students who come to school with good skills and high expectations. But how should this be done? Without particulars this conclusion can fade into banality, suggesting, as Alan Ryan has wryly put it in *Liberal Anxieties and Liberal Education*, that these students "will hardly be able to work at all unless everyone else exercises the utmost sensitivity to [their] anxieties." Sensitivity is nice, but it is an awful lot to expect, and even then, would it instill trust?

That is exactly what Geoffrey Cohen, Lee Ross, and I wondered as we took up the question of how a teacher or a mentor could give critical feedback across the "racial divide" and have that feedback be trusted. We reasoned that an answer to this question might yield insights about how to instill trust more broadly in the schooling environment. Cohen's hunch was that niceness alone wouldn't be enough. But the first question had to be whether there was in fact a racial divide between teachers and students, especially in the elite college environment in which we worked.

We set up a simple experiment. Cohen asked black and white Stanford students one at a time to write essays about their favorite teachers, for possible publication in a journal on teaching. They were asked to return several days later for feedback on their essays. Before each student left the first writing session, Cohen put a Polaroid snapshot of the student on top of his or her essay. His ostensible purpose was to publish the picture if the essay was published. His real purpose was to let the essay writers know that the evaluator of their writing would be aware of their race. When they returned days later, they were given constructive but critical feedback. We looked at whether different ways of giving this feedback engendered different degrees of trust in it.

We found that neither straight feedback nor feedback preceded by the "niceness" of a cushioning statement ("There were many good things about your essay") was trusted by black students. They saw these criticisms as probably biased, and they were less motivated than white students to improve their essays. White students took the criticism at face value—even as an indication of interest in them. Black students, however, faced a different meaning: the "ambiguating" possibility that the criticism was motivated by negative stereotypes about their group as much as by the work itself. Herein lies the power of race to make one's world insecure—quite apart from whatever actual discrimination one may experience.

But this experiment also revealed a way to be critical across the racial divide: tell the students that you are using high standards (this signals that the criticism reflects standards rather than race), and that your reading of their essays leads you to believe that they can meet those standards (this signals that you do not view them stereotypically). This shouldn't be faked. High standards, at least in a relative sense, should be an inherent part of teaching, and critical feedback should be given in the belief that the recipient can reach those standards. These things go without saying for many students. But they have to be made explicit for students under stereotype threat. The good news of this study is that when they *are* made explicit, the students trust and respond to criticism. Black students who got this kind of feedback saw it as unbiased and were motivated to take their essays home and work on them even though this was not a class for credit. They were more motivated than any other group of students in the study—as if this combination of high standards and assurance was like water on parched land, a much needed but seldom received balm.

REASSESSING THE TEST-SCORE GAP

THERE is, of course, another explanation for why black college students haven't fared well on predominantly white campuses: they aren't prepared for the competition. This has become an assumption of those who oppose affirmative action in college admissions. Racial preference, the argument goes, brings black students onto campuses where they simply aren't prepared to compete.

The fact most often cited in support of the underpreparation explanation is the lower SAT scores of black students, which sometimes average 200 points below those of other students on the same campus. The test-score gap has become shorthand for black students' achievement problems. But the gap must be assessed cautiously.

First, black students have better skills than the gap suggests. Most of the gap exists because the proportion of blacks with very high SAT scores is smaller than the corresponding proportions of whites and Asians. Thus when each group's scores are averaged, the black average will be lower than the white and Asian averages. This would be true even if the same admissions cut-off score were used for each group—even if, for example, affirmative action were eliminated entirely. Why a smaller proportion of blacks have very high scores is, of course, a complex question with multiple answers, involving, among other things, the effects of race on educational access and experience as well as the processes dwelt on in this article. The point, though, is that blacks' test-score deficits are taken as a sign of underpreparation, whereas in fact virtually all black students on a given campus have tested skills within the same range as the tested skills of other students on the campus.

In any case, the skills and preparation measured by these tests also turn out not to be good determinants of college success. As the makers of the SAT themselves tell us, although this test is among the best of its kind, it measures only about 18 percent of the skills that influence first-year grades, and even less of what influences subsequent grades, graduation rates, and professional success.

Indulge a basketball analogy that my colleagues Jay Rosner and Lee Ross and I have developed. Suppose that you were obliged to select a basketball team on the basis of how many of ten free throws a player makes. You'd regret having to select players on the basis of a single criterion. You'd know that free-throw shooting involves only a few of the skills that go into basketball—and, worse, you'd know that you'd never pick a Shaquille O'Neal.

You'd also wonder how to interpret a player's score. If he made ten out of ten or zero out of ten, you'd be fairly confident about making a judgment. But what about the kid who makes five, six, or seven? Middling scores like these could be influenced by many things other than underlying potential for free-throw shooting or basketball playing. How much practice was involved? Was the kid having a good or a bad day? Roughly the same is true, I suggest, for standardized-test scores. Are they inflated by middle-class advantages such as prep courses, private schools, and tours of European cathedrals? Are they deflated by race-linked experiences such as social segregation and being consistently assigned to the lower tracks in school?

In sum, black college students are not as underprepared in academic skills as their group score deficit is taken to suggest. The deficit can appear large, but it is not likely to be the sole cause of the troubles they have once they get on campus.

Showing the insufficiency of one cause, of course, does not prove the sufficiency of another. My colleagues and I believed that our laboratory experiments had brought to light an overlooked cause of poor college performance among non-Asian minorities: the threat to social trust brought about by the stereotypes of the larger society. But to know the real-life importance of this threat would require testing *in situ*, in the buzz of everyday life.

To this end Steven Spencer, Richard Nisbett, Kent Harber, Mary Hummel, and I undertook a program aimed at incoming first-year students at the University of Michigan. Like virtually all other institutions of higher learning, Michigan had evidence of black students' underachievement. Our mission was clear: to see if we could improve their achievement by focusing on their transition into college life.

We also wanted to see how little we could get away with—that is, to develop a program that would succeed broadly without special efforts. The program (which started in 1991 and is ongoing) created a racially integrated "living and learning" community in a 250-student wing of a large dormitory. It focused students on academic work (through weekly "challenge" workshops), provided an outlet for discussing the personal side of college life (through weekly rap sessions), and affirmed the students' abilities (through, for example, reminding them that their admission was a vote of confidence). The program lasted just one semester, although most students remained in the dormitory wing for the rest of their first year.

Still, it worked: it gave black students a significant academic jump start. Those in the program (about 15 percent of the entering class) got better first-year grades than black students outside the program, even after controlling for differences between these groups in the skills with which they entered college. Equally important, the program greatly reduced underperformance: black students in the program got first-year grades almost as high as those of white students in the general Michigan population who entered with comparable test scores. This result signaled the achievement of an academic climate nearly as favorable to black students as to white students. And it was achieved through a concert of simple things that enabled black students to feel racially secure.

One tactic that worked surprisingly well was the weekly rap sessions—black and white students talking to one another in an informal dormitory setting, over pizza, about the personal side of their new lives in college. Participation in these sessions reduced students' feelings of stereotype threat and improved grades. Why? Perhaps when members of one racial group hear members of another racial group express the same concerns they have, the concerns seem less racial. Students may also learn that racial and gender stereotypes are either less at play than they might have feared or don't reflect the worst-feared prejudicial intent. Talking at a personal level across group lines can thus build trust in the larger campus community. The racial segregation besetting most college campuses can block this experience, allowing mistrust to build where cross-group communication would discourage it.

Our research bears a practical message: even though the stereotypes held by the larger society may be difficult to change, it is possible to create niches in which negative stereotypes are not felt to apply. In specific classrooms, within specific programs, even in the climate of entire schools, it is possible to weaken a group's sense of being threatened by negative stereotypes, to allow its members a trust that would otherwise be difficult to sustain. Thus when schools try to decide how important black-white test-score gaps are in determining the fate of black students on their campuses, they should keep something in mind: for the greatest portion of black students—those with strong academic identities—the degree of racial trust they feel in their campus life, rather than a few ticks on a standardized test, may be the key to their success.

Stereotype

Ziva Kunda

Stereotype Maintenance and Change

As should be clear by now, negative stereotypes can have devastating effects. There have been ample demonstrations throughout history of open and intended, often murderous discrimination arising from negative group stereotypes. The social psychological research documented in this chapter has focused on more subtle influences on judgment whose consequences can nevertheless be quite pernicious. Stereotypes can influence the way members of stigmatized groups are perceived, understood, and treated by others. Even people who have no prejudicial intent can inadvertently view stereotyped individuals through the lenses of negative stereotypes, without even realizing that they are doing so. For their part, stereotyped individuals often assume that they are operating under a cloud of stereotype-based suspicion of inferiority, and this can cause them to experience enough anxiety to undermine their performance.

As you contemplate the vast social costs of mistaken negative stereotypes, you may be wondering if anything can be done to correct such misperceptions. Is it possible to change people's stereotypes? This question has also intrigued many social psychologists. Their research efforts have given rise to another question, namely, Why is it so difficult to bring about stereotype change? These issues are discussed next.

The Contact Hypothesis

Early intuitions suggested that if we come to meet members of groups that are unfairly stereotyped in negative terms, we'll soon recognize and correct our errors. If non-Blacks

Excerpted from *Social Cognition: Making Sense of People*, Chapter 8, pp. 380-391. © 1999 by The MIT Press, Cambridge, Mass. Reprinted by permission.

encounter enough intelligent, hard-working, and mild mannered African Americans, surely they will realize that it is inappropriate to view this group as unintelligent, lazy, and aggressive. These ideas gave rise to the *contact hypothesis,* which held that social contact between members of majority and minority groups will reduce prejudice. From the start, it was recognized that not any contact will do. Walking through an urban inner city or visiting Chinatown seems highly unlikely to change anyone's view of the ethnic minorities that reside there. Having an African American janitor seems unlikely to do the trick either. Rather, Gordon Allport suggested in 1954, to reduce prejudice through contact, the contact must be among people of equal status in pursuit of common goals. If, for example, a prejudiced White person has to cooperate at work with an African American teammate, this would eventually lead to liking and respect for this teammate which would then generalize into a more positive view of African Americans.

Although the contact hypothesis seemed intuitively appealing, it proved very difficult to change stereotypes through contact. In their classic Robber's Cave experiments, Muzafer Sherif and his colleagues created a sense of rivalry and hostility among two groups of boys, and then attempted to change their negative views of each other and eliminate their mutual dislike (Sherif et al. 1961). Sherif and his colleagues recruited well-adjusted middle-class White boys for a summer camp. Initially the boys did not know each other, and were unaware that they were participating in an experiment. After living together in the same cabin for a few days, the boys were separated into two groups. The investigators asked each boy who his best friend was, and made sure that the two would end up in different groups. The two groups were kept completely apart for a while, as each engaged in various activities designed to create group spirit. Once each group had acquired strong group spirit, the investigators initiated a series of activities intended to produce friction among them—a sports tournament, a competitive treasure hunt, and so on. Pretty soon, the boys were referring to members of the other groups as "stinkers," "sneaks," and "cheats." They began showing their mutual animosity by making threatening posters, planning raids, and burning the other group's banner after a game.

Having successfully created two hostile groups, the investigators began addressing the true purpose of the study—getting rid of the hostility. They began by creating opportunities for pleasant social contact such as watching movies together and eating in the same dining room. This proved to be a total failure.

The social events only provided an opportunity for the rival groups to berate and attack each other. They shoved each other in the line for food, threw paper and food at each other, and made rude comments. The investigators then turned to a more elaborate tactic. They created a series of urgent situations that forced the boys to work together. These included a breakdown in the water supply that required the boys to search the water line for the trouble spot, a failure of their truck to start that required the boys to all pull it together with a rope, and an opportunity to rent a movie that the two groups could only afford if they pooled their resources. Although the two groups were able to work together harmoniously on these tasks, their joint efforts did not lead to an immediate reduction in hostility. Initially, as soon as the task was completed, the boys returned to bickering and name calling. But gradually the friction and hostility between the groups was reduced, until, by the time the camp ended, they were seeking opportunities to mingle, entertain, and treat each other.

Recall that the rival groups in this study were made up of essentially similar boys with no prior history of hostility. Even for such groups, intergroup hostility was not reduced through sheer contact on an equal footing in a pleasant situation. And even cooperative contact did not lead to an immediate reduction in hostility. The outlook for groups with a long history of dislike and well-entrenched negative stereotypes of each other seemed even less promising. Indeed, extensive research on the contact hypothesis gives little reason for optimism. For contact to reduce prejudice, the members of the two groups must have equal status, an opportunity to get to know each other, exposure to evidence that disconfirms the stereotypes, shared goals, and active cooperation. And even then, contact is not always effective at reducing prejudice. Negative stereotypes often resist change even in the face of intense manipulations involving cooperation with members of the stereotyped group over long periods of time (for a review, see Stephan 1985).

Why do our group stereotypes so often remain unchanged even in the face of contact with group members whose behavior and attributes are nothing like our stereotypic expectations? One reason is that we may simply not realize that such individuals disconfirm our stereotypes because our interpretation of their behavior can be biased by our stereotypes; we may view their neutral and innocent behaviors as consistent with our negative stereotypes. But even when we recognize that individuals clearly disconfirm the stereotype of their group, we may still fail to generalize from them to the group as a whole

because we consider them atypical of their group, as discussed next.

Subtyping Counterstereotypic Individuals

When you encounter a wealthy African American, an aggressive housewife, a respectful teenager, or a member of any other social group who disconfirms your stereotype of that group, you may hang onto your stereotype by "fencing off" this individual (Allport 1954; Rothbart and John 1985; Weber and Crocker 1983). Yes, a White American might say to himself, my African American neighbor Marcus is wealthy and successful, but you can't really learn anything from him about what African Americans in general are like because he is so atypical of African Americans; he belongs to an unusual subgroup of African Americans, African American executives. Much like one views ostriches as an unusual kind of bird that teaches little about the size and flying capabilities of birds in general, one may view African American executives as an unusual kind of African American that teaches little about the behavior and attributes of African Americans in general. By allocating counterstereotypic individuals like Marcus to a subtype that is considered atypical and unrepresentative of the group as a whole, one may be able to maintain one's global stereotype of the group even though one knows that some group members do not fit the bill.

Through this mechanism, one may be able to maintain a negative stereotype of African Americans and a strong dislike for this group even though one's favorite entertainer is Bill Cosby, one's favorite singer is Michael Jackson, and one's favorite athlete is Michael Jordan (all of whom, one knows quite well, are African Americans). These liked and respected individuals can be dismissed as irrelevant to the stereotype of the group as a whole if they are viewed as belonging to atypical subtypes such as African American entertainers, African American singers, or African American athletes. In the same vein, the notion of subtyping explains how one can be a prejudiced bigot despite proclaiming that "Some of my best friends are Jews [or Blacks, or members of any other stigmatized group]." The "best friends" are simply fenced off as atypical of their still disliked group.

A landmark article by Renee Weber and Jennifer Crocker suggested that we may be less likely to change our stereotypes when we are confronted with individuals who disconfirm them if we can readily subtype these counterstereotypic individuals (Weber and Crocker 1983). In one study, these investigators attempted to change participants' stereotype of lawyers as well-dressed, industrious, and intelligent. In one set of conditions, participants read descriptions of 30 lawyers, each described by three sentences that implied different attributes. Participants in all conditions saw the same set of 90 sentences, which included 30 that implied attributes inconsistent with the stereotype of lawyers (e.g., "Larry has difficulty analyzing problems and developing logical solutions" implies unintelligent), 15 sentences that implied attributes consistent with the stereotype (e.g., "Ken often skips lunch and works overtime to finish projects" implies industrious), and 45 sentences that implied attributes irrelevant to the stereotype of lawyers (e.g., religious). In different conditions this identical set of sentences was distributed differently among the 30 lawyers. Most important, in the *dispersed* condition, the 30 counterstereotypic sentences were dispersed across all lawyers, so each had one disconfirming attribute. In contrast, in the *concentrated* condition, the 30 counterstereotypic attributes were all concentrated in 10 lawyers, such that this third of the lawyers each had 3 disconfirming attributes, whereas the remaining two-thirds had no disconfirming attributes.

Concentrating the disconfirming attributes within a small subgroup should make it easier to designate this group to an atypical subtype and, thereby, to dismiss its relevance to the overall stereotype. Indeed, participants in the concentrated condition appeared to show less stereotype change than did participants in the dispersed condition, who could not readily subtype the disconfirming individuals. Put differently, participants generalized less from the same examples of unlawyerly behavior when these examples were concentrated in a small subgroup of the observed lawyers than when they were dispersed across the entire sample. Other researchers have since replicated this finding (e.g., Johnston and Hewstone 1992). When we can, we subtype counterstereotypic individuals, and this enables us to maintain our global stereotypes.

It is easier to subtype and dismiss counterstereotypic individuals if they all share another common attribute that provides a good reason for viewing them as atypical. If, for example, the poorly dressed lawyers we encounter are all Black, it is easy to explain why they should differ from lawyers in general—perhaps they are pro bono lawyers, perhaps they come from impoverished backgrounds. With this explanation in mind, it seems reasonable to subtype them as atypical of lawyers as a whole, and it is then unnecessary to generalize from them to other lawyers. Indeed, several studies have shown that people are less likely to generalize from group members who disconfirm the stereotype on one dimension to the group as a whole when all of these counterstereotypic individuals also violate the stereo-

type on another dimension (Rothbart and Lewis 1988; Weber and Crocker 1983; Wilder, Simon, and Faith 1996). Put differently, individuals who disconfirm the stereotype of their group on one dimension are most likely to lead us to modify our stereotype if they are typical of their group's stereotype in all other ways. As assertive woman is most likely to provoke people into changing their stereotype of women as unassertive if she seems feminine in all other ways—wears makeup and feminine clothes, is warm and caring, and so on. An assertive woman who, in addition, dresses and behaves in a manner that violates the stereotype of women may provoke less stereotype change because she can so readily be subtyped as atypical and dismissed as irrelevant.

The subtyping of counterstereotypic individuals often results from an active attempt to maintain our stereotypes. We may be motivated to preserve our stereotypes because these help us to justify our social order, our own discriminatory behavior, or our sense of superiority to others (Allport 1954; Fein and Spencer 1997). But we may attempt to dismiss the relevance of counterstereotypic individuals to our stereotypes even in the absence of such motives. An individual who violates a well-entrenched stereotype may seem so surprising and improbable that we may attempt to explain this individual away, much like we do when we come across information that challenges any other expectancy that we harbor (Hastie 1984; Snyder 1984; Wong and Weiner 1981). For these reasons, when we encounter a member of a stereotyped group who violates our stereotype, we may ask ourselves, in effect, "Do I have any good reason for believing that this person is atypical of the group as a whole?" If the answer is positive, we may feel justified in not generalizing from the individual to the group. Recall that when we ask ourselves such one-sided questions, we tend to engage in an equally one-sided search for answers, which often biases us toward confirming our hypotheses (Klayman and Ha 1987; see chapter 3). Therefore, we will often find good reason for dismissing counterstereotypic individuals as irrelevant.

As discussed above, if the counterstereotypic individuals possess another atypical attribute, this provides a good reason for subtyping and dismissing them as unrepresentative of their group. More recent research has shown that the additional attribute characterizing a stereotype-disconfirming individual can facilitate subtyping even if it is not atypical of the stereotype to being with. We may be able to use even neutral information about a counterstereotypic person as grounds for viewing this person as atypical of his or her group (Kunda and Oleson 1995). For example, if we come across an outspoken, assertive woman who violates our stereotype of women as compliant and unassertive, we may feel compelled to revise our stereotype if we have no additional information about her. But we may be able to use any additional information about her as grounds for subtyping and dismissing her as atypical of women in general.

If we know, for example, that this assertive woman had (or did not have) brothers, that her parents were supportive (or unsupportive), that she was attractive (or unattractive), or if we have any other knowledge about her background, we may attempt to use this knowledge to explain why women with this particular attribute are, unlike most women, assertive. We are so good at generating explanations relating just about any attribute to just about any outcome that we should have little trouble coming up with a good explanation (e.g., Andersen and Sechler 1986; see chapter 3). We may theorize, for example, that women with brothers are likely to be assertive because they had the benefit of growing up with assertive role models. Or we may theorize that women without brothers are likely to be assertive because they had the benefit of growing up without being oppressed at home by domineering males. In either case, having successfully assigned the woman to an atypical subtype, we need not generalize from her to other women.

In one study designed to test these ideas, participants read an interview with a lawyer in which he came across as quite introverted, which challenged their stereotype of lawyers as outgoing (Kunda and Oleson 1995). Participants given no additional information about this lawyer did generalize from him to lawyers in general; they rated lawyers, on average, as more introverted than did control participants who had read no interview. A different pattern emerged for two additional groups that were given additional information about this introverted lawyer. One group was told that he worked for a small law firm, the other that he worked for a large law firm. Pretests had shown that lawyers who worked for small or large firms were not expected to differ in their introversion from other lawyers. In other words, participants in these two were given one of two opposite attributes that were both neutral in their implications for lawyers' introversion.

Although both these attributes were initially neutral, it is not difficult to construct an explanation for why either might make lawyers especially likely to be introverted. One may reason, for example, that either kind of lawyer may be able to get by despite being introverted—small-firm lawyers because they don't need to deal with many people and large-firm lawyers because in large firms some lawyers may be able to specialize in tasks that require few interpersonal skills. Either attribute, then, may be used as grounds for viewing the introverted lawyer as belonging to an atypical subtype. Indeed, unlike participants given no additional information about the introverted lawyer, those who were also told that he worked for a small or large firm did not feel compelled to generalize from him; their stereotype of lawyers remained unchanged. In sum, participants generalized from a counterstereotypic individual when given no additional information about him. But providing them with an additional neutral attribute sufficed to undercut this generalization. In the process, the neutral attributes also lost their neutrality; they came to be viewed as associated with introversion. Together, these findings suggest that the neutral attributes undermined generalization from the counterstereotypic individual because they served as grounds for subtyping this individual as atypical.

Even if we have no further information that can be used as grounds for subtyping a counterstereotypic person, we may still be able to dismiss this person as an irrelevant exception if the person's deviation from our stereotype is extreme enough (Kunda and Oleson 1997). Consider Colin Powell, the African American general who orchestrated the successful execution of the Persian Gulf War, or Margaret Thatcher who ruled Britain with an iron fist. These individuals may violate our stereotypes of their groups so extremely that we may feel justified in viewing them as exceptions that don't prove the rule. We may believe that the sheer extremity of their deviance from our stereotypes provides us with a good enough reason for dismissing them as atypical and irrelevant.

In a series of studies that examined these ideas, participants read about a person who violated their stereotype either extremely or only moderately (Kunda and Oleson 1997). In one study, participants' stereotype of public relations (PR) agents as extraverted was challenged by a PR agent who was either extremely or only moderately introverted. In another study, participants' stereotypes of feminists as assertive were challenged by a feminist who was either extremely or only moderately unassertive. Stereotype change was assessed by comparing ratings of the stereotyped group made by these participants to those made by control participants who had not been exposed to any group member. In both cases, the person who deviated from the stereotype only moderately provoked greater stereotype change than did the person who deviated extremely. Indeed, the extremely unassertive feminist provoked no stereotype change at all, whereas the moderately unassertive one did lead participants to view feminists as less assertive. If we want to change people's stereotypes of African Americans, we are more likely to

succeed by introducing them to moderately successful African American individuals than by introducing them to extremely successful ones such as Colin Powell or Bill Cosby. These famous individuals deviate so extremely from their group's stereotype that people may view the sheer extremity of this deviation as a good enough reason for dismissing their relevance to the stereotype.

It is ironic that the more individuals deviate from the stereotype of their group, the less likely they are to bring about stereotype change. One disturbing implication is that the more inaccurate our stereotype of a group, the less likely it is to change spontaneously following encounters with group members. This is because the more inaccurate our stereotype, the more discrepant it will be from the typical group member. Put differently, the typical group member will deviate more extremely from more inaccurate stereotypes, and so will be dismissed more readily as an exception. This may be one reason why it is so difficult to change racial stereotypes through contact with individuals who disconfirm them (Stephan 1985). These stereotypes may be so inaccurate that average group members are perceived as extreme exceptions to the rule. It also follows that the individuals whose stereotypes one would like most to change, namely those holding extremely inaccurate negative stereotypes, will be the least likely to reduce the negativity of their stereotypes following exposure to group members who disconfirm them. For such extreme perceivers, the average group member will seem like an extreme and irrelevant deviant. Indeed, in these studies, extreme individuals became, if anything, even more extreme in their stereotypes following exposure to individuals who disconfirmed them.

On the positive side, the finding that people who moderately disconfirm perceivers' stereotypes of their group can provoke stereotype change is encouraging. In everyday life we may be more likely to encounter such moderate violations of our stereotypes than we are to encounter extreme violations. There are far more moderately assertive women than there are Margaret Thatchers. This may be why stereotypes can and do evolve over time.

Despite the difficulty of changing stereotypes through short-term interventions, examination of historical records and of the findings of longitudinal research suggest that over more extended time periods, dramatic changes in stereotypes can occur. Consider a group widely viewed as dirty, drunken, incompetent, brawling, slum-dwellers. You may be surprised to hear that this was the stereotype of the Irish in the United States in the mid-eighteen hundreds, when job ads specifying "No Irish need apply" were common (Sowell 1981). The stereotype of Irish Americans has clearly undergone dramatic change.

Other stereotypes have changed substantially as well. In a series of studies termed "The Princeton trilogy," different generations of Princeton students were asked to rate several ethnic groups on the same set of adjectives in 1933, 1951, and 1969 (Katz and Braly 1933; Gilbert 1951; Karlins, Coffman, and Waters 1969). Many of the stereotypes appeared to have changed considerably over this period. For example, there was a substantial decline in the extent to which Jews were seen as shrewd and mercenary, and an increase in the extent to which they were seen as ambitious and intelligent. And there was a dramatic decline in the extent to which Blacks were seen as superstitious and lazy,

and an increase in the extent to which they were seen as musical. Admittedly, these changes may reflect not only actual changes in stereotypes but also changes in norms toward sanctioning open expression of prejudice (in itself, an encouraging development). Yet, when considered along with historical reports of stereotype change over the long run and experimental demonstrations that stereotype can be changed, these findings point to an optimistic outlook. Groups that are currently stereotyped inappropriately in negative terms may look forward with hope to a future in which they are subject to less prejudice and discrimination. As they gain greater insight into how people use their stereotypes and how they may come to change them, social psychologists may help bring this future about.

Unit 7

Key Points to Consider

❖ In your opinion, what is the likely effect on aggressive behavior of playing violent video games? On what do you base your opinion? How would you respond to someone with the opposite view? How could you resolve this conflict?

❖ What do you think of the argument that something about the culture of the South makes violent actions more likely to occur? Do you see any relevance between the issues dealt with in the first article and the hypothesis about violence and honor in the South? Explain.

❖ What do you think is the relationship between self-esteem and aggressive behavior? How and why would one's feelings about the self affect whether or not aggressive behavior occurs?

 **Links** **www.dushkin.com/online/**

These sites are annotated on pages 4 and 5.

The evidence that human beings are capable of great violence is all around us—all you have to do is read a newspaper or watch the evening news. Every day, people are shot, stabbed, beaten, or otherwise treated in a violent manner by friends, family, or strangers. People are attacked for the color of their skin, their political ideas, their membership in a rival gang, or just because they were in the wrong place at the wrong time. Nations war against other nations, and in civil conflicts nations war against themselves. Faced with millions and millions of victims, it is hard to disagree with the conclusion that the capacity for aggression is fundamental to human nature.

Of course, it may depend on what you mean by aggression. As it turns out, coming up with one clear definition of aggression has been very difficult. For example, does aggression require a clear intention to harm? That is, must I intend to hurt you in order for my behavior to be called aggressive? Must aggression be physical in nature, or can my verbal attacks on you also be labeled aggressive? Does aggression have to be directed toward a human being? What about violence toward animals, or even inanimate objects, such as when I become angry during a round of golf and bend my putter around a tree? Even after decades of research on this topic, social psychologists still disagree on what exactly defines an aggressive act.

Although social psychology does not completely ignore the role of biological factors in aggression, its usual focus is on identifying the environmental factors that influence aggressive behavior. One approach to understanding a form of aggression known as hostile aggression (aggression carried out for its own sake) has been to identify situational factors that cause unpleasant emotional states, which might then cause aggressive actions. For example, the failure to reach an important goal might lead to the unpleasant feeling of frustration, and these feelings can then trigger aggression. Hot and uncomfortable environments might also contribute to unpleasant emotional states, and thus contribute to heightened aggression.

In contrast to hostile aggression, which is carried out for its own sake, instrumental aggression is carried out in order to attain some other goal or objective. This form of aggression is often explained in terms of social learning theory, which holds that people can learn to carry out aggressive actions when they observe others doing so, and when those others are rewarded for their actions. Thus, this theory contends that people frequently learn to use aggression as a tool for getting something they want. One place where such behaviors can be learned, of course, is the mass media, and many studies (and congressional hearings) have been carried out to determine the role of television and other media in teaching violence to children.

The first selection in this section, "Good Clean Fun?" takes an interesting approach. The author—a long-time player of violent video games—reports on his first-hand experience with the effect that such play has had on his ability to handle real guns effectively. His findings are interesting, and a little disturbing. The second selection, "Violence and Honor in the Southern United States," examines a fascinating phenomenon—the fact that ever since homicide records have been kept, the murder rate in the South has been substantially higher than in any other region. This article considers the possibility that something about the historic cultural norms in the South is responsible for such high levels of homicide.

The next article, "Self-esteem, Narcissism, and Aggression: Does Violence Result From Low Self-esteem or From Threatened Egotism?" examines a controversial topic in social psychology: does violent behavior stem from low self-esteem or not? The authors argue that it does not, and that a better predictor of aggression is having high but unstable self-esteem, a state of affairs that makes the individual more likely to feel threatened.

In the final article, "Anatomy of a Violent Relationship," researchers Neil Jacobson and John Gottman describe some of the results of their investigations of conflict among violent couples. Among other interesting findings, they report that male abusers can be seen as falling into one of two groups: the emotionally explosive "Pit Bulls" and the colder, more deliberately abusive "Cobras."

good clean fun?

I've played videogames all my life. And for just as long, I've defended their merits against the public outcry over everything from maladjusted teens to the killings at Columbine. Then I met Dave Grossman, an army lieutenant-colonel with a psychology degree. In the backwoods of Mississippi, he handed me a gun. This is what happened next

by Clive Thompson

The sun beats down like a hammer on the Mississippi firing range as Lt.-Col. Dave Grossman crouches on the ground. The heat is furious and he's beginning to sweat a bit, his army crew cut glistening as he punches in the combination to open his safety box. Inside are two guns. Grossman pulls out a .22-caliber pistol.

This, he tells me, is the same model that fourteen-year-old Michael Carneal stole from his neighbor's house in Paducah, Kentucky, on December 1, 1997. Carneal took the gun to a high-school prayer meeting and opened fire on the group. "He fired eight shots and got eight hits on eight different kids. He killed three and paralyzed one for life," Grossman notes grimly in his slight Arkansas accent. It was an astonishing piece of marksmanship—a hit ratio that many highly trained police officers can't achieve. Last year, for example, four experienced New York City cops shot at unarmed Amadou Diallo, firing forty-one bullets from barely fifteen feet away; fewer than half hit their mark.

But perhaps more startling about Carneal is another salient fact: He'd never shot a handgun before. "So how did he get such incredible aim?" Grossman asks. "Where did he get that killing ability?"

His answer: videogames. In a controversial book out this fall, *Stop Teaching our Kids to Kill*, the forty-three-year-old Gross-

man details how Carneal had trained for hours and hours on point-and-shoot games. The teenager had practiced killing literally thousands of people *virtually;* he'd learned to aim for the head in order to dispatch each victim with just one shot.

Videogames have long been blamed for provoking violence, but rarely by someone of Grossman's background and expertise. A military man and Pulitzer-nominated authority on the psychology of killing, Grossman shot to prominence after the Columbine school massacre. In countless media appearances, he has argued that modern videogames are eerily similar to the training tools that military and law enforcement agencies use to teach soldiers and officers to kill. Kids learn these skills, he writes in his book, "much the same way as the astronauts on Apollo 11 learned how to fly to the moon without ever leaving the ground." The proof, he argues, is in the profusion of mass high-school shootings in recent years, where kids with limited experience in using guns have displayed excellent aim and tactical maneuvers, not to mention a view of murder as fun.

I am here to test Grossman's theory. I have never even held a gun, let alone fired one. But for two decades, I've been avidly playing videogames, including the wickedly violent arcade shooters that Grossman considers the most military-like "murder simulators." I'm particularly good at these—I

can usually finish *Area 51* or *Time Crisis* for only about three bucks in quarters. If Grossman is right, I should be as deadly as Michael Carneal.

I look down the range at my target, a human-shaped silhouette. It's twenty feet away, roughly the same distance from which Carneal shot his victims. In the blazing heat sweat drips slowly down the small of my back.

I raise the barrel of the gun.

THE VIDEOGAME DEBATE HAS BEEN GOING on for years, but Grossman has arguably brought it to a new level. He is a peculiar combination of ultra-pundit (known for his crisp sound bites on violence) and career soldier. Unlike other critics, who typically hail from the media-literacy or family-values camps. he has direct experience in the domain of killing. During his twenty-three-year stint in the army (from which he retired in 1998), he participated in the Panama invasion. He has taught the psychology of killing ("killology") at the West Point military academy and the University of Arkansas. Today, as founder and director of the Killology Research Group in Arkansas, he works full time training police officers—and remains an enthusiastic ambassador of military culture. He says

Interplay, the publisher of *Kingpin,* is one of several videogame makers being sued in the Carneal case. In the wake of Columbine, the company tried to pull one of its more brutal magazine ads, which announced in boldface type: YOU'RE GONNA DIE!

"roger" and "check" instead of "OK," and calls everyone "brother."

Grossman's epiphany about videogames came through a circuitous route. Research for his psychology PhD eventually became the source of his 1995 book *On Killing,* which examines a little-known aspect of war: that soldiers, even highly trained ones, are profoundly resistant to shooting people.

As Grossman points out, surveys of World War II veterans show that eighty percent of riflemen never once fired a gun during active combat, even when enemy bullets were flying around them. During the American Civil War, according to data collected after battles, many soldiers only pretended to fire their weapons, loading them again and again without actually discharging a shot. On some level, it seems, they simply couldn't bear the prospect of shooting other human beings. Had they done so, casualties would have obviously been much higher.

Faced with armies full of reluctant gunners, the U.S. military began devising new techniques to definitively train men to shoot—and shoot to kill. The answer lay in classic "operant conditioning" methods made famous by American psychologist B.F. Skinner in the fifties. In a series of experiments, Skinner trained rats to push on a bar, after which they were rewarded with food. Positive or negative reinforcement, he argued, could make any form of activity virtually automatic, overriding conscious objections.

For the military, this meant setting up realistic shooting simulations. Soldiers were put into mock combat situations, filled with noise and riot; they were taught to fire at pop-up silhouettes until it became a twitch instinct. The conditioning worked well. By the Korean War, Grossman found, such training brought the firing ratio up to fifty-five percent. In Vietnam, the number skyrocketed to ninety-five percent.

In the eighties, the armed forces began using an even more powerful and cheaper training tool: video- and computer-graphics-based simulations. Many were modeled directly on videogames. One popular military sim was a barely-modified version of the early Nintendo game *Duck Hunt.*

Which is when Grossman began to look away from the battlefields and into the ar-

cades. If the army was using game-like sims to train its killers, were the arcades doing the same thing inadvertently, to youth?

An incendiary chapter in his 1995 book blames Hollywood violence and the rise of super-realistic videogames for the seismic increase of "serious assault" cases in the U.S.—which had nearly doubled between 1977 and 1993, from 240 to 440 incidents per 100,000 people. In Grossman's analysis, different forms of entertainment provide different elements of violence training. Hollywood and TV desensitize youth to the consequences of violence, a proposition generally backed by study after study. More controversial is the role he assigns to videogames as teachers of gun-handling skills. It is a theory supported by scant scientific evidence; Grossman bases his claims entirely on military research and his personal experience. In his own pistol-training classes at West Point, he says, some recruits displayed an uncanny facility with weapons. "Out of every class of about twenty kids, you'll often get one or two that are extraordinary shots but who'd never fired a gun before. And almost without fail, if you ask them, Where did you get to be such a good pistol shot?, they'll look you in the eye and say, *Duck Hunt.* Or *Time Crisis.* The skills transfer over immediately."

Still, for all their explosiveness, Grossman's ideas would probably languish in obscurity if not for the Michael Carneals of the world.

High-school shootings in the U.S. have been going on for years. In fact, the 1992 to 1993 academic year was the worst in sheer numbers, with nearly fifty deaths. But they were almost all one-on-one incidents, either revenge- or gang-related. In 1997, however, the peculiarly large-scale shootings began, during which the killers fired indiscriminately at groups of people they barely knew. Consider a partial list: In October 1997, Luke Woodham shot up his high school in Pearl, Mississippi, killing two and injuring seven. A few months later, Carneal went on his prayer-group rampage. In March 1998, two kids opened fire on a school in Jonesboro, Arkansas, killing five and injuring ten. Not long after, a student in Springfield, Oregon, cut loose in a crowded cafeteria, murdering two and injuring eighteen. And then came the most

violent one of all—the April 1999 shootings at Columbine, which left a stunning thirteen dead and twenty injured.

Grossman figured his prophecy was coming true. It had also hit home. In a brutal coincidence, he actually lives in Jonesboro, across town from where its school shootings occurred; he was even summoned to the middle school to help counsel traumatized teachers. The ensuing weeks and months saw Grossman appear regularly in the media, from *60 Minutes* to *The New York Times.* An expert strategist, he decided the time was ripe to strike. This summer, he and co-author Gloria De-Gaetano (a media literacy consultant) quickly completed work on *Stop Teaching Our Kids to Kill,* which slams violent games, movies and TV, and demands that they be legally restricted to adults only. Grossman has also trained lawyers nationwide in how to launch class-action suits against videogame companies on behalf of families whose children are killed in school shootings, as well as consulting on draft laws for videogames. The ripple effects are already here: This spring, the parents of three of Michael Carneal's victims sued, among others, several videogame companies that they felt had incited the rampage.

Now, as the media prepare for still more shootings, Grossman has arguably become the most prominent player in the videogame debate. "This whole industry is going down, and going down hard," he says with conviction.

But a question remains: Is he right?

I TAKE A DEEP BREATH AND START FIRING LIKE mad, squeezing the trigger again and again until my finger aches, blasting round after round. Things are looking good: My aim is steady, my heart rate low. As I fire, bodies drop on impact—chunks of flesh flying off in all directions.

It's the day before my meeting with Grossman, and I've decided to go for a warm-up at a local arcade in Pearl, the Mississippi town I've come to to speak with him. I'm holding a plastic pistol in front of Midway's *House of the Dead,* blowing away endless platoons of zombies. A few days before, over the phone, Grossman spoke about the sheer physicality of guns like this one—arguing that they make games like *House of the Dead* preternaturally similar to a Fire Arms Training Simulator, which police officers use to hone their twitch-shooting instincts. Warming up on this stuff, he'd figured, would get me "really fired up" for the main event.

Indeed, from the time I first suggested this experiment, Grossman has displayed an almost perverse enthusiasm for it. He urged me to fly down from New York the following weekend to join him in Pearl, where he was due to guest-lecture at a po-

> **Adults can do whatever they want,"** Grossman says. **"They can have guns, pornography, alcohol, drugs, sex, cars. But if anybody gives those things to a child, then they're a criminal. So why would we market murder simulators to children?"**

lice sharpshooter conference (taking place just a few miles from the high school that had its own shooting in 1997).

When we meet for lunch, he pulls out ads he has collected for various videogame companies, gleefully poking fun at them. One, for *Quake,* features a photo of a human foot with a toe tag; the caption says, HE PRACTICED ON A PC. Another, an ad for a force-feedback joystick, reads, PSYCHIATRISTS SAY IT IS IMPORTANT TO FEEL SOMETHING WHEN YOU KILL. He slaps his thigh. "These things are mass-murder simulators—and in their own ads, they're saying so!"

I'm not so sure. I've been a long-time defender of videogames, on TV panels and in radio debates. Games need defending, I've always felt, simply because they're the chief pastime of the young, unathletic geek, a cohort with whom I feel a personal sympathy. For these kids, gaming is a crucial refuge in a teenage world that glorifies physical power and beauty. Videogame critics frequently come from outside this geek demographic—as does Grossman—and thus inevitably err in their analysis of it. They ignore, for example, the social aspect of games—the robust culture of camaraderie and information-swapping that surrounds them. Or they focus on a few gory games that comprise a small portion of the market, such as *Quake.* During the Columbine coverage, clueless journalists cited *Doom* as if it were actually a current game, when nobody I know had played it for about four years.

Perhaps most problematically, critics assume that players are hopeless dupes of the videogame experience—that they are unable to critically assess what they plan and are doomed only to be "influenced" by it. These critics rarely look at games as pieces of a living, breathing culture. In fact, you could argue that the tongue-in-cheek irony so prevalent in shooting games and their cartoonishly over-the-top gore are more of a comment on violence than a true enactment of it. Indeed, as gaming critic J.C. Herz once noted, the gun-toting protagonists of videogames are inevitably policemen, marines or soldiers—not mercenaries or lawless killers. What sort of social comment is that? As I sit here blowing away zombies in *House of the Dead,* my primary reaction

is, as always, to giggle. Part of the fun is simply the deep surreality of the action.

To his credit, Grossman gives these arguments their due. Sure, games are useful socially, which is why he doesn't have any problem with non-violent ones. He also sees the irony of the gorier titles. But he doesn't think young children do. "They accept it on a different level," he says.

I was skeptical of Grossman's theory, but something happened at the Pearl arcade that gave me pause. I'm halfway through a round of *L.A. Machinegunners* when I notice a young man in fatigues watching me. I introduce myself, and discover that he's Sgt. Scott Sargent, a U.S. military reservist out recruiting. A recruiter in an *arcade?* I ask him if he wants to join me for a game.

Soon, Sargent and I are merrily annihilating virtual terrorists on the streets of L.A., using throbbing, simulated machine guns. Watching him, I see that Grossman's theory seems to apply in reverse. Sargent has had extensive training on real-life weaponry, but he's never played *Machinegunners* until now. Nonetheless, he's astonishingly good. And *Machinegunners* is one of the most difficult shooters to play—my wife becomes nauseated just watching the vertiginous, rapidly shifting angles. Despite my long experience playing this game, Sargent is better than I am, racking up more kills and sustaining fewer injuries.

As the round ends, I ask him how the game compares to real life. He pauses for a second, fingering the machine-gun controls that have simulated recoil when you fire. I've always assumed the game recoil is a pale shadow of a real one. Apparently, this is not so. "It's actually very similar to the kick of an M-16," Sargent says. "I've trained with those things for years. It feels almost exactly the same."

THE NEXT DAY, TRAINING IS OVER. I'M AT the range, holding one of Grossman's pistols.

Several National Rifle Association officials and five police officers, here for a sharpshooting competition, stand in a semicircle behind me, eyeing me worriedly. I can hardly blame them: The prospect of a neophyte blasting away is clearly unset-

tling. It's obvious that I don't even know how to correctly hold the thing; one officer has to gently suggest a two-handed approach. He stands next to me to make sure I keep the gun pointed down-range and to tell me when to fire. Grossman looks on with excitement. "Imagine it's *House of the Dead,*" he calls out.

After everyone is safely a few paces back, the officer gives the nod. He leans over and touches a lever on my pistol. "The safety is down," he announces. "It's ready to fire."

For a second, I feel an odd sensation of danger, as if I'm only now realizing how deadly this thing really is. It's like driving along the edge of a cliff and suddenly visualizing yourself veering off into space. I have a brief, unbidden thought that at any moment I could swivel around and shoot three or four of the cops in the gut. I banish the notion immediately, then grip the gun more firmly and focus.

Guns are a peculiarly modernist combination of form and function, which is part of their allure. They have no extraneous elements: Just point and shoot. I squint down the range at the silhouette target.

I squeeze the trigger.

Bang.

A hole appears in the upper left shoulder of the target. Whoa: I've hit it squarely, though I aimed too high. I fire again, and again. I'm nervous, far more than I expected, and trembling like a leaf. Perhaps it's because five cops are staring at me. Perhaps it's because I'm trying to fire as quickly as possible, to emulate the speed of Carneal and the other teen killers, who had little time to line up their shots.

Yet for all my panic, it's quickly become apparent that I'm actually doing quite well. After only a few shots, I have learned to correct my high aim. Within thirty seconds I've fired off every round and reloaded. Grossman urges me to try some head shots. This is harder, but again, after an initial error, I can see the holes popping in the head of the silhouette and the sun peeking through.

By now it's clear that whatever else about his theories I might question, Grossman's right about one thing: The .22-caliber pistol is remarkably similar in feel to an arcade gun—the kick is miniscule and it's only slightly heavier. In fact, arcade guns have a heavy cord dangling from them, so after hours of playing, you feel an added weight. You tend to develop muscles that can clearly hold a .22 quite steady.

We decide to take things up a notch. "Now," Grossman says, "I want you to try something with a bit more kick to it." He hands me a much bigger gun—his .45-caliber Springfield pistol, the weapon carried by the FBI. A .22 is a potentially lethal gun, as Michael Carneal proved, but ultimately it's pretty lightweight stuff. A .45, however, can really mess someone up.

Including me. The first shot shocks me with the power of its kick, and the bullet flies harmlessly over the top of the target. I swallow deeply. My hands are shaking badly. Far more than the .22, this gun is very, very real, and nothing like an arcade toy. The way it kicks around, it's like it has a mind of its own.

Still, what happens next is revealing. Despite my nervousness, I automatically compensate for my panic. Even as my hands tremble, even as I sweat under the gaze of the cops, even as my mind races, my aim instantly improves. Some subconscious part of my brain takes over, and by the second shot I'm again hitting perfectly in the chest area. Shot after shot rips through the target, and I realize in a flash that this is what training is *supposed* to do—allow you to perform well even under great stress, or when your mind is occupied with other details. Some form of Skinner's operant conditioning, it seems, is in effect.

Then the hammer clicks on the empty chamber. The last shot has been fired. I hand the gun back to Grossman, and he races off to examine my targets.

According to Grossman, the accuracy of neophyte soldiers in training is relatively low. After one week of pistol training, fifty percent of recruits can hit the man-shaped silhouette "with some regularity," and one-quarter can concentrate their shots in the central chest area. Only five percent can place their shots in a small, silver-dollar-sized area. I've checked these stats with other police trainers; they agree the estimates are sound.

As for me? Grossman brings my targets. The shots are all in the center-chest area, the "9" and "10" scoring rings. It's unsettling, yet riveting to look at these close up. The bullet holes are clustered in what seems to be a shockingly tight radius. If this were a real person, hell, I'd have blown their torso to shreds with the first few shots alone.

Grossman seems thrilled. "I would say it was head-and-shoulders above the average first-time shooter." I'm not on par with the best he's seen, he says, but I'm shooting as well as a trainee would at the end of a week of training—a *week*. He gestures to the target. "That would be an A. You're scholarship material. You were rocking and rolling!"

Now comes the inevitable question. Grossman grins at me. "To shoot like you did with that .45 is truly extraordinary. And you've never fired a gun before. Where did you learn to do that?"

O N THE FLIGHT BACK FROM MISSISSIPPI, MY shooting targets crammed into a garment bag, I replay the experience in my head—what it means, what it doesn't. I'm still relatively unsettled by my aptitude with deadly force, and impressed by how well Grossman's theory has played out. But I'm also disappointed. On some level, I realize, I didn't want to prove him even partially right. Too frequently, critics assume all gamers are sociopathic freaks. I hardly wanted to push that stereotype further.

But even if Grossman's idea about gun training is correct, it still can't explain what's going on in American high schools—specifically, the motivations of the killers. Hand-eye co-ordination is one thing; seething rage is quite another. Sure, kids may be *able* to go on mass rampages, but why would they want to?

Investigators studying the Columbine shooting admitted this fall that they were still baffled by what motivated Dylan Klebold and Eric Harris. "I've been working on this nonstop daily since April 20th and I can't tell you why it happened," lead investigator Kate Battan told *Salon* magazine. The killers' hatred, it seems, was freefloating in the traditional manner of persecuted teens. Jocks, gays, other nerds, popular kids, minorities, racists—everyone was up for grabs. None of this would shock anyone who went through an even mildly bad adolescence—they know that high school is, socially and psychologically, a shark tank, pitting clique against clique. In that context, it's hard to finger *House of the Dead* as a singular cause of teen angst. On the contrary, teensploitation TV fare like *Manchester Prep* or *Popular*—with their phalanxes of glossy, milk-fed socialites and ugly, brainy losers—is probably more likely to blur your sense of reality. And though largely devoid of physical violence, shows like that are quite capable of training you in the art of teen psychological warfare, a battle in which no gun license is necessary.

Guns themselves, of course, are another obvious issue in recent shootings—and another wrinkle that makes Grossman's theory seem overly pat. Videogame guns don't kill people; real ones do. Yet Grossman, a soldier who wholeheartedly supports the NRA, isn't out there fighting for enhanced gun-control laws. Rather, he thinks current laws are adequate. He also claims kids' access to guns hasn't increased, so guns can't solely be responsible for the rise in shootings. "I grew up with a twelve-gauge shotgun in my bedroom," he notes.

Perhaps most damaging to Grossman's case, however, are academic videogame researchers, some of whom say he has no science to back up his theories. A recent survey by media think-tank Mediascope found that only sixteen studies exist that probe the relationship between videogames and aggression, and their results are mixed. Even if every study agreed that games are homicidal in their impact, sixteen studies is a scientifically insignificant number, say the scientists. It doesn't yet prove anything.

Jeanne Funk, author of several videogame studies and a respected psychologist from the University of Toledo, sighs when I mention Grossman's name. She admires *On Killing*, but thinks his videogame theories have no serious scientific foundation. "He says things have been proven when they haven't," she says. "The fact is, we're just beginning to examine this issue. We don't know. The data are *so* thin." In pushing his ideas, Grossman relies instead on the thousands of studies that successfully link violent TV shows with aggression, and on the military's experience using simulators. But neither, Funk argues, are easily applicable to gaming. Videogames could have benevolent effects; on the other hand, that could be far, far worse than Grossman's worst nightmares. "But we have nothing to go on right now," she insists.

This, ultimately, is the most frustrating part of the issue. Surrounded by all the firing guns, panicked parents and the media frenzy, simple answers are more seductive than further debate. But every time I'm tempted to dismiss Grossman, I open my closet and pull out those silhouette targets. I check out the cluster of holes in the chest. I remember the jolt of the .45.

Violence and Honor in the Southern United States

Richard E. Nisbett

Dov Cohen

THE U.S. SOUTH HAS LONG BEEN viewed as a place of romance, leisure, and gentility. Southerners have been credited with warmth, expressiveness, spontaneity, close family ties, a love of music and sport, and an appreciation for the things that make life worth living—from cuisine to love.

But there has also been the claim that there is a darker strain to southern life. For several centuries, the southern United States has been regarded as more violent than the northern part of the country.[1] This belief has been shared by foreign visitors, northerners, and southerners with experience outside the South. Duels, feuds, bushwhackings, and lynchings are more frequently reported in the correspondence, autobiographies, and newspapers of the South than of the North from the eighteenth century on.[2] The rates of homicide in some areas of the South in the nineteenth century make the inner city of today look almost like a sanctuary. According to one accounting, in the plateau region of the Cumberland Mountains between 1865 and 1915, the homicide rate was 130 per 100,000[3]—more than ten times today's national homicide rate and twice as high as that of our most violent cities.

Not only homicide but also a penchant for violence in many other forms are alleged to characterize the South. The autobiographies of southerners of the eighteenth and nineteenth centuries often included accounts of severe beatings of children by parents and others.[4] And southern pastimes and games often involved violence that is as shocking to us today as it was at the time to northerners. In one game called "purring," for example, two opponents grasped each other firmly by the shoulders and began kicking each other in the shins at the starting signal. The loser was the man who released his grip first.[5] Even more horrifying to modern (and to contemporaneous northern) sensibilities was a favorite sport of frontiersmen called fighting "with no holds barred," which meant that weapons were banned but nothing else was. Contestants could and did seek to maim their opponents.[6] Thus gouged-out eyes and bitten-off body parts were common outcomes of such fights.

Cases of southern violence often reflect a concern with blows to reputation or status—with "violation of personal honor"—and the tacit belief that violence is an appropriate response to such an affront. The journalist Hodding Carter has written that in the 1930s he served on a jury in Louisiana that was hearing a case concerning a man who lived next to a gas station where the hangers-on had been teasing him for some time. One day he opened fire with a shotgun, injuring two of the men and killing an innocent bystander. When Carter proposed a verdict of guilty, the other eleven jurors protested: "He ain't guilty. *He wouldn't of been much of a man if he hadn't shot them fellows.*"[7] A historian has written of the same period that it was impossible to obtain a conviction for murder in some parts of the South if the defendant had been insulted and had issued a warning that the insult had to be retracted.[8] And until the mid-1970s, Texas law held that if a man found his wife and her lover in a "compromising position" and killed them, there was no crime—only a "justifiable homicide."

The young men of the South were prepared for these violent activities by a socialization process designed to make them physically courageous and ferocious in defense of their reputations: "From an early age small boys were taught to think much of their own honor, and to be active in its defense. Honor in this society meant a pride of manhood in masculine courage, physical strength and warrior virtue. Male children were trained to defend their honor without a moment's hesitation."[9]

Even very young children were encouraged to be aggressive, learning that "they were supposed to grab for things, fight on the carpet to entertain parents, clatter their toys about, defy parental commands, and even set upon likely visitors in friendly roughhouse."[10] Children themselves rigor-ously enforced the code of honor. A boy who dodged a stone rather than allow himself to be hit and then respond in kind ran the risk of being ostracized by his fellows.[11]

The southerners' "expertise" in violence is reflected in their reputed success as soldiers.[12] Southerners have been alleged, at least since Tocqueville's commentary on America, to be more proficient in the arts of war than northerners and to take greater pride in their military prowess. Twentieth-century scholars have documented the southern enthusiasm for wars, their overrepresentation in the national military establishment, and their fondness for military content in preparatory schools and colleges.[13]

Explanations for Southern Violence

There are many "Souths"—the Cavalier South of seventeenth- and eighteenth-century Virginia, founded by the inheritors of the medieval knightly tradition of horsemanship and skill in battle; the mountain South, originating in eastern Appalachia and moving southward and westward decade by decade; the plantation South, based on growing cotton; and the western South, based on the herding of cattle in dry plains and hills that could sustain no other form of agriculture. Of the explanations that we will cite for southern violence, certain ones apply plausibly to some of these regions but less plausibly to others.

Four major explanations have been offered for the southern tendency to prefer violence: the higher temperature of the South and consequently the quicker tempers of southerners, the tradition of slavery, the greater poverty of the South, and the putative "culture of honor" of the South. We argue that the role of "honor" is independent of, and probably greater than, any role played by the other three.

Temperature. It has been suggested that at least a part of the violence of the South can be accounted for by the characteristically higher temperatures of the South.[14] It is indeed possible to show that variation in temperature in a locality is associated with the number of violent crimes there,[15] and we will examine the role played by temperature in the most dramatic form of violence, namely homicide.

Slavery. Slavery has long been held responsible for the violence of the South.[16] Abigail Adams was of the opinion that whites inflicted on themselves the same sort of violent treatment that they accorded their slaves.[17] Thomas Jefferson concurred in his *Notes on Virginia*, as did many other thoughtful southerners. John Dickinson, an eighteenth-century revolutionary from the eastern shore of Maryland, believed that the institution of slavery led to southern "pride, selfishness, peevishness, violence."[18] Toc-queville also believed that slavery was responsible for the South's violence, but he emphasized, rather than the "contagion" from treatment of the slaves, the idleness encouraged by slavery:

As [the Kentuckian] lives in an idle independence, his tastes are those of an idle man . . . and the energy which his neighbor devotes to gain turns with him to a passionate love of field sports and military exercises; he delights in violent bodily exertion, he is familiar with the use of arms, and is accustomed from a very early age to expose his life in single combat.[19]

At several points in this book we will assess the evidence for and against both aspects of slavery as explanations for southern violence.

Poverty. A third explanation for the greater violence of the South has to do with poverty. The South is poorer than any other region of the country and always has been; in each region of the country and in every sort of population unit, from rural county to large city, poverty is associated with higher homicide rates.

A variant of the economic explanation focuses not on absolute income or wealth but rather on disparities in income. Some argue that inequality in wealth breeds violence. We will attempt to assess the role of poverty and inequality in the violence of the South both in rates of homicide and in preference for violence as a means of conflict resolution.

Violence and the Culture of Honor

We believe that the most important explanation for southern violence is that much of the South has differed from the North in a very important economic respect and that this has carried with it profound cultural consequences. Thus the southern preference for violence stems from the fact that much of the South was a lawless, frontier region settled by people whose economy was originally based on herding. As we shall see, herding societies are typically characterized by having "cultures of honor" in which a threat to property or reputation is dealt with by violence.

Virtue, Strength, and Violence

Cultures of honor have been independently invented by many of the world's societies. These cultures vary in many respects but have one element in common: The individual is prepared to protect his reputation—for probity or strength or both—by resort to violence. Such cultures seem to be particularly likely to develop where (1) the individual is at economic risk from his fellows and (2) the state is weak or nonexistent and thus cannot prevent or punish theft of property. And those two conditions normally occur together: Herding, for example, is the main viable form of agriculture in remote areas, far from government enforcement mechanisms.

Some cultures of honor emphasize the individual's personal honesty and integrity in the sense that honor is usually meant today. That has always been one of the major meanings of the concept. Dr. Samuel Johnson, the eighteenth-century compiler of the first English dictionary, defined honor as "nobility of soul, magnanimity, and a scorn of meanness." This is "honour which derives from virtuous conduct."[20] Honor defined in those terms is prized by virtually all societies; the culture of honor, however, differs from other cultures in that its members are prepared to fight or even to kill to defend their reputations as honorable men.

The culture of honor also differs from others in an even more important respect. In addition to valuing honor defined as virtuous conduct, it values—often far more—honor defined as respect of the sort "which situates an individual socially and determines his right to precedence."[21] Honor in this sense is based not on good character but on a man's strength and power to enforce his will on others. Again, almost all societies value honor defined as precedence or status. The culture of honor differs from other cultures in that violence will be used to attain and protect this kind of honor. Honor, as we use the term in this book, is well captured by ethnographer David Mandelbaum's characterization of the Arabic and Persian word for honor—*izzat*. "It is a word often heard in men's talk, particularly when the talk is about conflict, rivalry, and struggle. It crops up as a kind of final explanation for motivation, whether for acts of aggression or beneficence."[22]

A key aspect of the culture of honor is the importance placed on the insult and the necessity to respond to it. An insult implies that the target is weak enough to be bullied. Since a reputation for strength is of the essence in the culture of honor, the individual who insults someone must be forced to retract; if the instigator refuses, he must be punished—with violence or even death. A particularly important kind of insult is one directed at female members of a man's family.

In the Old South, as in the ancient world, "son of a bitch" or any similar epithet was a most damaging blow to male pride.... To attack his wife, mother, or sister was to assault the man himself. Outsider violence against family dependents, particularly females, was a breach not to be ignored without risk of ignominy. An impotence to deal with such wrongs carried

all the weight of shame that archaic society could muster.[23]

Herding Economies and the Culture of Honor

The absence of the state makes it possible for an individual to commit violence with impunity, but it is not a sufficient condition for creating a culture that relies on violence to settle disputes. Hunting-gathering societies appear to have relatively low levels of violence, even though their members are not usually subjects of any state.[24] And farmers, even when they live in societies where the state is weak, typically are not overly concerned with their reputation for strength nor are they willing to defend it with violence.[25]

Herding and Vulnerability to Loss. There is one type of economy, however, that tends to be associated worldwide with concerns about honor and readiness to commit violence to conserve it. That is the economy based on herding of animals.[26] Together with some anthropologists, we believe that herding societies have cultures of honor for reasons having to do with the economic precariousness of herdsmen.[27] Herdsmen constantly face the possibility of loss of their entire wealth—through loss of their herds. Thus a stance of aggressiveness and willingness to kill or commit mayhem is useful in announcing their determination to protect their animals at all costs.

Herding and Sensitivity to Insults. Herdsmen adopt a stance of extreme vigilance toward any action that might imply that they are incapable of defending their property. Early in his career, in fact, the herdsman in some cultures may deliberately pick fights to show his toughness. As the ethnographer J. K. Campbell wrote of Mediterranean herding culture:

The critical moment in the development of the young shepherd's reputation is his first quarrel. Quarrels are necessarily public. They may occur in the coffee shop, the village square, or most frequently on a grazing boundary where a curse or a stone aimed at one of his straying sheep by another shepherd is an insult which inevitably requires a violent response.[28]

Herding and the Uses of Warfare

People who herd animals usually live in places such as mountains, semideserts, and steppes, where because of the ecology, crop farming is inadequate to provide for basic food needs. They have little surplus and sometimes experience genuine want. Thus they are often tempted to take the herds of other groups. As a consequence, "theft and

raiding are endemic to pastoral peoples."[29] Or, as one herdsman of the Middle East put it, "Raids are our agriculture."[30] Thus skill at warfare is valuable to a herdsman in a way that it is not to a hunter-gatherer or a farmer. It is no accident that it is the herding peoples of Europe who have been reputed to be the best soldiers over the centuries, that "to the Scots, as to the Swiss, Swedes, Albanians, Prussians and other people of Europe's margins and infertile uplands, war has been something of a national industry."[31]

In addition to the "marginal" northern Europeans, many if not most Mediterranean groups—including the traditional cultures of such peoples as the Andalusians of southern Spain, the Corsicans, Sardinians, Druze, Bedouins, Kabyle of Algeria, and Sarakatsani of Greece—are characterized as holding to a version of the culture of honor.[32] These groups all have economies that are greatly dependent on herding. Many other traditional societies of Africa[33] and the steppes of Eurasia and North America[34] also have (or had) herding economies and cultures of honor.

There are some interesting natural experiments that show that people who occupy the same general region but differ in occupation also differ in their predilections toward toughness, violence, and warfare. Anthropologist Robert Edgerton studied two neighboring tribes in East Africa, each of which included a group of herders and a group of farmers. Edgerton reported that in both tribes, the pastoralists exhibited "a syndrome that can best be described as *machismo*," whereas farmers manifested "the insistent need to get along with . . . neighbors."[35]

In North America, the Navajo and the Zuni also inhabit similar ecological niches, but the Navajo are herders and the Zuni are farmers. The Navajo are reputed to be great warriors (right up to the present—they served in large numbers and with distinction in World War II). The Zuni are more peaceable and have not been noted as warriors at any time in their history.[36]

An even better natural experiment came with the introduction of the horse to the American Indians of the Plains. Prior to the arrival of the horse, the tribes of the Plains had been relatively peaceful; after its introduction, many tribes began to behave like herders everywhere. They reckoned their wealth in terms of the number of horses they owned, they staged raids on their neighbors, and they began to glorify warfare.[37]

Herding and the Weakness of the State

Since herding usually takes place in regions where geography and low population density conspire against the ability of law enforcement officials to reach their targets, defense against enemies is left up to the individual and the small community in which he lives.

For many people in such circumstances, the prevailing form of law is the feud—with the threat of deadly consequences for family members as the primary means of maintaining order. Hence it should be no surprise that the feuding societies of the world are preponderantly herding societies.[38]

The Scotch-Irish and the Herding Economy in Europe and America

What has the reputed violence of the U.S. South to do with the culture of honor as it might be evidenced by a Greek shepherd, an East African warrior, or a Navajo? In our view, a great deal.

The northern United States was settled by farmers—Puritans, Quakers, Dutch, and Germans. These people were cooperative, like farmers everywhere, and modern in their orientation toward society. They emphasized education and quickly built a civilization that included artisans, tradespeople, businesspeople, and professionals of all sorts.

In contrast, the South was settled primarily by people from the fringes of Britain—the so-called Scotch-Irish.[39] These people had always been herders because the regions where they lived—Ireland, Scotland, Wales—were not in general suitable for more-intensive forms of agriculture.[40]

The Celts and Their Descendants

The Scottish and the Irish were descendants of the Celts, who had kept cattle and pigs since prehistoric times and had never practiced large-scale agriculture.[41] Like other herding peoples, the Celts reckoned their wealth in terms of animals, not land, and were accustomed to intertribal warfare and cattle raiding.[42] The Romans feared the Celts because of their ferocity (though the Romans were not impressed with the Celts' organizational abilities). Over centuries of war, including Julius Caesar's famous battles with the Gauls, the Celts were driven into Britain. Subsequent wars—with Vikings, Danes, Angles, Saxons, and other Germanic peoples—drove them to the least hospitable fringe areas. The battles really never ceased, however, especially along the Scottish frontier with England and between the Scottish and Irish in Ulster.

One cannot know how relevant the distant past of this culture is. But it may be worth noting that the Celtic peoples did not develop the characteristics of farmers until their emigration to America.[43] They did not undergo the transformation common elsewhere in Europe from serf to peasant to bourgeois farmer. When they engaged in agriculture at all, it was generally of the horticultural or slash-and-burn variety in which

a field was cultivated for three or four years and then left to lie fallow for a decade or more.[44] Such a method is the most efficient one when, as is true in most of the range of the Celtic peoples, the soil is unproductive. An important characteristic of this method of farming is that it does not encourage permanence on the land. Periodic movement was common,[45] a fact to bear in mind when one contemplates the behavior of the Scotch-Irish after they came to America.

The Scotch-Irish in the U.S. South and West

The immigration of the Scotch-Irish to North America began in the late seventeenth century and was completed by the early nineteenth century. The group was composed largely of Ulster Scots, Irish, and both lowland and highland Scots.[46] The impoverished, deeply Roman Catholic Irish who came later in the nineteenth century, as well as the Presbyterian, often highly educated Scots, were culturally very different from these earlier immigrants, who were both more secular and more inclined to violence as a means of settling disputes.[47]

Their new land, if anything, served to reinforce the herding economy practiced by the Scotch-Irish immigrants.[48] With its mountains and wide-open spaces, America, especially the Appalachians and the South, was ideally suited to the herding life and to horticulture.[49] The Scotch-Irish tended to seek out relatively unproductive lands to homestead, but even when they found themselves on highly productive land, they tended to farm in low-efficiency, horticultural fashion rather than in the more efficient agrarian manner that involves clearing the land of stumps, rotating crops, and making the sort of improvements that would have made movement away from the land hard to contemplate.[50]

The geography and low population density probably served to increase culture-of-honor tendencies in another respect as well: Because of the remoteness and ruggedness of the frontier, the law was as weak in America as it had been in Britain: "In the absence of any strong sense of order as unity, hierarchy, or social peace, backsettlers shared an idea of order as a system of retributive justice. The prevailing principle was *lex talionis,* the rule of retaliation."[51] Or, as a North Carolina proverb stated, "Every man should be sheriff on his own hearth."

The southerner, thus, was of herding origin, and herding remained a chief basis of the economy in the South for many decades. Not until the invention of the cotton gin in the early nineteenth century would there be a viable economic competitor to herding. The cotton gin made possible the plantation South. But by the early nineteenth century, the characteristic cultural forms of the Celtic

herding economy were well established, and at no time in the nineteenth century did southern folkways even in the farming South converge on those of the North.[52]

When we refer to "the South" in this book, we always mean to include the states of the deep South as well as the mountain states of Tennessee, Kentucky, and West Virginia; but many of our generalizations hold, often with equal force, to the West. The herding economy moved with the Scotch-Irish to the West—that is, to Texas and Oklahoma and the mostly southern portions of the mountain West that were settled by southerners. Again, the herding economy was basic because of the ecology. Thus, it should not be surprising that the westerner, like the southerner, shared the common characteristics of herding peoples everywhere: He used violence to protect his herd and his property; he was hypersensitive to insult because of its implications for his strength and ability to defend himself; he was skilled in the arts of combat; and he was careful to train his children, especially boys, to be capable of violence when needed.

Though we have relied on the findings of the ethnographer and historian, their methods are limited in their capacity to address these issues. Even the best-considered assertions by scholars can be challenged as mistaken subjective interpretations by other scholars. Moreover, quantitative social scientists themselves have presented conflicting evidence. Some maintain, on the basis of one type of data or another, collected by one method or another, that there is no culture of honor, no greater violence, and no attitudinal network supportive of violence existing in the South today—if there ever was. . . .

Notes

1. Gastil, 1989, p. 1473.
2. Fischer, 1989; Redfield, 1880, cited in Gastil, 1989, p. 1473.
3. Caudill, 1962, p. 46.
4. Fischer, 1989, p. 689.
5. McWhiney, 1988, p. 154.
6. Gorn, 1985, p. 20.
7. Carter, 1950, p. 50, emphasis in original.
8. Brearley, 1934.
9. Fischer, 1989, p. 690.
10. Wyatt-Brown, 1982, p. 138.
11. McWhiney, 1988, p. 203.
12. Napier, 1989.
13. May, 1989, p. 1108.
14. Anderson, 1989.
15. Anderson, 1989; Cotton, 1986; Reifman, Larrick, and Fein, 1991; Rotton and Frey, 1985.
16. Gastil, 1971.
17. Ammerman, 1989, p. 660.
18. Quoted in Wyatt-Brown, 1982, p. 153.
19. Tocqueville, [1835] 1969, p. 379.

20. Johnson, 1839.
21. Pitt-Rivers, 1965, p. 36.
22. Mandelbaum, 1988, p. 20.
23. Wyatt-Brown, 1982, p. 53.
24. Farb, [1968] 1978; O'Kelley and Carney, 1986.
25. Edgerton, 1971; Farb, [1968] 1978, pp. 121–122.
26. Edgerton, 1971, pp. 16–17; Farb, [1968] 1978, pp. 9–10; Galaty, 1991, p. 188; Lowie, 1954; Peristiany, 1965, p. 14.
27. See, for example, O'Kelley and Carney, 1986, pp. 65–81.
28. Campbell, 1965, p. 148.
29. O'Kelley and Carney, 1986, p. 65.
30. Black-Michaud, 1975, p. 199.
31. Keegan, 1944, p. 167.
32. Black-Michaud, 1975; Gilmore, 1990; Peristiany, 1965; Fisek, 1983.
33. Galaty and Bonte, 1991.
34. Lowie, 1954; Farb, [1968] 1978.
35. Edgerton, 1971, pp. 18, 297.
36. Farb, [1968] 1978, pp. 258–259.
37. Farb, [1968] 1978, p. 9–10; Lowie, 1954.
38. Black-Michaud, 1975.
39. Fischer, 1989; McWhiney, 1988; Wyatt-Brown, 1982, p. 38.
40. Blethen and Wood, 1983, p. 7.
41. Chadwick, 1970, p. 25; McWhiney, 1988, p. xxiv.
42. Corcoran, 1970, p. 25; Chadwick, 1970, p. 37.
43. Cunliffe, 1979, p. 198.
44. Blethen and Wood, 1983, p. 20.
45. McWhiney, 1988, p. 9.
46. Fischer, 1989, pp. 613–634; McWhiney, 1988, p. xli.
47. McWhiney, 1988, esp. pp. xxxvii and xli.
48. McWhiney, 1988, pp. xli ff; Wyatt-Brown, 1982, p. 36.
49. Fitzpatrick, 1989, p. 71.
50. Blethen and Wood, 1983, p. 20.
51. Fischer, 1989, p. 765.
52. Fischer, 1989.

Self-Esteem, Narcissism, and Aggression: Does Violence Result From Low Self-Esteem Or From Threatened Egotism?

Roy F. Baumeister,[1] Brad J. Bushman, and W. Keith Campbell

Department of Psychology, Case Western Reserve University, Cleveland, Ohio (R.F.B., W.K.C.), and Department of Psychology, Iowa State University, Ames, Iowa (B.J.B.)

Abstract

A traditional view holds that low self-esteem causes aggression, but recent work has not confirmed this. Although aggressive people typically have high self-esteem, there are also many nonaggressive people with high self-esteem, and so newer constructs such as narcissism and unstable self-esteem are most effective at predicting aggression. The link between self-regard and aggression is best captured by the theory of threatened egotism, which depicts aggression as a means of defending a highly favorable view of self against someone who seeks to undermine or discredit that view.

Keywords

aggression; violence; self-esteem; narcissism

For decades, the prevailing wisdom has held that low self-esteem causes aggression. Many authors have cited or invoked this belief or used it as an implicit assumption to explain their findings regarding other variables (e.g., Gondolf,

1985; Levin & McDevitt, 1993; Staub, 1989). The origins of this idea are difficult to establish. One can search the literature without finding any original theoretical statement of that view, nor is there any seminal investigation that provided strong empirical evidence that low self-esteem causes aggression. Ironically, the theory seemed to enter into conventional wisdom without ever being empirically established.

The view of low self-esteem that has emerged from many research studies does not, however, seem easily reconciled with the theory that low self-esteem causes aggression. A composite of research findings depicts people with low self-esteem as uncertain and confused about themselves, oriented toward avoiding risk and potential loss, shy, modest, emotionally labile (and having tendencies toward depression and anxiety), submitting readily to other people's influence, and lacking confidence in themselves (see compilation by Baumeister, 1993).

None of these patterns seems likely to increase aggression, and some of them seem likely to discourage it. People with low self-esteem are oriented toward avoiding risk and loss, whereas attacking someone is eminently risky. People with low self-esteem lack confidence of success, whereas aggression is usually undertaken in the expectation of defeating the other person. Low self-esteem in-

volves submitting to influence, whereas aggression is often engaged in to resist and reject external influence. Perhaps most relevant, people with low self-esteem are confused and uncertain about who they are, whereas aggression is likely to be an attempt to defend and assert a strongly held opinion about oneself.

PAINTING THE PICTURE OF VIOLENT MEN

An alternative to the low-self-esteem theory emerges when one examines what is known about violent individuals. Most research has focused on violent men, although it seems reasonable to assume that violent women conform to similar patterns. Violent men seem to have a strong sense of personal superiority, and their violence often seems to stem from a sense of wounded pride. When someone else questions or disputes their favorable view of self, they lash out in response.

An interdisciplinary literature review (Baumeister, Smart, & Boden, 1996) found that favorable self-regard is linked to violence in one sphere after another. Murderers, rapists, wife beaters, violent youth gangs, aggressive nations, and other categories of violent people are all marked by strongly held views of their own superiority. When large groups of people differ in self-esteem, the group with the higher self-esteem is generally the more violent one.

When self-esteem rises or falls as a by-product of other events, aggressive tendencies likewise tend to covary, but again in a pattern precisely opposite to what the low-self-esteem theory predicts. People with manic depression, for example, tend to be more aggressive and violent during their manic stage (marked by highly favorable views of self) than during the depressed phase (when self-esteem is low). Alcohol intoxication has been shown to boost self-esteem temporarily, and it also boosts aggressive tendencies. Changes in the relative self-esteem levels of African-American and white American citizens have been accompanied by changes in relative violence between the groups, and again in the direction opposite to the predictions of the low-self-esteem view. Hence, it appears that aggressive, violent people hold highly favorable opinions of themselves. Moreover, the aggression ensues when these favorable opinions are disputed or questioned by other people. It therefore seems plausible that aggression results from threatened egotism.

AGGRESSION, HOSTILITY, AND SELF-REGARD

Thus, the low-self-esteem theory is not defensible. Should behavioral scientists leap to the opposite conclusion, namely, that high self-esteem causes violence? No. Although clearly many violent individuals have high self-esteem, it is also necessary to know whether many exceptionally nonviolent individuals also have high self-esteem.

Perhaps surprisingly, direct and controlled studies linking self-esteem to aggression are almost nonexistent. Perhaps no one has ever bothered to study the question, but this seems unlikely. Instead, it seems more plausible that such investigations have been done but have remained unpublished because they failed to find any clear or direct link. Such findings would be consistent with the view that the category of people with high self-esteem contains both aggressive and nonaggressive individuals.

One of the few studies to link self-esteem to hostile tendencies found that people with high self-esteem tended to cluster at both the hostile and the non-hostile extremes (Kernis, Grannemann, & Barclay, 1989). The difference lay in stability of self-esteem, which the researchers assessed by measuring self-esteem on several occasions and computing how much variability each individual showed over time. People whose self-esteem was high as well as stable—thus, people whose favorable view of self was largely impervious to daily events—were the least prone to hostility of any group. In contrast, people with high but unstable self-esteem scored highest on hostility. These findings suggest that violent individuals are one subset of people with high self-esteem. High self-esteem may well be a mixed category, containing several different kinds of people. One of those kinds is very nonaggressive, whereas another is quite aggressive.

The view that individuals with high self-esteem form a heterogeneous category is gaining ground among researchers today. Some researchers, like Kernis and his colleagues, have begun to focus on stability of self-esteem. Others are beginning to use related constructs, such as narcissism. Narcissism is defined by grandiose views of personal superiority, an inflated sense of entitlement, low empathy toward others, fantasies of personal greatness, a belief that ordinary people cannot understand one, and the like (American Psychiatric Association, 1994). These traits seem quite plausibly linked to aggression and violence, especially when the narcissist encounters someone who questions or disputes his or her highly favorable assessment of self. Narcissism has also been linked empirically to high but unstable self-esteem, so narcissism seems a very promising candidate for aggression researchers to study.

We have recently undertaken laboratory tests of links among self-esteem, narcissism, and aggression (Bushman & Baumeister, 1998). In two studies, participants were insulted (or praised) by a confederate posing as another participant, and later they were given an opportunity to aggress against that person (or another person) by means of sounding an aversive blast of loud noise. In both studies, the highest levels of aggression were exhibited by people who had scored high on narcissism and had been insulted. Self-esteem by itself had no effect on aggression, and neither did either high or low self-esteem in combination with receiving the insult. These results confirmed the link between threatened egotism and aggression and contradicted the theory that low self-esteem causes violence.

Narcissism has thus taken center stage as the form of self-regard most closely associated with violence. It is not, however, entirely fair to depict narcissists as generally or indiscriminately aggressive. In our studies (Bushman & Baumeister, 1998), narcissists' aggres-sion did not differ from that of other people as long as there was no insulting provocation. Narcissism is thus not directly a cause of aggression and should instead be understood as a risk factor that can contribute to increasing a violent, aggressive response to provocation. The causal role of the provocation itself (in eliciting aggression by narcissists) is clearly established by the experimental findings.

Moreover, even when the narcissists were insulted, they were no more aggressive than anyone else toward an innocent third person. These patterns show that the aggression of narcissists is a specifically targeted, socially meaningful response. Narcissists are heavily invested in their high opinion of themselves, and they want others to share and confirm this opinion. When other people question or undermine the flattering self-portrait of the narcissist, the narcissist turns aggressive in response, but only toward those specific people. The aggression is thus a means of defending and asserting the grandiose self-view.

Do laboratory studies really capture what happens out in the real world, where violence often takes much more serious and deadly forms than pushing a button to deliver a blast of aversive noise? To answer this question, we conducted another study in which we obtained self-esteem and narcissism scores from incarcerated violent felons (Bushman, Baumeister, Phillips, & Gilligan, 1999). We assumed that the prisoners' responses to some items (e.g., "I certainly feel useless at times") would be affected by being in prison as well as by the salient failure experience of having been arrested, tried, convicted, and sentenced. These factors would be expected to push all scores toward low self-esteem and low narcissism.

Despite any such tendency, however, the prisoners' scores again pointed toward high narcissism as the major cause of aggression. The self-esteem scores of this group were comparable to the scores of published samples. The narcissism scores, meanwhile, were significantly higher than the published norms from all other studies. In particular, the prisoners outscored the baselines from other (nonincarcerated) groups to the largest degree on subscales measuring entitlement and superiority. (Again, though, the fact that the participants were in prison might have artificially lowered scores on some items, such as vanity, exhibitionism, and authority.) These findings suggest that the dangerous aspects of narcissism are not so much simple vanity and self-admiration as the inflated sense of being superior to others and being entitled to special privileges. It is apparently fine to love oneself quietly—instead, the interpersonal manifestations of narcissism are the ones associated with violence.

DEEP DOWN INSIDE

A common question raised about these findings is whether the apparent egotism of aggressive, violent people is simply a superficial form of bluster that is put on to conceal deep-rooted insecurities and self-doubts. This question is actually an effort to salvage the low-self-esteem theory, because it suggests that aggressive people really do have low self-esteem but simply act as if they do not. For example, perhaps murderers and wife beaters really perceive themselves as inferior beings, and their aggressive assertion of superiority is just a cover-up.

The question can be handled on either conceptual or empirical grounds. Empirically, some investigators have sought to find this inner core of self-doubt and reported that they could not do so. For example, Olweus (1994) specifically rejected the view that playground bullies secretly have low self-esteem, and Jankowski (1991) likewise concluded that members of violent gangs do not carry around a load of inner insecurities or self-doubts. Likewise, a number of experts who study narcissism have reported that they could not support the traditional clinical view of an egotistical outer shell concealing inner self-loathing. Virtually all studies that have measured self-esteem and narcissism have found positive correlations between the two, indicating that narcissists have high self-esteem.

Even if such evidence could be found, though, the view that low self-esteem causes aggression would still be wrong. It is by now clear that overt low self-esteem does not cause aggression. How can hidden low self-esteem cause aggression if nonhidden low self-esteem has no such effect? The only possible response is that the hidden quality of that low self-esteem would be decisive. Yet focusing the theory on the hidden quality of low self-esteem requires one to consider what it is that is hiding it—which brings the analysis back to the surface veneer of egotism. Thus, again, it would be the sense of superiority that is responsible for aggression, even if one could show that the sense of superiority is only on the surface and conceals an underlying low self-esteem. And no one has shown that, anyway.

CONCLUSION

It is time to abandon the quest for direct, simple links between self-esteem and aggression. The long-standing view that low self-esteem causes violence has been shown to be wrong, and the opposite view implicating high self-esteem is too simple. High self-esteem is a characteristic of both highly aggressive individuals and exceptionally nonaggressive ones, and so attempts at direct prediction tend to be inconclusive. Moreover, it is unwarranted to conclude that self-views directly cause aggression. At best, a highly favorable self-view constitutes a risk factor for turning violent in response to perceptions that one's favorable view of self has been disputed or undermined by others.

Researchers have started trying to look more closely at the people with high self-esteem in order to find the aggressive ones. Patterns of narcissism and instability of self-esteem have proven successful in recent investigations, although more research is needed. At present, the evidence best fits the view that aggression is most likely when people with a narcissistically inflated view of their own personal superiority encounter someone who explicitly disputes that opinion. Aggression is thus a means of defending a highly favorable view of self against someone who seeks (even unwittingly) to deflate it. Threatened egotism, rather than low self-esteem, is the most explosive recipe for violence.

Further research can benefit by discarding the obsolete view that low self-esteem causes violence and building on the findings about threatened egotism. It would be helpful to know whether a highly favorable view of self contributes to violent response by increasing the perception of insult (i.e., by making people oversensitive) or instead by simply producing a more aggressive response to the same perceived provocation. Further, research on whether narcissistic individuals would aggress against people who know bad information about them (but have not specifically asserted it themselves) would shed light on whether it is the critical view itself or the expression of it that is decisive. Another question is what exactly narcissistic people hope to accomplish by responding violently to an insult: After all, violence does not really refute criticism in any meaningful way, but it may discourage other people from voicing similar criticisms. The emotion processes involved in egotistical violence also need to be illuminated: How exactly do the shameful feelings of being criticized transform into aggressive outbursts, and does aggression genuinely make the aggressor feel better?

Recommended Reading

Baumeister, R. (1997). *Evil: Inside human violence and cruelty.* New York: W.H. Freeman.

Baumeister, R., Smart, L., & Boden, J. (1996). (See References)

Bushman, B., & Baumeister, R. (1998). (See References)

Kernis, M., Grannemann, B., & Barclay, L. (1989). (See References)

Note

1. Address correspondence to R. Baumeister, Department of Psychology, Case Western Reserve University, Cleveland, OH 44106-7123; e-mail: rfb2@po.cwru.edu.

References

American Psychiatric Association. (1994). *Diagnostic and statistical manual of mental disorders* (4th ed.). Washington, DC: Author.

Baumeister, R. (1993). *Self-esteem.* New York: Plenum Press.

Baumeister, R., Smart, L., & Boden, J. (1996). Relation of threatened egotism to violence and aggression: The dark side of high self-esteem. *Psychological Review, 103,* 5–33.

Bushman, B., & Baumeister, R. (1998). Threatened egotism, narcissism, self-esteem, and direct and displaced aggression: Does self-love or self-hate lead to violence? *Journal of Personality and Social Psychology, 75,* 219–229.

Bushman, B., Baumeister, R., Phillips, C., & Gilligan, J. (1999). *Narcissism and self-esteem among violent offenders in a prison population.* Manuscript submitted for publication.

Gondolf, E. (1985). *Men who batter.* Holmes Beach, FL: Learning Publications.

Jankowski, M.S. (1991). *Islands in the street: Gangs and American urban society.* Berkeley: University of California Press.

Kernis, M., Grannemann, B., & Barclay, L. (1989). Stability and level of self-esteem as predictors of anger arousal and hostility. *Journal of Personality and Social Psychology, 56,* 1013–1022.

Levin, J., & McDevitt, J. (1993). *Hate crimes.* New York: Plenum Press.

Olweus, D. (1994). Bullying at school: Long-term outcomes for the victims and an effective school-based intervention program. In R. Huesmann (Ed.), *Aggressive behavior: Current perspectives* (pp. 97–130). New York: Plenum Press.

Staub, E. (1989). *The roots of evil.* New York: Cambridge University Press.

ANATOMY OF A Violent RELATIONSHIP

By Neil S. Jacobson, Ph.D., and John M. Gottman, Ph.D.

Each year at least 1.6 million U.S. women are beaten by their husbands

Yet we know surprisingly little about why so many men erupt into violence, and why they feel such a need to control their women with brutal behavior.

Here, two leading marriage researchers plunge into the red-hot core of domestic abuse—observing violent couples in the heat of conflict—and surface with some startling answers.

Don was having a miserable day. There were rumors of layoffs at work, and his supervisor had been on his case for coming in late. Not only was he sick of not getting credit for doing his work well, he was sure he was about to get caught in some kind of vise he could not control. Now Don was test-driving the car he had asked his wife, Martha, to pick up from the garage. As he listened to his car's motor, he knew instantly that she had been hoodwinked. That damn rattle was still there when he drove up hills! By the time he pulled into their driveway, he was so mad that he almost hit Martha's car.

"What is it with you?" Don railed as he walked into the house. "Couldn't you tell that the damn car still wasn't running right?"

Martha, who was cooking dinner, responded calmly. "Is something wrong with the car? It sounded fine to me."

"Couldn't you tell you'd been had by the garage mechanics? Are you really that stupid?" he continued.

Martha started defending herself. "Wait a minute. I may know nothing about cars, but I resent being called 'stupid.'"

From *Psychology Today*, March/April 1998, pp. 60–65, 81, 84. Excerpted from *When Men Batter Women: New Insights into Ending Abusive Relationships.* Reprinted with the permission of Simon & Schuster. © 1998 by Neil Jacobson and John Gottman.

Don continued railing against the mechanics and against Martha for not standing up to them. He was beginning to see red, and he warned her to shut up.

But Martha didn't shut up. "If you're such a big man, why didn't you stand up to the mechanics the last time they gypped you?"

Don punched Martha in the face—hard. It was not the first punch of their marriage. But she deserved it, he told himself as he continued to hit her and yell at her. All he had wanted, he said, was a little empathy about his problems—and here she was siding with the enemy. Only a small part of him, a dim whisper in his brain, wanted to beg her forgiveness, and by the next day he would manage to squelch even that dim light of remorse.

How does a marital argument like this, one that seems to start out in near-ordinary frustration, escalate so quickly into violence? This question had come up time and again in our work as creators of couples-therapy techniques and in our two decades as social scientists studying marriage. We knew that the existing studies of the dynamics of battering didn't provide

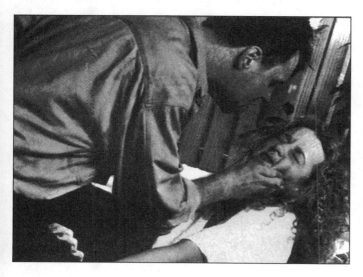

Esbin-Anderson/The Image Works

adequate answers, because they relied on after-the-fact reports by batterers and their victims, reports which are often biased and easily distorted. Particularly with battering, abundant psychological research shows that people are simply not reliable observers of their own or their intimate partner's behavior. So we decided to do something that no one had ever done before—directly observe the arguments of violent couples ourselves.

Using a simple public service announcement asking for couples experiencing marital conflict, we were able to obtain a sample of 63 battering couples, as well as a control group of couples who were equally dissatisfied with their marriage but had no history of violence. All these volunteers agreed to come into the laboratory, have electrodes hooked up to their bodies to record heart rate

and other vital signs, and be videotaped in the midst of arguments. (We also provided important safeguards, including exit interviews to ensure the woman's safety, and referrals to battered women's shelters.)

As you'll see, in the eight years of this study we made a number of myth-shattering discoveries:

- Batterers share a common profile: they are unpredictable, unable to be influenced by their wives, and impossible to prevent from battering once an argument has begun.
- Battered women are neither passive nor submissive; sometimes they are as angry as the batterers. But women almost never batter men.
- Batterers can be classified into two distinct types, men whose temper slowly simmers until it suddenly erupts into violence, and those who strike out immediately. This difference has important implications for women leaving abusive relationships.
- Emotional abuse plays a vital role in battering, undermining a woman's confidence.
- Domestic violence can decrease on its own—but it almost never stops.
- Battered women do leave at high rates, despite the increased danger they face when leaving the relationship.

Battering's Beginnings

Battering is physical aggression with a purpose: to control, intimidate, and subjugate another human being. It is always accompanied by emotional abuse, often involves injury, and virtually always causes fear in the battered woman. In our study, battering couples had at least two episodes of kicking or hitting with a fist, or at least one incident of potentially lethal violence, such as strangling.

Can women ever be batterers? In our study, we found that some battered women defend themselves, and hit or push as often as their husbands do. Some people claim that there is a huge underground movement of battered husbands. However, statistics on violent women do not take into account the impact and function of the violence. According to research conducted by Dina Vivian, Ph.D., at the State University of New York at Stonybrook, women are much more likely to be injured and in need of medical care than men, and much more likely to be killed by their husbands than the reverse. Women are the ones who are beaten up. These injuries help to sustain the fear, which is the force that provides battering with its power.

What about couples who periodically have arguments that escalate into pushing and shoving, but not beyond? We discovered large numbers of these couples, and we found that the husbands almost never become batterers.

While it is important to know about this low-level violence, we were concerned with the dynamics of severely violent couples.

Arguments under The Microscope

Through our research, we were able to reconstruct hundreds of violent arguments. Although we knew we would not directly observe violence between our subjects, we could observe their nonviolent arguments in the laboratory, ask them about these encounters, then judge their accounts of violent arguments by the accuracy of these reports.

When we put violent arguments under a microscope this way, we discovered a number of familiar themes. One of the most startling was our inability to predict when batterers would cross over into violence. While emotional abuse often preceded physical abuse, it was such a common occurrence in the relationship that it did not serve as an accurate warning sign. Further, there was no way for the battered woman to control when emotional abuse would turn into physical abuse. Martha could have shut up when Don told her to. But would this have stopped Don from hitting her? We have discovered that once an episode starts, there is nothing that the woman can do to affect its course.

Despite this inability, the women in our study did not become passive or submissive. Even when the batterers reacted to everyday requests with emotional abuse, the women typically responded calmly and assertively. We found that they wanted to inject as much normalcy into their lives as possible, and they didn't want to give up on their dream of the family life that they wanted.

However, in all the videotapes we made, never did we hear a batterer say anything like, "That's a good point," or "I never thought of that,"—comments that most married men (and women) say all the time during an argument. Instead, we observed that batterers became more aggressive when their wives asserted themselves. When Martha challenged him, we saw that Don responded violently in an attempt to maintain his dominance, no matter what the costs.

Another way that batterer's arguments diverged from those of nonviolent couples—perhaps the key difference—is that nonviolent couples have what we call "a withdrawal ritual," where at some point the escalation process stops or reverses itself. Some couples take breaks, other couples compromise, still others do both. In battering couples, the women are typically quite willing to stop at a point where they start to sense danger, but once the husbands are "activated," violence follows. Although the violence is unpredictable, we were able to identify certain warning signs. When belligerence and contempt during an argument were combined with attempts to squelch, control, or dominate a wife's behavior, that was a sign that a batterer was close to crossing the line. Don's contemptuous way of asking Martha whether she was "really that stupid," and his attempt to dominate her by telling her to shut up, demonstrate a classic prelude to battering.

Surprisingly, both in the lab and at home, battered women expressed as much belligerence and contempt as their husbands did. Like most people, battered women get angry when they are insulted and degraded. We saw much effort on the part of the women to contain their anger, but it tended to leak out anyway. Nevertheless, their initial responses—like Martha's retort to Don about not standing up to the mechanics—could hardly be considered provocations to violence.

The Slow Burn: "Pit Bulls"

Men like Don metabolize anger in a kind of slow burn: it gradually increases but never lets up. We call them "Pit Bulls" because they grow more and more aggressive until they finally attack. These men, we have found, constitute about 80 percent of batterers.

Pit Bulls have unrelenting contempt for women, and yet are extremely dependent on them. This creates a unique dynamic in their behavior. In many unhappy marriages, when one partner (usually the woman) requests change, the other one (usually the man) resists change, and eventually the woman's requests become demands, and the man's avoidance becomes withdrawal. But Pit Bulls often both demand and withdraw. We can see this in the incessant demands that Don made of Martha. Everything she did (including getting the car fixed) was wrong because nothing she did was quite enough for Don. Martha had to watch every move she made, give up her friends and family, account for all of her time, avoid Don's jealousy, and try to satisfy what he called his "simple need for a little empathy." Yet even as she walked on eggshells, she was attacked for being a "stupid bitch." Don blamed Martha for his own neediness, and punished her for it almost every day they were together.

Through this scrutiny and these constant demands, Pit Bulls establish control. Control is important to these men because they genuinely feel that they will be abandoned if they do not maintain constant vigilance over their wives. One particularly sinister form of control they use is known as "gaslighting." This technique—which gets its name from the film *Gaslight*, in which Charles Boyer convinces Ingrid Bergman she is going insane—involves a systematic denial of the wife's experience of reality. For example, when one of our subjects slapped his wife in front of a neighbor, he denied that he had done it, telling her that this kind of behavior was inconsistent with his personality, and that her accusations of abuse came from

Can Batterers JUST STOP?

"Why do women stay?" That question haunts anybody who has observed domestic violence. But a far more practical question is, How can the men be stopped? Maryland psychologist Steven Stosny, Ph.D., has developed a remarkable and effective treatment program for battering men. Even a year after treatment, an astonishing 86 percent have ended the physical abuse, and 73 percent have stopped the verbal and emotional abuse. The national dropout rate for battering programs is one out of two; Stosny's is only one out of four.

Treating batterers is something that most therapists shy away from. How did you get into it?

I became interested in spouse and child abuse at the age of two. I grew up in a violent family, where we had police and ambulances coming to the door. It took a while for me to get up the courage to get into this field, and when I started a group with severe batterers, I wanted to learn how they got that way, to learn how to prevent abuse. I was surprised when they stopped being abusive.

So how do you approach batterers?

Our program is based on the idea that most batterers can't sustain attachment, and because of this, they become flooded with feelings of guilt, shame, and abandonment, which they regulate with aggression. We teach them a five-step technique called HEALS. First, we start with the concept of *Heal.* Our clients learn that blame is powerless, but compassion is true power, and has the ability to heal. Next, you *Explain* to yourself the core hurt that anger is masking: feeling unimportant, disregarded, guilty, devalued, rejected, powerless, and unlovable. All abusive behavior is motivated by these core hurts. Then you *Apply* self-compassion. Let's say your wife calls you a brainless twit, and you feel she doesn't love you. You want to punish her for reminding you that you're unlovable. We teach men to replace this core feeling with self-compassion. "She feels unloving, but she still loves me. My instinct might be to call her a filthy slut, but she said what she said because she's hurt and feeling bad." Then you move into a feeling of *Love,* for yourself and your wife. And finally, you solve the problem by presenting your true position without blaming or attacking the other person: you say, "I care about you, but I have a problem with your calling me a brainless twit." You are healing your core hurt through love rather than anger.

So you're saying the batterer is really trying to heal his hurt core, and he can do it with compassion instead of abuse. Still, how can someone used to physical aggression learn to be so rational?

We call it teaching Mr. Hyde to remember what Dr. Jekyll learned. These men have to learn emotional regulation and the rewards of change based on compassion. We ask them to remember an incident that made them angry, to feel the anger again, and follow the steps of HEALS 12 times a day for four weeks. It almost works like a vaccination. You feel the core hurt for five seconds at a time when you practice, and you develop an immunity to it.

Why is your dropout rate so low?

It's a 12-week program, and if they don't do their homework, they go to jail. We have surprisingly little resistance. I also say "If you don't feel much better about yourself, we'll give you your money back. You'll like yourself better when you're compassionate." I've treated over 1200 abusers in my career, and even the antisocial ones—no matter how justified they felt at the time—never felt proud of hurting someone they loved. Our group is about becoming proud.

Does this work even for the true sociopaths, the ones Jacobson and Gottman call Cobras?

These people are not afraid of the criminal justice system and they don't usually come to treatment. Most people in treatment are different. They're the dependent personalities who only hurt ones they love, and who get over-involved in the relationship. If sociopaths and people with antisocial personality disorders do come into treatment, they don't learn compassion. But they do learn to use emotional regulation techniques to keep from getting upset. Some of them use this as another form of superiority—you're going to get hysterical and I'm not—but it's better than beating up their wives in front of the children. It's a form of harm reduction.

Why does this work better than traditional treatment?

Most treatment programs focus on how men's domination causes domestic violence. We say that the real gender variable is that culture doesn't teach men to regulate their negative emotions, or sustain trust, compassion, and love. Numerous studies have shown that. We socialize girls and women to have an emotional vocabulary, and this has nothing to do with education level. We look into the eyes of little girls and reward them when they cry or express other emotions, but when a little boy expresses emotions, we call him a sissy. Boys are taught to keep vulnerable emotions sub-

merged, and don't develop an emotional vocabulary.

And if you can't tell sadness from loneliness from disappointment from rejection from being devalued, the bad feelings get overloaded easily. The strongest emotion is anger.

What about the women? Do you counsel them at all?

We put the safety of the victim first. We say, "We're sure you're not going to be abused any more, but it's very unlikely you'll have a good relationship with your abuser." We tell the women that there's more to life than not being abused. And we have a higher separation rate than the average. While 75 percent of women and children in shelters go back to their husbands, out of 379 couples to go through our program so far, 46 percent of them have left their spouses.

How do you treat substance abusers?

We conduct our treatment simultaneously with substance abuse treatment. Even though this hurts our treatment outcomes— 98 percent of our recidivism is from alcohol and drugs—it's important because the nervous system bounce makes a person more irritable when coming off a drug, and I prefer they have some skills first.

Roland Maiuro, Ph.D., of the University of Washington, has been conducting a controlled study using the antidepressant Paxil to treat abusers. Maiuro found that abusers has consistently low serotonin levels, which were perhaps rendered even lower by their negative patterns of behavior. Have you seen Prozac-like drugs work with batterers?

I always tell abusers to try antidepressants. Anything that increases serotonin will reduce shame. And shame causes anger and aggression. I'll bet money that when studies like Maiuro's come out, we will see a significant reduction in violence. The problem is getting them to take it.

They'll take any illicit drug, but they won't take Prozac. But Prozac and HEALS will work best. It may even get the sociopaths.

How can we prevent domestic violence from happening in the first place?

If you treat it in the early stages you can prevent murders from happening. But you can't do this with a gender war. Community meetings against domestic violence have one or two men, and few minorities. Saying you're against domestic violence scares off people, and attracts the ones who really believe in the battle of the sexes. By demonizing the batterer, it makes him more isolated.

But if we make community organization about being for the creation of safe and secure families, they will have a much broader appeal.

her own disturbed mind. Although her face still hurt from the slap, she thought to herself that maybe she had made it all up. The neighbor, a friend of the husband's, went along and said he didn't see anything.

This technique of denying the woman's reality can be so effective that, when used in combination with methods to isolate the woman from other people, it causes battered women to doubt their own sanity. This is the ultimate form of abuse: to gain control of the victim's mind.

Lightning Strikes: "Cobras"

When Don and Martha started arguing, Don's heart rate would go up, he would sweat, and he'd exhibit other signs of emotional arousal. Most people show this response. However, we were astonished to find that as some batterers become more verbally aggressive, there is a decrease in heart rate. Like the cobra who becomes still and focused before striking its victim at over 100 miles an hour, these men calm themselves internally and focus their attention while striking swiftly at their wives with vicious verbal aggression.

When we separated these calm batterers from those who became internally aroused, we found other profound differences between the two groups. These "Cobras"—who constituted about 20 percent of our sample—were more likely to have used or threatened to use a knife or a gun on their wives, and were more severely violent than the other batterers. Only three percent of Pit Bulls had a history of extramarital violence, while 44 percent of Cobras did. And while about 33 percent of Pit Bills qualified for a diagnosis of "antisocial personality disorder"—which includes a long history of impulsive criminal behavior, childhood episodes of lying, stealing, fire setting, and cruelty to animals—fully 90 percent of the Cobras met the criteria. Finally, even though both groups abused alcohol at high rates, Cobras were more likely to be dependent on illegal drugs, such as cocaine and heroin, and were much less emotionally attached to their wives.

George was a typical Cobra. In the year prior to entering our research project, George had threatened to kill Vicky numerous times. One night several weeks before coming to see us, George came home late after he'd been out drinking and found Vicky and their two year-old daughter Christi sharing a pizza. Vicky was angry with him for missing dinner, and ignored him when he arrived. Her silence angered him, and he shouted, "You got a problem?" When she remained silent, he slammed his fist into the pizza, knocked her off the chair, dragged her across the room by her hair, held her down, and spat pizza in her face. He then beat her up, yelling, "You've ruined my life!"

The contrast between this incident and the altercation between Don and Martha over the car shows how Cobras are far more emotionally aggressive towards their wives at the start of their arguments than Pit Bulls. While Don became increasingly heated and less controlled over the course of the argument, George escalated the situation extremely rapidly, using both physical and verbal abuse in the service of control, intimidation, and subjugation. He was in Vicky's face twice as fast as she ever expected. This quick response is typical of the way Cobras control their wives—a tactic which they use because it often quiets the partner quickly and with minimal effort.

Another main difference between Cobras and Pit Bulls is that Cobras come from more chaotic family backgrounds. In our study, 78 percent of the Cobras came from violent families, compared to 51 percent of Pit Bulls. (In the population at large, 20 to 25 percent of children grow up in violent homes.) George's childhood was a classic example. He was beaten and neglected by both parents, and sexually abused by his prostitute mother's male customers. Like other Cobras, he came from a background that seriously crushed the implicit trust that every child has in his or her parents. This horrible childhood background, we believe, had somehow led the Cobras to vow to themselves that no one would ever control them again.

MEN CAN CHANGE

An astonishing 54 percent of our male volunteers showed decreases in violence during the second of two follow-up years. In fact, some men no longer met our standards for being included in our violent group. But

> **Batterers subscribe to an "honor code" that makes them unable to accept any influence—no matter how gentle—from women.**

this decrease in violence may be misleading. Once control is established over a woman through battering, perhaps it can be maintained by continued emotional abuse with intermittent battering used as a terrifying reminder of what is possible in the marriage. Cobras' violence was so severe that it may have been easier for them than for the Pit Bulls to maintain control through emotional abuse alone. Still, only seven percent of batterers in our study stopped their violence altogether in the two-year follow-up period.

We did observe several examples of husbands stopping the violence when it was unsuccessful in controlling their wives. George stopped beating Vicky as soon as she responded to his bullying with anger of her own.

WHEN WOMEN WON'T LEAVE

Three years after our two-year follow-up, we recontacted many of the battered women and their husbands. Despite the greater incidence of mental illness, drug addiction, emotional abuse, and severe violence in Cobra relationships, the typical pattern among the Cobra couples was for the wives to be committed to the marriages. While almost half of Pit Bull marriages dissolved within two years, by the five-year follow-up point, only 25 percent of women married to Cobras had left them; these women not only recognized the danger of trying to leave them, but often were quite attached to them.

Why would a woman be attached to a man as dangerous as George? Surprisingly, Vicky—like 80 percent of women married to Cobras—tested normal on our personality scales. However, she described her childhood as a "war zone" where her father would one day be absent and disengaged, and then suddenly become physically abusive toward Vicky's mother and all of the kids. She ran away from home to find a better life. And when she became pregnant by George, she tried to build her dream life. With her dashing new husband, she would finally have the home she had always wanted.

But when Vicky realized her dream of a normal, nonabusive relationship would never come to pass with George, she made the decision to leave. With Vicky and other battered women, "giving up the dream" was a pivotal step in shifting from fear to contempt and a determination to leave. Battered women need to be helped to "give up the dream" sooner, and this process should occur in conjunction with a careful safety plan and the support of an experienced helper.

Once Vicky implemented her safety plan, which included restraining orders against George and notifying his employer, the Navy, she found that George lost interest in her and went on to new pursuits. We found that Cobras will not pursue women who leave them unless it is easy and causes them little hassle to do so. But there are exceptions, and this is where help from an expert is essential.

Pit Bulls are the opposite of Cobras: easier to leave in the short run, but harder to leave in the long run. When Martha left Don and called it a trial separation, Don had little problem with it. But when she continued the separation for more than a month, he began to abuse and stalk her.

After three years of this, Martha consistently and forcefully asserted her rights. She divorced him. She hung up on him. She ended a definitive conversation with a "F___ you!" and refused to talk to him. Don might have killed her at this time. Pit Bulls have a great capacity to minimize, deny, or distort reality, and they can often justify to themselves stalking, continued abuse, and at times even murder. But Martha got lucky. Don began to leave her alone when it was clear that she would no longer be responsive to his threats. By that time, she had decided that even death was preferable to being under Don's spell.

EMERGING FROM HELL

We began this study with the goal of learning about the relationship between batterers and battered women, and we learned a great deal. We expected to focus on the men, especially when we came upon the distinction between Pit Bulls and Cobras. But during our exit interviews, we found the women in our study to be resourceful and courageous, and over time we began to realize that our work was also about the heroic struggle of battered women. These women start with a dream and truly descend into hell, and for a period of time seem stuck there. But they do not give up. They continue to struggle. Our main cause for optimism is that many of them emerge from hell and live to love again.

Unit 8

Key Points to Consider

❖ What kind of motivations lead people to volunteer their time and energy to help others? Would you call these motivations "egoistic" or "altruistic"? What factors seem to be especially important in determining whether people continue their volunteering or not? How do the results of the research in "The Effects of 'Mandatory Volunteerism' on Intentions to Volunteer" relate to this issue of people's motivation for helping?

❖ Are humans (or any species) capable of truly altruistic behavior? What would constitute evidence of "pure" altruism? Have you ever acted in a purely altruistic way?

 **Links** **www.dushkin.com/online/**

These sites are annotated on pages 4 and 5.

Early in the semester, you volunteer to participate in a psychology experiment being conducted at your school. When you arrive at the appointed time and place you are greeted by the experimenter, who explains that the research project requires you to complete a series of questionnaires measuring different aspects of your personality. The experimenter gives you the questionnaires and then returns to his office for the 30 minutes it will take you to complete them. After 5 minutes or so, you hear a loud crash in the hallway, and then you hear what sounds like a person groaning softly. What do you do?

Most of us have a very clear idea about what we would do—we would leave the room, look for the person who apparently fell, and try to help him or her. And sure enough, when research like this is conducted, that is what happens . . . some of the time. When students are alone in the room when the crash occurs, they are quite likely to help, just as we might expect. When several students are in the room together, however, they are less likely to help; in fact, the more people in the room, the less helping occurs. Thus, there is something about being in a group of people that makes us less likely to respond to the needs of another during an emergency. Strange.

Strange it may be, but research like this is one example of the kind of work that is done by social psychologists who study helping behavior. This particular kind of experiment is an attempt to understand a phenomenon known as "bystander intervention"—when bystanders actively get involved during an emergency to try to help the victim. Research has consistently demonstrated that having a large number of bystanders can actually reduce the amount of aid that is given, in part because each person takes less and less responsibility for helping the victim.

Other approaches to helping have tried to uncover the different kinds of motivations that lead people to help. Some people seem to help, for example, because they have a strong sense of obligation to care for others who are in need; this sense of obligation is often created early in life. Sometimes people help in order to reduce the level of arousing distress they feel when they see a victim; thus, helping the other person actually serves to help oneself as well. Helping that also provides a benefit to the helper is usually termed "egoistic" helping. There is also evidence that sometimes people help simply for the goal of easing another's burden, and they are not doing so to achieve personal gain. Helping of this kind is usually referred to as "altruistic" helping, because its ultimate goal is to benefit another.

In the first selection in this unit, "Volunteerism and Society's Response to the HIV Epidemic," psychologists Mark Snyder and Allen Omoto focus on a particular form of helping: volunteerism. Each year millions of people donate their time and energy to their communities in some way, and in

this selection the authors consider the various motives that can lead people to volunteer, and the motives that can lead them to continue volunteering over the long haul.

In "Morals, Apes, and Us," author Marc Hauser examines recent research that has studied our nearest genetic relatives: gorillas, chimpanzees, and orangutans. If the claims of evolutionary psychology are accurate, then we might well expect to find evidence in our evolutionary "cousins" of some emotions and behaviors that we also see in humans—in particular, the presence of moral emotions such as empathy and altruistic helping. As the article makes clear, however, clear-cut evidence is hard to find.

In "Cause of Death: Uncertain(ty)," Robert Cialdini discusses the theory mentioned at the beginning of this overview—the bystander intervention model. He describes the model itself, what led to its initial formulation, and how it has been tested. He also provides some very specific, practical advice about how to ensure that you can get help during an emergency.

Finally, in "The Effects of 'Mandatory Volunteerism' on Intentions to Volunteer," the authors examine a fairly recent phenomenon: schools requiring students to perform a certain amount of volunteer work as part of their studies. Their research suggests the interesting conclusion that at least some of the time such mandatory helping actually reduces the likelihood that the students will offer such help in the future.

Volunteerism and Society's Response to the HIV Epidemic

Mark Snyder and Allen M. Omoto

Mark Snyder is Professor of Psychology at the University of Minnesota. **Allen M. Omoto** is Assistant Professor of Psychology at the University of Kansas. Address correspondence to Mark Snyder, Department of Psychology, University of Minnesota, 75 East River Road, Minneapolis, MN 55455-0344, or Allen M. Omoto, Department of Psychology, 426 Fraser Hall, University of Kansas, Lawrence, KS 66045-2160.

In 1981, the Centers for Disease Control reported the first case of what would come to be known as AIDS. Now, barely a decade later, there are over 200,000 confirmed cases of AIDS in the United States and an estimated 1.5 million Americans infected with HIV (the virus that causes AIDS). The World Health Organization projects that, by the year 2000, 30 to 40 million adults and children worldwide will have been infected with HIV, and most of them are expected to develop AIDS.[1] Clearly, with neither a vaccine nor a cure in sight, the full impact of AIDS, as devastating and profound as the epidemic has been, has yet to be felt, and will surely touch all of our lives.

Society has responded to the HIV epidemic on a number of fronts, including at least three for which the skills and expertise of psychologists, as scientists and practitioners, can be tapped: (a) providing psychological services for persons living with AIDS (PWAs), (b) developing behavior change campaigns to reduce the likelihood of HIV transmission, and (c) implementing public education programs to address matters of prejudice and discrimination associated with AIDS and PWAs.[2] In our research, we are examining a remarkable social phenomenon born of the HIV epidemic—AIDS volunteerism and its implications for each of these fronts.

A critical component of society's response has been the development of community-based grass-roots organizations of volunteers involved in caring for PWAs and in educating the public about HIV, AIDS, and PWAs. Volunteers fill many roles; some provide emotional and social support as "buddies" to PWAs, whereas others help PWAs with their household chores or transportation needs. Volunteers also staff information, counseling, and referral hotlines; make educational presentations; raise funds; and engage in social, legal, and political advocacy. In the United States, AIDS volunteer programs have emerged in every state, in cities large and small, and in rural areas as well. AIDS volunteerism is a compelling testimonial to human kindness and to the power of communities of "ordinary people" to unite and organize in response to extraordinary events.[3]

As remarkable as AIDS volunteerism is, it actually is part of a pervasive social phenomenon in American society. A recent Gallup Poll estimated that, in 1989, 98.4 million American adults engaged in some form of volunteerism, with 25.6 million giving 5 or more hours per week to volunteer work—volunteer services worth some $170 billion.[4] In addition to working on HIV-related issues, volunteers provide companionship to the elderly, health care to the sick, tutoring to the illiterate, counseling to the troubled, food to the hungry, and shelter to the homeless.

Although the study of helping has long been a mainstay of research in the psychological sciences, volunteerism is a form of prosocial action about which there is little systematic literature.[5] Volunteerism is, however, marked by several distinctive features. Volunteers typically seek out their opportunities to help, often deliberate long and hard about the form and the extent of their involvements, and may carefully consider how different volunteer opportunities fit with their own needs, goals, and motivations. Many forms of volunteerism also entail commitments to ongoing helping relationships that have considerable duration and require sizable personal costs in time, energy, and expense.

We view AIDS volunteerism not only as an intriguing social phenomenon, but also as paradigmatic of sustained and potentially costly helping behavior. In one survey,[6] we found that AIDS volunteers overwhelmingly had actively sought out their volunteer opportunities (over 80% indicated that they had approached their AIDS organizations on their own initiative). Moreover, their involvement represented a substantial and recurring time commitment (on average, 4 hr per week) that extended over a considerable length of time (1½ years on average, and often spanning several years). Finally, these volunteers were giving of themselves in trying and stressful circumstances (spending time with PWAs and confronting the tragic realities of serious illness and death) and doing so at some personal cost (with many reporting feeling stigmatized as a result of their AIDS work).

THREE STAGES OF THE VOLUNTEER PROCESS

In our research, we are seeking to understand the social and psychological aspects of volunteerism. Our research is grounded in a three-stage conceptual model of the *volunteer process,* a model that specifies psychological and behavioral features associated with each stage and speaks to activity at three levels of analysis: the individual volunteer, the organizational context, and the broader social system.[7]

The first stage of the volunteer process involves *antecedents* of volunteerism and addresses the questions "who volunteers?" and "why do they volunteer?" In the case of AIDS, considerations at the antecedents stage focus on the attitudes, values, and motivations that dispose people to serve as AIDS volunteers, as well as the needs and

From *Current Directions in Psychological Science,* August 1992, pp. 113–116. © 1992 by the American Psychological Society. Reprinted by permission of Blackwell Publishers.

goals that AIDS volunteer work may fulfill for individuals.

The second stage concerns *experiences* of volunteers and the dynamics of the helping relationships that develop between volunteers and the people with whom they work. In the specific case of AIDS, it is important to recognize that these relationships are carried out against the stressful backdrop of chronic illness and even death. Of additional concern are the effects of AIDS volunteers on the general treatment and coping processes of PWAs, as well as changes that occur in volunteers themselves.

The third stage focuses on *consequences* of volunteerism and is concerned with how volunteer work affects volunteers, members of their social networks, and society at large. For AIDS volunteers, it is possible that their work has not only beneficial effects on personal attitudes, knowledge, and behaviors, but also negative consequences of stigmatization and social censure. When it comes to societal issues, moreover, AIDS volunteerism may possess the potential for encouraging social change as volunteers transmit their new attitudes and behavior to their friends and associates and, by extension, to the broader social system.

BASIC RESEARCH AND PRACTICAL PROBLEMS

In our research, we are engaged in a coordinated program of cross-sectional and longitudinal field studies coupled with experiments conducted in the laboratory and sampling from diverse populations of volunteers and nonvolunteers. Thus, we have conducted a national survey of currently active AIDS volunteers, querying them about their motivations for volunteering, their experiences, and the consequences of their involvement in AIDS volunteerism, thereby generating cross-sectional data relevant to the three stages of the volunteer process. In an extended longitudinal study, we are also tracking new volunteers over the course of their service providing emotional support and living assistance to PWAs; in this long-term study, we are examining the same people at all stages of the volunteer process. Finally, we are conducting laboratory experiments and field intervention studies, each relevant to one or more stages of the volunteer process.

At each stage of our conceptual model, relevant psychological theories and the evidence of basic research are helping us to frame research questions, the answers to which, we hope, will have implications for addressing practical issues related to volunteerism, as well as

for building bridges between basic research and practical application. To illustrate the ways in which our research builds these bridges, let us examine two important practical matters that are rooted in different stages of the volunteer process and the theoretically informed answers to them derived from our program of research. Specifically, we examine issues of volunteer recruitment and retention.

The Recruitment of Volunteers

Recruitment is one of the key concerns at the antecedents stage. There are many formidable barriers that can keep prospective volunteers from getting involved; in the case of AIDS, not only are there limits of time and energy but also, for many people, fear of AIDS and death and concerns about stigmatization. What, then, motivates people to volunteer to staff an AIDS hotline or to be buddies for PWAs?

Guided by a functionally oriented theory of motivation (which proposes that apparently similar acts of volunteerism may reflect markedly different underlying motivations), we have been examining the motivations of AIDS volunteers. We have utilized exploratory and confirmatory factor analytic techniques in developing and validating a self-report inventory to assess five primary motivations for AIDS volunteerism, each one reliably measured by five different items.[8] The first set of motivations involves personal *values* (e.g., "because of my humanitarian obligation to help others"). The second set invokes considerations related to *understanding* (e.g., "to learn about how people cope with AIDS"). The third set taps *community concern* and reflects people's sense of obligation to or concern about a community or social grouping (e.g., "because of my concern and worry about the gay community"). The fourth set concerns *personal development* and centers on issues of personal growth (e.g., "to challenge myself and test my skills"). The fifth category assesses *esteem enhancement* and includes considerations about current voids or deficits in one's life (e.g., "to feel better about myself").[9]

The development of this motivational inventory has made possible a more thorough analysis of the psychology of AIDS volunteerism. This work has revealed that, despite what appears to be a commonality of purpose in being a volunteer, there is striking individual-to-individual variability in the motivations that are most and least important. An appreciation of different motivations, moreover, has great practical import for volunteer recruitment. Because vol-

unteering serves different psychological functions for different people, volunteer organizations would be well advised to tailor their recruitment messages to particular motivations of selected sets of potential volunteers. In recruiting volunteers who would be motivated by esteem enhancement, for instance, recruitment appeals could stress how AIDS volunteerism provides many opportunities for people to work through personal fears, anxieties, and doubts rather than, say, stressing humanitarian obligations and images of kindness (which could be used to appeal to prospective volunteers motivated by value-based concerns).

The Retention of Volunteers

Why do some volunteers continue to donate their time and services, and why do others stop? A persistent frustration in volunteer programs is the high rate of attrition (i.e., dropout) of volunteers. As difficult as it may be to recruit volunteers, it is sometimes even more difficult to ensure their continued service. Considerations of the experiences and consequences stages of the process may shed light on matters of attrition and longevity of service because the experiences associated with volunteer work and the consequences that result from it likely influence volunteers' effectiveness, their satisfaction, and the length of time they ultimately remain active. To examine some of these possibilities, we recontacted one set of AIDS volunteers a year after they had told us about their work. At that time, approximately one half of the original sample was still active with their AIDS organizations, and we proceeded to ask both quitters and stayers about their experiences as volunteers and the consequences of their work.[8]

We found no differences between the quitters and stayers in reported satisfaction with their service and commitment to the purposes of their AIDS organizations. Where quitters and stayers differed, however, was in their perceptions of the costs of their volunteer work. Despite having engaged in satisfying and rewarding volunteer work, quitters more than stayers said they felt that volunteering had taken up too much time and—an important point—caused them to feel embarrassed, uncomfortable, or stigmatized. The negative consequences and not the rewards of the work, then, distinguished quitters from volunteers who continued to serve.

Bringing our analysis full circle, we also found that initial motivations for volunteering were related to attrition and length of service. To the extent that people espoused esteem enhancement or personal development reasons for their work (rather than community concern, values, or understanding), they were likely to still be active volunteers at our 1-year follow-up; moreover, esteem enhancement and understanding motivations proved valuable as predictors of the total length of service of these volunteers. Thus, volunteer attrition seemed not to be associated with the relatively "self-less" or other-focused motivations, as one might expect, but with more "selfish" desires of feeling good about oneself and acquiring knowledge and skills. Good, and perhaps romanticized, intentions related to humanitarian concern simply may not be strong enough to sustain volunteers faced with the tough realities and personal costs of working with PWAs. Therefore, volunteer organizations, in combating attrition, may want to remind volunteers of the personal rewards of their work rather than underscoring how volunteer efforts benefit clients and society. Similarly, volunteers may be better prepared for their work by having the potential costs of volunteerism made explicit to them at the outset; in this way, volunteers could be "prepared for the worst" and thereby "inoculated" against the negative impact of the personal costs of their service.

CONCLUSIONS

To conclude, let us explicitly address a recurring theme in our research—the relation between basic research and practical problems. Our research is simultaneously basic and applied. As much as it informs applied concerns with the current and potential roles of volunteerism in society's response to AIDS, our work also speaks directly to theoretical concerns about the nature of helping relationships and, more generally, the dynamics of individual and collective action in response to societal needs. With a dual focus on applied and theoretical concerns, our program of research embodies the essential components of *action research,* in which basic and applied research mutually inform and enrich one another and, under optimal circumstances, basic research is advanced and effective social action is undertaken.[10]

It is said that a society is judged by how it responds in times of need. Clearly, the age of AIDS is a time of the greatest need. The HIV epidemic represents not only a medical crisis, but also a broader set of challenges to individuals and to society. Among these challenges are those to researchers in the social and behavioral sciences. By all accounts, the number of AIDS cases will only increase in the years ahead, and, as medical advances extend the life expectancy of PWAs, more and more people will be living with AIDS and living *longer* with AIDS. As the HIV epidemic continues and intensifies, so too will the importance of contributions of theory-based research relevant to all facets of AIDS. Ultimately, when the history of the HIV epidemic is written, we hope that the psychological sciences will have proven themselves integral to society's collective response to AIDS.

Acknowledgments—This research and the preparation of this manuscript have been supported by grants from the American Foundation for AIDS Research (No. 000741-5 and 000961-7) and from the National Institute of Mental Health (No. 1 RO1 MH47673) to Mark Snyder and Allen M. Omoto. We thank the volunteers and staff of the Minnesota AIDS Project (Minneapolis, MN) and the Good Samaritan Project (Kansas City, MO) for their cooperation and participation in this research.

Notes

1. AIDS spreading faster than thought, *The Kansas City Star,* p. A-3 (February 12, 1992).

2. G.M. Herek and E.K. Glunt, An epidemic of stigma: Public reaction to AIDS, *American Psychologist, 43,* 886–891 (1988); S.F. Morin, AIDS: The challenge to psychology, *American Psychologist, 43,* 838–842 (1988).

3. P.S. Arno, The nonprofit sector's response to the AIDS epidemic: Community-based services in San Francisco, *American Journal of Public Health, 76,* 1325–1330 (1988); S.M. Chambré, The volunteer response to the AIDS epidemic in New York City: Implications for research on voluntarism, *Nonprofit and Voluntary Sector Quarterly, 20,* 267–287 (1991); J.A. Dumont, Volunteer visitors for patients with AIDS, *The Journal of Volunteer Administration, 8,* 3–8 (1989); P.M. Kayal, Gay AIDS voluntarism as political activity, *Nonprofit and Voluntary Sector Quarterly, 20,* 289–331 (1991); S.C. Ouellette Kobasa, AIDS and volunteer associations: Perspectives on social and individual change, *The Milbank Quarterly, 68* (S2), 280–294 (1990); D. Lopez and G.S. Getzel, Strategies for volunteers caring for persons with AIDS, *Social Casework, 68,* 47–53 (1987).

4. Independent Sector, *Giving and Volunteering in the United States* (Gallup Organization for Independent Sector, Washington, DC, 1990).

5. For perspectives on the literature on volunteerism, see S.M. Chambré, Kindling points of light: Volunteering as public policy, *Nonprofit and Voluntary Sector Quarterly, 18,* 249–268 (1989); E.G. Clary and M. Snyder, A functional analysis of altruism and prosocial behavior: The case of volunteerism, *Review of Personality and Social Psychology, 12,* 119–148 (1991); J. Van Til, *Mapping the Third Sector: Voluntarism in a Changing Social Economy* (Foundation Center, New York, 1988).

6. A.M. Omoto, M. Snyder, and J.P. Berghuis, The psychology of volunteerism: A conceptual analysis and a program of action research, in *The Social Psychology of HIV Infection,* J.B. Pryor and G.D. Reeder, Eds. (Erlbaum, Hillsdale, NJ, 1992).

7. A.M. Omoto and M. Snyder, Basic research in action: Volunteerism and society's response to AIDS, *Personality and Social Psychology Bulletin, 16,* 152–165 (1990); Omoto, Snyder, and Berghuis, note 6.

8. M. Snyder and A.M. Omoto, Who helps and why? The psychology of AIDS volunteerism, in *Helping and Being Helped: Naturalistic Studies,* S. Spacapan and S. Oskamp, Eds. (Sage, Newbury Park, CA, 1991); M. Snyder and A.M. Omoto, AIDS volunteers: Who volunteers and why do they volunteer? in *Leadership and Management,* V.A. Hodgkinson and R.D. Sumariwalla, Eds. (Independent Sector, Washington, DC, 1991).

9. Similar sets of motivations have also emerged from other attempts to measure the motives of AIDS volunteers. See, e.g., M.J. Williams, Gay men as "buddies" to persons living with AIDS and ARC, *Smith College Studies in Social Work, 59,* 38–52 (1988); L.M. Wong, S.C. Ouellette Kobasa, J.B. Cassel, and L.P. Platt, *A new scale identifies 6 motives for AIDS volunteers,* poster presented at the annual meeting of the American Psychological Society, Washington DC (June 1991). On the motivations served by volunteerism in general, see E.G. Clary, M. Snyder, and R.D. Ridge, Volunteers' motivations: A functional strategy for the recruitment, placement, and retention of volunteers, *Nonprofit Management and Leadership* (in press).

10. K. Lewin, *Field Theory in Social Science* (Harper, New York, 1951; original work published 1944); Omoto and Snyder, note 7.

Recommended Reading

Omoto, A.M., Snyder, M., and Berghuis, J.P. (1992). The psychology of volunteerism: A conceptual analysis and a program of action research. In *The Social Psychology of HIV Infection,* J.B. Pryor and G. D. Reeder, Eds. (Erlbaum, Hillsdale, NJ).

Snyder, M., and Omoto, A.M. (1991). Who helps and why? The psychology of AIDS volunteerism. In *Helping and Being Helped: Naturalistic Studies,* S. Spacapan and S. Oskamp, Eds. (Sage, Newbury Park, CA).

Morals, Apes, and Us

Can animals learn to share, cooperate, punish, and show empathy?

By Marc D. Hauser

Nearly four years ago, a visitor to Brookfield Zoo, outside Chicago, captured an extraordinary event on video. A 3-year-old boy fell into a gorilla enclosure and was knocked unconscious. Within moments, Binti Jua, a female gorilla, approached, picked up the unconscious boy, and cradled him in her arms. Then she walked over and gently put the boy down in front of the caretaker's door. The event captured the nation's heart as newspaper headlines blared: "Gorilla Saves Boy."

Most reports suggested that Binti rescued the boy because she felt empathy for him. Although there is no ambiguity about what the gorilla did, there are a lot of questions about why. Did she realize the boy was unconscious? Was she concerned about his well-being? Would she have acted in the same way toward a conscious boy, a cat, a teddy bear, or a bag of potato chips?

Despite what the headlines implied about Binti's moral fiber, the answer is by no means clear. Studies by developmental psychologists Susan Carey and Frank Keil, for example, have shown that children don't fully grasp the distinction between a dead being and a live one until they are almost 10 years old. And to date, no study of ape intelligence comes close to showing that orangutans, gorillas, or chimpanzees have the mental sophistication of a 10-year-old human. We can only guess why Binti did what she did. And one incident is not enough to warrant conclusions.

But Binti's actions do raise the public and scientific interest in the broad question of what mental traits cause us to behave morally and to what extent other animals possess those tools. As a psychologist, I'm interested in the techniques we use to get at these questions: Can other creatures share, cooperate, punish cheaters, show empathy, and act altruistically?

In a 1988 study, University of Zurich ethologist Eduard Stammbach set up an experiment with long-tailed macaque monkeys to test their ability to rein in aggressive behavior and act cooperatively. First each monkey was trained to press a lever on a machine to receive a popcorn treat. Once each animal knew what to do and when, subgroups were created. Then a low-ranking member in each subgroup was trained to press a set of levers in a specific sequence that caused the machine to deliver enough popcorn for three individuals. During the training, the machine began releasing popcorn only to the low-ranking specialist.

At first, high-ranking individuals threatened low-ranking individuals to keep them away from the dispenser altogether. Then the high-ranking individuals learned that the low-ranking individuals had a unique skill, so they followed them to the machine and waited to grab all the popcorn. Before long the low-ranking specialists stopped operating the machine. But their strike didn't last long. Some higher-ranking individuals changed their behavior. Rather than chasing specialists away or eating all their popcorn, they began to inhibit their aggression. They approached peacefully and allowed the lower-ranking specialists to eat a portion of the popcorn. Further, some high-ranking individuals started grooming specialists more often, even during periods when the machine was inoperative. Although this attitude change enabled low-ranking specialists to access food that would normally be unobtainable, it had no impact on their dominance rank within the group. Specialists kept their low rank but were allowed a moment at the high table when their skills were of use to the royalty.

Other experiments have found that monkeys even have a rudimentary sense of ownership and respect for property. Although these might seem to be strictly human concerns, territorial animals such as sunfish, lizards, sparrows, and gibbons are invested in these issues. The space that a territory owner defends is like its property, and an intruder's respect reveals its acknowledgment of ownership and property rights.

In a 1991 study, for example, University of Zurich ethologists Hans Kummer and Marina Cords tested macaques that had something other macaques wanted—a see-through tube filled with raisins. The tube was either fixed to a wall or freestanding. If it was freestanding, it was attached to a long or a short piece of rope, or no rope at all. A subordinate animal was allowed first crack at the tube in all the various placements. Then researchers observed how the more dominant individuals reacted. Although dominants often take resources away from subordinates, the experiments re-

Reprinted with permission from *Discover* magazine, February 2000, pp. 50-55 © 2000 by The Walt Disney Company.

Possession is nine-tenths of the law: When monkeys held their food tubes close, they weren't attacked and robbed

vealed rules underlying their responses. Consistently, dominants took ownership of fixed tubes more often than free tubes, and took over free tubes when the subordinates failed to carry them. Staying close to the tube and looking at it were not sufficient cues of ownership from the dominant's perspective. A dominant macaque would appear to inhibit its impulse to grab the tube if a subordinate held it close to its body. Here, then, is an intriguing example of how inhibition plays a crucial role in maintaining social conventions among monkeys.

But in any social situation with conventions, individuals often find that it pays to break the rules. Would such rule-breakers be punished? To explore this possibility; I conducted experiments on the island of Gayo Santiago, a research station near Puerto Rico that is home to some 800 rhesus monkeys. This particular species has an interesting convention: Unlike long-tailed macaques, which don't share food, rhesus monkeys tend to call out when they find food. In the study, my colleagues and I located lone individuals and presented them with a small stash of food. Their first response was to look around, presumably to decide if there were enemies near. A few individuals waited and waited and then, as if assuming an infantry combat crouch, moved cautiously toward the food. Only half the discoverers called out. When they were detected by other group members, some were aggressively attacked. Our initial suspicion was that those who were being attacked were lower-ranking than those who were not. This hunch turned out to be false. Surprisingly, both high- and low-ranking individuals were attacked. Whether or not they were attacked seemed to depend on their vocal behavior. Silent discoverers who were caught with food were attacked more often and more severely than those who cried out. It was as if individuals were being punished for being inappropriately silent,

for deceptively withholding information about a rich food source.

In a second experiment, we tested peripheral males, outsiders shifting between groups. Of 26 outsider males who were shown food, not one called out. They beelined to the food and either consumed it on the spot or gobbled a few pieces and then moved to a new location with a stash. Even if other monkeys discovered them with the food, the outsiders were never attacked. Thus, it seemed that members of an established rhesus community abide by a rule that says: Attack members that find food and don't share it. And the corollary seems to be: Why bother risking harm by assaulting one-time transgressors?

Thus research indicates that animals can inhibit their impulses and punish those who violate community rules. But what about empathy? What about Binti? Unless we can establish that animals understand the thoughts and feelings of others, we cannot assume that their behavior is moral as humans understand the word. Codes of moral behavior are founded on beliefs of right and wrong. How we form those beliefs is based on an idea of justice, a consideration of how particular actions affect others. And to understand how our behavior affects others requires empathy.

Ethologist Frans de Waal has offered several observations of apparent empathy among nonhuman primates in his 1996 book *Good Natured: The Origins*

of Right and Wrong in Humans and Other Animals. Richer insights come, however, from a series of studies published about 40 years ago, when standards for animal welfare were minimal. Today the experiments would be deemed unethical, but they do provide a window on animal emotion that has yet to be opened by more recent scientific observations.

One experiment was designed by psychologist Robert Miller and his colleagues to see if a monkey could interpret another monkey's facial expression, a presumed indicator of emotion. First, a researcher trained rhesus monkeys to pull a lever to avoid getting shocked after hearing a specific sound. Then one of the monkeys —the "actor"—was put in a room with a lever and a live television image of a second animal—the "receiver"—that was out of sight and earshot. The receiver was exposed to the sound that indicated a shock was coming but lacked a lever to avoid it.

The assumption underlying this experiment was that the receiver would hear the sound, anticipate the shock, and show fear on its face. If the actor understood the receiver's facial expressions, then it would use this information to pull its lever. If the actor failed, both animals received a shock. Because shock trials were presented randomly and neither animal could hear the other, there was no way to predict the timing of a response except by using the receiver's image in the monitor. As it turned out, the actor pulled the lever significantly more when the receiver heard the sound. Miller concluded that the actor was able to read the receiver's facial expressions. Moreover, he and his colleagues suggested that the animals behaved cooperatively: To avoid the shock, the receiver gave a signal and the actor read the receiver's signal.

Did the receivers intend to provide information to the actors? Was this a

Some monkeys in established communities abide by this rule: Attack those that find food and don't share

Some experiments in the 1960s tried to determine if monkeys would act altruistically toward one another

cooperative effort? The receivers, to be sure, must have felt helpless and afraid. But to establish that they were signaling the actors, one would have to demonstrate that they were aware of the actors' presence. And, given the design of the experiment, they certainly were not. Rather, each receiver's response was elicited by the sound, perhaps as reflexively as we kick out our foot in response to the doctor's tiny mallet. It seems likely that the actors picked up on a change in the activity of the receivers, one that was consistent enough to predict the shock. But using an expression to predict a response is not the same as seeing the expression as an indication of another's emotions at the time.

This experiment left many loose ends. Although it is clear that rhesus monkeys can learn to avoid shock by attending to a facial expression, we don't know if this response is motivated by empathy, and empathy is necessary for altruism. One has to feel what it would be like to be someone else, to feel someone else's fear, pain, or joy. We don't know whether the actors were even aware of the receivers' feelings. There was no reason for the actors to care. From the actors' perspective, all that mattered was that the image displayed on the video monitor functioned as a reliable predictor of shock. A better experiment would

have allowed the actors to see what was happening to the receiver but restrict the shock to the receiver alone.

In a 1964 study, Jules Masserman and his colleagues ran a different experiment, again with rhesus monkeys. An actor was trained to pull one of two chains to receive its food in response to a brief flash of blue or red light. Next, a receiver was housed nearby, where the actor could see it. The experimenter then changed the consequences of responding to the color of the flash. Pulling in response to one delivered food; pulling in response to the other delivered both food to the actor and a severe shock to the receiver. Most actors pulled the chain delivering the shock far less often than the chain delivering food only. Two of the 15 actors even stopped pulling both chains for between 5 to 12 days. When the actors were paired with new receivers, most continued to refrain from pulling the chain that delivered the shock. And pairs that knew each other well tended to show more altruistic behavior than pairs that were unfamiliar.

What is most remarkable about this last experiment is the possibility that some monkeys refrained from eating to avoid injuring another. Perhaps the actors empathized, imagining what it would be like to receive the shock. Alternatively, perhaps seeing another mon-

key grimace in pain is unpleasant or threatening, and rhesus monkeys will do whatever they can to avoid unpleasant conditions. Or perhaps the actor worried that one day it might be the recipient of a shock. Although refraining from eating appears to be a response of empathy or sympathy, it may actually be a selfish response.

As the experiments show, animals are by no means robots driven solely by instinctual responses. They are sensitive to their social and ecological environments, and under certain conditions they can inhibit one response and favor another. Moreover, they can punish others and sometimes alleviate another's pain. But no experiment to date has provided evidence that animals are aware of others' beliefs or intentions. And without such awareness, there can be no ethical judgment.

Asking what it means to be moral challenges us to think about how our own capacity for moral agency came about. Monkeys employ rulelike strategies for promoting the welfare of a group, including maintaining peace, observing boundaries, and sharing food. And they can abide by these rules without necessarily understanding them. Humans are a different kind of animal: We can consciously evaluate whether behavior is right or wrong, but we tend to do so depending on the conventions of our society. In that regard, the roots of our moral intuition are entwined with the self-interest shown by other animals. What we don't know is exactly when the uniquely human capacity for empathy and justice emerged in our ancestors and how cultures build on a universal moral sense. What is certain is that our moral potential is still far from fully realized. As Agesilaus, a Spartan king, said, "If all men were just, there would be no need of valor."

CAUSE OF DEATH: UNCERTAIN(TY)

Richard B. Cialdini
Arizona State University

All the weapons of influence discussed in this book work better under some conditions than under others. If we are to defend ourselves adequately against any such weapon, it is vital that we know its optimal operating conditions in order to recognize when we are most vulnerable to its influence. We have already had a hint of one time when the principle of social proof worked best with the Chicago believers. It was a sense of shaken confidence that triggered their craving for converts. In general, when we are unsure of ourselves, when the situation is unclear or ambiguous, when uncertainty reigns, we are most likely to look to and accept the actions of others as correct (Tesser, Campbell, & Mickler, 1983; Wooten & Reed, 1998).

In the process of examining the reactions of other people to resolve our uncertainty, however, we are likely to overlook a subtle, but important fact: Those people are probably examining the social evidence, too. Especially in an ambiguous situation, the tendency for everyone to be looking to see what everyone else is doing can lead to a fascinating phenomenon called *pluralistic ignorance*. A thorough understanding of the pluralistic ignorance phenomenon helps explain a regular occurrence in our country that has been termed both a riddle and a national disgrace: the failure of entire groups of bystanders to aid victims in agonizing need of help.

The classic example of such bystander inaction and the one that has produced the most debate in journalistic, political, and scientific circles began as an ordinary homicide case in New York City's borough of Queens. A woman in her late twenties, Catherine Genovese, was killed in a late-night attack on her street as she returned from work. Murder is never an act to be passed off lightly, but in a city the size and tenor of New York, the Genovese incident warranted no more space than a fraction of a column in the *New York Times*. Catherine Genovese's story would have died with her on that day in March 1964 if it hadn't been for a mistake.

The metropolitan editor of the *Times*, A. M. Rosenthal, happened to be having lunch with the city police commissioner a week later. Rosenthal asked the commissioner about a different Queens-based homicide, and the commissioner, thinking he was being questioned about the Genovese case, revealed something staggering that had been uncovered by the police investigation. It was something that left everyone who heard it, the commissioner included, aghast and grasping for explanations. Catherine Genovese had not experienced a quick, muffled death. It had been a long, loud, tortured, *public* event. Her assailant had chased and attacked here in the street three times over a period of 35 minutes before his knife finally silenced her cries for help. Incredibly, 38 of her neighbors watched from the safety of their apartment windows without so much as lifting a finger to call the police.

Rosenthal, a former Pulitzer Prize winner reporter, knew a story when he heard one. On the day of his lunch with the commissioner, he assigned a reporter to investigate the "bystander angle" of the Genovese incident. Within a week, the *Times* published a long, front-page article that was to create a swirl of controversy and speculation. The initial paragraphs of that report provided the tone and focus of the story:

> For more than half an hour 38 respectable, law-abiding citizens in Queens watched a killer stalk and stab a woman in three separate attacks in Kew Gardens.
>
> Twice the sound of their voices and the sudden glow of their bedroom lights interrupted him and frightened him off. Each time he returned, sought her out, and stabbed her again. Not one person telephoned the police during the assault; one witness called after the woman was dead.
>
> That was two weeks ago today. But Assistant Chief Inspector Frederick M. Lussen, in charge of the borough's detectives and a veteran of 25 years of homicide investigations, is still shocked.
>
> He can give a matter-of-fact recitation of many murders. But the Kew Gardens slaying baffles him—not because it is a murder, but because "good people" failed to call the police. (Ganzberg, 1964, p. 7)

As with Assistant Chief Inspector Lussen, shock and bafflement were the standard reactions of al-

most everyone who learned the story's details. The shock struck first, leaving the police, the newspeople, and the reading public stunned. The bafflement followed quickly. How could 38 "good people" fail to act under those circumstances? No one could understand it. Even the murder witnesses themselves were bewildered. "I don't know," they answered one after another. "I just don't know." A few offered weak reasons for their inaction. For example, two or three people explained that they were "afraid" or "did not want to get involved." These reasons, however, do not stand up to close scrutiny: A simple anonymous call to the police could have saved Catherine Genovese without threatening the witnesses' future safety or free time. No, it wasn't the observers' fear or reluctance to complicate their lives that explained their lack of action; something else was going on there that even they could not fathom.

Confusion, though, does not make for good news copy. So the press as well as the other media—several papers, TV stations, and magazines that were pursuing followup stories—emphasized the only explanation available at the time: The witnesses, no different from the rest of us, hadn't cared enough to get involved. Americans were becoming a nation of selfish, insensitive people. The rigors of modern life, especially city life, were hardening them. They were becoming "The Cold Society," unfeeling and indifferent to the plight of their fellow citizens.

In support of this interpretation, news stories began appearing regularly in which various kinds of public apathy were detailed. Also supporting such an interpretation were the remarks of a range of armchair social commentators, who, as a breed, seem never to admit to bafflement when speaking to the press. They, too, saw the Genovese case as having large-scale social significance. All used the word *apathy*, which, it is interesting to note, had been in the headline of the *Times*'s front-page story, although they accounted for the apathy differently. One attributed it to the effects of TV violence, another to repressed aggressiveness, but most implicated the "depersonalization" of urban life with its "megalopolitan societies" and its "alienation of the individual from the group." Even Rosenthal, the newsman who first broke the story and who ultimately made it the subject of a book, subscribed to the city-caused apathy theory.

> Nobody can say why the 38 did not lift the phone while Miss Genovese was being attacked, since they cannot say themselves. It can be assumed, however, that their apathy was indeed one of the big-city variety. It is almost a matter of psychological survival, if one is surrounded and pressed by millions of people, to prevent them from constantly imping-

ing on you, and the only way to do this is to ignore them as often as possible. Indifference to one's neighbor and his troubles is a conditioned reflex in life in New York as it is in other big cities. (A. M. Rosenthal, 1964, pp. 82–83)

As the Genovese story grew—aside from Rosenthal's book, it became the focus of numerous newspaper and magazine pieces, several television news documentaries, and an off-Broadway play—it attracted the professional attention of a pair of New York-based psychology professors, Bibb Latané and John Darley (1968b). They examined the reports of the Genovese incident and, on the basis of their knowledge of social psychology, hit on what had seemed like the most unlikely explanation of all— the fact that 38 witnesses were present. Previous accounts of the story had invariably emphasized that no action was taken, *even though* 38 individuals had looked on. Latané and Darley suggested that no one had helped precisely *because* there were so many observers.

The psychologists speculated that, for at least two reasons, a bystander to an emergency will be unlikely to help when there are a number of other bystanders present. The first reason is fairly straightforward. *With several potential helpers around, the personal responsibility of each individual is reduced:* "Perhaps someone else will give or call for aid, perhaps someone else already has." So with everyone thinking that someone else will help or has helped, no one does. The second reason is the more psychologically intriguing one; it is founded on the principle of social proof and involves the pluralistic ignorance effect. Very often an emergency is not obviously an emergency. Is the man lying in the alley a heart-attack victim or a drunk sleeping one off? Is the commotion next door an assault requiring the police or an especially loud marital spat where intervention would be inappropriate and unwelcome? What is going on? In times of such uncertainty, the natural tendency is to look around at the actions of others for clues. We can learn from the way the other witnesses are reacting whether the event is or is not an emergency.

What is easy to forget, though, is that everybody else observing the event is likely to be looking for social evidence, too. Because we all prefer to appear poised and unflustered among others, we are likely to search for that evidence placidly, with brief, camouflaged glances at those around us. Therefore everyone is likely to see everyone else looking unruffled and failing to act. As a result, and by the principle of social proof, the event will be roundly interpreted as a nonemergency. This, according to Latané and Darley (1968b) is the state of pluralistic ignorance "in which each person decided that since nobody is concerned, nothing is wrong. Meanwhile, the danger may be mounting to the point where a single individual, uninfluenced by the seeming clam of others, *would* react."[1]

A Scientific Approach

The fascinating upshot of Latané and Darley's reasoning is that, for an emergency victim, the idea of "safety in numbers" may often be completely wrong. It might be that someone in need of emergency aid would have a better chance of survival if a single bystander, rather than a crowd, were present. To test this unusual thesis. Darley, Latané, their students, and colleagues performed a systematic and impressive program of research that produced a clear set of findings (for a review, see Latané & Nida, 1981). Their basic procedure was to stage emergency events that were observed by a single individual or by a group of people. They then recorded the number of times the emergency victim received help under those circumstances. In their first experiment (Darley & Latané, 1968), a New York college student who appeared to be having an epileptic seizure received help 85 percent of the time when there was a single bystander present but only 31 percent of time with five bystanders present. With almost all the single bystanders helping, it becomes difficult to argue that ours is "The Cold Society" where no one cares for suffering others. Obviously it was something about the presence of other bystanders that reduced helping to shameful levels.

Other studies have examined the importance of social proof in causing widespread witness "apathy." They have done so by planting within a group of witnesses to a possible emergency people who are rehearsed to act as if no emergency were occurring. For instance, in another New York-based experiment (Latané & Darley, 1968a), 75 percent of lone individuals who observed smoke seeping from under a door reported the leak; however, when similar

---

[1] The potentially tragic consequences of the pluralistic ignorance phenomenon are starkly illustrated in a UPI news release from Chicago:

A university coed was beaten and strangled in daylight hours near one of the most popular tourist attractions in the city, police said Saturday.

The nude body of Lee Alexis Wilson, 23, was found Friday in dense shrubbery alongside the wall of the Art Institute by a 12-year-old boy playing in the bushes.

Police theorized she may have been sitting or standing by a fountain in the Art Institute's south plaza when she was attacked. The assailant apparently then dragged her into the bushes. She apparently was sexually assaulted, police said.

Police said thousands of persons must have passed the site and one man told them he heard a scream about 2 P.M. but did not investigate because no one else seemed to be paying attention.

leaks were observed by three-person groups, the smoke was reported only 38 percent of the time. The smallest number of bystanders took action, though, when the three-person groups included two individuals who had been coached to ignore the smoke; under those conditions, the leaks were reported only 10 percent of time. In a similar study conducted in Toronto (A. S. Ross, 1971), single bystanders provided emergency aid 90 percent of the time, whereas such aid occurred in only 16 percent of the cases when a bystander was in the presence of two passive bystanders.

Social scientists now have a good idea of when bystanders will offer emergency aid. First, and contrary to the view that we have become a society of callous, uncaring people, once witnesses are convinced that an emergency situation exists, aid is very likely. Under these conditions, the number of bystanders who either intervene themselves or summon help is quite comforting. For example, in four separate experiments done in Florida (R. D. Clark & Word, 1972, 1974), accident scenes involving a maintenance man were staged. When it was clear that the man was hurt and required assistance, he was helped 100 percent of the time in two of the experiments. In the other two experiments, where helping involved contact with potentially dangerous electric wires the victim still received bystander aid in 90 percent of the instances. In addition, these extremely high levels of assistance occurred whether the witnesses observed the event singly or in groups.

The situation becomes very different when, as in many cases, bystanders cannot be sure that the event they are witnessing is an emergency. Then a victim is much more likely to be helped by a lone bystander than by a group, especially if the people in the group are strangers to one another (Latané & Rodin, 1969). It seems that the pluralistic ignorance effect is strongest among strangers: Because we like to look graceful and sophisticated in public and because we are unfamiliar with the reactions of those we do not know, we are unlikely to give off or correctly read expressions of concern when in a group of strangers. Therefore, a possible emergency is viewed as a nonemergency and a victim suffers.

A close look at this set of research findings reveals an enlightening pattern. All the conditions that decrease an emergency victim's chances for bystander aid exist normally and innocently in the city, in contrast to rural areas:

1. Cities are more clamorous, distracting, rapidly changing places where it is difficult to be certain of the nature of the events one encounters.
2. Urban environments are more populous; consequently, people are more likely to be with others when witnessing a potential emergency situation.

3. City dwellers know a much smaller percentage of fellow residents than do people who live in small towns; therefore, city dwellers are more likely to find themselves in a group of strangers when observing an emergency.

These three natural characteristics of urban environments—their confusion, their populousness, and their low levels of acquaintanceship—fit in very well with the factors shown by research to decrease bystander aid. Without ever having to resort to such sinister concepts as "urban depersonalization" and "megalopolitan alienation," then, we can explain why so many instances of bystander inaction occur in our cities.

Devictimizing Yourself

Explaining the dangers of modern urban life in less ominous terms does not dispel them. Furthermore, as the world's populations move increasingly to the cities—half of all humanity will be city dwellers within a decade—there will be a growing need to reduce those dangers. Fortunately, our newfound understanding of the bystander "apathy" process offers real hope. Armed with this scientific knowledge, an emergency victim can increase enormously the chances of receiving aid from others. The key is the realization that groups of bystanders fail to help because the bystanders are unsure rather than unkind. They don't help because they are unsure an emergency actually exists and whether they are responsible for taking action. When they are sure of their responsibilities for intervening in a clear emergency, people are exceedingly responsive!

Once it is understood that the enemy is the simple state of uncertainty, it becomes possible for emergency victims to reduce this uncertainty, thereby protecting themselves. Imagine, for example, you are spending a summer afternoon at a music concert in a park. As the concert ends and people begin leaving, you notice a slight numbness in one arm but dismiss it as nothing to be alarmed about. Yet, while moving with the crowd to the distant parking areas, you feel the numbness spreading down to your hand and up one side of your face. Feeling disoriented, you decide to sit against a tree for a moment to rest. Soon you realize that something is drastically wrong. Sitting down has not helped; in fact, the control and coordination of your muscles has worsened, and you are starting to have difficulty moving your mouth and tongue to speak. You try to get up but can't. A terrifying thought rushes to mind: "Oh, God, I'm having a stroke!" Groups of people are passing by and most are paying no attention. The few who notice the odd way you are slumped against the tree or the strange look on your face check the social evidence around them and, seeing that no one else is reacting with concern, walk on convinced that nothing is wrong.

Were you to find yourself in such a predicament, what could you do to overcome the odds against receiving help? Because your physical abilities would be deteriorating, time would be crucial. If, before you could summon aid, you lost your speech or mobility or consciousness, your chances for assistance and for recovery would plunge drastically. It would be essential to try to request help quickly. What would be the most effective form of that request? Moans, groans, or outcries probably would not do. They might bring you some attention, but they would not provide enough information to assure passersby that a true emergency existed.

If mere outcries are unlikely to produce help from the passing crowd, perhaps you should be more specific. Indeed, you need to do more than try to gain attention; you should call out clearly your need for assistance. You must not allow bystanders to define your situation as a nonemergency. Use the word "Help" to show your need for emergency aid, and don't worry about being wrong. Embarrassment is a villain to be crushed. If you think you are having a stroke, you cannot afford to be worried about the possibility of overestimating your problem. The difference is that between a moment of embarrassment and possible death or lifelong paralysis.

Even a resounding call for help is not your most effective tactic. Although it may reduce bystanders' doubts that a real emergency exists, it will not remove several other important uncertainties within each onlooker's mind: What kind of aid is required? Should I be the one to provide the aid, or should someone more qualified do it? Has someone else already gone to get professional help, or is it my responsibility? While the bystanders stand gawking at you and grappling with these questions, time vital to your survival could be slipping away.

Clearly, then, as a victim you must do more than alert bystanders to your need for emergency assistance; you must also remove their uncertainties about how that assistance should be provided and who should provide it. What would be the most efficient and reliable way to do so?

Based on the research findings we have seen, my advice would be to isolate one individual from the crowd: Stare, speak, and point directly at that person and no one else: "You, sir, in the blue jacket, I need help. Call an ambulance." With that one utterance you would dispel all the uncertainties that might prevent or delay help. With that one statement you will have put the man in the blue jacket in the role of "rescuer." He should now understand that emergency aid is needed; he should understand that he, not someone else, is responsible for providing the aid; and, finally, he should understand exactly how to provide it. All the scientific evidence indicates that the result should be quick, effective assistance.

In general, then, your best strategy when in need of emergency help is to reduce the uncertainties of those around you concerning your condition and their responsibilities. Be as precise as possible about your need for aid. Do not allow bystanders to come to their own conclusions because, especially in a crowd, the principle of social proof and the consequent pluralistic ignorance effect might well cause them to view your situation as a nonemergency. Of all the techniques in this book designed to produce compliance with a request, this one is the most important to remember. After all, the failure of your request for emergency aid could mean your life. . . .

THE EFFECTS OF "MANDATORY VOLUNTEERISM" ON INTENTIONS TO VOLUNTEER

Arthur A. Stukas,[1] Mark Snyder,[2] and E. Gil Clary[3]

[1]Univeristy of Northern Colorado, [2]University of Minnesota, and [3]College of St. Catherine

Abstract—*With the widespread emergence of required community-service programs comes a new opportunity to examine the effects of requirements on future behavioral intentions. To investigate the consequences of such "mandatory volunteerism" programs, we followed students who were required to volunteer in order to graduate from college. Results demonstrated that stronger perceptions of external control eliminated an otherwise positive relation between prior volunteer experience and future intentions to volunteer. A second study experimentally compared mandates and choices to serve and included a premeasured assessment of whether students felt external control was necessary to get them to volunteer. After being required or choosing to serve, students reported their future intentions. Students who initially felt it unlikely that they would freely volunteer had significantly lower intentions after being required to serve than after being given a choice. Those who initially felt more likely to freely volunteer were relatively unaffected by a mandate to serve as compared with a choice. Theoretical and practical implications for understanding the effects of requirements and constraints on intentions and behavior are discussed.*

For decades now, psychologists have sought to understand the factors that lead people to help others in need (see Krebs & Miller, 1985). Initial work focused on helping in emergencies or other short-term "spontaneous helping" situations in which a potential helper is faced with an unexpected need for help, calling for an immediate decision to act, and an opportunity to provide one and only one relatively brief act of help (e.g., Latané & Darley, 1970). More recently, students of helping behavior have increasingly come to recognize that, to gain a fuller understanding of who helps and why, they must also study helping that is planned and sustained over time (e.g., Clary, Snyder, Ridge, et al., 1998; Cnaan & Goldberg-Glen, 1991; Omoto & Snyder, 1995; Smith, 1994; Snyder & Omoto, 1992). The prototypical example of planned, sustained helping is volunteerism. Every year, millions of people volunteer their time and effort to act as tutors for children and adults, com-

panions for the lonely, and health care providers for the sick; in 1995 alone, an estimated 23 million American adults spent at least 5 hr each week in volunteer service (Independent Sector, 1996).

However, even though many people do volunteer, many do not (51% of 1995 survey respondents had not volunteered in the past 12 months; Independent Sector, 1996). Indeed, society has recognized that extra effort may be necessary to inspire its members to help, and consequently the United States has created federal programs such as the Peace Corps and VISTA. Recently, the call to volunteer has become even louder as those in need of help see public supports eliminated. To promote citizen participation, various institutions have started to use their authority to require, as opposed to "inspire," individuals to engage in community service. In particular, many educational institutions have sought to increase levels of "volunteer" activity by requiring community service of their students (Keith, 1994). Moreover, governments have gone so far as to establish community-service requirements as conditions of graduation from high school (e.g., the State of Maryland; Sobus, 1995).

In addition to directly enhancing the welfare of the community, an implicit, if not always explicit, goal of these "mandatory volunteerism" programs is to increase levels of future volunteerism, thereby ensuring a continuing pool of volunteers from which the community can draw in times of need (Sobus, 1995). Many service-learning proponents believe that requiring students to volunteer will accomplish this goal by promoting the personal, social, and civic development of students and the internalization of prosocial values that lead to intentions to volunteer (Giles & Eyler, 1994; Sobus, 1995). However, mandating volunteerism with such aims in mind raises the question of whether behavior performed under external pressure actually leads to internalization of prosocial values and future behavioral intentions (e.g., Deci & Ryan, 1985, 1987).

Indeed, it can be argued that requirements to volunteer may reduce interest in volunteer activities by altering individuals' perceptions of why they help. If mandated students begin to perceive that they help only when required or rewarded, then their intentions to freely engage in volunteer service in the future may be reduced (e.g., Batson, Coke, Jasnoski, & Hanson, 1978; Clary, Snyder, & Stukas, 1998; Kunda & Schwartz,

Address correspondence to Arthur A. Stukas, Department of Psychology, McKee 0014, University of Northern Colorado, Greeley, CO 80639; e-mail: aastuka@bentley.unco.edu.

1983). In keeping with this theory, Piliavin and Callero (1991) reported that blood donors who gave blood for the first time under coercion expressed lesser intentions to continue donating in the future than those who were not coerced. Requirements (and other coercive techniques) may also engender psychological reactance (Brehm & Brehm, 1981); limiting an individual's freedom to act may lead to desires to reestablish that freedom, which can be accomplished by derogating the forced activity and by refusing to perform it once the mandate has been lifted.

Most theories about the undermining of interest in an activity suggest that this effect may be strongest for individuals with initial interest in the activity (e.g., Lepper, Greene, & Nisbett, 1973). One important indicator of interest in volunteering is previous involvement in volunteer activities, and we expect that experienced individuals may be most likely to suffer from required service programs; in other words, predictions of an inhibiting effect presuppose that individuals possess established behavioral intentions and habits that can be inhibited by a requirement. Given that a principal defining characteristic of volunteerism is its sustained nature, it is not unreasonable to expect that prior volunteer experience may play a pivotal role in determining how people respond to mandatory volunteerism programs. Certainly, under ordinary circumstances, prior experience is an influential determinant of later intentions. For example, Charng, Piliavin, and Callero (1988) have shown that continued experience as a blood donor can lead to the role of blood donor becoming a central part of the self-concept and donating becoming habitual and routine. We do not doubt that the same process occurs for other types of volunteerism. However, when requirements to serve are placed on experienced volunteers, their intentions to continue to engage in voluntary action may be short-circuited.

Although an inhibiting effect can be theorized to occur for those persons with established histories of volunteer action, we suggest that prior experience itself may not be the sole predictor of the consequences of mandatory volunteerism. Indeed, survey research indicates that many students have a positive attitude toward instituting community-service requirements at their schools (e.g., Independent Sector, 1992), and may not feel particularly "forced" into volunteerism because they are already advocates of such service-learning programs. Other students, however, have a less positive attitude and may feel that these programs are unnecessary and that they will volunteer when and if they have the time and inclination; these students might feel forced to serve.

Given students' varied reactions to mandatory volunteerism, we hypothesized that the effects of prior experience on intentions to volunteer following required service are moderated by perceptions of the external control being exerted by the requirements. Feeling forced to volunteer may weaken the positive relation between past experience and future intentions. Thus, in a study testing this hypothesis, we predicted that when individuals perceived lower levels of external control, their prior experience and future intentions would be positively related; that is, as prior experience increased, so too would intentions to volunteer in the future. However, we expected that when individuals perceived higher levels of external control,

prior experience and future intentions would be unrelated or perhaps even negatively related; in other words, as prior experience increased, future intentions would remain relatively constant or perhaps even decrease. This pattern of results would demonstrate that under high levels of perceived external control, individuals with the most prior experience (who would otherwise have the highest future intentions) suffer the greatest inhibiting effect on their intentions to volunteer.

STUDY 1

In 1993, the University of St. Thomas in St. Paul, Minnesota, incorporated a new graduation requirement into its undergraduate business program: All students were required to engage in 40 hr of community service. A noncredit, tuition-free course, coordinated by a business faculty member, was designed to track students' fulfillment of the requirement and to help them choose an appropriate service opportunity (e.g., being a companion to an elderly person or a tutor to an illiterate child). The introduction of this requirement provided us with a "real world" laboratory in which we could follow students, all of whom were required to volunteer, over the course of their service and examine the factors that affected their intentions to volunteer subsequently.

Method

Participants

A total of 371 business majors (192 men and 179 women) who were required to enroll in the service-learning course (Business 200, or B200) completed initial and follow-up surveys as a component of the course.[1] Data were collected from six separate classes between the fall of 1993 and the spring of 1995.

Procedure

Participants completed surveys, administered during the first and last class meetings of B200, which marked the beginning and end of their mandated service performed over the course of 12 weeks. The initial survey included measures of prior volunteer experience and the extent to which participants felt they were engaging in service only because they were required, as well as other measures. The follow-up survey included among its items measures of future intentions to volunteer.

---

1. The 371 participants came from a pool of 612 business majors who were enrolled in B200 during the time period of this study. Thirty-six of these students did not attend the orientation session and thus did not complete the initial survey. Of those students who completed the initial survey, 64.4% also completed the follow-up survey. The 35.6% of students who did not complete the final survey had been excused by the instructor from the final session of the course, when the final survey was administered, and failed to return a mailed follow-up survey. On average, these students were significantly older, were more likely to be male, and had more of their time set aside for a paid job than students who completed the final survey. For an additional 39 students, data for one or more of the variables included in our analyses were missing; these students were included only in those analyses for which it was appropriate.

Thus, to assess just how much participants felt they were performing their community service because of the mandate, we developed a two-item measure ($r = .46$, $p < .01$) for use in the pretest: "I am participating in B200 only because it is required of me" and "Even if I weren't in the B200 program, I would be volunteering" (reverse coded). The combined scale ranged from 2 to 14 (with higher scores indicating greater perceptions of external control[2]) and had a mean of 8.3 and a standard deviation of 3.4.

At the end of the program, participants were asked to indicate the likelihood (on a 7-point scale; 1 = *extremely unlikely*, 7 = *extremely likely*) that they would volunteer at several points in the future. Our behavioral-intentions index was an average of responses to six items: "I will work at the same site next semester," "I will volunteer somewhere else next semester," "I will be a volunteer 1 year from now," "I will be a volunteer 3 years from now," "I will be a volunteer 5 years from now," and "I will be a volunteer 10 years from now." The internal consistency (alpha) of this index was .82.

Results

We predicted that for students who perceived lower levels of external control, prior volunteer experience would be an influential and positive determinant of later intentions to continue their work in the future; by contrast, students who felt higher levels of external control would demonstrate a much weaker relation between experience and intentions, mostly because experienced volunteers would have comparatively lower intentions. We employed hierarchical regression to investigate this hypothesis.

Specifically, the strategy used to test such moderated effects involved entering the *past experience* factor (estimated total number of months volunteered in one's lifetime; $M = 12$ months, $SD = 18$ months[3]) on the first step of the regression analysis and then entering the *external control* factor on the second step and the *interaction* term (a multiplicative product of the first two scores) on the third step. Moderation was indicated by a significant increase in the r^2 value from Step 2 to Step 3 (Baron & Kenny, 1986).

The results of this analysis demonstrated that past experience had a main effect on intentions: Students with more experience were more likely to intend to volunteer in the future at the program's end than were students who began with less experience, $r^2 = .036$, $F(1, 330) = 12.28$, $p < .001$. There was also a main effect of perceptions of external control on intentions (after experience had already been entered into the equation); students who felt more external control upon starting

B200 were less likely to intend to volunteer at its finish, r^2 improvement = .177, $F(1, 329) = 74.10$, $p < .001$.

Our primary hypothesis, however, was that the effects of experience on students' intentions would be moderated by perceptions of external control, and, indeed, we found a statistically significant interaction of experience and external control, r^2 improvement = 0.21, $F(1, 328) = 8.86$, $p < .01$. When students perceived the service-learning program to be more controlling of their behavior, the positive relation between past volunteer experience and future intentions was weakened; thus, students who had the greatest past experience and who also felt controlled did not have the highest future intentions—instead, their intentions were undermined by the requirement. For those students who did not feel controlled, past experience was positively correlated with future intentions (i.e., students with the most experience were most likely to intend to volunteer in the future). To provide a graphic representation of this analysis, we plotted regression lines for three levels of external control: the mean, 1 standard deviation above the mean, and 1 standard deviation below the mean (as recommended by Cohen & Cohen, 1983, p. 323) (see Fig. 1).

As is apparent from this graph, students with lower levels of perceived external control (plotted at external control = 4.9) demonstrated a positive relation between prior experience and future intentions (the upwardly sloping regression line). Students at higher levels of perceived external control (external control = 11.7) demonstrated a slightly negative relation between prior experience and future intentions (the downwardly sloping regression line). For students at the mean of the external-control scale (external control = 8.3), prior experience and future intentions were essentially unrelated (the middle regression line, which is almost flat).

Discussion

The findings of this field study demonstrated that in the context of a mandatory volunteerism program, behavioral intentions to engage in volunteer work in the future were positively related to past histories of volunteerism—but only for students who did not feel that the program had overly controlled their behavior. These results support the findings of earlier research demonstrating that external constraints to act, in the form of requirements or rewards, may reduce interest in an activity (e.g., Batson et al., 1978; Kunda & Schwartz, 1983). This research has consistently shown that such decrements in interest result most strongly for individuals with prior interest in an activity. Indeed, in our study, when external constraints were perceived to be controlling, an inhibiting effect was strongest for participants with greater prior experience as volunteers—individuals for whom such an inhibiting effect was possible.

Conducting this research with students in an actual mandatory volunteerism program gives us confidence that we have assessed reactions to requirements as they exist in actual educational environments. Yet investigating these effects in the field with actual required volunteers also meant that we were unable to conduct a true experiment; all participants were ex-

---

2. Correlates of perceptions of external control were investigated. Higher perceptions of control were significantly associated with fewer months of prior experience ($r = -.13$) age ($r = .11$), and the motivations measured by our (Clary, Snyder, Ridge, et al., 1998) Volunteer Functions Inventory (r from $-.15$ to $-.50$). A significant gender difference in perceptions of control indicated that men had higher perceptions of control ($M = 8.87$) than women ($M = 7.45$), $t(330) = -3.87$, $p < .000$.

3. Six individuals with outlying scores on the experience variable (more than 6 years of prior experience) had their scores altered to 73 months, as recommended by Tabachnick and Fidell (1996, p. 69).}

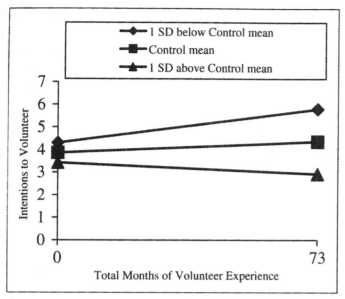

Fig. 1. Future intentions to volunteer regressed on prior volunteer experience at three levels of perceived external control.

posed to the same mandatory volunteerism program, and we could not randomly assign students to conditions and compare those who had been mandated to volunteer with those who had been assigned to choose to volunteer. However, the students entered the program with sufficient variability in their assessments of whether they would be volunteering regardless of the requirement, and our statistical analysis of the moderating effects of perceptions of control allowed us to make comparisons that are functionally similar to those that would be available from an experimental manipulation of mandated and freely chosen volunteerism.[4] Nevertheless, with our second study, we did conduct an experimental examination in which participants were randomly assigned to be required or freely allowed to volunteer; in this way, we could more conclusively demonstrate whether or not future intentions to volunteer were inhibited by requirements to serve.

STUDY 2

In Study 2, we used experimental methods in the laboratory to explicitly compare two routes to volunteerism, requirements and free choices. One possible outcome of an explicit comparison of the effects of required and more freely chosen service is that future intentions will be much higher after volunteer activity is freely chosen than after volunteer activity is required. That is, if service is not required but instead "induced" with an eye toward maintaining students' perceptions of self-determination, students may be less likely to demonstrate the ill effects of feeling controlled.

Given the results of our first study, it seemed likely, however, that individuals' reactions to a manipulation of mandated versus freely chosen volunteerism might depend on their initial

feelings about whether external control would be necessary to get them to volunteer. That is, we thought those who would freely volunteer (without a requirement) might not be differentially affected by being mandated or given a choice; they might be unlikely to have their intentions undermined by a requirement. Those who initially felt that a requirement would be necessary to get them to volunteer might feel more externally controlled by a mandate than a choice; consequently, they could have their intentions undermined by a requirement but not a free choice.

Therefore, in this second study, we examined not only the situational effects of mandates and choices to volunteer, but also whether such effects were moderated by preexisting person-centered judgments about externally controlled volunteerism. In a pretest, long before students were invited to the laboratory, we measured their perceptions about whether they would volunteer freely or only if controlled.[5] Our prediction was that students who thought a high degree of external control would be necessary to get them to volunteer would have much lower intentions to volunteer after being required to serve than after being given a choice; we also expected that students who thought they were likely to volunteer freely (i.e., who thought little external control would be necessary to get them to volunteer) would have higher intentions to volunteer and that their intentions would be relatively unaffected by being mandated to serve (as compared with freely choosing to do so).

Method

Participants

Sixty-three University of Minnesota psychology undergraduates (35 men and 28 women) participated in the study for extra credit.

Procedure

At the start of the semester, participants completed measures related to their inclinations to volunteer freely. Specifically, they responded on 7-point scales to the following questions: "To what extent do you believe that you would only volunteer if it were required of you?" and "To what extent do you believe that when you volunteer it will be because you freely choose to do so?" (reverse coded). Answers to these two items were correlated at $r = .31$ and were averaged into a scale with higher scores indicating greater preexisting perceptions of external control.

Several weeks later, we recruited participants by telephone for a study of "leisure time activities." Upon arrival at the laboratory, they were told that the specific activities under consideration were entertainment (watching music videos) and volunteerism (reading textbooks for the blind). It was emphasized that this volunteer activity was common on campus and

---

4. This examination of the moderating effect of external control on the relation between past experience and prospectively measured future intentions involved predicting a higher order interaction between variables. Such predictions, in some ways, also reduce the threats to internal validity in our nonexperimental design (Cook & Campbell, 1979).

5. Because the effects of control existed even for participants lowest in experience in our first study, we chose not to reexamine the effects of experience in Study 2 and focused instead on subjectively perceived and objectively manipulated control.

that students had the opportunity to continue reading for the blind in the future if they so desired; thus, this was a true volunteer position. All participants were told that the protocol was to allow them to choose the activity they wanted to perform, to perform the activity for 30 min, and then to complete a questionnaire about their attitudes toward the activity.

However, we randomly assigned half of the participants to be told next that because of a scarcity of individuals in the volunteerism condition, they would be forced to read for the blind (mandate condition); we persuaded the other half to choose volunteerism through an induced-compliance technique (i.e., we told them that they did not have to select reading for the blind but it would really help if they did; all students agreed to volunteer in this choice condition). We then taught participants to read a textbook into a tape recorder, and they did so for 15 min.

Afterward, they completed dependent measures. As a manipulation check, students responded to several items designed to examine whether they felt controlled by our choice and mandate conditions.[6] Specifically, they responded to the following two items on 7-point scales: "To what extent did you freely choose to engage in today's task?" and "To what extent do you believe that you read to the blind today only because it was required of you?" (reverse scored). These two items were averaged to form a scale with higher scores indicating greater perceptions of free choice. Participants in the choice condition ($M = 4.72$) were more likely to feel that they had freely chosen to read to the blind than participants in the mandate condition ($M = 3.58$), $t(61) = 3.08$, $p < .01$.

Participants also responded to the following seven items designed to assess their intentions to volunteer: "How likely is it that you will engage in some form of volunteer work this quarter?" "...next quarter?" "...next summer?" "...in the next year?" "How likely is it that you will be a volunteer 3 years from now?" "...5 years from now?" and "...10 years from now?" These items were averaged to form a scale with high scores indicating greater future intentions to volunteer; this scale had excellent internal consistency (alpha = .88).

Results

To investigate whether preexisting perceptions of external control moderated how the conditions of choice and mandate influenced future intentions to volunteer, we performed a median split on the external-control scale. We then performed a planned contrast to examine our hypothesis that individuals with greater perceptions of external control (i.e., those who were not prepared to volunteer freely) would respond differentially to the choice and mandate conditions, whereas individuals with lower perceptions of external control (i.e., those who were prepared to volunteer freely) would be relatively unaffected by the manipulation, as suggested by the results of Study 1. Thus, this contrast compared students who had high

perceptions of external control and were forced to read to the blind (−3), students who had high perceptions of external control and chose to read to the blind (−1), students who had low perceptions of external control and were forced to read to the blind (+2), and students who had low perceptions of external control and chose volunteerism (+2).

This planned comparison was significant, $t(53) = 2.88$, $p < .01$: Mean intention to volunteer in the future was 4.04 for the high-external-control/mandate group, 4.99 for the high-external-control/choice group, 5.03 for the low-external-control/mandate group, and 5.49 for the low-external-control/choice group (Fig. 2). As expected, individuals who had higher perceived external control had lower intentions to volunteer in the future after being required than after being led to freely choose to volunteer. Individuals who had lower perceived external control (who had higher intentions overall) were relatively unaffected by the mandate versus choice conditions.[7]

Discussion

The results of this experiment demonstrated not only that participants had different initial perceptions of whether it would take control to get them to volunteer or whether they would do so freely, but also that those who had different initial perceptions responded differently to mandates to serve and choices to serve. That is, participants who were more inclined against freely volunteering subsequently reported greater future intentions to volunteer when they completed service that was chosen rather than mandated. In contrast, mandates and choices seem not to have differentially affected participants who were initially inclined toward volunteering freely; regardless of the context under which their service was initiated, these individuals reported greater future intentions to volunteer than did those who were initially less likely to volunteer freely.

These results confirm the hypothesis, suggested by Study 1, that required volunteerism is more likely to reduce the intentions of those who perceive that they are being controlled than those who perceive themselves as volunteering freely. That is, compared with conditions of free choice, mandatory volunteerism does have a greater negative impact—but only on those individuals who feel less inclined to volunteer of their own free will.

GENERAL DISCUSSION

Taken together, the field study and the laboratory experiment presented here suggest that whereas earlier laboratory research found that intentions to help (in more short-term or spontaneous helping situations) were undermined by external inducements (Batson et al., 1978; Kunda & Schwartz, 1983), there may actually be important boundary conditions to this effect.

---

6. Six individuals whose scores on these items were outliers within their particular condition were eliminated from further analyses after the t test checking the manipulation.

7. Although it may appear that our significant contrast value is largely attributable to a main effect of perceived external control, we also performed a contrast that explicitly compared individuals with high perceived external control under conditions of mandate and choice (contrast: −1, 1, 0, 0). This contrast was also significant, $t(53) = 2.03$, $p < .05$.

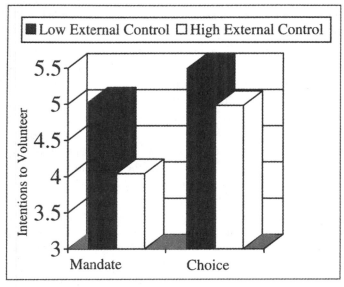

Fig. 2. Future intentions to volunteer after mandated and chosen volunteer activity as a function of perceived external control.

In our first study, we found that a required program undermined the relationship between past experience and future intentions only for those individuals who felt more externally controlled by the program. Students' subjective perceptions of how much a requirement controlled their behavior were a strong moderator of their reactions to the program (e.g., Deci & Ryan, 1987), and stronger perceptions of external control had greater inhibiting effects on those students with the most prior volunteer experience (e.g., Lepper et al., 1973). In our second study, individuals' preexisting feelings about whether they would freely choose to volunteer or not moderated whether a requirement to volunteer (as compared with a choice) affected future intentions to volunteer. This finding, that readiness to volunteer moderated the effects of requirements and choices to volunteer, goes beyond theories about the effects of subjective perceptions of external control (e.g., Deci & Ryan, 1987) to suggest that assessments individuals provide in advance can predict whether they will be negatively affected by requirements to volunteer.

Thus, given these converging results in experimental and nonexperimental investigations conducted in the laboratory and field, it may be the case that requirements to volunteer undermine the future behavioral intentions only of those individuals who currently do not feel free to volunteer (perhaps for a variety of reasons, which may involve interest or available time and resources). That is, only those individuals who would not otherwise be volunteering (Study 1) or who feel that it would take external control to get them to volunteer (Study 2) may find their future intentions undermined by a requirement to volunteer.

Perhaps such subjective assessments are viable moderators of reactions to requirements only for activities that, like volunteering, are typically planned and chosen. Indeed, few activities so overtly suggest a conceptualization of individuals as active, purposeful, and agenda setting (Snyder & Cantor, 1998; Snyder, Clary, & Stukas, in press). Planned helpfulness, as typically construed, represents a phenomenon in which the sa-

lient (external) cues for action are less demanding than the cues in short-term or emergency intervention situations, and usually involves processes that encourage people to look inward for guidance in deciding whether to get involved in helping (e.g., Clary & Snyder, 1991; Clary, Snyder, Ridge, et al., 1998; Omoto & Snyder, 1995; Snyder & Cantor, 1998; Snyder et al., in press). When the typically planned helpfulness of volunteerism is turned into the required helpfulness of mandatory volunteerism, individual agendas may be placed at odds with the agenda of the institution establishing the requirement. Future intentions to volunteer may depend importantly on whether individuals' personal agendas are in harmony or in conflict with the agenda behind the requirement.

The two investigations presented here demonstrate how basic theoretical research can be linked to applied and practical attempts to understand real-world social issues (Snyder, 1993). By using psychological theories about the effects of external inducements to act on future behavioral intentions, not only have we been able to advance theory (by identifying important boundary conditions), but we are also positioned to suggest possible routes for reducing the negative impact of requirements to volunteer. For example, institutions that choose to impose community-service requirements may reduce inhibiting effects by giving students a sense of freedom and autonomy in meeting their requirements. Allowing participants to design the focus and specific details of their service may effectively solve this problem; students themselves may be able to come up with the most creative ways to serve within the frameworks of their existing personal agendas. With such practical and theoretical benefits, action research on volunteerism may be beneficial both to psychological science and to society.

Acknowledgments—This research was supported by grants from the Gannett Foundation and the Aspen Institute's Nonprofit Research Fund to Mark Snyder and E. Gil Clary, and by grants from the National Science Foundation and National Institute of Mental Health to Mark Snyder. This article was written while Mark Snyder held the Chaire Francqui Interuniversitaire au Titre étranger at the Université de Louvain (Louvain-la-Neuve, Belgium). We wish to acknowledge the assistance of the Business 200 program at the University of St. Thomas and its director, Jan Kormann, in making this research possible. We also thank Craig Hunter and Frank Condon, who served as research assistants for Study 2. Portions of this article were presented at the July 1996 meeting of the American Psychological Society in San Francisco and at the May 1998 meeting of the American Psychological Society in Washington, D.C.

REFERENCES

Baron, R., & Kenny, D. (1986). The moderator-mediator variable distinction in social psychological research: Conceptual, strategic, and statistical considerations. *Journal of Personality and Social Psychology, 51,* 1173–1182.

Batson, C. D., Coke, J. S., Jasnoski, M. L., & Hanson, M. (1978). Buying kindness: Effect of an extrinsic incentive for helping on perceived altruism. *Personality and Social Psychology Bulletin, 4,* 86–91.

Brehm, S. S., & Brehm, J. (1981). *Psychological reactance: A theory of freedom and control.* New York: Academic Press.

Charng, H., Piliavin, J. A., & Callero, P. L. (1988). Role identity and reasoned action in the prediction of repeated behavior. *Social Psychological Quarterly, 51,* 303–317.

Clary, E. G., & Snyder, M. (1991). A functional analysis of altruism and prosocial behavior: The case of volunteerism. In M. Clark (Ed.), *Prosocial behavior* (pp. 119–148). Newbury Park, CA: SAGE.

Clary, E. G., Snyder, M., Ridge, R. D., Copeland, J., Stukas, A. A., Haugen, J., & Miene, P. (1998). Understanding and assessing the motivations of volunteers: A functional approach. *Journal of Personality and Social Psychology, 74,* 1516–1530.

Clary, E. G., Snyder, M., & Stukas, A. A. (1998). Service-learning and psychology: Lessons from the psychology of volunteers' motivations. In R. G. Bringle & D. K. Duffy (Eds.), *With service in mind: Concepts and models for service-learning in psychology* (pp. 35–50). Washington, DC: American Association of Higher Education.

Cnaan, R. A., & Goldberg-Glen, R. S. (1991). Measuring motivation to volunteer in human services. *Journal of Applied Behavioral Science, 27,* 269–284.

Cohen, J., & Cohen, P. (1983). *Applied multiple regression/correlation analysis for the behavioral sciences* (2nd ed.). Hillsdale, NJ: Erlbaum.

Cook, T. D., & Campbell, D. T. (1979). *Quasi-experimentation: Design & analysis issues for field settings.* Boston: Houghton Mifflin.

Deci, E. L., & Ryan, R. M. (1985). *Intrinsic motivation and self-determination in human behavior.* New York: Plenum Press.

Deci, E. L., & Ryan, R. M. (1987). The support of autonomy and the control of behavior. *Journal of Personality and Social Psychology, 53,* 1024–1037.

Giles, D. E., Jr., & Eyler, J. (1994). The impact of a college community service laboratory on students' personal, social, and cognitive outcomes. *Journal of Adolescence, 17,* 327–339.

Independent Sector. (1992). *Volunteering and giving among American teenagers 12 to 17 years of age: Findings from a national survey.* Washington, DC: Author.

Independent Sector. (1996). *Giving and volunteering in the United States: Findings from a national survey, 1995.* Washington, DC: Author.

Keith, N. Z. (1994). School-based community service: Answers and some questions. *Journal of Adolescence, 17,* 311–320.

Krebs, D. L., & Miller, D. T. (1985). Altruism and aggression. In G. Lindzey & E. Aronson (Eds.), *Handbook of social psychology* (3rd ed., Vol. 2, pp. 1–71). New York: Random House.

Kunda, Z., & Schwartz, S. (1983). Undermining intrinsic moral motivation: External reward and self-presentation. *Journal of Personality and Social Psychology, 45,* 763–771.

Latané, B., & Darley, J. M. (1970). *The unresponsive bystander: Why doesn't he help?* New York: Appleton.

Lepper, M. R., Greene, D., & Nisbett, R. E. (1973). Undermining children's intrinsic interest with extrinsic reward: A test of the "overjustification" hypothesis. *Journal of Personality and Social Psychology, 28,* 129–137.

Omoto, A. M. & Snyder, M. (1995). Sustained helping without obligation: Motivation, longevity of service, and perceived attitude change among AIDS volunteers. *Journal of Personality and Social Psychology, 68,* 671–686.

Piliavin, J. A., & Callero, P. L. (1991). *Giving blood: The development of an altruistic identity.* Baltimore: Johns Hopkins University Press.

Smith, D. H. (1994). Determinants of voluntary association participation and volunteering: A literature review. *Nonprofit and Voluntary Sector Quarterly, 23,* 243–263.

Snyder, M. (1993). Basic research and practical problems: The promise of a "functional" personality and social psychology. *Personality and Social Psychology Bulletin, 19,* 251–264.

Snyder, M., & Cantor, N. (1998). Understanding personality and social behavior: A functionalist strategy. In D. Gilbert, S. Fiske, & G. Lindzey (Eds.) *The handbook of social psychology: Vol. 1* (4th ed., pp. 635–679). Boston: McGraw-Hill.

Snyder, M., Clary, E. G., & Stukas, A. A. (in press). The functional approach to volunteerism. In G. R. Maio & J. M. Olson (Eds.), *Why we evaluate: Functions of attitudes.* Hillsdale, NJ: Erlbaum.

Snyder, M. & Omoto, A.M. (1992). Who helps and why? The psychology of AIDS volunteerism. In S. Spacapan & S. Oskamp (Eds.), *Helping and being helped: Naturalistic studies* (pp. 213–239). Newbury Park, CA: SAGE.

Sobus, M. S. (1995). Mandating community service: Psychological implications of requiring prosocial behavior. *Law and Psychology Review, 19,* 153–182.

Tabachnick, B. G., & Fidell, L. S. (1996). *Using multivariate statistics* (3rd ed.). New York: Harper Collins.

(RECEIVED 11/18/97; REVISION ACCEPTED 6/30/98)

Unit Selections

Key Points to Consider

❖ What are the most important characteristics of a group experiencing groupthink? How do those characteristics ultimately influence the decisions reached by the group? Other than the Bay of Pigs and *Challenger* disasters, can you think of any well-known group decisions that might be examples of groupthink? Can you think of any examples from groups in your own life?

❖ How successful do you think problem-solving groups like those in the Herbert Kelman article will be in reducing group tensions? On what do you base your answer? Can you think of any other techniques that could be helpful?

❖ What do you think of Daniel Goleman's argument that it is *emotional* intelligence which best separates average from truly effective leaders? What does he mean by emotional intelligence? Would you agree that this is truly a form of intelligence? Why?

 **Links** **www.dushkin.com/online/**

These sites are annotated on pages 4 and 5.

In 1961 President John F. Kennedy and a group of his senior advisers held a series of secret meetings to plan a dramatic military action. The plan under consideration was an invasion of Cuba, and the goal was to overthrow the Communist regime of Fidel Castro. This was not to be a massive invasion, however, utilizing the United States' heavy superiority in numbers and technology; such a move would be too provocative. Instead, the plan called for the United States to secretly train and equip a relatively small force of anti-Castro Cubans—exiles driven from their homeland because of Castro's rise to power. This small force of about 1,400 men would begin the invasion by landing at the Bahia de Cochinos, or the Bay of Pigs. Seizing control of radio stations, they would broadcast news of Cuba's liberation and would then sweep across the country picking up support from the Cuban people until they would constitute a force so compelling that Castro could not endure.

They never had a chance. Supplies that were supposed to sustain the invaders failed to arrive; the tiny invading force was completely overwhelmed by the larger, better-trained Cuban military; and the anticipated uprising by the Cuban people never happened. Within 3 days the entire force had been captured or killed. Instead of a dramatic military success, the United States, and President Kennedy, suffered a humiliating political defeat in the eyes of the world; in fact, the phrase "Bay of Pigs" has come to signify any plan or action that comes to a disastrous end. In the aftermath of this debacle, moreover, it seemed painfully obvious that the plan was doomed from the start. The nagging question, then, was how could some of the smartest people in the country come to agree on a plan that in retrospect seemed to have no chance at all of succeeding? How could the group go so wrong?

That question is one of the many that social psychology has asked about groups, and the processes that occur when people meet in groups. In fact, a very interesting line of research into how groups can reach such bad decisions—a phenomenon known as "groupthink"—was directly inspired by the Bay of Pigs fiasco. According to this approach, highly cohesive groups frequently develop a mindset characterized by secretiveness, overconfidence, and illusions of invulnerability; this in turn can lead them into decisions that overlook what should be obvious flaws. Other approaches to group decision making have focused on another common phenomenon: the fact that when groups have to choose a course of action, they often make a choice that is more extreme than the decision that each individual would make alone. That is, one effect of group discussion is to polarize the attitudes of the group members.

In addition to the issue of how groups make decisions, another topic of interest has been the impact that groups can have on the behavior of the individuals who make up the group. For example, it frequently happens that individuals work faster and more productively when in the presence of others than they do when they are alone—at least if the task they are working on is relatively simple, or if it is a task with which they have had a lot of practice. In contrast, on a new task, or one which is very complex, the presence of other people can hurt performance. Researchers who study this phenomenon, called social facilitation, have identified a variety of possible explanations for its occurrence.

The selections in this unit represent several different approaches to the study of group processes. The first selection, "Building Cooperation, Empathy, and Compassion in the Classroom," is by Elliot Aronson, and he argues that there is a simple and effective solution to much of the violence which occurs in our schools: the use of cooperative learning tasks such as the "jigsaw classroom." Such approaches would make the educational experience much more humane for millions of students, and would replace the typically competitive classroom environment with one based on cooperation.

In "Group Decision Fiascoes Continue: Space Shuttle *Challenger* and a Revised Groupthink Framework," the authors use the decision to launch the ill-fated space shuttle *Challenger* as an example of groupthink. They trace how some of the cognitive biases that characterize groupthink were present during the discussions leading up to the decision to launch.

The next selection deals with the problem of international conflict. In "Group Processes in the Resolution of International Conflicts: Experiences From the Israeli-Palestinian Case," Herbert Kelman describes his ongoing project designed to help foster greater cooperation between Israelis and Palestinians in the Middle East. By using insights gained from social psychology, Kelman has created interactive problem-solving workshops that help foster greater understanding and cooperation between these two traditionally antagonistic groups.

The final article in this section, "What Makes a Leader?," is concerned with the characteristics that are common to effective leaders of groups. Daniel Goleman argues that to a considerable degree what separates the average leader from the gifted leader is "emotional intelligence." That is, while IQ and technical skills are important, most leaders possess these qualities; what distinguishes the best leaders are such characteristics as self-awareness, self-regulation, motivation, empathy, and social skill.

Group Processes

Building Cooperation, Empathy, and Compassion in the Classroom

Elliot Aronson

University of California at Santa Cruz

In William Wharton's provocative novel *Birdy,* one of the protagonists, Alfonso, a Sergeant in the army, develops an instant dislike for an overweight enlisted man, a clerk typist named Ronsky. There are a great many things that Alfonso dislikes about Ronsky. At the top of his list is Ronsky's annoying habit of continually spitting. He spits all over his own desk, his typewriter, and anyone who happens to be in the vicinity. Alfonso cannot stand the guy and has fantasies of punching him out. Several weeks later, Alfonso learns that Ronsky had taken part in the Normandy invasion and had watched, in horror, as several of his buddies were cut down before they even had a chance to hit the beach. It seems that his constant spitting was a concrete manifestation of his attempt to get the bad taste out of his mouth. On learning this, Alfonso sees his former enemy in an entirely different light. He sighs with regret and says to himself: "Before you know it, if you're not careful, you can get to feeling for everybody and there's nobody left to hate."

Do you like your job? If you do, then you probably work in a place where the people involved like one another, work well together, are supportive of one another, and are respectful of one another's minor idiosyncrasies and different styles of working. You are in a working situation where you feel respected and feel like an important member of a team—no matter what your job is.

Let me put some meat on those bare bones, by going into detail in my description of a highly supportive hypothetical work environment: In this well-functioning office, the people who work closely with one another are attentive to and supportive of individual differences in ways of working. For example, your immediate coworkers know that, after a meeting, Ned likes to shut himself in his office to work alone for a while. On the other hand, you and Chris enjoy working out some bugs in the project over coffee in the cafeteria or while exercising in the company gym. Sue and Sandy say they get their best ideas on their noontime walk. When the team comes back together, everyone has something valuable to say. The boss is a straight-up guy, too. Even though he supervises close to a hundred employees, he knows your name and remembers that you like to play the banjo. He can be a tough taskmaster—sometimes a little too tough—but he listens well and is almost always fair.

There's some petty office politics, of course—that can hardly be avoided. But it's no big deal and doesn't keep you awake at night. Most people just ignore it. It helps a lot that the men and women at your company get along pretty well together. There is a little competitiveness and a little envy but, for the most part, people root for each other, cooperate with each other, and are pleased by the success of a colleague. People can relax and even occasionally make innocent jokes, and nobody minds. Most people are happily married or happily single; no one's on the prowl.

You enjoy the Friday casual day, when everyone knocks off work early for the company get-together with pizza and basketball. Some of the basketball players were varsity athletes in high school or college. They're still really good and still love to play, but there aren't any company sports heroes or anything dumb like that. Nobody lionizes them like they did in high school; here they're just regular guys. The superstars in your organization are the ones who come up with creative ideas and support others in developing their ideas; they are also the ones who land the big contracts or really shine at their jobs. You can see that they're on the fast track to upper management. But even if you're not one of them, you still feel good about your role because you are always aware that you have something important to contribute, and the success of the superstars enhances things for everyone.

When things aren't going so great at home, you can always count on your coworkers to give you a sense of perspective and cheer you up. Things have been tense at home since your loudmouthed brother-in-law came to visit; your daughter's hair is a different color every week; and your son says he wants to use all the money he saved from his summer job to buy a motorcycle. By contrast, work seems like a refuge, filled with "normal" people who understand how trying home life can be. And if you have a really serious problem, the company has professional counselors you can talk to.

Things aren't perfect. There is often a lot of pressure and too much unnecessary drudge work. Occasionally, it's hard to rip yourself out of bed early in the morning to go to work, but you know they'd miss you if you didn't show up. Even with the deadlines and the ridiculous paperwork, you feel good about your job. You feel comfortable; you know you belong there. And that makes all the difference.

Now try to imagine a truly unpleasant work environment—a work environment from hell. You and your coworkers are constantly competing against one another in order to impress management. When you come up with a good idea, you can feel a chill in the air; instead of congratulating you and supporting your idea, your coworkers seem annoyed that they hadn't come up with that idea themselves. When you screw up at a work assignment, your coworkers are quick to smirk; sometimes they tease you or taunt you. Although you always considered yourself a warm and supportive person, after a few months in this environment, you even find yourself experiencing pangs of envy when one of your associates does well and feelings of joy when one of them commits a stupid blunder. Within your office, there are a definite in-group and out-group. Interestingly enough, people in the in-group are not necessarily the most skillful, the hardest-working, or the most productive workers. Indeed, the people in the out-group may be very good at what they do, but they also tend to be rather shy or awkward; they don't dress fashionably. One is obese.

You are in neither the in-group nor the out-group, but somewhere in between. When you go to eat in the company cafeteria, you are always at a loss as to where to sit. You wish you would feel welcome by the in-group members—but you aren't. You don't want to associate with those in the out-group out of fear that doing so might lower your status in the office. You would like to be in the in-group, but it's not clear how one accomplishes that. Some of your coworkers in the in-group are actually untalented at their jobs, but they are good at things that strike you as irrelevant to the work that needs doing: One is a good golfer; one is a good basketball player; one is flirtatious and looks good in tight sweaters. Even the boss seems to favor these colleagues.

Sound wacky? It is. In such an atmosphere, no business could hope to retain its best employees—or succeed. But that's precisely the way it is at most high schools. Do you know of any high schools where the academically brightest and most cooperative students are the ones who are invariably liked best by their peers, where members of the debating team or the philosophy club are generally held in higher esteem than members of the football team? Do you know of any high school where off-beat, idiosyncratic behavior is actively encouraged or even tolerated?

It is almost a cliché for us middle-aged people to sigh wistfully and say, "I wish I were young again," but I suspect that most of us are choosing not to remember many of the harsher aspects of our teenage existence. If push ever came to shove, very few of us would really want to go back to high school. Nobody wants to deal with the academic demands of six different teachers, the emotional turmoil of adolescent hormones, feelings of inferiority if you're not a jock, a superstar, or physically attractive, loneliness if you don't have your own tight group to hang with, plus coping with parents who "just don't get it" and may be unreasonable, unsupportive, or unsympathetic. It is no wonder that students often prefer their after-school job at a fast-food restaurant to studying Renaissance art or the physics of space flight. What is more rewarding about frying burgers than learning about art or astrophysics? As illustrated by the hypothetical example at the beginning of this chapter, a positive work environment, even at a fairly menial job, can offer far more than a negative school environment. As employees, young people often experience the kind of teamwork, camaraderie, and responsibility that is often missing at their school.

A truly positive work environment is as exciting for what it is not as for what it is. In a positive work environment, there is an absence of put-downs, taunting, and exclusion. People don't go around humiliating one another. No one gets lionized for irrelevant and unattainable (for the rest of us) attributes—like being a fast runner or having bulging muscles or bulging breasts. People are respected for who they are. Differences are not simply tolerated, they are celebrated.

REDUCING COMPETITION/ FOSTERING COOPERATION

What can schools do to make the classroom environment as appealing to young people as their after-school jobs? You can't do it by adding prayer in the classrooms or posting the Ten Commandments on the bulletin board. You can't do it by forcing kids to call their teachers "sir" and "ma'am." You can't do it even by adding wonderful classes on Renaissance art or medieval history—as valuable as these courses might be. The best way I know to accomplish this is to restructure students' academic experience. I'm not talking about the content of the courses, but about the atmosphere created by the process of learning. In many respects, how a topic is learned is more important than the content of what is learned.

There are many ways to convey information to students. The teacher can lecture on a topic like World War II. Or students can read the facts about World War II in a textbook. The teacher can assign students to do their own research in the library, or have students interview people who served in the military or lived through the war period in the United States, Europe, and Asia. The teacher might require students to work individually or in groups. Students might be required to take a test, write a term paper, or give a talk to demonstrate what they have learned. One could use the format of a quiz show where the teacher asks questions and the students show their quickness and mastery of the subject by raising their hands as soon as they know the answer.

Each of these methods of conveying information sends a different message to students. Teachers who lecture send the message that they are an expert source of information.

Teachers who dispatch students to the library send the message that it is useful for students to become skillful researchers, as well as learn about the topic at hand. Teachers who require students to interview a war veteran convey the implicit message that not all important information is contained in books. Teachers who run their class like a competitive quiz show indicate that quickness as well as knowledge is important.

The point is that students learn something from the process (the manner in which the product is attained or communicated) even while they are focusing on the content of the assignment. If students are required to take lecture notes, read textbooks, raise their hands as soon as they know the answer, and take tests graded on a curve, then the academic environment is designed to encourage students to compete against each other. When the grades come out, some students are big winners, some big losers, and most fall in the nameless middle zone. Students who have six classes like this may come to see life as competition—outside the classroom as well as inside it.

That's the atmosphere in most classrooms in this country—separating winners from losers. Perhaps that is why most of us tend to treat losing like a contagious disease. Most youngsters want to keep as far away from it as possible. The winners and those in the middle ground try to differentiate themselves from the losers. They don't associate with them; they taunt them; they want the losers to just "get lost." But, unless they drop out of school, losers don't disappear. In most cases, they simply suffer in silence, retreating further and further from the mainstream. The more they are ignored or taunted, the further away they drift. On rare, but significant, occasions, they explode—doing serious damage to themselves or others.

Many schools have attempted to counteract the negative influences of excessive competitions. It would be hard to find a preschool or elementary school that did not actively encourage children to share, work harmoniously with others, and behave respectfully and cooperatively. Many elementary schools now have students sit in small groups at tables, rather than in rows of individual desks. Many schools focus a lot of attention on children with academic or behavior problems, going out of their way to include them as full and valued members of the class.

On the other hand, it would be hard to find a high school or middle school that goes out of its way to demonstrate a high value on inclusion and cooperation among all students. It is true that some schools have attempted to reduce the competitive atmosphere in the academic arena by eliminating tracking, opening Advanced Placement classes to all students, and doing away with class rankings and valedictorians. But these attempts miss the mark. Indeed, many parents and students view these strategies as an empty exercise in political correctness that serves only to penalize serious students who work hard. After all, no one would seriously entertain the idea of randomly assigning students to the starting lineup of the school's varsity football team, or playing intramural sports without scores or team rankings.

Attempts to enforce cooperation in the classroom can also backfire if not carefully designed. Simply assigning students to work together in groups to produce a joint report does not guarantee true cooperation. Most often the group dynamics of an unstructured "cooperative" situation of this sort mirror the larger competitive classroom dynamic. The one or two most able or most motivated students put themselves forward to do most of the work, while simultaneously resenting the fact that they are carrying the load for the entire group. The less able or less motivated students end up doing little, learning little, and feeling inadequate. These so-called "cooperative groups" are cooperative in name only.

THE JIGSAW CLASSROOM

The problem with cooperative learning assignments is not that they don't work. It is that they need to be carefully structured to work as intended. One successful model, with a three-decade track record, is the jigsaw classroom. "Jigsaw" is a specific type of group learning experience that requires everyone's cooperative effort to produce the final product. Just as in a jigsaw puzzle, each piece—each student's part—is essential for the production and full understanding of the final product. If each student's part is essential, then each student is essential. That is precisely what makes this strategy so effective.

Here is how it works: The students in a history class, for example, are divided into small groups of five or six students each. Suppose their task is to learn about World War II. In one jigsaw group let us say that Sara is responsible for researching Hitler's rise to power in prewar Germany. Another member of the group, Steven, is assigned to cover concentration camps; Pedro is assigned Britain's role in the war; Melody is to research the contribution of the Soviet Union; Bill will handle Japan's entry into the war; Clara will read about the development of the atom bomb.

Eventually each student will come back to his or her jigsaw group and will try to present a vivid, interesting, well-organized report to the group. The situation is specifically structured so that the only access any member has to the other five assignments is by listening intently to the report of the person reciting. Thus, if Bill doesn't like Pedro, or if he thinks Sara is a nerd, if he heckles them, or tunes out while they are reporting, he cannot possibly do well on the test that follows. In order to increase the probability that each report will be factual and accurate, the students doing the research do not immediately take it back to their jigsaw group. After doing their research, they must first meet with the other students (one from each of the jigsaw groups) who had the identical assignment. For example, those students assigned to the atom bomb topic will meet together to work as a team of specialists, gathering information, discussing ideas, becoming experts on their topic, and rehearsing their presentations. We call this the "expert" group. It is particularly useful for those students who might have initial difficulty learning or organizing their part of the assignment—for it allows them to benefit from paying attention to and rehearsing with other "experts," to pick up strategies of presentation, and generally to bring themselves up to speed.

After this meeting, when each presenter is up to speed, the jigsaw groups reconvene in their initial heterogeneous configuration. The atom bomb expert in each group teaches the other group members what she has learned about the development of the atom bomb. Each student in each group educates the whole group about his or her specialty. Students are then tested on what they have learned from their fellow group members about World War II.

What is the benefit of the jigsaw classroom? First and foremost, it is a remarkably efficient way to learn the material. But even more important, in terms of the present discussion, the jigsaw process encourages listening, engagement, and empathy by giving each member of the group an essential part to play in the academic activity. Group members must work together as a team to accomplish a common goal. Each person depends on all the others. No student can achieve his or her individual goal (learning the material, getting a good grade) unless everyone works together as a team. Group goals and individual goals complement and bolster each other. This "cooperation by design" facilitates interaction among all students in the class, leading them to value one another as contributors to their common task.

In 1971, it was my privilege to witness this process unfold in Austin, Texas, in the very first jigsaw classroom ever held. My graduate students and I invented the jigsaw strategy that year, as a matter of absolute necessity, to help defuse a highly explosive situation. The city's schools had recently been desegregated and, because Austin had always been residentially segregated, white youngsters, African-American youngsters, and Mexican-American youngsters found themselves in the same classrooms for the first time in their lives. Within a few weeks, long-standing suspicion, fear, distrust, and antipathy between groups produced an atmosphere of turmoil and hostility, exploding into inter-ethnic fistfights in corridors and schoolyards across the city. The school superintendent called me in to see if we could do anything to help students learn to get along with one another. After observing what was going on in classrooms for a few days, my students and I concluded that intergroup hostility was being exacerbated by the competitive environment of the classroom.

Let me explain. In every classroom we observed, the students worked individually and competed against one another for grades. Here is a description of a typical fifth-grade classroom that we observed:

> The teacher stands in front of the class, asks a question, and waits for the children to indicate that they know the answer. Most frequently, six to ten youngsters raise their hands. But they do not simply raise their hands, they lift themselves a few inches off their chairs and stretch their arms as high as they can in an attempt to attract the teacher's attention. To say they are eager to be called on is an incredible understatement. Several other students sit quietly with their eyes averted, as if trying to make themselves invisible. These are the ones who don't know the answer. Understandably, they are trying to avoid eye contact with the teacher because they do not want to be called on.
>
> When the teacher calls on one of the eager students, there are looks of disappointment, dismay, and unhappiness on the faces of the other students who were avidly raising their hands but were not called on. If the selected student comes up with the right answer, the teacher smiles, nods approvingly, and goes on to the next question. This is a great reward for the child who happens to be called on. At the same time that the fortunate student is coming up with the right answer and being smiled upon by the teacher, an audible groan can be heard coming from the children who were striving to be called on but were ignored. It is obvious they are disappointed because they missed an opportunity to show the teacher how smart and quick they are. Perhaps they will get an opportunity next time. In the meantime, the students who didn't know the answer breathe a sigh of relief. They have escaped being humiliated this time.

The teacher may have started the school year with a determination to treat every student equally and encourage all of them to do their best, but the students quickly sorted themselves into different groups. The "winners" were the bright, eager, highly competitive students who fervently raised their hands, participated in discussions, and did well on tests. Understandably, the teacher felt gratified that these students responded to her teaching. She praised and encouraged them, continued to call on them, and depended on them to keep the class going at a high level and at a reasonable pace.

Then there were the "losers." At the beginning, the teacher called on them occasionally, but they almost invariably didn't know the answer, were too shy to speak, or couldn't speak English well. They seemed embarrassed to be in the spotlight; some of the other students made snide comments—sometimes under their breath, occasionally out loud. Because the schools in the poorer section of town were substandard, the African-American and the Mexican-American youngsters had received a poorer education prior to desegregation. Consequently, in Austin, it was frequently these students who were among the losers. This tended unfairly to confirm the unflattering stereotypes that the white kids had about minorities. They considered them stupid or lazy. The minority students also had preconceived notions about white kids—that they were pushy show-offs and teacher's pets. These stereotypes were also confirmed by the way most of the white students behaved in the competitive classroom.

After a while, the typical classroom teacher stopped trying to engage the students who weren't doing well. She felt it was kinder not to call on them and expose them to ridicule by the other students. In effect, she made a silent pact with the "losers"; she would leave them alone as long as they weren't disruptive. Without really meaning to, she gave up on these students, and so did the rest of the class. Without really meaning to, the teacher contributed to the difficulty the students were experiencing. After a while, these students tended to give up on themselves as well—perhaps believing that they *were* stupid—because they sure weren't getting it.

It required only a few days of intensive observation and interviews for us to have a pretty good idea of what was going on in these classrooms. We realized that we needed to do something drastic to shift the emphasis from a relentlessly competitive atmosphere to a more cooperative one. It was in this context that we invented the jigsaw strategy. Our first intervention was with fifth-graders. First we helped several fifth-grade teachers devise a cooperative jigsaw structure for the students to learn about the life of Eleanor Roosevelt. We divided the students into small groups, diversified in terms of race, ethnicity, and gender, and made each student responsible for a certain portion of Roosevelt's biography. Needless to say, at least one or two of the students in each group were already viewed as "losers" by their classmates.

Carlos was one such student. Carlos was very shy and felt insecure in his new surroundings. English was his second language. He spoke it quite well, but with a slight accent. Try to imagine his experience: After attending an inadequately funded, substandard neighborhood school consisting entirely of Mexican-American students like himself, he was suddenly bused across town to the middle-class area of the city and catapulted into a class with Anglo students who spoke English fluently, seemed to know much more than he did about all the subjects taught in the school, and who were not reluctant to let him know it.

When we restructured the classroom so that students were now working together in small groups, this was terrifying to Carlos at first. He could no longer slink down in his chair and hide in the back of the room. The jigsaw structure made it necessary for him to speak up when it was his turn to recite. Carlos gained a little confidence by rehearsing with the others who were also studying Eleanor Roosevelt's work with the United Nations, but he was understandably reticent to speak when it was his turn to teach the students in his jigsaw group. He blushed, stammered, and had difficulty articulating the material that he had learned. Skilled in the ways of the competitive classroom, the other students were quick to pounce on Carlos's weakness and began to ridicule him.

One of my research assistants was observing that group and heard some members of Carlos's group make comments such as, "Aw, you don't know it, you're dumb, you're stupid. You don't know what you're doing. You can't even speak English." Instead of admonishing them to "be nice" or "try to cooperate," she made one simple but powerful statement. It went something like this: "Talking like that to Carlos might be fun for you to do, but it's not going to help you learn anything about what Eleanor Roosevelt accomplished at the United Nations—and the exam will be given in about fifteen minutes." What my assistant was doing was reminding the students that the situation had changed. The same behavior that might have been useful to them in the past, when they were competing against each other, was now going to cost them something very important: the chance to do well on the upcoming exam.

Needless to say, old dysfunctional habits do not die easily. But they do die. Within a few days of working with jigsaw, Carlos's groupmates gradually realized that they needed to change their tactics. It was no longer in their own best interest to rattle Carlos; he wasn't the enemy—he was on their team. They needed him to perform well in order to do well themselves. Instead of taunting him and putting him down, they started to gently ask him questions. The other students began to put themselves in Carlos's shoes so they could ask questions that didn't threaten him and would help him recite what he knew in a clear and understandable manner. After a week or two, most of Carlos's groupmates had developed into skillful interviewers, asking him relevant questions to elicit the vital information from him. They became more patient, figured out the most effective way to work with him, helped him out, and encouraged him. The more they encouraged Carlos, the more he was able to relax; the more he was able to relax, the quicker and more articulate he became. Carlos's groupmates began to see him in a new light. He became transformed in their minds from a "know-nothing loser who can't even speak English" to someone they could work with, someone they could appreciate, maybe even someone they could like. Moreover, Carlos began to see *himself* in a new light, as a competent, contributing member of the class who could work with others from different ethnic groups. His self-esteem grew and as it grew, his performance improved even more; and as his performance continued to improve, his groupmates continued to view him in a more and more favorable light.

Within a few weeks, the success of the jigsaw was obvious to the classroom teachers. They spontaneously told us of their great satisfaction about the way the atmosphere of their classrooms had been transformed. Adjunct visitors (such as music teachers and the like) were little short of amazed at the dramatically changed atmosphere in the classrooms. Needless to say, this was exciting to my graduate students and me. But, as scientists, we were not totally satisfied; we were seeking firmer, more objective evidence—and we got it. Because we had randomly introduced the jigsaw intervention into some classrooms and not others, we were able to compare the progress of the jigsaw students with that of the students in traditional classrooms in a precise, scientific manner. After only eight weeks there were clear differences, even though students spent only a small portion of their class time in jigsaw groups. When tested objectively, jigsaw students expressed significantly less prejudice and negative stereotyping, were more self-confident, and reported that they liked school better than children in traditional classrooms. Moreover, this self-report was bolstered by hard behavioral data: For example, the students in jigsaw classrooms were absent less often than those in traditional classrooms. In addition, academically, the poorer students in jigsaw classes showed enormous improvement over the course of eight weeks; they scored significantly higher on objective exams than the poorer students in traditional classes, while the good students continued to do well—as well as the good students in traditional classes.

COOPERATION: JIGSAW AND BASKETBALL

You might have noticed a rough similarity between the kind of cooperation that goes on in a jigsaw group and the kind of cooperation that is necessary for the smooth functioning of an athletic team. Take a basketball team,

for example. If the team is to be successful, each player must play his or her role in a cooperative manner. If each player was hell-bent on being the highest scorer on the team, then each would shoot whenever the opportunity arose. In contrast, on a cooperative team, the idea is to pass the ball crisply until one player manages to break clear for a relatively easy shot. If I pass the ball to Sam, and Sam whips a pass to Harry, and Harry passes to Tony who breaks free for an easy layup, I am elated even though I did not receive credit for either a field goal or an assist. This is true cooperation.

As a result of this cooperation, athletic teams frequently build a cohesiveness that extends to their relationship off the court. They become friends because they have learned to count on one another. There is one difference between the outcome of a typical jigsaw group and that of a typical high school basketball team, however—and it is a crucial difference. In high school, athletes tend to hang out with each other and frequently exclude nonathletes from their circle of close friends. In short, the internal cohesiveness of an athletic team often goes along with the exclusion of everyone else.

In the jigsaw classroom, we circumvented this problem by the simple device of shuffling groups every eight weeks. Once a group of students was functioning well together, once the barriers had been broken down and the students showed a great deal of liking and empathy for one another, we would re-form the groupings. At first, the students would resist this re-forming of groups. Picture the scene: Debbie, Carlos, Tim, Patty, and Jacob have just gotten to know and appreciate one another and they are doing incredibly good work as a team. Why should they want to leave this warm, efficient, and cozy group to join a group of relative strangers?

Why, indeed? After spending a few weeks in the new group, the students invariably discover that the new people are just about as interesting, friendly, and wonderful as their former group. The new group is working well together and new friendships form. Then the students move on to their third group, and the same thing begins to happen. As they near the end of their time in the third group, it begins to dawn on most students that they didn't just luck out and land in groups with four or five terrific people. Rather, they realize that just about *everyone* they work with is a good human being. All they need to do is pay attention to each person, to try to understand him or her, and good things will emerge. That is a lesson well worth learning.

ENCOURAGING GENERAL EMPATHY

Students in the jigsaw classroom become adept at empathy. They come to understand students like Carlos with empathy. Empathy is what Bill Clinton is getting at when he utters that well-known phrase, "I feel your pain." When we watch a movie, empathy is what brings tears or joy in us when sad or happy things happen to a character. But why should we care about a character in a movie? We care because we have learned to feel and experience what that character experiences—as if it were happening to us. As infants and children, we experience empathy for members of our family and close friends. But most of us do not experience empathy for our sworn enemies. Thus, when watching an adventure movie such as *Star Wars*, most youngsters will cheer wildly when spaceships manned by members of the Evil Empire are blown to smithereens. Who cares what happens to Darth Vader's followers?

Is empathy a trait we are born with or is it something we learn? I believe we are born with the capacity to feel for another person. It is part of what makes us human. I also believe that empathy is a skill that can be enhanced with practice. If I am correct, then it should follow that working in jigsaw groups would lead to a sharpening of a youngster's general empathic ability because to do well in the group, the child needs to practice feeling what her groupmates feel. To test this notion, one of my graduate students, Diane Bridgeman, conducted a clever experiment in which she showed a series of cartoons to 10-year-old children. Half of the children had spent two months participating in jigsaw classes; the others had spent that time in traditional classrooms. In one series of cartoons, a little boy is looking sad as he waves good-bye to his father at the airport. In the next frame, a letter carrier delivers a package to the boy. When the boy opens the package and finds a toy airplane inside, he bursts into tears. Diane Bridgeman asked the children why they thought the little boy burst into tears at the sight of the airplane. Nearly all of the children could answer correctly—because the toy airplane reminded him of how much he missed his father. Then Diane asked the crucial question: "What did

the letter carrier think when he saw the boy open the package and start to cry?"

Most children of this age make a consistent error; they assume that everyone knows what they know. Thus, the youngsters in the control group thought that the letter carrier would know the boy was sad because the gift reminded him of his father leaving. But the children who had participated in the jigsaw classroom responded differently. Because they were better able to take the perspective of the letter carrier—to put themselves in his shoes—they realized that he would be confused at seeing the boy cry over receiving a nice present because the letter carrier hadn't witnessed the farewell scene at the airport.

Offhand, this might not seem very important. After all, who cares whether kids have the ability to figure out what is in the letter carrier's mind? In point of fact, we should all care—a great deal. Here's why: The extent to which children can develop the ability to see the world from the perspective of another human being has profound implications for empathy, prejudice, aggression, and interpersonal relations in general. When you can feel another person's pain, when you can develop the ability to understand what that person is going through, it increases the probability that your heart will open to that person. Once your heart opens to another person, it becomes virtually impossible to bully that other person, to taunt that other person, to humiliate that other person—and certainly to kill that other person. If you develop the general ability to empathize, then your desire to bully or taunt *anyone* will decrease. Such is the power of empathy.

Recall that as a lead-in to this chapter, I quoted form the novel *Birdy* that touching statement by Alfonso: "Before you know it, if you're not careful, you can get to feeling for everybody and there's nobody left to hate." Yes, that is the power of the jigsaw method—it builds empathy among students who frequently disliked and distrusted one another and were motivated to reject, taunt, and fight with one another. After experiencing jigsaw for a couple of months, they literally ran out of people to hate.

WHAT DO THE STUDENTS SAY ABOUT JIGSAW?

Cooperative learning strategies are effective. Students learn the material as well as, or better than, students in traditional classrooms. We have almost thirty years of scientific research that clearly demonstrates this. The data also show that through cooperative learning the classroom becomes a positive social atmosphere where students learn to like and respect one another, and where taunting and bullying are sharply reduced. Students involved in jigsaw tell us that they enjoy school more and show us that they do by attending class more regularly. It goes without saying that the scientific results are important. But on a personal level, what is perhaps even more gratifying is to witness, firsthand, youngsters actually going through the transformation. Tormentors evolve into supportive helpers and anxious "losers" begin to enjoy learning and feel accepted for who they are. Occasionally, I am privileged to receive spontaneous, unsolicited letters from young men and young women who, many years earlier, had undergone such a transformation. To give you some of the flavor of this experience, I would like to share one such letter with you.

Dear Professor Aronson:
I am a senior at——University. Today I got a letter admitting me to the Harvard Law School. This may not seem odd to you, but let me tell you something. I am the sixth of seven children my parents had—and I am the only one who ever went to college, let alone graduate, or go to law school.

By now, you are probably wondering why this stranger is writing to you and bragging to you about his achievements. Actually, I'm not a stranger although we never met. You see, last year I was taking a course in social psychology and we were using a book you wrote called *The Social Animal,* and when I read about prejudice and jigsaw—and then, I realized that I was in that very first class you ever did jigsaw in—when I was in the fifth grade. And as I read on, it dawned on me that I was the boy that you called Carlos. And then I remembered you when you first came to our classroom and how I was scared and how I hated school and how I was so stupid and didn't know anything. And you came in—it all came back to me when I read your book—you were very tall—about 6 1/2 feet—and you had a big black beard and you were funny and made us all laugh.

And, most important, when we started to do work in jigsaw groups, I began to realize that I wasn't really that stupid. And the kids I thought were cruel and hostile became my friends and the teacher acted friendly and nice to me and I actually began to love school, and I began to love to learn things and now I'm about to go to Harvard Law School.

You must get a lot of letters like this but I decided to write anyway because let me tell you something. My mother tells me that when I was born I almost died. I was born at home and the cord was wrapped around my neck and the midwife gave me mouth to mouth and saved my life. If she was still alive, I would write to her too, to tell her that I grew up smart and good and I'm going to law school. But she died a few years ago. I'm writing to you because, no less than her, you saved my life too.

Sincerely, XXXX XXX

I think you will agree that it is a beautiful letter. For me, it is just about he most moving letter I have ever received. But when I read the signature I was startled to discover that it did not belong to the boy that I had in mind— the boy who in my previous writings I had referred to as "Carlos." The young man who wrote me that lovely letter was mistaken.

I have a clear memory of sitting there with the letter in my hand thinking about that young man and how wrong he was. But after a few minutes, I fell into a reverie in which I began to realize that perhaps that young man was not mistaken after all. That is, although I had a specific fifth-grader in mind when I wrote about Carlos, there are a great many children who come pretty close to fitting that description. In my reverie, I began to grasp the implications of the possibility that there are thousands of youngsters all over America who think they are Carlos. And, in the deepest possible way, they *are* all Carlos. Carlos is any child who has been the unhappy recipient of put-downs, taunting, rejection, and loss of self-esteem—but who has managed to turn that around because the structure of the classroom changed, creating a different set of responses. To the child involved, it feels like a miracle. To the social psychologist, it is another vivid example of the power of the situation: What looks like a small, simple change in the structure of a social environment can have an enormous impact on the experience of the people in that environment. . . .

Group Decision Fiascoes Continue:

Space Shuttle Challenger and a Revised Groupthink Framework

Gregory Moorhead, Richard Ference
and Chris P. Neck

In this article, the authors review the events surrounding the tragic decision to launch the space shuttle Challenger. Moorhead and his colleagues assert that the decision-making process demonstrates *groupthink,* a phenomenon wherein cohesive groups become so concerned with their own process that they lose sight of the true requirements of their task. The authors review the events in light of this concept, suggesting that the groupthink concept needs to be expanded to consider time pressures, which were surely present in the Challenger situation, as well as the kind of leadership patterns that exist in a group.

In 1972, a new dimension was added to our understanding of group decision making with the proposal of the groupthink hypothesis by Janis (1972). Janis coined the term "groupthink" to refer to "a mode of thinking that people engage in when they are deeply involved in a cohesive in-group, when the members' striving for unanimity override their motivation to realistically appraise alternative courses of action" (Janis, 1972, p. 8). The hypothesis was supported by his hindsight analysis of several political-military fiascoes and successes that are differentiated by the occurrence or non-occurrence of antecedent conditions, groupthink symptoms, and decision-making defects.

In a subsequent volume, Janis further explicates the theory and adds an analysis of the Watergate transcripts and various published memoirs and accounts of principals involved, concluding that the Watergate cover-up decision also was a result of groupthink (Janis, 1983). Both volumes propose prescriptions for preventing the occurrence of groupthink, many of which have appeared in popular press, in books on executive decision making, and in management textbooks. Multiple advocacy decision-making procedures have been adopted at the executive levels in many organizations, including the executive branch of the government. One would think that by 1986, 13 years after the publication of a popular book, that its prescriptions might be well ingrained in our management and decision-making styles. Unfortunately, it has not happened.

On January 28, 1986, the space shuttle Challenger was launched from Kennedy Space Center. The temperature that morning was in the mid-20's, well below the previous low temperatures at which the shuttle engines had been tested. Seventy-three seconds after launch, the Challenger exploded, killing all seven astronauts aboard, and becoming the worst disaster in space flight history. The catastrophe shocked the nation, crippled the American space program, and is destined to be remembered as the most tragic national event since the assassination of John F. Kennedy in 1963.

The Presidential Commission that investigated the accident pointed to a flawed decision-making process as a primary contributory cause. The decision was made the night before the launch in the Level I Flight Readiness Review meeting. Due to the work of the Presidential Commission, information concerning that meeting is available for analysis as a group decision possibly susceptible to groupthink.

In this paper, we report the results of our analysis of the Level I Flight Readiness Review meeting as a decision-making situation that displays evidence of groupthink. We review the antecedent conditions, the groupthink symptoms, and the possible decision-making defects, as suggested by Janis (1983). In addition, we take the next and more important step by going beyond the develop-

From *Psychology Is Social: Readings and Conversations in Social Psychology, 3/e,* edited by Edward Krupat, chapter 5, pp. 185–195, published by HarperCollins, 1994. Originally from *Human Relations,* 1991, pp. 539–550. © 1991 by Plenum Publishing Corporation. Reprinted by permission.

ment of another example of groupthink to make recommendations for renewed inquiry into group decision-making processes.

THEORY AND EVIDENCE

The meeting(s) took place throughout the day and evening from 12:36 p.m. (EST), January 27, 1986 following the decision to not launch the Challenger due to high crosswinds at the launch site. Discussions continued through about 12:00 midnight (EST) via teleconferencing and Telefax systems connecting the Kennedy Space Center in Florida, Morton Thiokol (MTI) in Utah, Johnson Space Center in Houston, and the Marshall Space Flight Center. The Level I Flight Readiness Review is the highest level of review prior to launch. It comprises the highest level of management at the three space centers and at MTI, the private supplier of the solid rocket booster engines.

To briefly state the situation, the MTI engineers recommended not to launch if temperatures of the O-ring seals on the rocket were below 53 degrees Fahrenheit, which was the lowest temperature of any previous flight. Laurence B. Mulloy, manager of the Solid Rocket Booster at Marshall Space Flight Center, states:

> The bottom line of that, though, initially was that Thiokol engineering, Bob Lund, who is the Vice President and Director of Engineering, who is here today, recommended that 51-L [the Challenger] not be launched if the O-ring temperatures predicted at launch time would be lower than any previous launch, and that was 53 degrees (*Report of the Presidential Commission on the Space Shuttle Accident*, 1986, p. 91–92).

This recommendation was made at 8:45 p.m., January 27, 1986 (*Report of the Presidential Commission on the Space Shuttle Accident*, 1986). Through the ensuing discussions the decision to launch was made.

Antecedent Conditions

The three primary antecedent conditions for the development of groupthink are: a highly cohesive group, leader preference for a certain decision, and insulation of the group from qualified outside opinions. These conditions existed in this situation.

Cohesive Group. The people who made the decision to launch had worked together for many years. They were familiar with each other and had grown through the ranks of the space program. A high degree of *esprit de corps* existed between the members.

Leader Preference. Two top level managers actively promoted their pro-launch opinions in the face of opposition. The commission report states that several managers at space centers and MTI pushed for launch, regardless of the low temperatures.

Insulation from Experts. MTI engineers made their recommendations relatively early in the evening. The top level decision-making group knew of their objections but did not meet with them directly to review their data and concerns. As Roger Boisjoly, a Thiokol engineer, states in his remarks to the Presidential Commission:

> and the bottom line was that the engineering people would not recommend a launch below 53 degrees Fahrenheit. . . . From this point on, management formulated the points to base their decision on. There was never one comment in favor, as I have said, of launching by any engineer or other nonmanagement person. . . . I was not even asked to participate in giving any input to the final decision charts (*Report of the Presidential Commission on the Space Shuttle Accident, 1986,* p. 91–92).

This testimonial indicates that the top decision-making team was insulated from the engineers who possessed the expertise regarding the functioning of the equipment.

Janis identified eight symptoms of groupthink. They are presented here along with evidence from the *Report of the Presidential Commission on the Space Shuttle Accident* (1986).

Invulnerability. When groupthink occurs, most of all of the members of the decision-making group have an illusion of invulnerability that reassures them in the face of obvious dangers. This illusion leads the group to become overly optimistic and willing to take extraordinary risks. It may also cause them to ignore clear warnings of danger.

The solid rocket joint problem that destroyed Challenger was discussed often at flight readiness review meetings prior to flight. However, Commission member Richard Feynman concluded from the testimony that a mentality of overconfidence existed due to the extraordinary record of success of space flights. Every time we send one up it is successful. Involved members may seem to think that on the next one we can lower our standards or take more risks because it always works (*Time*, 1986).

The invulnerability illusion may have built up over time as a result of NASA's own spectacular history. NASA had not lost an astronaut since 1967 when a flash fire in the capsule of Apollo 1 killed three. Since that time NASA had a string of 55 successful missions. They had put a man on the moon, built and launched Skylab and the shuttle, and retrieved defective satellites from orbit. In the minds of most Americans and apparently their own, they could do no wrong.

Rationalization. Victims of groupthink collectively construct rationalizations that discount warnings and other forms of negative feedback. If these signals were taken seriously when presented, the group members would be forced to reconsider their assumptions each time they re-commit themselves to their past decisions.

In the Level I flight readiness meeting when the Challenger was given final launch approval, MTI engineers presented evidence that the joint would fail. Their argument was based on the fact that in the coldest previous launch (air temperature 30 degrees) the joint in question experienced serious erosion and that no data existed as to how the joint would perform at colder temperatures. Flight center officials put forth numerous technical rationalizations faulting MTI's analysis. One of these rationalizations was that the engineer's data were inconclusive. As Mr. Boisjoly emphasized to the Commission:

> I was asked, yes, at that point in time I was asked to quantify my concerns, and I said I couldn't. I couldn't quantify it. I had no data to quantify it, but I did say I knew that it was away from goodness in the current data base. Someone on the net commented that we had soot blow-by on SRM-22 [Flight 61-A, October, 1985] which was launched at 75 degrees. I don't remember who made the comment, but that is where the first comment came in about the disparity between my conclusion and the observed data because SRM-22 [Flight 61-A, October 1985] had blow-by at essentially a room temperature launch. I then said that SRM-15 [Flight 51-C, January, 1985] had much more blow-by indication and that it was indeed telling us that lower temperature was a factor. I was asked again for data to support my claim, and I said I have none other than what is being presented (*Report of the Presidential Commission on the Space Shuttle Accident*, 1986, p. 89).

Discussions became twisted (compared to previous meetings) and no one detected it. Under normal conditions, MTI would have to prove the shuttle boosters readiness for launch, instead they found themselves being forced to prove that the boosters were unsafe. Boisjoly's testimony supports this description of the discussion:

> This was a meeting where the determination was to launch, and it was up to us to prove beyond a shadow of a doubt that it was not safe to do so. This is in total reverse to what the position usually is in a preflight conversation or a flight readiness review. It is usually exactly the opposite of that (*Report of the Presidential Commission on the Space Shuttle Accident*, 1986, p. 93).

Morality. Group members often believe, without question, in the inherent morality of their position. They tend to ignore the ethical or moral consequences of their decision.

In the Challenger case, this point was raised by a very high level MTI manager, Allan J. McDonald, who tried to stop the launch and said that he would not want to have to defend the decision to launch. He stated to the Commission:

> I made the statement that if we're wrong and something goes wrong on this flight, I wouldn't want to have to be the person to stand up in front of board in inquiry and say that I went ahead and told them to go ahead and fly this thing outside what the motor was qualified to (*Report of the Presidential Commission on the Space Shuttle Accident*, 1986, p. 95).

Some members did not hear this statement because it occurred during a break. Three top officials who did hear it ignored it.

Stereotyped Views of Others. Victims of groupthink often have a stereotyped view of the opposition of anyone with a competing opinion. They feel that the opposition is too stupid or too weak to understand or deal effectively with the problem.

Two of the top three NASA officials responsible for the launch displayed this attitude. They felt that they completely understood the nature of the joint problem and never seriously considered the objections raised by the MTI engineers. In fact they denigrated and badgered the opposition and their information and opinions.

Pressure on Dissent. Group members often apply direct pressure to anyone who questions the validity of these arguments supporting a decision or position favored by the majority. These same two officials pressured MTI to change its position after MTI originally recommended that the launch not take place. These two officials pressured MTI personnel to prove that it was not safe to launch, rather than to prove the opposite. As mentioned earlier, this was a total reversal of normal preflight procedures. It was this pressure that top MTI management was responding to when they overruled their engineering staff and recommended launch. As the Commission report states:

> At approximately 11 p.m. Eastern Standard Time, the Thiokol/NASA teleconference resumed, the Thiokol management stating that they had reassessed the problem, that the temperature effects were a concern, but that the data was admittedly inconclusive (p. 96).

This seems to indicate the NASA's pressure on these Thiokol officials forced them to change their recommendation from delay to execution of the launch.

Self-Censorship. Group members tend to censor themselves when they have opinions or ideas that deviate from the apparent group consensus. Janis feels that this reflects each member's inclination to minimize to himself or herself the importance of his or her own doubts and counter-arguments.

The most obvious evidence of self-censorship occurred when a vice president of MTI, who had previously presented information against launch, bowed to pressure from NASA and accepted their rationalizations for launch. He then wrote these up and presented them to NASA as the reasons that MTI had changed its recommendation to launch.

Illusion of Unanimity. Group members falling victim to groupthink share an illusion of unanimity concerning judgments made by members speaking in favor of the majority view. This symptom is caused in part by the preceding one and is aided by the false assumption that any participant who remains silent is in agreement with the majority opinion. The group leader and other members support each other by playing up points of convergence in their thinking at the expense of fully exploring points of divergence that might reveal unsettling problems.

No participant from NASA ever openly agreed with or even took sides with MTI in the discussion. The silence from NASA was probably amplified by the fact that the meeting was a teleconference linking the participants at three different locations. Obviously, body language which might have been evidenced by dissenters was not visible to others who might also have held a dissenting opinion. Thus, silence meant agreement.

Mindguarding. Certain group members assume the role of guarding the minds of others in the group. They attempt to shield the group from adverse information that might destroy the majority view of the facts regarding the appropriateness of the decision.

The top management at Marshall knew that the rocket casings had been ordered redesigned to correct a flaw 5 months previous to this launch. This information and other technical details concerning the history of the joint problem was withheld at the meeting.

Decision-Making Defects

The result of the antecedent conditions and the symptoms of groupthink is a defective decision-making process. Janis discusses several defects in decision making that can result.

Few Alternatives. The group considers only a few alternatives, often only two. No initial survey of all possible alternatives occurs. The Flight Readiness Review team had a launch/no-launch decision to make. These were the only two alternatives considered. Other possible alternatives might have been to delay the launch for further testing, or to delay until the temperatures reached an appropriate level.

No Re-Examination of Alternatives. The group fails to reexamine alternatives that may have been initially discarded based on early unfavorable information. Top NASA officials spent time and effort defending and strengthening their position, rather than examining the MTI position.

Rejecting Expert Opinions. Members make little or no attempt to seek outside experts' opinions. NASA did not seek out other experts who might have some expertise in this area. They assumed that they had all the information.

Rejecting Negative Information. Members tend to focus on supportive information and ignore any data or information that might cast a negative light on their preferred alternative. MTI representatives repeatedly tried to point out errors in the rationale the NASA officials were using to justify the launch. Even after the decision was made, the argument continued until a NASA official told the MTI representative that it was no longer his concern.

No Contingency Plans. Members spend little time discussing the possible consequences of the decision and, therefore, fail to develop contingency plans. There is no documented evidence in the Rogers Commission Report of any discussion of the possible consequences of an incorrect decision.

The major categories and key elements of the groupthink hypothesis have been presented (albeit somewhat briefly) along with evidence from the discussions prior to the launching of the Challenger, as reported in the President's Commission to investigate the accident. The antecedent conditions were present in the decision-making group, even though the group was in several physical locations. The leaders had a preferred solution and engaged in behaviors designed to promote it rather than critically appraise alternatives. These behaviors were evidence of most of the symptoms leading to a defective decision-making process.

DISCUSSION

This situation provides another example of decision making in which the group fell victim to the groupthink syndrome, as have so many previous groups. It illus-

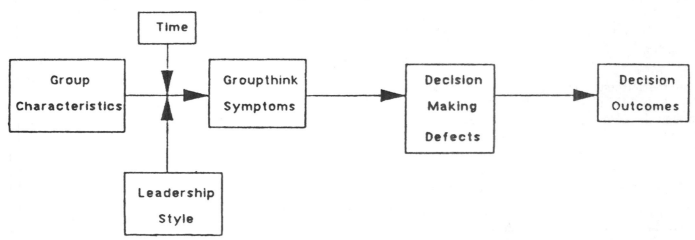

Figure 1 Revised groupthink framework

trates the situation characteristics, the symptoms of groupthink, and decision-making defects as described by Janis. This situation, however, also illustrates several other aspects of situations that are critical to the development of groupthink model. First, the element of time in influencing the development of groupthink has not received adequate attention. In the decision to launch the space shuttle Challenger, time was a crucial part of the decision-making process. The launch had been delayed once, and the window for another launch was fast closing. The leaders of the decision team were concerned about public and congressional perceptions of the entire space shuttle program and its continued funding and may have felt that further delays of the launch could seriously impact future funding. With the space window fast closing, the decision team was faced with a launch now or seriously damage the program decision. One top level manager's response to Thiokol's initial recommendation to postpone the launch indicates the presence of time pressure:

> With this LCC (Launch Commit Criteria), i.e., do not launch with a temperature greater [sic] than 53 degrees, we may not be able to launch until next April. We need to consider this carefully before we jump to any conclusions (Report of the Presidential Commission on the Space Shuttle Accident, 1996, p. 96).

Time pressure could have played a role in the group choosing to agree and to self-censor their comments. We propose that in certain situations when there is pressure to make a decision quickly, the elements may combine to foster the development of groupthink.

The second revision needs to be in the role of the leadership of the decision-making group. In the space shuttle Challenger incident, the leadership of the group varied from a shared type of leadership to a very clear leader in the situation. This may indicate that the leadership role needs to be clearly defined and a style that demands open disclosure of information, points of opposition, complaints, and dissension. We propose the leadership style is a crucial variable that moderates the relationship between the group characteristics and the development of the symptoms. Janis (1983) is a primary form of evidence to support the inclusion of leadership style in the enhanced model. His account of why the *same* group succumbed to groupthink in one decision (Bay of Figs) and not in another (Cuban Missile Crisis) supports the depiction of leadership style as a moderator variable. In these decisions, the only condition that changed was the leadership style of the President. In other words, the element that seemed to distinguish why groupthink occurred in the Bay of Pigs decision and not in the Cuban Missile Crisis situation is the president's change in his behavior.

These two variables, time and leadership style, are proposed as moderators of the impact of the group characteristics on groupthink syndrome. This relationship is portrayed graphically in Fig. 1. In effect, we propose that the groupthink symptoms result from the group characteristics, as proposed by Janis, but only in the presence of the moderator variables of time and certain leadership styles.

Time, as an important element in the model, is relatively straightforward. When a decision must be made within a very short time frame, pressure on members to agree, to avoid time-consuming arguments and reports from outside experts, and to self-censor themselves may increase. These pressures inevitably cause group members to seek agreement. In Janis's original model, time was included indirectly as a function of the antecedent condition, group cohesion. Janis (1983) argued that time pressures can adversely affect decision quality in two ways. First, it affects the decision makers' mental efficiency and judgment, interfering with their ability to concentrate on complicated discussions, to absorb new information, and to use imagination to anticipate the future consequences of alternative courses of action. Second, time pressure is a source of stress that will have the effect of inducing a policy-making group to become more cohesive and more likely to engage in groupthink.

Leadership style is shown to be a moderator because of the importance it plays in either promoting or avoiding the development of the symptoms of the groupthink. The leader, even though she or he may not promote a preferred solution, may allow or even assist the group seeking agreement by not forcing the group to critically appraise all alternative courses of action. The focus of this leadership variable is on the degree to which the leader allows or promotes discussion and evaluation of alternatives. It is not a matter of simply not making known a preferred solution; the issue is one of stimulation of critical thinking among the group.

Impact on Prescriptions for Prevention

The revised model suggests that more specific prescriptions for prevention of groupthink can be made. First, group members need to be aware of the impact that a short decision time frame has on decision processes. When a decision must be made quickly, there will be more pressure to agree, i.e., discouragement of dissent, self-censorship, avoidance of expert opinion, and assumptions about unanimity. The type of leadership suggested here is not one that sits back and simply does not make known her or his preferred solution. This type of leader must be one that requires all members to speak up with concerns, questions, and new information. The leader must know what some of these concerns are and which members are likely to have serious doubts so that the people with concerns can be called upon to voice them. This type of group leadership does not simply assign the role of devil's advocate and step out of the way. This leader actually plays the role or makes sure that others do. A leader with the required style to avoid groupthink is not a laissez-faire leader or non-involved participative leader. This leader is active in directing the activities of the group but does not make known a preferred solution. The group still must develop and evaluate alternative courses of action, but under the direct influence of a strong, demanding leader who forces critical appraisal of all alternatives.

Finally, a combination of the two variables suggests that the leader needs to help members to avoid the problems created by the time element. For example, the leader may be able to alter an externally imposed time frame for the decision by negotiating an extension or even paying late fees, if necessary. If an extension is not possible, the leader may need to help the group eliminate the effects of time on the decision processes. This can be done by forcing attention to issues rather than time, encouraging dissension and confrontation, and scheduling special sessions to hear reports from outside experts that challenge prevailing views within the group.

Janis presents, in both editions of his book, several recommendations for preventing the occurrence of groupthink. These recommendations focus on the inclusion of outside experts in the decision-making process, all members taking the role of devil's advocate and critically appraising all alternative courses of action, and the leader not expressing a preferred solution. The revised groupthink framework suggests several new prescriptions that may be helpful in preventing further decision fiascoes similar to the decision to launch the space shuttle Challenger.

References

Time. Fixing NASA. June 9, 1986.

Janis, I. L. (1983). *Victims of groupthink.* Boston: Houghton Mifflin.

Janis, I. L. (1983). *Groupthink* (2nd ed., revised). Boston: Houghton Mifflin.

Report of the Presidential Commission on the Space Shuttle Accident. Washington, D.C.: July 1986.

Group Processes in the Resolution of International Conflicts

Experiences From the Israeli–Palestinian Case

Herbert C. Kelman
Harvard University

For over 20 years, politically influential Israelis and Palestinians have met in private, unofficial, academically based, problem-solving workshops designed to enable the parties to explore each other's perspective, generate joint ideas for mutually satisfactory solutions to their conflict, and transfer insights and ideas derived from their interaction into the policy process. Most of the work takes place in small groups, but the focus is on promoting change in the larger system. This article discusses 5 ways in which the workshop group serves as a vehicle for change at the macrolevel. It does so by functioning as a microcosm of the larger system, as a laboratory for producing inputs into the larger system, as a setting for direction interaction, as a coalition across conflict lines, and as a nucleus for a new relationship.

The Israeli–Palestinian conflict has long been cited as a typical case of a protracted, intractable conflict. The origins of the conflict go back to the birth of modern political Zionism at the end of the 19th century. Violence first erupted in the 1920s, and, in various forms and with varying degrees of intensity, it has pervaded the relationship between the two peoples since that time. The psychological core of the conflict has been its perception by the two sides as a zero-sum conflict around national identity and national existence, which has led over the years to mutual denial of the other's identity and systematic efforts to delegitimize the other (Kelman, 1978, 1987). Under the circumstances, the parties had been reluctant for a long time to go to the negotiation table and, indeed, to offer each other the assurances and enticements that would make negotiations safe and promising in their eyes.

Nevertheless, in response to a strong initiative from the U.S. administration, Israelis and Palestinians finally entered into a process of direct negotiations, starting with the Madrid Conference in the fall of 1991. The mere fact that the parties were negotiating represented a significant departure in the history of the conflict, but the official talks themselves, which continued in Washington, DC, for nearly two years, did not develop their own momentum and seemed to arrive at an impasse (cf. Kelman, 1992a). In the meantime, however, secret talks between representatives of Israel's Labor Party-led government (elected in June 1992) and the Palestine Liberation Organization, held in Oslo in 1993, produced a dramatic agreement that was signed by the parties on the White House lawn in September 1993. The Oslo accord took the form of an exchange of letters of mutual recognition between the official representatives of the two peoples, followed by a Declaration of Principles (DOP) that stipulated the establishment of a Palestinian authority in Gaza and Jericho as the first step in Palestinian self-rule. Despite the shortcomings of the DOP and despite the fact that the most difficult political issues were left to be resolved in the final-status negotiations, which were scheduled to begin in May 1996, the Oslo accord represents a fundamental breakthrough in the Israeli–Palestinian con-

Editor's note. Michael G. Wessells served as action editor for this article.

Author's note. This article is based on an address delivered on August 13, 1995, at the 103rd Annual Convention of the American Psychological Association in New York, on receipt of the 1995 Distinguished Group Psychologist Award from Division 49 (Group Psychology and Group Psychotherapy). The award citation read, "Involved in study, research, publication and action, he exemplifies the very best in social science. As a group psychologist, he has studied and practiced conflict resolution in real life terms, and has expanded the reach and influence of group therapeutic understanding. In making a singular contribution to Middle East peace, he models the most creative blends of academics and practice."

The action research program on which this article is based is carried out in collaboration with Nadim Rouhana of Boston College under the auspices of the Program on International Conflict Analysis and Resolution (PICAR) at the Harvard Center for International Affairs. It is supported by grants from the Nathan Cummings Foundation, the Charles R. Bronfman Foundation, the Carnegie Corporation, and the U.S. Information Agency. PICAR (Herbert C. Kelman, Director; Donna Hicks, Deputy Director) is supported by a grant from the William and Flora Hewlett Foundation.

Correspondence concerning this article should be addressed to Herbert C. Kelman, Department of Psychology, William James Hall, Harvard University, Cambridge, MA 02138. Electronic mail may be sent via Internet to hck@wjh.harvard.edu.

flict. That breakthrough derives, in my view, from the mutual recognition of the other's nationhood and each side's commitment to negotiate and make peace with the body that symbolizes and legitimates that nationhood.

It would be foolhardy to insist that the peace process set into motion by the Oslo accords is irreversible. At this writing (October 1996), the indications are that, under the current Likud-led government in Israel, the process will be slowed down but neither reversed nor entirely halted. On the other hand, slowing down the process can seriously undermine the achievement of a final peace agreement. As we have already seen, it may provoke acts of violence and counterviolence, creating an atmosphere unconducive to negotiations, and it may create new facts on the ground—such as the expansion of Israeli settlements in the West Bank—leaving no room for an agreement on the basis of territorial compromise. Although I remain optimistic about the ultimate success of the Israeli–Palestinian peace process, I am less prepared now than three years ago to predict that a peace agreement will be signed by the end of the century. But even if the current phase of the peace process were to fail, the Oslo accord has fundamentally changed the character of the conflict. What is irreversible is the fact that the unthinkable has not only been thought, but it has been acted on—the fact that the two parties have recognized each other's national identity and have, in their negotiations and interactions, acknowledged each other's legitimacy. In this sense, the Oslo accord is a breakthrough that is at least as significant as Anwar Sadat's trip to Jerusalem, which led to the Egyptian–Israeli peace agreement.

What are the forces that led to this breakthrough? On a long-term basis, the Six-Day War of 1967 created a new geopolitical and strategic situation in the Middle East, which led to the gradually evolving recognition on all sides that a historic compromise of the Palestine problem in the form of some version of a two-state solution would best serve their national interests (cf. Kelman, 1988). The powerful political obstacles to such a solution were finally overcome by short-term strategic and micropolitical considerations that can be traced to the Gulf War and the end of the Cold War. The combination of these long-term and short-term developments made negotiations necessary from the point of view of both Israeli and Palestinian interests. But a significant factor contributing to the breakthrough was the conclusion, on both sides, that negotiations were not only necessary but also possible—that they could yield an acceptable agreement without jeopardizing their national existence. This sense of possibility evolved out of interactions between the two sides that produced the individuals, the ideas, and the political atmosphere required for productive negotiations.

A variety of unofficial contacts between the two sides played a significant role in creating this sense of possibility and the climate conducive to negotiations. It is in this context that the third-party efforts in which my colleagues and I have been engaged since the early 1970s contributed to the evolving peace process (Kelman, 1995). Our work illustrates the potential contributions of social psychology and the scholar–practitioner model (Kelman 1992b) to the interdisciplinary, multifaceted task of analyzing and resolving protracted international and ethnic conflicts.

This article focuses on the ways in which the microprocess of the small-group meetings that my colleagues and I organize can serve as a vehicle for change at the macrolevel. To set the stage for this discussion, the article briefly (a) places our work in the context of the emerging field of conflict resolution, (b) describes our particular approach to conflict resolution at the international level, and (c) discusses our efforts to contribute to the Israeli–Palestinian peace process.

The Conflict Resolution Field

In the past two decades or so, the world has witnessed the development and proliferation of a variety of new approaches to conflict resolution, which together constitute a new field of theory and practice (see Kelman, 1993b). The precise boundaries of this emerging field are difficult to draw, and practitioners differ in their view of what should be included and what should be excluded.

Practitioners of conflict resolution work at different levels—ranging from the interpersonal to the international. They operate in different domains, such as the court system, public policy, labor–management relations, interethnic relations, or international diplomacy. They derive their ideas from a variety of sources, such as law, psychotherapy, management theories, group dynamics, peace research, decision theory, the study of conflict resolution in traditional societies, and theoretical models from the entire range of social science disciplines. Despite the diversity in level, domain, and intellectual origins that characterizes the work in this field, there are certain common insights and approaches to practice that run through all of its manifestations. Thus, with different degrees of emphasis, they all call for a nonadversarial framework for conflict resolution, an analytic approach, a problem-solving orientation, direct participation by the parties in conflict in jointly shaping a solution, and facilitation by a third party trained in the process of conflict resolution.

Interaction among scholar–practitioners working at different levels and in different domains is instructive and enriching and contributes significantly to the refinement of theory and technique. At the same time, it is important to keep in mind that the application of general principles requires sensitivity to the unique features of the context in which they are applied. Thus, in my own work over the years on international and intercommunal conflict, I have called attention to the need for knowledge about and experience with the particular features and issues of conflict at these levels and to the danger of direct transfer of experiences from the interpersonal and interorganizational levels to the international arena.

Interactive Problem Solving

The unofficial third-party approach to international and ethnic conflict resolution that my colleagues and I have been developing and applying derives from the pioneering efforts of Burton (1969, 1979, 1984). I have used the term *interactive problem solving* to describe the approach, which finds its fullest expression in problem-solving workshops (Kelman, 1972, 1979, 1986, 1991, 1992b, 1996; Kelman & Cohen, 1986). Within this framework, I have done some work on the Cyprus conflict, and, through the work of my students, associates, and colleagues, I have maintained an active interest in a number of other protracted identity group conflicts around the world, such as the conflicts in Northern Ireland, Sri Lanka, Rwanda–Burundi, the former Yugoslavia, and the former Soviet Union. The primary regional focus of my action research program, however, has been on the Middle East. In particular, since the early 1970s, my colleagues and I have conducted an intensive program of problem-solving workshops and related activities on the Israeli–Palestinian conflict.

Problem-solving workshops are intensive meetings between politically involved but entirely unofficial representatives of conflicting parties—for example, Israelis and Palestinians or Greek and Turkish Cypriots (see Kelman, 1993a). Workshop participants are often politically influential members of their communities. Thus, in our Israeli–Palestinian work, participants have included parliamentarians; leading figures in political parties or movements; former military officers or government officials; journalists or editors specializing in the Middle East; and academic scholars who are major analysts of the conflict for their societies and some of whom have served in advisory, official, or diplomatic positions.[1] The workshops take place under academic auspices and are facilitated by a panel of social scientists who are knowledgeable about international conflict, group process, and the Middle East region.

The discussions are completely private and confidential. There is no audience, no publicity, and no record, and one of the central ground rules specifies that statements made in the course of a workshop cannot be cited with attribution outside of the workshop setting. These and other features of the workshop are designed to enable and encourage workshop participants to engage in a type of communication that is usually not available to parties involved in an intense conflict relationship. The third party creates an atmosphere, establishes norms,

and makes occasional interventions, all conducive to free and open discussion, in which the parties address each other rather than third parties or their own constituencies and in which they listen to each other in order to understand their differing perspectives. They are encouraged to deal with the conflict analytically rather than polemically—to explore the ways in which their interaction helps to exacerbate and perpetuate the conflict, rather than to assign blame to the other side while justifying their own. This analytic discussion helps the parties penetrate each other's perspective and understand each other's concerns, needs, fears, priorities, and constraints.

Once both sets of concerns are on the table and have been understood and acknowledged, the parties are encouraged to engage in a process of joint problem solving. They are asked to work together in developing new ideas for resolving the conflict in ways that would satisfy the fundamental needs and allay the existential fears of both parties. They are then asked to explore the political and psychological constraints that stand in the way of such integrative, win–win solutions and that, in fact, have prevented the parties from moving to (or staying at) the negotiating table. Again, they are asked to engage in a process of joint problem solving, designed to generate ideas for "getting from here to there." A central feature of this process is the identification of steps of mutual reassurance—in the form of acknowledgments, symbolic gestures, or confidence-building measures—that would help reduce the parties' fears of engaging in negotiations in which the outcome is uncertain and risky. Problem-solving workshops also contribute to mutual reassurance by helping the parties develop—again, through collaborative effort—a non-threatening, deescalatory language and a shared vision of a desirable future.

Workshops have a dual purpose. First, they are designed to produce changes in the workshop participants themselves—changes in the form of more differentiated images of the enemy (see Kelman 1987), a better understanding of the other's perspective and of their own priorities, greater insight into the dynamics of the conflict, and new ideas for resolving the conflict and for overcoming the barriers to a negotiated solution. These changes at the level of individual participants are a vehicle for promoting change at the policy level. Thus, the second purpose of workshops is to maximize the likelihood that the new insights, ideas, and proposals developed in the course of the interaction are fed back into the political debate and the decision-making process in each community. One of the central tasks of the third party is to structure the workshop in such a way that new insights and ideas are likely both to be generated and to be transferred effectively to the policy process.

The composition of the workshop is crucial in this context: Great care must be taken to select participants who, on the one hand, have the interest and capacity to engage in the kind of learning process that workshops provide and, on the other hand, have the positions and

---

[1] For a description of the recruitment process, see Kelman (1992b) and Rouhana and Kelman (1992b) and Rouhana and Kelman (1994).

credibility in their own communities that enable them to influence the thinking of political leaders, political constituencies, or the general public. It should be noted that the third party's role, although essential to the success of problem-solving workshops, is strictly a facilitative role. The critical work of generating ideas and infusing them into the political process must be done by the participants themselves. A basic assumption of our approach is that solutions emerging out of the interaction between the conflicting parties are most likely to be responsive to their needs and to engender their commitment.[2]

Contributions to the Israeli–Palestinian Peace Process

Most of the Israeli–Palestinian work that my colleagues and I carried out over the years took place during the prenegotiation phase of the conflict. The primary purpose was to help create a political atmosphere that would encourage the parties to move to the negotiating table. Moreover, until 1990, the workshops that we organized were all one-time events. Although some Israelis and Palestinians, as individuals, participated in several such events, each workshop was self-contained. Because of financial, logistical, and political constraints, we were not able to bring the same group of participants together for more than one occasion.

In 1990, however, we took a major step forward in our work by organizing, for the first time, a continuing workshop (see Rouhana & Kelman, 1994). A group of highly influential Israelis and Palestinians committed themselves initially to a series of three workshop meetings over the course of a year. The first meeting took place in November 1990 and, at the end of the third meeting (in August 1991), the participants decided to continue the process.

In the meantime, external events instigated a second major new development in our work. With the convening of the Madrid Conference in the fall of 1991 and the opening of an official Israeli–Palestinian peace process, our own work moved from the prenegotiation to the negotiation phase of the conflict. We had no doubt—and the participants in the continuing workshop agreed—that there was still a great need for maintaining an unofficial process alongside of the official one. However, with the onset of official negotiations, the purpose and focus of our work had to change (Rouhana & Kelman, 1994). When negotiations are in progress, workshops can contribute to overcoming obstacles to staying at the table and negotiating productively, to creating a momentum for the negotiations, to addressing long-term issues that are not yet on the negotiating table, and to beginning

the process of peace-building that must accompany and follow the process of peacemaking.

As Nadim Rouhana and I began to formulate, along with the Israeli and Palestinian participants, the functions of the continuing workshop in the new phase of the peace process, we confronted another new development, which created both opportunities and complications. Our unofficial process was steadily moving closer to the official process. When the official negotiating teams were established, four of the six Palestinian members of the continuing workshop were appointed to key positions on them. With the Labor Party's victory in the Israeli election in 1992, several of our Israeli participants gained increasing access to the top decision makers. (In fact, eventually, one was appointed to the cabinet and another to a major diplomatic post.) These developments clearly enhanced the political relevance of the continuing workshop, but the overlap between the official and unofficial processes also created some ambiguities and role conflicts.

The meetings of the continuing workshop after the start of the official negotiations focused on the obstacles confronting the peace process at the negotiating table and on the ground but also addressed the question of the functions and composition of the continuing workshop in the new political environment. Altogether, this continuing workshop met over a three-year period. Its final session took place in August 1993, ending just a day or so before the news of the Israeli–Palestinian breakthrough that was achieved in Oslo began to emerge.

In the wake of the Oslo accord, signed in September 1993, there has been general recognition of the role that unofficial efforts have played, directly or indirectly, in laying the groundwork for the Israeli–Palestinian breakthrough. In this context, various observers—within and outside of the Middle East—have acknowledged the contributions of the activities in which my colleagues and I have been engaged over the years. In my own assessment, there are three ways in which our work, along with that of many others, has contributed (Kelman, 1995).

1. Workshops have helped to develop cadres prepared to carry out productive negotiations. Over the years, dozens of Israelis and dozens of Palestinians, many of them political influentials or preinfluentials, have participated in our workshops and related activities, including the continuing workshop in the early 1990s. Many of these individuals were involved in the discussions and negotiations that led up to the Oslo accord. Many have continued to be involved in the peace process, and some have served in the Israeli cabinet, Knesset, and foreign ministry and in leading positions in the various Palestinian political agencies.

2. The sharing of information and the formulation of new ideas in the course of our workshops have provided important substantive inputs into the ne-

[2] For a more detailed discussion of the workshop ground rules, the nature of the interaction between participants, and the role of the third party, see Kelman (1979), Kelman (1992b), and Rouhana and Kelman (1994).

gotiations. Through the public and private communications of workshop participants—and to some degree also through the communications of members of the third party—some of the insights and ideas on which productive negotiations could be built were injected into the two political cultures. These included shared assumptions, mutual sensitivities, and new conceptions of the process and outcome of negotiations, all of which were developed in the course of workshop interactions.

3. Workshops have fostered a political atmosphere that has made the parties open to a new relationship. Our workshops, along with various other Israeli–Palestinian meetings and projects, have done so by encouraging the development of more differentiated images of the enemy, of a deescalatory language and a new political discourse that is attentive to the other party's concerns and constraints, of a working trust that is based on the conviction that both parties have a genuine interest in a peaceful solution, and of a sense of possibility regarding the ultimate achievement of a mutually satisfactory outcome.

The Oslo agreement, of course, represented only the beginning of what has already been and will almost certainly continue to be a long and difficult process, confronting obstacles and periodic setbacks. Therefore, unofficial efforts alongside the official negotiations continue to be needed. Accordingly, when we decided to close the continuing workshop in the late fall of 1993, we immediately initiated a new project, which built on the experience and achievements of the preceding work. This new project has taken the form of a joint working group on Israeli–Palestinian relations, which held its first meeting in May 1994. The initial emphasis of the group has been on systematic exploration of the difficult political issues—including Israeli settlements, Palestinian refugees, Jerusalem, and the precise nature of Palestinian self-determination—that have been deferred to the final-status negotiations. For the first time in our work, we hope to produce and disseminate one or more joint concept papers, which will frame these issues in terms of the future relationship between the two societies that is envisaged as the long-term outcome of the final agreement.

The Role of Group Processes in Conflict Resolution

Having presented a brief description of our microlevel approach and its contribution to conflict resolution at the macrolevel, I now want to highlight the role that interaction within the small group plays in the larger process.

Most of our work takes place in the context of small groups, composed of three to six representatives of the two sides and two to four third-party facilitators. The focus of all of our efforts is on promoting change in the

larger system, but direct interaction in the small-group setting can produce important inputs into the political thinking, the political debate, and the decision-making processes within the two societies and into the formal negotiations between them. Thus, changes at the individual level resulting from interaction in the small group become vehicles for change at the system level.

In the following sections, I discuss five ways in which the workshop group serves as a vehicle for change in the larger system. It does so by functioning as a microcosm of the larger system, as a laboratory for producing inputs into the larger system, as a setting for direct interaction, as a coalition across conflict lines, and as a nucleus for a new relationship. These five functions of the group are not meant to represent different theories or even different dimensions of group process. They are merely different ways of looking at the role of group processes in our intervention model. By looking at the group process from these different angles, I hope to provide a fuller and more nuanced picture of how our micro-process contributes to change at the macrolevel.

The Group as a Microcosm

The group assembled for a workshop can be viewed as a microcosm of the larger system. It is a microcosm not in the sense of a small-scale *model* that reproduces all of the forces of the larger system but in the sense of an *arena* in which the forces of the larger system may manifest themselves. We make no attempt to reproduce the larger system in our workshops. In fact, we try to create an environment that differs significantly from the one in which the conflicting parties normally interact—an environment governed by a different set of norms, in which participants are both free and obligated to speak openly, listen attentively, and treat each other as equals. Nor do we try to represent the entire political spectrum in our workshops. We look for participants who are part of the mainstream in their communities and close to the political center but who are interested in exploring the possibilities of a negotiated, mutually satisfactory solution to the conflict.

The group is a microcosm of the larger system because, despite their relative moderation, the participants share the fundamental concerns, fears, memories, and aspirations of their respective communities. As they interact with each other around the issues in conflict, they reflect their own community's perspectives, priorities, and limits of what is negotiable, not only in what they say but also in how they say it and how they act toward each other. As a result, some of the dynamics of the larger conflict are acted out in the interactions within the workshop group. Participants' interactions in the group context often reflect the nature of the relationship between their communities—their mutual distrust, their special sensitivities and vulnerabilities, their differences in power and minority—majority status—and demonstrate the self-perpetuating character of interactions among conflicting societies.

The advantage of the workshop is that it creates an atmosphere, a set of norms, and a working trust among the participants that enable them to observe and analyze these conflict dynamics at or very near the moment they occur. Such analyses are facilitated by third-party interventions in the form of process observations, which suggest possible ways in which interactions between the parties "here and now" may reflect the dynamics of the conflict between their communities (Kelman, 1979). The insights that such observations can generate are comparable to the "corrective emotional experiences" that play an important role in individual and, particularly, group psychotherapy (Alexander & French, 1946, pp. 66–68; Frank & Ascher, 1951), although our interventions are always at the intergroup rather than the interpersonal level. That is, interactions between workshop participants are relevant to our purposes only insofar as they can tell us something about the dynamics of the interaction between their communities.

In summary, the character of the workshop group as a microcosm of the larger system makes it a valuable learning experience: It provides opportunities for the participants to gain important insights into the dynamics of the conflict. I turn next to the role of the group in transmitting what is learned into the larger system.

The Group as a Laboratory

The workshop group can also be conceived as a laboratory for producing inputs into the larger system. The metaphor of the laboratory is particularly appropriate because it captures the two roles that workshops play in the macroprocess. A workshop is a specially constructed space in which the parties can engage in a process of exploration, observation, and analysis and in which they can create new products to be fed into the political debate and decision making in the two societies.

Providing a space for exploring issues in the conflict, mutual concerns, and ideas for conflict resolution is one of the key contributions of problem-solving workshops. The opportunity for joint informal exploration—playing with ideas, trying out different scenarios, obtaining a sense of the range of possible actions and of the limits for each party, and discovering potential tradeoffs—enhances the productivity of negotiations and the quality of the outcome. Such opportunities, however, are not readily available in official negotiations, in which the participants operate in representative roles, are instructed and closely monitored by their governments, are concerned about the reactions of various constituencies and third parties, and are in the business of producing binding agreements. Problem-solving workshops, by virtue of their nonbinding character, are ideally suited to fill this gap in the larger diplomatic process. The setting, the atmosphere, the ground rules, the governing norms, the agenda, and the interventions of the third party all help to make the workshop group a unique laboratory for the process of open, noncommittal exploration that does not often occur elsewhere in the system, neither in the official negotiations nor in the spontaneous interactions between the conflicting parties.

The process of exploration and joint thinking yields new products, which can be exported into the political process within and between the two communities. This is the second sense in which the laboratory metaphor captures the function of workshops. Indeed the group constitutes a workshop in the literal sense of that term: It is a specially constructed space for shaping products that are then brought back into the two communities. The sharing of perspectives, the conflict analysis, and the joint thinking encouraged in workshops enable the participants to come up with a variety of products in the form of new information, new insights, and new ideas that can advance the negotiation process: differentiated images of the other, which suggest that there is someone to talk to on the other side and something to talk about; understanding of the needs, fears, priorities, and constraints on the other side and, indeed, on one's own side; insight into the escalatory and self-perpetuating dynamics of the conflict relationship; awareness of change and the readiness for change on the other side; ideas for mutual reassurance and other ways of improving the atmosphere for negotiation; ideas for the overall shape of a mutually satisfactory solution; and ideas for redefining the conflict and reframing issues so as to make them more amenable to resolution. These products must then be exported into the political arena. It is essential, therefore, that the individuals selected as workshop participants have not only an interest in mutual exploration and learning, and skills for generating ideas and creative problem solving, but also the capacity and opportunity to utilize what they learn and to inject the workshop products into their respective communities in ways that make a political difference.

In sum, I have described the workshop group as a special space—a laboratory—in which a significant part of the work of peacemaking can be carried out. The unique contribution of the workshop to this larger process is that it provides a carefully designed environment in which constructive social interaction between the parties can take place. Let me, therefore, turn to the third image of the workshop: the group as a setting for direct interaction.

The Group as a Setting for Direct Interaction

Although international conflict and conflict resolution are societal and intersocietal processes, which cannot be reduced to the level of individual behavior, there are certain processes central to conflict resolution—such as empathy or taking the perspective of the other (which is at the heart of social interaction), learning and insight, and creative problem solving—that, of necessity, take place at the level of individuals and interactions between individuals. These psychological processes are by no means the whole of conflict resolution, but they must occur somewhere in the system if there is to be movement toward a mutually satisfactory and stable peace. Problem-solving workshops provide a setting for these processes to occur by bringing together representatives of the conflicting parties for direct interaction under conditions of confidentiality and equality and under an alternative set of norms in contrast to the norms that usually govern interactions between conflicting parties.

The context, norms, ground rules, agenda, procedures, and third-party interventions in workshops are all designed to encourage (and permit) a special kind of interaction, marked by an emphasis on addressing each other (rather than one's constituencies, third parties, or the record) and on listening to each other, an analytical focus, adherence to a "no-fault" principle, and a problem-solving orientation. This kind of interaction allows the parties to explore each other's concerns, penetrate each other's perspective, and take cognizance of each other's constraints (Kelman, 1992b). As a result, they are able to offer each other the reassurances needed for productive negotiation and mutual accommodation and to come up with solutions responsive to both sides' needs and fears.

The nature of the interaction fostered in problem-solving workshops has some continuities with a therapeutic model (Kelman, 1991). Workshop features that reflect such a model are the analytical character of the discourse, the use of here-and-now experiences as a basis for learning about the dynamics of the conflict, and the encouragement of mutual acknowledgments that have both a reassuring and a healing effect. Unlike therapy groups, however, workshops focus not on individuals and their interpersonal relations but on how their interaction may illuminate the dynamics of the conflict between their communities.

An underlying assumption of the workshop process is that products of social interaction have an emergent quality (Kelman, 1992b). In the course of direct interaction, the parties are able to observe firsthand their differing reactions to the same events and the different perspectives these reflect, the differences between the way they perceive themselves and the way the other perceives them, and the impact that their statements and actions have on each other. Out of these observations, they can jointly shape new insights and ideas that could not have been predicted from what they initially brought to the interaction. Certain kinds of solutions to the conflict can emerge only from the confrontation of assumptions, concerns, and identities during face-to-face communication.

The emergence of ideas for solution to the conflict out of the interaction between the parties (in contrast, e.g., to ideas proposed by third parties) has several advantages. Such ideas are more likely to be responsive to the fundamental needs and fears of both parties; the parties are more likely to feel committed to the solutions they produce themselves; and the process of producing these ideas in itself contributes to building a new relationship between the parties, initially between the pronegotiation elements on the two sides and ultimately between the two societies as wholes. Let me turn then to the function of the workshop group in building relationships of both kinds.

The Group as a Coalition Across Conflict Lines

The workshop group can be conceived as a coalition across conflict lines—as part of a process of building a coalition between those elements on each side that are interested in a negotiated solution (Kelman, 1993a). This does not mean that workshop participants are all committed doves. Often, they are individuals who, out of pragmatic considerations, have concluded that a negotiated agreement is in the best interest of their own community. Workshops, then, can be seen as attempts to strengthen the hands of the pronegotiation elements on each side in their political struggle within their own communities and to increase the likelihood that the pronegotiation elements on the two sides will support and reinforce each other in pursuing their common interest in a negotiated solution.

Because the coalition formed by a workshop group (and by the entire array of joint efforts by the pronegotiation forces on the two sides) cuts across a very basic conflict line, it is almost by definition an uneasy coalition. It must function in the face of the powerful bonds that coalition members have to the very groups that the coalition tries to transcend. The coalition may well be perceived as threatening the national community that is so important to the identity, the long-term interests, and the political effectiveness of each coalition partner. As a result, the coalition work is complicated by participants' concern about their self-images as loyal members of their group; by their concern about their credibility at home and, hence, their long-term political effectiveness; by significant divergences in the perspectives of the two sets of coalition partners; and by the fact that even committed proponents of negotiation share the memories, concerns, fears, and sensitivities of their identity group.

Participants' bonds to their national communities create inevitable barriers to coalition work, which require systematic attention if problem-solving workshops are to achieve their goals. Thus, mutual distrust is an endemic condition that complicates coalition work. Even among individuals who have worked together for some time and have achieved a considerable level of working trust, old fears and suspicions that have deep historical roots are easily rearoused by events on the ground or by words and actions of a participant on the other side. Coalition work, therefore, requires a continuing process of mutual testing and reestablishment of working trust. A second impediment to coalition work is alienating language— the use of words or a manner of speaking that the other side finds irritating, patronizing, insulting, threatening, or otherwise oblivious to its sensitivities. One of the valuable outcomes of workshops is growing sensitivity to the meaning of particular words to the other side. Nevertheless, alienating language does crop up, both because participants speak from the perspectives and out of the experiences of their own communities and because the pragmatic terms in which peace is justified to one's domestic audiences (and perhaps to one's self) may appear dehumanizing or delegitimizing to the other side. Examples are the Israeli emphasis on the Palestinian "demographic threat" and the Palestinian emphasis on Israel's superior power as reasons for seeking a compromise. Finally, fluctuations in the political and psychological climate may affect one or the other party, creating a lack of synchronism in the readiness for coalition work between the two sides.

The uneasy quality of a coalition across conflict lines is an inevitable reality, insofar as coalition members are bona fide representatives of their national groups—as they must be if the coalition is to achieve its goal of promoting a negotiated agreement. This reality creates barriers to coalition work, and it is part of the task of the third party to help overcome them. But it is not only difficult to overcome these barriers, it may in fact be counterproductive to overcome them entirely. It is important for the coalition to remain uneasy in order to enhance the value of what participants learn in the course of workshops and of what they can achieve upon reentry into their home communities.

Experimental research by Rothbart and associates (Rothbart & John, 1985; Rothbart & Lewis, 1988) suggests that direct contact between members of conflicting groups may have a paradoxical effect on intergroup stereotypes. If it becomes apparent, in the course of direct interaction with representatives of the other group, that they do not fit one's stereotype of the group, there is a tendency to differentiate these particular individuals from their group: to perceive them as nonmembers. Since they are excluded from the category, the stereotype about the category itself can remain intact. This process of differentiating and excluding individual members of the other group from their category could well take place in workshops in which a high degree of trust develops between the parties. Therefore, it is essential for the participants to reconfirm their belongingness to their national categories—thus keeping the coalition uneasy—if they are to demonstrate the possibility of peace not just between exceptional individuals from the two sides but between the two enemy camps.

An even more important reason why a coalition across conflict lines must, of necessity, remain uneasy relates to what is often called the *reentry problem* (see, e.g., Kelman, 1972; Walton, 1970). If a workshop group

> became overly cohesive, it would undermine the whole purpose of the enterprise: to have an impact on the political decisions within the two communities. Workshop participants who become closely identified with their counterparts on the other side may become alienated from their own co-nationals, lose credibility, and hence forfeit their political effectiveness and their ability to promote a new consensus within their own communities. One of the challenges for problem-solving workshops, therefore, is to create an atmosphere in which participants can begin to humanize and trust each other and to develop an effective collaborative relationship, without losing sight of their separate group identities and the conflict between their communities. (Kelman, 1992b, p. 82)

The Group as a Nucleus for a New Relationship

Our work is based on the proposition that in conflicts such as that between Palestinians and Israelis—conflicts about national identity and national existence between two peoples destined to live together in the same small space—conflict resolution must aim toward the ultimate establishment of a new cooperative and mutually enhancing relationship and must involve a process that paves the way to such a relationship. Nothing less will work in the long run, and, even in the short run, only a process embodying the principle of reciprocity that is at the center of a new relationship is likely to succeed. Perhaps the greatest strength of problem-solving workshops is their potential contribution to transforming the relationship between the conflicting parties.

Interaction in the workshop group both promotes and models a new relationship between the parties. It is based on the principles of equality and reciprocity. The participants are encouraged to penetrate each other's perspective and to gain an understanding of the other's needs, fears, and constraints. They try to shape solutions that are responsive to the fundamental concerns of both sides. They search for ways of providing mutual reassurance. Such ideas often emerge from acknowledgments that participants make to each other in the course of their interaction: acknowledgments of the other's humanity, national identity, view of history, authentic links to the land, legitimate grievances, and commitment to peace.

Out of these interactions, participants develop increasing degrees of empathy, of sensitivity and responsiveness to the other's concerns, and of working trust, which are essential ingredients of the new relationship to which conflict resolution efforts aspire. The working trust and responsiveness both develop out of the collaborative work in which the group is engaged and, in turn, help to enhance the effectiveness of that work. Thus, workshop participants can transmit to their respective communities not only ideas toward transformation of the relationship between the communities but also the results of their own experience: They can testify that a cooperative, mutually enhancing relationship is possible and can point to some of the conditions that promote such a relationship.

The joint working group on Israeli–Palestinian relations, which my colleague Nadim Rouhana and I are currently cochairing, is explicitly based on the conception of the group as the nucleus of a new relationship between the two societies. The main purpose of the working group is to focus on the peace-building processes that must follow successful peacemaking and to explore the nature of the long-term relationship envisaged in the aftermath of the final political agreement. At this point, as I mentioned earlier, we are addressing the difficult political issues—settlements, refugees, Jerusalem, Palestinian self-determination—that have been deferred to the final-status negotiations, in the light of the future relationship between the societies. That is, we try to assess different options for resolving these issues from the point of view of their congruence with a long-term relationship that is based on peaceful coexistence, cooperation, and mutual benefit.

Furthermore, we see the working group itself as a model and perhaps even as the seed of an institutional mechanism that a new relationship calls for. In our view, a mutually beneficial relationship between two units that are as closely linked and as interdependent as the Israeli and Palestinian communities requires the development of a civil society across the political borders. A useful institutional mechanism for such a civil society would be an unofficial joint forum for exploring issues in the relationship between the two communities within a problem-solving framework. It is not entirely unrealistic to hope that our current working group may evolve into or at least serve as a model for such an institution. This scenario thus provides an illustration of the way in which a group like our Israeli–Palestinian working group can serve not only as a means for promoting a new relationship between the parties but also as a model and manifestation of that new relationship.

REFERENCES

Alexander, F., & French, T. M. (1946). *Psychoanalytic therapy*. New York: Ronald Press.

Burton, J. W. (1969). *Conflict and communication: The use of controlled communication in international relations*. London: Macmillan.

Burton, J. W. (1979). *Deviance, terrorism and war: The process of solving unsolved social and political problems*. New York: St. Martin's Press.

Burton, J. W. (1984). *Global conflict: The domestic sources of international crisis*. Brighton, England: Wheatsheaf.

Frank, J. D., & Ascher, E. (1951). Corrective emotional experiences in group therapy. *American Journal of Psychiatry, 108*, 126–131.

Kelman, H. C. (1972). The problem-solving workshop in conflict resolution. In R. L. Merritt (Ed.), *Communication in international politics* (pp. 168–204). Urbana: University of Illinois Press.

Kelman, H. C. (1978). Israelis and Palestinians: Psychological prerequisites for mutual acceptance. *International Security, 3*, 162–186.

Kelman, H. C. (1979). An interactional approach to conflict resolution and its application to Israeli–Palestinian relations. *International Interactions, 6*, 99–122.

Kelman, H. C. (1986). Interactive problem solving: A social–psychological approach to conflict resolution. In W. Klassen (Ed.), *Dialogue toward interfaith understanding* (pp. 293–314). Tantur/Jerusalem: Ecumenical Institute for Theological Research.

Kelman, H. C. (1987). The political psychology of the Israeli–Palestinian conflict: How can we overcome the barriers to a negotiated solution? *Political Psychology, 8*, 347–363.

Kelman, H. C. (1988, Spring). The Palestinianization of the Arab–Israeli conflict. *The Jerusalem Quarterly, 46*, 3–15.

Kelman, H. C. (1991). Interactive problem solving: The uses and limits of a therapeutic model for the resolution of international conflicts. In V. D. Volkan, J. V. Montville, & D. A. Julius (Eds.), *The psychodynamics of international relationships, Volume II: Unofficial diplomacy at work* (pp. 145–160). Lexington, MA: Lexington Books.

Kelman, H. C. (1992a). Acknowledging the other's nationhood: How to create a momentum for the Israeli–Palestinian negotiations. *Journal of Palestine Studies, 22*(1), 18–38.

Kelman, H. C. (1992b). Informal mediation by the scholar/practitioner. In J. Bercovitch & J. Z. Rubin (Eds.), *Mediation in international relations: Multiple approaches to conflict management* (pp. 64–96). New York: St. Martin's Press.

Kelman, H.C. (1993a). Coalitions across conflict lines: The interplay of conflicts within and between the Israeli and Palestinian communities. In S. Worchel & J. Simpson (Eds.), *Conflict between people and groups* (pp. 236–258). Chicago: Nelson-Hall.

Kelman, H. C. (1993b). Foreword. In D. J. D. Sandole & H. van der Merwe (Eds.), *Conflict resolution theory and practice: Integration and application* (pp. ix–xii). Manchester, England: Manchester University Press.

Kelman, H C. (1995). Contributions of an unofficial conflict resolution effort to the Israeli–Palestinian breakthrough. *Negotiation Journal, 11*, 19–27.

Kelman, H. C. (1996). Negotiation as interactive problem solving. *International Negotiations, 1*, 99–123.

Kelman, H. C., & Cohen, S. P. (1986). Resolution of international conflict: An interactional approach. In S. Worchel & W. G. Austin (Eds.), *Psychology of intergroup relations* (2nd ed., pp. 323–342). Chicago: Nelson Hall.

Rothbart, M., & John, O. P. (1985). Social categorization and behavioral episodes: A cognitive analysis of the effects of intergroup contact. *Journal of Social Issues, 41*(3), 81–104.

Rothbart, M., & Lewis, S. (1988). Inferring category attributes from exemplar attributes: Geometric shapes and social categories. *Journal of Personality and Social Psychology, 55*, 861–872.

Rouhana. N. N., & Kelman, H. C. (1994). Promoting joint thinking in international conflicts: An Israeli–Palestinian continuing workshop. *Journal of Social Issues, 50*(1), 157–178.

Walton, R. E. (1970). A problem-solving workshop on border conflicts in Eastern Africa. *Journal of Applied Behavioral Science, 6*, 453–489.

IQ and technical skills are important, but emotional intelligence is the sine qua non of leadership.

What Makes a Leader?

BY DANIEL GOLEMAN

EVERY BUSINESSPERSON knows a story about a highly intelligent, highly skilled executive who was promoted into a leadership position only to fail at the job. And they also know a story about someone with solid—but not extraordinary—intellectual abilities and technical skills who was promoted into a similar position and then soared.

Such anecdotes support the widespread belief that identifying individuals with the "right stuff" to be leaders is more art than science. After all, the personal styles of superb leaders vary: some leaders are subdued and analytical; others shout their manifestos from the mountaintops. And just as important, different situations call for different types of leadership. Most mergers need a sensitive negotiator at the helm, whereas many turnarounds require a more forceful authority.

I have found, however, that the most effective leaders are alike in one crucial way: they all have a high degree of what has come to be known as *emotional intelligence*. It's not that IQ and technical skills are irrelevant. They do matter, but mainly as "threshold capabilities"; that is, they are the entry-level requirements for executive positions. But my research, along with other recent studies, clearly shows that

Daniel Goleman is the author of Emotional Intelligence *(Bantam, 1995) and* Working with Emotional Intelligence *(Bantam, 1998). He is cochairman of the Consortium for Research on Emotional Intelligence in Organizations, which is based at Rutgers University's Graduate School of Applied and Professional Psychology in Piscataway, New Jersey. He can be reached at Goleman@javanet.com.*

emotional intelligence is the sine qua non of leadership. Without it, a person can have the best training in the world, an incisive, analytical mind, and an endless supply of smart ideas, but he still won't make a great leader.

In the course of the past year, my colleagues and I have focused on how emotional intelligence operates at work. We have examined the relationship between emotional intelligence and effective performance, especially in leaders. And we have observed how emotional intelligence shows itself on the job. How can you tell if someone has high emotional intelligence, for example, and how can you recognize it in yourself? In the following pages, we'll explore these questions, taking each of the components of emotional intelligence—self-awareness, self-regulation, motivation, empathy, and social skill—in turn.

Evaluating Emotional Intelligence

Most large companies today have employed trained psychologists to develop what are known as "competency models" to aid them in identifying, training, and promoting likely stars in the leadership firmament. The psychologists have also developed such models for lower-level positions. And in recent years, I have analyzed competency models from 188 companies, most of which were large and global and included the likes of Lucent Technologies, British Airways, and Credit Suisse.

In carrying out this work, my objective was to determine which personal capabilities drove outstanding performance within these organizations, and to what degree they did so. I grouped capabilities into three categories: purely technical skills like accounting and business planning; cognitive abilities like analytical reasoning; and competencies demonstrating emotional intelligence such as the ability to work with others and effectiveness in leading change.

To create some of the competency models, psychologists asked senior managers at the companies to identify the capabilities that typified the organization's most outstanding leaders. To create other models, the psychologists used objective criteria such as a division's profitability to differentiate the star performers at senior levels within their organizations from the average ones. Those individuals were then extensively interviewed and tested, and their capabilities were compared. This process resulted in the creation of lists of ingredients for highly effective leaders. The lists ranged in length from 7 to 15 items and included such ingredients as initiative and strategic vision.

When I analyzed all this data, I found dramatic results. To be sure, intellect was a driver of outstanding performance. Cognitive skills such as big-picture thinking and long-term vision were particularly important. But when I calculated the

Effective leaders are alike in one crucial way: they all have a high degree of emotional intelligence.

ratio of technical skills, IQ, and emotional intelligence as ingredients of excellent performance, emotional intelligence proved to be twice as important as the others for jobs at all levels.

Moreover, my analysis showed that emotional intelligence played an increasingly important role at the highest levels of the company, where differences in technical skills are of negligible importance. In other words, the higher the rank of a person considered to be a star performer, the more emotional intelligence capabilities showed up as the reason for his or her effectiveness. When I compared star performers with average ones in senior leadership positions, nearly 90% of the difference in their profiles was attributable to emotional intelligence factors rather than cognitive abilities.

Other researchers have confirmed that emotional intelligence not only distinguishes outstanding leaders but can also be linked to strong performance. The findings of the late David McClelland, the renowned researcher in human and organizational behavior, are a good example. In a 1996 study of a global food and beverage company, McClelland found that when senior managers had a critical mass of emotional intelligence capabilities, their divisions outperformed yearly earnings goals by 20%. Meanwhile, division leaders without that critical mass underperformed by almost the same amount. McClelland's findings, interestingly, held as true in the company's U.S. divisions as in its divisions in Asia and Europe.

In short, the numbers are beginning to tell us a persuasive story about the link between a company's success and the emotional intelligence of its leaders. And just as important, research is also demonstrating that people can, if they take the right approach, develop their emotional intelligence. (See "Can Emotional Intelligence Be Learned?")

Self-Awareness

Self-awareness is the first component of emotional intelligence—which makes sense when one con-

The Five Components of Emotional Intelligence at Work

	Definition	Hallmarks
Self-Awareness	the ability to recognize and understand your moods, emotions, and drives, as well as their effect on others	self-confidence realistic self-assessment self-deprecating sense of humor
Self-Regulation	the ability to control or redirect disruptive impulses and moods the propensity to suspend judgment—to think before acting	trustworthiness and integrity comfort with ambiguity openness to change
Motivation	a passion to work for reasons that go beyond money or status a propensity to pursue goals with energy and persistence	strong drive to achieve optimism, even in the face of failure organizational commitment
Empathy	the ability to understand the emotional makeup of other people skill in treating people according to their emotional reactions	expertise in building and retaining talent cross-cultural sensitivity service to clients and customers
Social Skill	proficiency in managing relationships and building networks an ability to find common ground and build rapport	effectiveness in leading change persuasiveness expertise in building and leading teams

siders that the Delphic oracle gave the advice to "know thyself" thousands of years ago. Self-awareness means having a deep understanding of one's emotions, strengths, weaknesses, needs, and drives. People with strong self-awareness are neither overly critical nor unrealistically hopeful. Rather, they are honest—with themselves and with others.

People who have a high degree of self-awareness recognize how their feelings affect them, other people, and their job performance. Thus a self-aware person who knows that tight deadlines bring out the worst in him plans his time carefully and gets his work done well in advance. Another person with high self-awareness will be able to work with a demanding client. She will understand the client's impact on her moods and the deeper reasons for her frustration. "Their trivial demands take us away from the real work that needs to be done," she might explain. And she will go one step further and turn her anger into something constructive.

Self-awareness extends to a person's understanding of his or her values and goals. Someone who is highly self-aware knows where he is headed and why; so, for example, he will be able to be firm in turning down a job offer that is tempting financially but does not fit with his principles or long-term goals. A person who lacks self-awareness is apt to make decisions that bring on inner turmoil by treading on buried values. "The money looked good so I signed on," someone might say two years into a job, "but the work means so little to me that I'm constantly bored." The decisions of self-aware people mesh with their values; consequently, they often find work to be energizing.

How can one recognize self-awareness? First and foremost, it shows itself as candor and an ability to assess oneself realistically. People with high self-awareness are able to speak accurately and openly—although not necessarily effusively or confessionally—about their emotions and the impact they have on their work. For instance, one manager I know of was skeptical about a new personal-shopper service that her company, a major department-store chain, was about to introduce. Without prompting from her team or her boss, she offered them an explanation: "It's hard for me to get behind the rollout of this service," she admitted, "because I really wanted to run the project, but I wasn't selected. Bear with me while I deal with that." The manager did indeed examine her feelings; a week later, she was supporting the project fully.

Such self-knowledge often shows itself in the hiring process. Ask a candidate to describe a time he got carried away by his feelings and did something he later regretted. Self-aware candidates will be frank in admitting to failure—and will often tell their tales with a smile. One of the hallmarks of self-awareness is a self-deprecating sense of humor.

Self-awareness can also be identified during performance reviews. Self-aware people know—and are comfortable talking about—their limitations and strengths, and they often demonstrate a thirst for constructive criticism. By contrast, people with low self-awareness interpret the message that they need to improve as a threat or a sign of failure.

Self-aware people can also be recognized by their self-confidence. They have a firm grasp of their capabilities and are less likely to set themselves up to fail by, for example, overstretching on assignments. They know, too, when to ask for help. And the risks they take on the job are calculated. They won't ask for a challenge that they know they can't handle alone. They'll play to their strengths.

Consider the actions of a mid-level employee who was invited to sit in on a strategy meeting with her company's top executives. Although she was the most junior person in the room, she did not sit there quietly, listening in awestruck or fearful silence. She knew she had a head for clear logic and the skill to present ideas persuasively, and she offered cogent suggestions about the company's strategy. At the same time, her self-awareness stopped her from wandering into territory where she knew she was weak.

Despite the value of having self-aware people in the workplace, my research indicates that senior executives don't often give self-awareness the credit it deserves when they look for potential leaders. Many executives mistake candor about feelings for "wimpiness" and fail to give due respect to employees who openly acknowledge their shortcomings. Such people are too readily dismissed as "not tough enough" to lead others.

In fact, the opposite is true. In the first place, people generally admire and respect candor. Further, leaders are constantly required to make judgment calls that require a candid assessment of capabilities—their own and those of others. Do we have the management expertise to acquire a competitor? Can we launch a new product within

Self-aware job candidates will be frank in admitting to failure—and will often tell their tales with a smile.

six months? People who assess themselves honestly—that is, self-aware people—are well suited to do the same for the organizations they run.

Self-Regulation

Biological impulses drive our emotions. We cannot do away with them—but we can do much to manage them. Self-regulation, which is like an ongoing inner conversation, is the component of emotional intelligence that frees us from being prisoners of our feelings. People engaged in such a conversation feel bad moods and emotional impulses just as everyone else does, but they find ways to control them and even to channel them in useful ways.

Imagine an executive who has just watched a team of his employees present a botched analysis to the company's board of directors. In the gloom that follows, the executive might find himself tempted to pound on the table in anger or kick over a chair. He could leap up and scream at the group. Or he might maintain a grim silence, glaring at everyone before stalking off.

But if he had a gift for self-regulation, he would choose a different approach. He would pick his words carefully, acknowledging the team's poor performance without rushing to any hasty judgment. He would then step back to consider the reasons for the failure. Are they personal—a lack of effort? Are there any mitigating factors? What was his role in the debacle? After considering these questions, he would call the team together, lay out the incident's consequences, and

Can Emotional Intelligence Be Learned?

For ages, people have debated if leaders are born or made. So too goes the debate about emotional intelligence. Are people born with certain levels of empathy, for example, or do they acquire empathy as a result of life's experiences? The answer is both. Scientific inquiry strongly suggests that there is a genetic component to emotional intelligence. Psychological and developmental research indicates that nurture plays a role as well. How much of each perhaps will never be known, but research and practice clearly demonstrate that emotional intelligence can be learned.

One thing is certain: emotional intelligence increases with age. There is an old-fashioned word for the phenomenon: maturity. Yet even with maturity, some people still need training to enhance their emotional intelligence. Unfortunately, far too many training programs that intend to build leadership skills—including emotional intelligence—are a waste of time and money. The problem is simple: they focus on the wrong part of the brain.

Emotional intelligence is born largely in the neurotransmitters of the brain's limbic system, which governs feelings, impulses, and drives. Research indicates that the limbic system learns best through motivation, extended practice, and feedback. Compare this with the kind of learning that goes on in the neocortex, which governs analytical and technical ability. The neocortex grasps concepts and logic. It is the part of the brain that figures out how to use a computer or make a sales call by reading a book. Not surprisingly—but mistakenly—it is also the part of the brain targeted by most training programs aimed at enhancing emotional intelligence. When such programs take, in effect, a neocortical approach, my research with the Consortium for Research on Emotional Intelligence in Organizations has shown they can even have a *negative* impact on people's job performance.

To enhance emotional intelligence, organizations must refocus their training to include the limbic system. They must help people break old behavioral habits and establish new ones. That not only takes much more time than conventional training programs, it also requires an individualized approach.

Imagine an executive who is thought to be low on empathy by her colleagues. Part of that deficit shows itself as an inability to listen; she interrupts people and doesn't pay close attention to what they're saying. To fix the problem, the executive needs to be motivated to change, and then she needs practice and feedback from others in the company. A colleague or coach could be tapped to let the executive know when she has been observed failing to listen. She would then have to replay the incident and give a better response; that is, demonstrate her ability to absorb what others are saying. And the executive could be directed to observe certain executives who listen well and to mimic their behavior.

With persistence and practice, such a process can lead to lasting results. I know one Wall Street executive who sought to improve his empathy—specifically his ability to read people's reactions and see their perspectives. Before beginning his quest, the executive's subordinates were terrified of working with him. People even went so far as to hide bad news from him. Naturally, he was shocked when finally confronted with these facts. He went home and told his family—but they only confirmed what he had heard at work. When their opinions on any given subject did not mesh with his, they, too, were frightened of him.

Enlisting the help of a coach, the executive went to work to heighten his empathy through practice and feedback. His first step was to take a vacation to a foreign country where he did not speak the language. While there, he monitored his reactions to the unfamiliar and his openness to people who were different from him. When he returned home, humbled by his week abroad, the executive asked his coach to shadow him for parts of the day, several times a week, in order to critique how he treated people with new or different perspectives. At the same time, he consciously used on-the-job interactions as opportunities to practice "hearing" ideas that differed from his. Finally, the executive had himself videotaped in meetings and asked those who worked for and with him to critique his ability to acknowledge and understand the feelings of others. It took several months, but the executive's emotional intelligence did ultimately rise, and the improvement was reflected in his overall performance on the job.

It's important to emphasize that building one's emotional intelligence cannot—will not—happen without sincere desire and concerted effort. A brief seminar won't help; nor can one buy a how-to manual. It is much harder to learn to empathize—to internalize empathy as a natural response to people—than it is to become adept at regression analysis. But it can be done. "Nothing great was ever achieved without enthusiasm," wrote Ralph Waldo Emerson. If your goal is to become a real leader, these words can serve as a guidepost in your efforts to develop high emotional intelligence.

offer his feelings about it. He would then present his analysis of the problem and a well-considered solution.

Why does self-regulation matter so much for leaders? First of all, people who are in control of their feelings and impulses—that is, people who are reasonable—are able to create an environment of trust and fairness. In such an environment, politics and infighting are sharply reduced and productivity is high. Talented people flock to the organization and aren't tempted to leave. And self-regulation has a trickle-down effect. No one wants to be known as a hothead when the boss is known for her calm approach. Fewer bad moods at the top mean fewer throughout the organization.

Second, self-regulation is important for competitive reasons. Everyone knows that business today is rife with ambiguity and change. Companies merge and break apart regularly. Technology transforms work at a dizzying pace. People who have mastered their emotions are able to roll with the changes. When a new change program is announced, they don't panic; instead, they are able to suspend judgment, seek out information, and listen to executives explain the new program. As the initiative moves forward, they are able to move with it.

Sometimes they even lead the way. Consider the case of a manager at a large manufacturing company. Like her colleagues, she had used a certain software program for five years. The program drove how she collected and reported data and how she thought about the company's strategy. One day, senior executives announced that a new program was to be installed that would radically change how information was gathered and assessed within the organization. While many people in the company complained bitterly about how disruptive the change would be, the manager mulled over the reasons for the new program and was convinced of its potential to improve performance. She eagerly attended training sessions—some of her colleagues refused to do so—and was eventually promoted to run several divisions, in part because she used the new technology so effectively.

I want to push the importance of self-regulation to leadership even further and make the case that it enhances integrity, which is not only a personal virtue but also an organizational strength. Many of the bad things that happen in companies are a function of impulsive behavior. People rarely plan to exaggerate profits, pad expense accounts, dip into the till, or abuse power for selfish ends. Instead, an opportunity presents itself, and people with low impulse control just say yes.

By contrast, consider the behavior of the senior executive at a large food company. The executive was scrupulously honest in his negotiations with local distributors. He would routinely lay out his cost structure in detail, thereby giving the distributors a realistic understanding of the company's pricing. This approach meant the executive couldn't always drive a hard bargain. Now, on occasion, he felt the urge to increase profits by withholding information about the company's costs. But he challenged that impulse—he saw that it made more sense in the long run to counteract it. His emotional self-regulation paid off in strong, lasting relationships with distributors that benefited the company more than any short-term financial gains would have.

The signs of emotional self-regulation, therefore, are not hard to miss: a propensity for reflection and thoughtfulness; comfort with ambiguity and change; and integrity—an ability to say no to impulsive urges.

Like self-awareness, self-regulation often does not get its due. People who can master their emotions are sometimes seen as cold fish—their considered responses are taken as a lack of passion.

People who have mastered their emotions are able to roll with the changes. They don't panic.

People with fiery temperaments are frequently thought of as "classic" leaders—their outbursts are considered hallmarks of charisma and power. But when such people make it to the top, their impulsiveness often works against them. In my research, extreme displays of negative emotion have never emerged as a driver of good leadership.

Motivation

If there is one trait that virtually all effective leaders have, it is motivation. They are driven to achieve beyond expectations—their own and everyone else's. The key word here is *achieve*. Plenty of people are motivated by external factors such as a big salary or the status that comes from having an impressive title or being part of a prestigious company. By contrast, those with leadership potential are motivated by a deeply embedded desire to achieve for the sake of achievement.

If you are looking for leaders, how can you identify people who are motivated by the drive to achieve rather than by external rewards? The first sign is a passion for the work itself—such people seek out creative challenges, love to learn, and take great pride in a job well done. They also display an unflagging energy to do things better. People with such energy often seem restless with the status quo. They are persistent with their questions about why things are done one way rather than another; they are eager to explore new approaches to their work.

A cosmetics company manager, for example, was frustrated that he had to wait two weeks to get sales results from people in the field. He finally tracked down an automated phone system that would beep each of his salespeople at 5 p.m. every day. An automated message then prompted them to punch in their numbers—how many calls and sales they had made that day. The system shortened the feedback time on sales results from weeks to hours.

That story illustrates two other common traits of people who are driven to achieve. They are forever raising the performance bar, and they like to keep score. Take the performance bar first. During performance reviews, people with high levels of motivation might ask to be "stretched"

The very word *empathy* seems unbusinesslike, out of place amid the tough realities of the marketplace.

by their superiors. Of course, an employee who combines self-awareness with internal motivation will recognize her limits—but she won't settle for objectives that seem too easy to fulfill.

And it follows naturally that people who are driven to do better also want a way of tracking progress—their own, their team's, and their company's. Whereas people with low achievement motivation are often fuzzy about results, those with high achievement motivation often keep score by tracking such hard measures as profitability or market share. I know of a money manager who starts and ends his day on the Internet, gauging the performance of his stock fund against four industry-set benchmarks.

Interestingly, people with high motivation remain optimistic even when the score is against them. In such cases, self-regulation combines with achievement motivation to overcome the frustration and depression that come after a setback or failure. Take the case of another portfolio manager at a large investment company. After several successful years, her fund tumbled for three consecutive quarters, leading three large institutional clients to shift their business elsewhere.

Some executives would have blamed the nosedive on circumstances outside their control; others might have seen the setback as evidence of personal failure. This portfolio manager, however, saw an opportunity to prove she could lead a turnaround. Two years later, when she was promoted to a very senior level in the company, she described the experience as "the best thing that ever happened to me; I learned so much from it."

Executives trying to recognize high levels of achievement motivation in their people can look for one last piece of evidence: commitment to the organization. When people love their job for the work itself, they often feel committed to the organizations that make that work possible. Committed employees are likely to stay with an organization even when they are pursued by headhunters waving money.

It's not difficult to understand how and why a motivation to achieve translates into strong leadership. If you set the performance bar high for yourself, you will do the same for the organization when you are in a position to do so. Likewise, a drive to surpass goals and an interest in keeping score can be contagious. Leaders with these traits can often build a team of managers around them with the same traits. And of course, optimism and organizational commitment are fundamental to leadership—just try to imagine running a company without them.

Empathy

Of all the dimensions of emotional intelligence, empathy is the most easily recognized. We have all felt the empathy of a sensitive teacher or friend; we have all been struck by its absence in an unfeeling coach or boss. But when it comes to business, we rarely hear people praised, let alone rewarded, for their empathy. The very word seems unbusinesslike, out of place amid the tough realities of the marketplace.

But empathy doesn't mean a kind of "I'm okay, you're okay" mushiness. For a leader, that is, it doesn't mean adopting other people's emotions as one's own and trying to please everybody. That would be a nightmare—it would make action impossible. Rather, empathy means thoughtfully considering employees' feelings—along with other factors—in the process of making intelligent decisions.

For an example of empathy in action, consider what happened when two giant brokerage companies merged, creating redundant jobs in all their divisions. One division manager called his people together and gave a gloomy speech that emphasized the number of people who would soon be fired. The manager of another division gave his people a different kind of speech. He was upfront about his own worry and confusion, and he promised to keep people informed and to treat everyone fairly.

The difference between these two managers was empathy. The first manager was too worried about his own fate to consider the feelings of his anxiety-stricken colleagues. The second knew intuitively what his people were feeling, and he acknowledged their fears with his words. Is it any surprise that the first manager saw his division sink as many demoralized people, especially the most talented, departed? By contrast, the second manager continued to be a strong leader, his best people stayed, and his division remained as productive as ever.

Empathy is particularly important today as a component of leadership for at least three reasons:

the increasing use of teams; the rapid pace of globalization; and the growing need to retain talent.

Consider the challenge of leading a team. As anyone who has ever been a part of one can attest, teams are cauldrons of bubbling emotions. They are often charged with reaching a consensus—hard enough with two people and much more difficult as the numbers increase. Even in groups with as few as four or five members, alliances form and clashing agendas get set. A team's leader must be able to sense and understand the viewpoints of everyone around the table.

That's exactly what a marketing manager at a large information technology company was able to do when she was appointed to lead a troubled team. The group was in turmoil, overloaded by work and missing deadlines. Tensions were high among the members. Tinkering with procedures was not enough to bring the group together and make it an effective part of the company.

So the manager took several steps. In a series of one-on-one sessions, she took the time to listen to everyone in the group—what was frustrating them, how they rated their colleagues, whether they felt they had been ignored. And then she directed the team in a way that brought it together: she encouraged people to speak more openly about their frustrations, and she helped people raise constructive complaints during meetings. In short, her empathy allowed her to understand her team's emotional makeup. The result was not just heightened collaboration among members but also added business, as the team was called on for help by a wider range of internal clients.

Globalization is another reason for the rising importance of empathy for business leaders. Cross-cultural dialogue can easily lead to miscues and misunderstandings. Empathy is an antidote. People who have it are attuned to subtleties in body language; they can hear the message beneath the words being spoken. Beyond that, they have a deep understanding of the existence and importance of cultural and ethnic differences.

Consider the case of an American consultant whose team had just pitched a project to a potential Japanese client. In its dealings with Americans, the team was accustomed to being bombarded with questions after such a proposal, but this time it was greeted with a long silence. Other members of the team, taking the silence as disapproval, were ready to pack and leave. The lead consultant gestured them to stop. Although he was not particularly familiar with Japanese culture, he read the client's face and posture and sensed not rejection but interest—even deep consideration. He was right: when the client finally spoke, it was to give the consulting firm the job.

Finally, empathy plays a key role in the retention of talent, particularly in today's information economy. Leaders have always needed empathy to develop and keep good people, but today the stakes are higher. When good people leave, they take the company's knowledge with them.

That's where coaching and mentoring come in. It has repeatedly been shown that coaching and mentoring pay off not just in better performance but also in increased job satisfaction and decreased turnover. But what makes coaching and mentoring work best is the nature of the relationship. Outstanding coaches and mentors get inside the heads of the people they are helping. They sense how to give effective feedback. They know when to push for better performance and when to hold back. In the way they motivate their protégés, they demonstrate empathy in action.

In what is probably sounding like a refrain, let me repeat that empathy doesn't get much respect in business. People wonder how leaders can make hard decisions if they are "feeling" for all the people who will be affected. But leaders with empathy do more than sympathize with people around them: they use their knowledge to improve their companies in subtle but important ways.

Social skill is friendliness with a purpose: moving people in the direction you desire.

Social Skill

The first three components of emotional intelligence are all self-management skills. The last two, empathy and social skill, concern a person's ability to manage relationships with others. As a component of emotional intelligence, social skill is not as simple as it sounds. It's not just a matter of friendliness, although people with high levels of social skill are rarely mean-spirited. Social skill, rather, is friendliness with a purpose: moving people in the direction you desire, whether that's agreement on a new marketing strategy or enthusiasm about a new product.

Socially skilled people tend to have a wide circle of acquaintances, and they have a knack for finding common ground with people of all kinds—a knack for building rapport. That doesn't mean they socialize continually; it means they work according to the assumption that nothing important gets done alone. Such people have a network in place when the time for action comes.

Social skill is the culmination of the other dimensions of emotional intelligence. People tend to be very effective at managing relationships when they can understand and control their own emotions and can empathize with the feelings of others. Even motiva-

Emotional intelligence can be learned. The process is not easy. It takes time and commitment.

tion contributes to social skill. Remember that people who are driven to achieve tend to be optimistic, even in the face of setbacks or failure. When people are upbeat, their "glow" is cast upon conversations and other social encounters. They are popular, and for good reason.

Because it is the outcome of the other dimensions of emotional intelligence, social skill is recognizable on the job in many ways that will by now sound familiar. Socially skilled people, for instance, are adept at managing teams—that's their empathy at work. Likewise, they are expert persuaders—a manifestation of self-awareness, self-regulation, and empathy combined. Given those skills, good persuaders know when to make an emotional plea, for instance, and when an appeal to reason will work better. And motivation, when publicly visible, makes such people excellent collaborators; their passion for the work spreads to others, and they are driven to find solutions.

But sometimes social skill shows itself in ways the other emotional intelligence components do not. For instance, socially skilled people may at times appear not to be working while at work. They seem to be idly schmoozing—chatting in the hallways with colleagues or joking around with people who are not even connected to their "real" jobs. Socially skilled people, however, don't think it makes sense to arbitrarily limit the scope of their relationships. They build bonds widely because they know that in these fluid times, they may need help someday from people they are just getting to know today.

For example, consider the case of an executive in the strategy department of a global computer manufacturer. By 1993, he was convinced that the company's future lay with the Internet. Over the course of the next year, he found kindred spirits and used his social skill to stitch together a virtual community that cut across levels, divisions, and nations. He then used this de facto team to put up a corporate Web site, among the first by a major company. And, on his own initiative, with no budget or formal status, he signed up the company to participate in an annual Internet industry convention. Calling on his allies and persuading various divisions to donate funds, he recruited more than 50 people from a dozen different units to represent the company at the convention.

Management took notice: within a year of the conference, the executive's team formed the basis for the company's first Internet division, and he was formally put in charge of it. To get there, the executive had ignored conventional boundaries, forging and maintaining connections with people in every corner of the organization.

Is social skill considered a key leadership capability in most companies? The answer is yes, especially when compared with the other components of emotional intelligence. People seem to know intuitively that leaders need to manage relationships effectively; no leader is an island. After all, the leader's task is to get work done through other people, and social skill makes that possible. A leader who cannot express her empathy may as well not have it at all. And a leader's motivation will be useless if he cannot communicate his passion to the organization. Social skill allows leaders to put their emotional intelligence to work.

It would be foolish to assert that good-old-fashioned IQ and technical ability are not important ingredients in strong leadership. But the recipe would not be complete without emotional intelligence. It was once thought that the components of emotional intelligence were "nice to have" in business leaders. But now we know that, for the sake of performance, these are ingredients that leaders "need to have."

It is fortunate, then, that emotional intelligence can be learned. The process is not easy. It takes time and, most of all, commitment. But the benefits that come from having a well-developed emotional intelligence, both for the individual and for the organization, make it worth the effort.

Test Your Knowledge Form

We encourage you to photocopy and use this page as a tool to assess how the articles in **Annual Editions** expand on the information in your textbook. By reflecting on the articles you will gain enhanced text information. You can also access this useful form on a product's book support Web site at **http://www.dushkin.com/ online/.**

NAME: _____ DATE: _____

TITLE AND NUMBER OF ARTICLE: _____

BRIEFLY STATE THE MAIN IDEA OF THIS ARTICLE: _____

LIST THREE IMPORTANT FACTS THAT THE AUTHOR USES TO SUPPORT THE MAIN IDEA:

WHAT INFORMATION OR IDEAS DISCUSSED IN THIS ARTICLE ARE ALSO DISCUSSED IN YOUR TEXTBOOK OR OTHER READINGS THAT YOU HAVE DONE? LIST THE TEXTBOOK CHAPTERS AND PAGE NUMBERS:

LIST ANY EXAMPLES OF BIAS OR FAULTY REASONING THAT YOU FOUND IN THE ARTICLE:

LIST ANY NEW TERMS/CONCEPTS THAT WERE DISCUSSED IN THE ARTICLE, AND WRITE A SHORT DEFINITION:

ANNUAL EDITIONS revisions depend on two major opinion sources: one is our Advisory Board, listed in the front of this volume, which works with us in scanning the thousands of articles published in the public press each year; the other is you—the person actually using the book. Please help us and the users of the next edition by completing the prepaid article rating form on this page and returning it to us. Thank you for your help!

ANNUAL EDITIONS: Social Psychology 01/02

ARTICLE RATING FORM

Here is an opportunity for you to have direct input into the next revision of this volume. We would like you to rate each of the 39 articles listed below, using the following scale:

1. Excellent: should definitely be retained
2. Above average: should probably be retained
3. Below average: should probably be deleted
4. Poor: should definitely be deleted

Your ratings will play a vital part in the next revision.
So please mail this prepaid form to us just as soon as you complete it.
Thanks for your help!

We Want Your Advice

RATING

ARTICLE

1. The Nature of the Self
2. Culture
3. Making Sense of Self-Esteem
4. I Am Somebody!
5. The "Vividness Problem"
6. The Seed of Our Undoing
7. How Culture Molds Habits of Thought
8. The Power of the Situation Over You
9. Inferential Hopscotch: How People Draw Social Inferences From Behavior
10. The New-Boy Network
11. Mindless Propaganda, Thoughtful Persuasion
12. How to Sell a Pseudoscience
13. A Social Psychological Perspective on the Role of Knowledge About AIDS in AIDS Prevention
14. Obedience in Retrospect
15. Liking: The Friendly Thief
16. Persuasion: What Will It Take to Convince You?
17. Suspect Confessions
18. Shyness: The New Solution
19. Linking Up Online
20. Isn't She Lovely?
21. What's Your Love Story?
22. Will Your Marriage Last?
23. Where Bias Begins: The Truth About Stereotypes
24. Breaking the Prejudice Habit

RATING

ARTICLE

25. Aversive Racism and Selection Decisions: 1989 and 1999
26. Thin Ice: "Stereotype Threat" and Black College Students
27. Stereotype
28. Good Clean Fun?
29. Violence and Honor in the Southern United States
30. Self-Esteem, Narcissism, and Aggression: Does Violence Result From Low Self-Esteem or From Threatened Egotism?
31. Anatomy of a Violent Relationship
32. Volunteerism and Society's Response to the HIV Epidemic
33. Morals, Apes, and Us
34. Cause of Death: Uncertain(ty)
35. The Effects of "Mandatory Volunteerism" on Intentions to Volunteer
36. Building Cooperation, Empathy, and Compassion in the Classroom
37. Group Decision Fiascoes Continue: Space Shuttle Challenger and a Revised Groupthink Framework
38. Group Processes in the Resolution of International Conflicts: Experiences From the Israeli-Palestinian Case
39. What Makes a Leader?

(Continued on next page)

BUSINESS REPLY MAIL
FIRST-CLASS MAIL PERMIT NO. 84 GUILFORD CT

POSTAGE WILL BE PAID BY ADDRESSEE

McGraw-Hill/Dushkin
530 Old Whitfield Street
Guilford, CT 06437-9989

ABOUT YOU

Name _____ Date _____

Are you a teacher? ☐ A student? ☐
Your school's name _____

Department _____

Address _____ City _____ State ___ Zip ___

School telephone # _____

YOUR COMMENTS ARE IMPORTANT TO US!

Please fill in the following information:
For which course did you use this book?
_____

Did you use a text with this *ANNUAL EDITION*? ☐ yes ☐ no
What was the title of the text?
_____

What are your general reactions to the *Annual Editions* concept?
_____

Have you read any particular articles recently that you think should be included in the next edition?
_____

Are there any articles you feel should be replaced in the next edition? Why?
_____

Are there any World Wide Web sites you feel should be included in the next edition? Please annotate.
_____

May we contact you for editorial input? ☐ yes ☐ no
May we quote your comments? ☐ yes ☐ no

W9-AAC-884